AF556115

Project Management

Project Management

R.B. KHANNA
Professor
Indian Institute of Planning and Management (IIPM)
Jaipur

PHI Learning Private Limited
Delhi-110092
2016

₹350.00

PROJECT MANAGEMENT
R.B. Khanna

© 2011 by PHI Learning Private Limited, Delhi. All rights reserved. No part of this book may be reproduced in any form, by mimeograph or any other means, without permission in writing from the publisher.

ISBN-978-81-203-4288-0

The export rights of this book are vested solely with the publisher.

Third Printing ... ... **May, 2016**

Published by Asoke K. Ghosh, PHI Learning Private Limited, Rimjhim House, 111, Patparganj Industrial Estate, Delhi-110092 and Printed by Raj Press, New Delhi-110012.

To my lovely granddaughter
Roshni

Contents

Part II PROJECT PLANNING

Preface

Time and cost overruns in projects are a matter of grave concern. The Government of India set up the Ministry of Statistics and Programme Implementation in the 1980s to oversee projects. A flash report of the ministry up to July 2009 states that out of 602 projects costing over ₹ 100 crore each, 329 were suffering from cost and time overruns and 74 had no fixed date of commissioning. The total cost overrun on these projects was ₹ 55,757 crore—or 10.4% of the original planned cost. The time overruns varied from 1 to 51 months. Why do so many projects fail to meet their deadlines in terms of cost, time and quality? It is mainly because they are ill-conceived and poorly managed.

Project management has mostly been viewed as a capital budgeting problem. In fact, the subject is included as a part of finance specialization in many MBA programmes. Some academic bodies do include it as a mandatory subject for the MBA programmes, but the stress is still on the financial aspects. Indian literature on the subject lays more emphasis on analysis and selection of projects than on their planning, execution, monitoring and control. This book attempts to correct this aberration. The book deals with all phases of project management, that is, project initiation, project planning, project execution, monitoring and control, and project closure. The book also carries examples illustrating the use of software packages which can be used effectively for better planning, scheduling, monitoring and controlling of projects.

The book is designed to serve as text for Project Management courses which are part of MBA programmes and undergraduate engineering programmes. Every effort has been made to keep the language and the text simple. Complex mathematical formulations and theoretical proofs and axioms have been omitted. The book is embellished with life-like examples and case studies and an attempt has been made to strike a balance between theoretical inputs and their applications to practical problems.

The book will also serve as a useful reference for practising managers. It is hoped that it will help in developing a better understanding of the nuances and issues involved in project management and will result in the elimination or considerable reduction of time and cost overruns.

A separate CD containing PowerPoint presentations for all chapters, solutions to all unsolved numerical problems and suggested discussion points for case studies is available as teaching resources for instructors on demand.

The book is organized in four parts. Part I deals with project initiation; Part II deals with project planning; Part III deals with project execution, monitoring and control; and Part IV deals with project audit and closure. A chapter dealing with the public investment projects in India is also included. A separate detailed text on social cost–benefit analysis has been included as an appendix to Chapter 3 of the book. The latest technique of critical chain and buffer management which is an improvement on CPM and PERT has been included separately as another appendix. Eight case studies on different real-world situations have been provided to help the students gain practical experience. An annexure giving some financial inputs has been included for the benefit of readers who may not have exposure to financial inputs.

I wish to place on record my thanks to my colleagues and friends who have encouraged me to write this book. Suggestions for improvement are most welcome and will be gratefully acknowledged. They may be forwarded by e-mail to rbkhanna@gmail.com.

R.B. Khanna

PART I Project Initiation

Chapter 1 Project Management—An Introduction
Chapter 2 Project Origination
Chapter 3 Project Feasibility

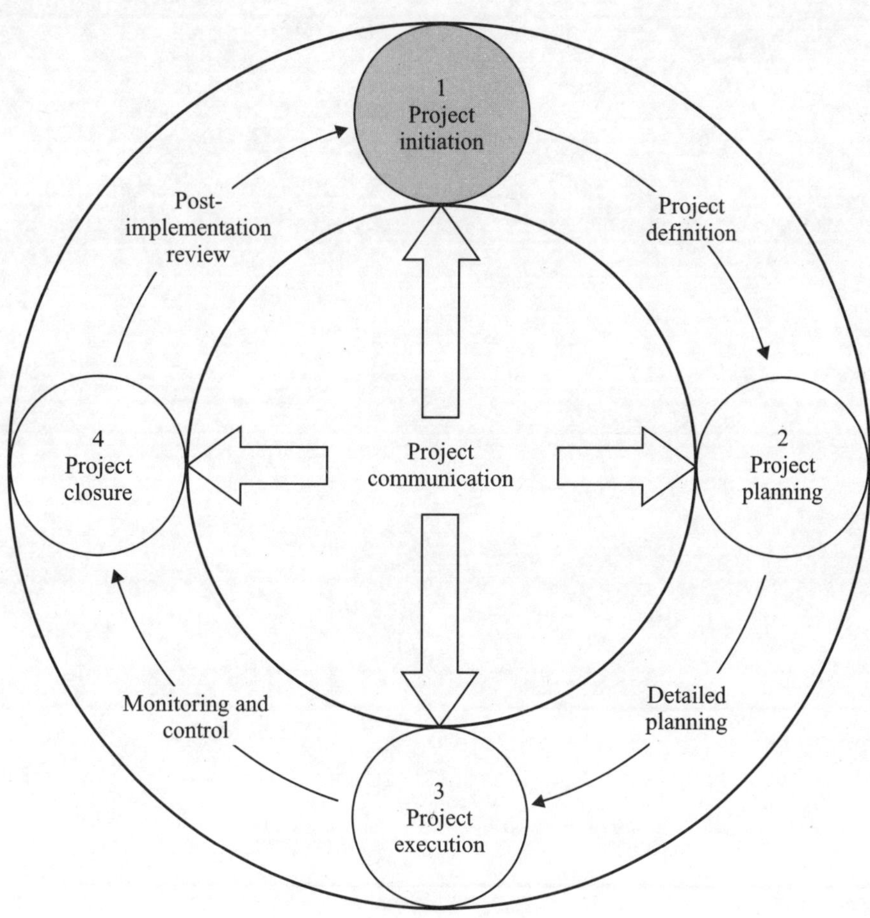

CHAPTER 1

Project Management
An Introduction

Project management is ... The art of creating the illusion that any outcome is the result of a series of predetermined, deliberate acts when, in fact, it was dumb luck.

—Harold Kerzner

LEARNING OBJECTIVES

After reading this chapter, you will be able to:

- Define a project and explain the characteristics of a project.
- Understand the difference between projects and operations.
- Explain the relationship between projects and capital budgeting.
- Understand the concept of project management and its importance.
- Understand the project life cycle.
- Explain the importance of projects in business strategy.

1.1 INTRODUCTION

We hear of projects every day. The Narmada Valley project, the ONGC oil refinery project at Bhatinda, the nuclear plant project at Rawatbhatta, the POSCO steel plant project in Orissa, Tata's car project in Gujarat splash across the pages of newspapers almost every day. The outcome of these projects are different—the Narmada Valley project resulted in a hydroelectric power plant, the ONGC's project will result in an oil refinery and the Tata's project will create a facility to produce cars—yet, they are all referred to as projects. What then is the common basis or the common elements in this varied group of activities? To understand the commonality running in these ventures, it is important for us to understand what a project is.

1.2 WHAT IS A PROJECT?

A project has been defined differently by different authorities. Some of the definitions are given as follows:

> *A project is a temporary endeavour undertaken to create a unique product, service or result.*
>
> —PMBOK

> *A coordinated effort, using a combination of human, technical, administrative, and financial resources, in order to achieve a specific goal within a fixed time period.*
>
> —Graham McLeod and Derek Smith

> *Project is a one-shot, time limited, goal oriented, major undertaking requiring commitment of varied skills and resources, a combination of human and non-human resources pooled together in a temporary organization to achieve a specific purpose.*
>
> —Project Management Institute of USA

We can see that there are common threads in each of these definitions. The attributes of a project may be described as temporary, unique and progressive elaboration.

Temporary

Projects are temporary in nature. 'Temporary' implies that they have a definite beginning and a definite end. The project ends when the objective is achieved, or it becomes obvious that the objective will not or cannot be achieved, or the need for the objective no longer exists and the project is terminated. Temporary does not imply that projects are short in duration. They may take considerable time to complete but they have a finite duration. They do not last forever and are not ongoing efforts.

Temporary, however, does not apply to the product, service or result created by a project. These are generally long lasting. For instance, the oil refinery resulting from the ONGC's project may have a long life span of 50 or 100 years. Projects often have deliberately planned or unintended social, economic and environmental impacts that far outlast the projects themselves.

The temporary nature of a project does extend to the opportunity for the project and to the project team and organization that carries out the project. The team and organization are disbanded and reassigned to other tasks on the completion of the project.

Unique

Project deliverables—what have to be delivered at the end of the project—are unique. Projects create a unique product, service or result. They may create a product that is quantifiable, a capability to provide a service such as a business function or a result such as outcomes or documents. For instance, a research and development project may yield results that can be applied and innovated upon.

We may question the uniqueness of a project. We could say that all housing projects produce a set of houses almost similar in design. While the activities involved are repetitive in nature, each housing project is unique as it is on a different site with its own typical problems. Different owners, different contractors, different designs, different sites and so on make each project unique. The repetitive nature of the activities involved does not detract from the uniqueness of the project.

Progressive elaboration

This is a feature of projects. It implies developing in steps and continuing in increments. The project scope may be described in broad terms to start with. But as the project team develops a better understanding, the scope may be defined more explicitly and in greater detail. However, the project scope, that is, the work to be done, should be controlled. The project scope, time and costs are interrelated. If the scope increases, the time required increases and consequently the cost also increases.

To sum up, we can say that a project has a definite goal. It has a definite beginning and a definite end. It requires resources and coordination. It is a temporary and unique activity which creates a product, service or result.

1.3 PROJECTS AND OPERATIONS

Organizations exist to fulfil the needs of society. These needs are fulfilled through products or services. The work of an organization may be categorized as projects and operations. Projects are unique and have a definite beginning and a definite end, while operations are ongoing. For instance, let us consider a steel plant. The construction of the steel plant is a project. It terminates when the plant is completed. The manufacture of steel is an operation of the firm. It is an ongoing process. Different goals or targets may be set for different periods in terms of both the products and quantities, but the process continues. Projects terminate when their goals are achieved. On the other hand, operations continue, adopting new sets of objectives and goals.

Sometimes, projects and operations tend to overlap. When organizations plan operations for a specific period, they may treat such operations as projects. They fall in the category of projects since they are temporary and unique. For example, Ferrari may undertake a project to produce a champion racing car for the Formula 1 races to be held five years later. Similarly, an organization may treat the launch of a product with a limited life as a project.

Some examples of projects are:

(a) Constructing a new facility
(b) Expanding an existing facility
(c) Creating new information systems and software
(d) Building a ship
(e) Constructing bridges
(f) Developing a new product or service
(g) Conducting a unique one-time event like the Olympic Games
(h) Implementing new business procedures (Enterprise Resource Planning systems)

The list is by no means exhaustive. It is emphasized that any endeavour that is temporary in nature and that produces a unique outcome can be termed as a project.

1.4 PROJECTS AND CAPITAL BUDGETING

Projects generally involve large capital outlays and are treated as capital investments from the financial point of view. In financial terms, projects are schemes typically involving a certain current outlay, or current and future outlay of funds in the expectation of a stream of benefits extending far into the future. Financial analysts treat projects as capital investments and concern themselves with the characteristics of such investments. These involve very substantial, large financial outlays with long-term effects. The size of the outlays often makes reversal of decisions costly in terms of sunk costs. However, that does not imply that projects cannot be terminated midway if they are found to be infeasible or if it is determined that the goals of the project cannot be met or the need for the goals no longer exists. Since the effects of such capital expenditure are long lasting, the outcomes are full of uncertainty and the risk associated with this uncertainty has to be taken into account. From a capital budgeting angle, the selection of projects becomes vital. Good project management will ensure that the goals of a project are achieved within the time frame and the costs as visualized, and a perfectly good solution may be achieved but for the wrong problem, if the selection of the project itself is incorrect. The choice of projects is a capital budgeting exercise aimed at increasing the shareholder's wealth and hence, projects which would give the maximum benefit should be selected. It may be observed that the term 'benefit' has been used instead of profit. Projects are undertaken not only by the private entrepreneur but also by the government and both have a social responsibility which extends beyond mere financial profits. Selection of projects involves a thorough analysis comprising market analysis, technical analysis, ecological analysis, financial analysis and economic or social cost–benefit analysis.

1.5 PROJECT MANAGEMENT

Project management is defined by the Project Management Institute (PMI) of USA as "the application of knowledge, skills, tools and techniques to project activities to meet project requirements. It is accomplished through the application and integration of the project management processes of initiating, planning, executing, monitoring and controlling and closing." Some other definitions are as follows:

> *Project management is the process of achieving project objectives through traditional organization structure and over the specialities of the individuals concerned. Project management is applicable for any unique, one-time or one-of-a-kind undertaking concerned with specific end objectives.*
>
> —Harold Kerzner
>
> *Project management is the application of skills, knowledge, tools and techniques to meet the needs and expectations of stakeholders for a project.* —Stephen Kim
>
> *Project management is the application of a collection of tools and techniques to direct the use of diverse resources towards the accomplishment of a unique, complex, one-time task, within time, cost and quality constraints. Each task requires a mix of these tools and techniques structured to fit the task environment and life cycle (from conception to completion) of the task.*
>
> —Richard P. Olsen

The aim of any project management team is to ensure that the product, service or result which the project has to deliver is completed as per the scope, within the time and costs allotted and in conformity with the desired quality. Project managers often talk of a 'triple constraint', namely, project scope, time and cost (Figure 1.1). A change in any one of these factors affects at least one other factor. Project quality depends on these three factors and is achieved by balancing them.

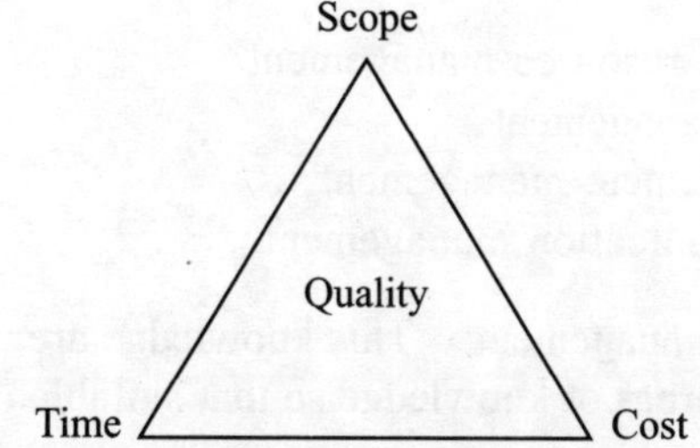

Figure 1.1 Triple constraint of a project.

Some organizations adopt a project management approach to other activities by defining them as projects in a manner consistent with the definition of a project. This is referred to as 'management by project' and the principles and processes applied to project management are applied to such activities. While all operational activities cannot be classified as projects and treated as such, the trend to treat more and more time-bound, unique activities as projects is on the increase.

Effective project management requires the knowledge and skills of the following areas of expertise:

1. Project management body of knowledge
2. Application area knowledge, standards and regulations
3. Understanding the project environment
4. General management knowledge and skills
5. Interpersonal skills

1.5.1 Project Management Body of Knowledge

It consists of knowledge that is unique to project management and overlaps other management areas. The PMI of USA describes the body of knowledge through five management process groups and nine knowledge areas. The management process groups are:

1. Initiating process group
2. Planning process group
3. Executing process group
4. Monitoring and controlling process group
5. Closing process group

The knowledge areas are:

1. Core areas:
   (i) Project scope management
   (ii) Project time management

(iii) Project cost management
(iv) Project quality management

2. Facilitating areas:

(i) Project human resource management
(ii) Projcct risk management
(iii) Project procurement management
(iv) Project communication management

3. Project integration management: This knowledge area helps to integrate the core areas and the facilitating areas of knowledge so that suitable outcomes to satisfy the needs can be arrived at.

1.5.2 Application Area Knowledge, Standards and Regulations

Application area knowledge is the special knowledge required in the area of the project and is not necessarily needed for all projects. For instance, a project for the construction of a bridge would require civil engineering knowledge. If we consider a project for building a hotel, the construction would definitely require civil engineering knowledge but would also need expertise and knowledge on hotel layouts and designs which satisfy the requirements of a hotel. The construction of a steel plant would require some knowledge and expertise from the metallurgical engineering field besides knowledge of civil engineering. Application areas may be in terms of functional areas, technical elements, management areas or industry groups. These areas of knowledge are required for a certain group of projects but are not necessarily common to all projects.

Standards are generally laid down by recognized bodies as guidelines or as characteristics that must be met. Each industry and profession has its standards and it is important to know the standards to which the project activities must conform. Regulations are generally statutory and mandatory requirements that are laid down by the government or regulatory bodies. Knowledge of pertinent regulations is necessary to manage projects. For instance, a housing project will have to conform to regulations of offsets to be left in front of buildings and area utilization.

1.5.3 Understanding the Project Environment

The project team must understand the social, cultural, physical, political and international environment in which projects are undertaken. These environmental factors affect and are affected by the project. Project managers should understand the effect of the project on people while at the same time recognizing how people will affect the project. It may be necessary to study the social, cultural, religious, ethnic, educational and other characteristics of the society which may have an interest in the project. The project team may have to familiarize themselves with the international and political factors that influence the project. Different local laws, regulations, tax regimes, language and customs, work culture and so on may have a profound influence on the project and it is important that the project team understands such implications in order to make a success of managing the project.

1.5.4 General Management Knowledge and Skills

General management includes planning, staffing, organizing, directing and controlling and is common to all projects. It includes knowledge of different functional areas such as finance, marketing, human resource management, procurement, sales, contract and commercial law, logistics and supply chain management, information systems management, health and safety practices and so on.

1.5.5 Interpersonal Skills

Projects are temporary in nature. The organization set up for a project is also temporary and the team is assembled when required. Working with such a team requires a high degree of interpersonal skills which include communication, leadership, motivation, negotiation and conflict management skills, and problem-solving skills.

1.6 IMPORTANCE OF PROJECT MANAGEMENT

Successful projects are those that achieve their objective within the specified time frame, at the specified cost and to the specified quality. Unfortunately, a large number of projects suffer from time and consequently cost overruns. This would be clear from the following box.

PROJECT COST AND TIME OVERRUNS

The problem is so acute in India that a Ministry of Statistics and Programme Implementation has been set up. A flash report of the ministry, dealing with projects of ₹ 100 crore and above, for July 2009 reveals the following statistics:

(a) Number of projects monitored	602
(b) Original estimate	₹ 5,44,656.88 crore
(c) Anticipated cost	₹ 6,00,414.11 crore
(d) Cost overruns	₹ 55,757.23 crore
(e) Projects ahead of schedule	13
(f) Projects on schedule	145
(g) Projects delayed	329
(h) Projects with no fixed date of commissioning	74
(i) Delay range	1–51 months
(j) Percentage of cost overruns in delayed projects	10.24%

Considering the magnitude of the problem, it is imperative that projects are managed properly.

Projects fail because they are mismanaged. Some of the causes of project failure are discussed in the following paragraphs.

Scope creep

Often, the scope of the project is not properly defined. While projects are characterized by progressive elaboration, this implies the clarity of detail and not a change or enhancement of scope at each step. Scope creep introduces a changing and ever-increasing scope of the project during its execution. It is little wonder that under such circumstances the plans fail resulting in time and cost overruns. For instance, the light combat aircraft project for the defence services got inordinately delayed as the service requirements kept changing from time to time.

Poor information gathering

Another major cause of project failure is the lack of proper information at the planning stage. If the time duration and costs of activities are not correctly estimated at the planning stage, the project is bound to have time and cost overruns.

Unrealistic planning and scheduling

Planners often tend to make ambitious plans which may be unrealistic to achieve. For instance, Indian planners often ignore the time delays that are likely to take place in the acquisition of land for projects. These acquisitions have a social and political impact and generally involve prolonged negotiations. An unrealistic time allotment for the vital activity of land acquisition can lead to time and cost overruns.

Lack of resources

This will affect a project adversely. If adequate labour, material, equipment or funds are not available the project is bound to be delayed. For instance, if two bulldozers are needed and one breaks down leaving only one available for work, the time required to complete the task will increase.

Lack of proper sponsorship

This is another factor that affects government projects adversely. Invariably, the project is controlled by a very high powered steering committee which rarely meets as its members are preoccupied with other tasks. Adequate authority is not vested with the project manager and the project management organization (PMO). A mismatch between authority, responsibility and accountability delays projects.

It is, therefore, important that projects are managed professionally and competently.

1.7 PROJECT HIERARCHY

Projects are part of programmes which themselves are part of plans at the international, national, state or regional level. The hierarchy is shown in Figure 1.2. A plan consists of various programmes. For instance, the national plan may consist of an education programme, a health programme, an industry programme and so on. The health programme may have a number of projects like setting up a general hospital, a medical college, a number of primary health centres and so on. Projects are divided into work packages like the construction and setting up of the operation theatre in a hospital project. The work packages are further broken down to specific activities, for example the electrification of the operation theatre or the plumbing of the operation theatre and so on. The details of activities vary with the level at which they are being dealt with.

The work packages are normally assigned to an identifiable person or authority responsible for their execution.

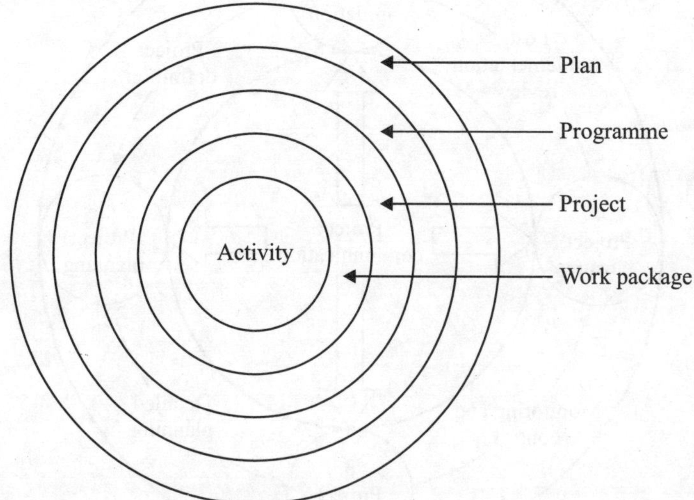

Figure 1.2 Project hierarchy.

1.8 PROJECT LIFE CYCLE

Projects can be divided into phases for better execution and control. These phases are referred to as project life cycle. The project life cycle describes the tasks that must be completed to produce a product, service or result. Different project life cycles exist for different products or services. For example, the life cycle activities required for a construction project would be different from those required for a software project. However, the project management life cycle defines how to manage the project and will always be the same irrespective of the project life cycle. The project life cycle defines the phases that connect the project from the beginning to its end. The phases are described differently by different authorities, but the generic phases remain the same and are:

1. Project initiation
2. Project planning
3. Project execution, monitoring and control
4. Project closure

The schematic representation of a project life cycle is shown in Figure 1.3.

Project phases end with some deliverables. A deliverable is defined as any measurable, tangible and verifiable outcome, result or item that must be produced. For example, a detailed list of activities to be performed is a deliverable of the activity definition process. The deliverables may or may not require the approval of the customer.

The phases of a project life cycle are generally sequential. The cost, staffing and resources required are low at the start, peak during the intermediate phases and taper off as the project draws to a conclusion, as illustrated in Figure 1.4.

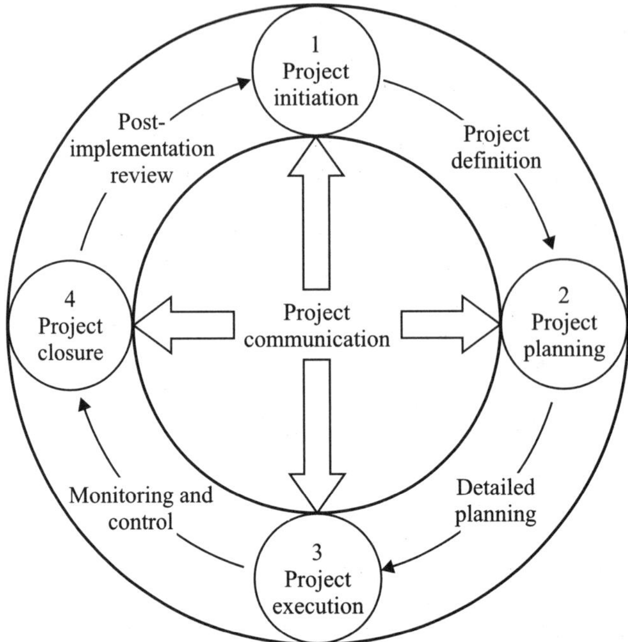

Figure 1.3 A schematic diagram of project life cycle.

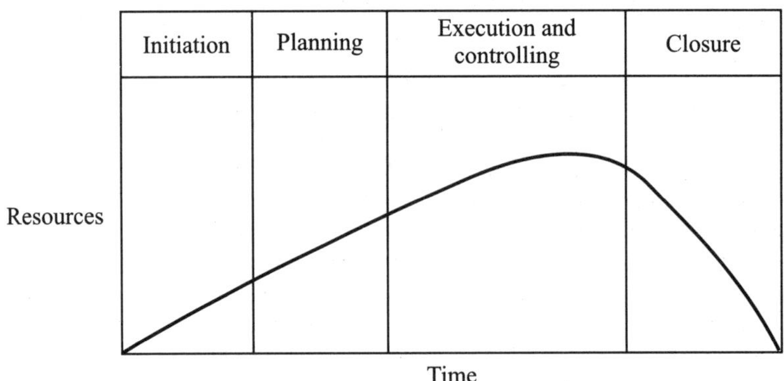

Figure 1.4 Typical project cost and staffing levels across the project life cycle.

The level of uncertainty is highest at the beginning of a project and it can be influenced by the stakeholders. The cost of making changes is also low at the beginning. As the project progresses, the risk increases and the influence of the stakeholders also decreases. The cost of making changes at later stages increases. This is shown in Figure 1.5.

The activities associated with each phase of the project life cycle are discussed in the following paragraphs.

1.8.1 Project Initiation

The key question during this phase is what will be covered by the project. It involves developing project proposals and selecting a project. Once the project is selected, other typical activities of this phase are:

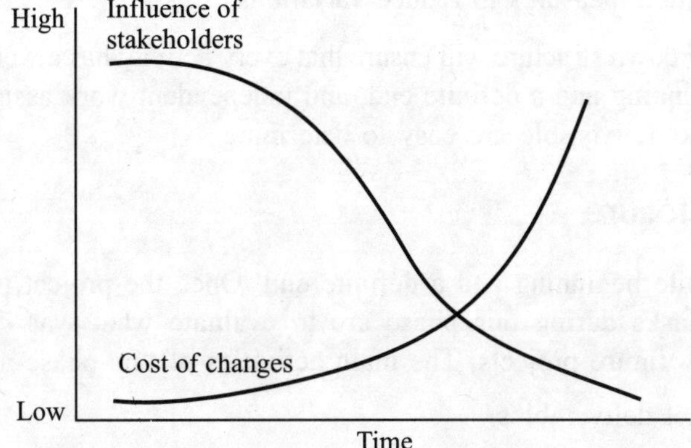

Figure 1.5 Stakeholders' influence over time.

1. State the problem.
2. Establish overall goals.
3. Define objectives.
4. Identify success criteria.
5. List assumptions, risks and obstacles.
6. Produce a project definition statement.

1.8.2 Project Planning

The plan provides answers to what, where, when, who and how issues. The typical activities of this phase are:

1. Identify project activities.
2. Estimate activity duration.
3. Develop a schedule.
4. Determine resource requirements.
5. Assign tasks and responsibilities.
6. Draw a project network/Gantt chart.

1.8.3 Project Execution, Monitoring and Control

The key tasks of this phase are to organize people, allocate resources and schedule activities. Typical activities of this phase include:

1. Organize the project team.
2. Develop a work breakdown structure.
3. Schedule and document work.
4. Level resources.

5. Establish management control and information systems so that actual progress can be measured vis-à-vis planned progress.
6. Initiate corrective measures to reduce variations.

A good work breakdown structure will ensure that every activity has a well-defined measurable output, a definite beginning and a definite end, and independent work assignment, and the cost and time taken for the deliverable are easy to determine.

1.8.4 Project Closure

A project has a definite beginning and a definite end. Once the project is completed, it must be closed. The key tasks during this phase are to evaluate what was done and to compile information for use in future projects. The main activities of this phase are:

1. Produce project deliverables.
2. Obtain customer acceptance.
3. Complete project documentation.
4. Issue project final report.

On completion, the project is handed over to the customer or sponsor for operations.

1.9 PROJECTS AND STRATEGIC MANAGEMENT

Projects are often undertaken for those activities which do not fall under the ambit of normal operations. Since they also involve large capital outlays, they should be in conformity and in furtherance of corporate strategy. Today's world is characterized by rapid change. In fact, the only thing that is permanent is change. An organization's ability to rapidly adapt to change, and more importantly drive it, is a key factor in its success and survival. Projects usher in change and every organization strives to complete projects within time, costs and quality. Project management skills can provide a strategic advantage to an organization as it can then outperform the competition and reduce risk.

A firm draws its strategy based on its mission and vision statement and as a result of environmental and internal assessment. A mission statement is an enduring statement of purpose that distinguishes one business from other similar firms. A mission statement identifies the scope of a firm's operations in production and marketing terms. It is a statement which defines the role that an organization plays in the society. It is a statement that defines what business the firm is in, who its customers are and how its core beliefs shape its decision-making. For example, the mission statement of ONGC is: "To stimulate, continue and accelerate efforts to develop and maximize the contribution of the energy sector to the economy of the country." ONGC is not just in the business of oil and natural gas but is in the business of energy sector.

The next step is to carry out an environmental scan. This involves analyzing the external environment for business opportunities as well as competitive threats. Political, economic, social and technological factors are considered. These factors throw up opportunities as well as threats for the business. For instance, the significant social change in the Indian social environment is the breakdown of the joint family system and the emergence of nuclear families. There is also a phenomenal rise in the number of working women. These changes have created a need for looking after small children and the elderly. An organization could see business opportunities to fulfil these needs. It may decide to set up childcare centres or geriatric centres. Similarly, the political emergence of the European Union has resulted in the removal of trade barriers within the Union and this may open up new business opportunities. An unstable political environment may pose a threat to business because of unstable policies and an uncertain future.

The opportunities and threats have to be combined with an organization's internal strengths and weaknesses. The organization must recognize its core competencies—things that it does better than anyone else. Based on experience, knowledge and know-how, core competencies provide an organization with sustainable competitive advantage. Products and services do not constitute core competencies as these can be easily copied. Core competencies generally constitute processes or a company's ability to do things better than its competitors. They can also be defined as 'the collective learning in an organization, especially how to coordinate diverse production skills and integrate multiple streams of technologies' (Prahlad and Hamel, 1990). For example, Canon's core competency is in the field of combining technologies related to fine optics, precision mechanics and microelectronics. It is a combination of these technologies that helps Canon to produce cameras, FAX machines, copiers and calculators.

The final step in the formulation of business strategy is to 'put it all together'. The mission of the organization, the opportunities and threats posed by the environment and the organization's internal strengths and weaknesses must be matched to define the long-range plans for the organization.

SUMMARY

A project is a temporary endeavour undertaken to produce a unique product, service or result. A project is temporary in nature in as much as it has a definite beginning and a definite end. The organization responsible for the project is also temporary and is wound up at the end of the project. However, the result of the project in the form of a product, service or other deliverable may be long lasting. The construction of an oil refinery is a project and ends when the refinery is finally handed over for operations. The operations of the refinery are ongoing and the refinery may have a life of 50 or 100 years. Projects are unique and also have the characteristic of progressive elaboration—that is, the scope is defined more elaborately as the project progresses.

Projects are different from operations. While operations are ongoing activities, projects have a definite beginning and a definite end. Projects generally involve large capital outlays. They may have long gestation periods and are prone to risk and uncertainty. The decisions are usually irreversible because of the large sums of capital involved.

Project management is the application of knowledge, skills, tools and techniques to meet project requirements. The aim of any project team is to complete the project as per its scope within the time and cost allotted and in conformity with the desired quality.

Effective project management requires the project management body of knowledge; knowledge of application area, standards and regulations; an understanding of the project environment; knowledge of general management and skills; and interpersonal skills.

Projects often fail because of scope creep, where the scope keeps changing and increasing as the project progresses. They also fail because of lack of proper information, unrealistic planning and scheduling and lack of resources. Another major cause of project failure is the lack of proper sponsorship and a mismatch between authority, responsibility and accountability between the project management organization and the sponsors.

The project life cycle consists of four distinct phases—project initiation, project planning, project execution, monitoring and control, and project closure.

Effective project management offers strategic advantage as an organization can then outperform its competition and reduce its risk.

QUESTIONS

1. What is a project? Explain its characteristics and features.
2. What is the difference between projects and operations?
3. What is project management? Explain the knowledge and skill areas required for effective project management.
4. What are the causes of project failure?
5. Explain the project life cycle.

CHAPTER 2

Project Origination

First comes thought; then organization of that thought, into ideas and plans; then transformation of those plans into reality. The beginning, as you will observe, is in your imagination.
—Napoleon Hill

LEARNING OBJECTIVES

After reading this chapter, you will be able to:

- Understand the origin of projects.
- Explain how strategic choices lead to projects.
- Study other sources of project ideas.
- Study methods for preliminary screening of projects.

2.1 INTRODUCTION

Projects are often undertaken for those activities which do not fall under the ambit of normal operations. How do projects originate? More often than not, their origin can be traced to the desire to solve an existing problem or to satisfy an unfulfilled societal need. Projects may also originate as a result of government policy. For example, the government may lay down that it shall not allow the export or import of certain items. We may then view this as an opportunity and seek projects or capital investments to take advantage of the same. Projects may originate to fulfil statutory requirements like pollution control and so on. Success lies in getting into the right business at the right time. The entrepreneur needs to be creative, sensitive to changes in the environment, and needs to have a realistic assessment of what the firm can do.

2.2 PROJECT ORIGINATION

Let us try and understand the process of project origination with the help of an example. Let us consider a city that has to host the Olympic Games. The city will need stadiums for different games, a games village, roads or rail networks to connect the village to all the games venues, additional infrastructure at its airport to take the extra air traffic during the games, hotel accommodation for the visitors and spectators both domestic and foreign, parking spaces and so on. Each one of these items can be considered as a project. There may also be some other considerations. For instance, we may like to consider what will happen to all these facilities once the games are over. Let us consider the games village. If we plan to utilize the housing afterwards for domestic use, we may have to design it accordingly so that it requires little or no modification for alternate use. The additional hotel accommodation may have to be used as office accommodation and so on.

Let us consider an oil discovery in some remote desert area by the national oil and gas agency. The agency will have to take into account whether there is a national demand for petroleum products or not. In case we are an oil-rich nation, then the discovered reserves may only be surplus to our requirement. We may then consider exporting the additional oil. Some of the questions that would crop up are—should we export crude or should we export refined petroleum products? If we decide on the former, we will have to plan to transport the crude to a seaport. Do we have suitable port facilities? Do we have a pipeline or other means of transporting the crude or oil products to the port?

On the other hand, if the oil products are required for our own consumption, do we have existing refining facilities which we can use or do we have to set up a new refinery? Can we exercise an option of exporting crude and importing refined petroleum products, and so on? Each of these options would require projects ranging from laying a pipeline to the construction of a refinery.

The attempt to satisfy unmet needs is the largest source of project ideas. The need for a project can be established through an environmental scan. The factors to be considered are politico-legal factors, economic factors, socio-demographic factors, technological factors and competition.

2.2.1 Politico-Legal Factors

Political stability is an important consideration for business. In case of political instability, one cannot be certain whether the new government will adhere to the policies of the old regime. Often changes in the political system have resulted in the takeover of private industries by the government. An entrepreneur can ill-afford such a situation. The industrial policies of the government, its programmes, its taxation regime, import–export policies, its repatriation policies and so on have an impact on enterprise. The factors could throw up opportunities or threats for the entrepreneur. For example, the emergence of the European Community with a common currency has facilitated trade with all the members. At the same time, since the members enjoy most favoured status, other nations producing similar products may find it difficult to enter the European market. Projects to produce products as substitutes of imported items are generally viewed favourably. Government plans may specify priorities for investments in particular sectors.

2.2.2 Economic Factors

We should consider the state of the economy and the overall growth rate. A growing economy is an indicator of favourable market conditions. We should also consider the growth of various sectors of the economy. The sectors with growth can throw up opportunities that can be exploited. For instance, a rapid growth in the electronics sector throws up opportunities to establish or expand existing capacities in the electronic industries. We should consider cyclic factors, inflation rates and the linkages with the world economy. The advent of information technology has reduced the world to a global village and the linkages of the economy of the country to the world economy cannot be ignored. The trade surplus or deficit and the exchange rate and its fluctuations should also be taken into account. Interest rates need to be considered as projects involve very large capital outlays and the cost of capital cannot be ignored.

2.2.3 Socio-demographical Factors

We must consider population trends, age distribution, income distribution, education profile of the population, employment of women and the changes in the family structure. For instance, in India the joint family system is increasingly giving way to nuclear families and the number of working women is on the rise. This inherently makes it difficult to look after the young children and the old members of the family. This social change throws up business opportunities in the field of childcare and geriatrics. The working woman needs things that will make her household chores faster and easier to perform. This may give opportunities in the white goods sector, like washing machines, microwave ovens and so on. One may even think of 'ready to cook' food, or providing housekeeping services and the like.

2.2.4 Technological Factors

The rapid emergence of new technologies has resulted in the shortening of the product life cycle. An entrepreneur who innovates products rapidly from new technologies will enjoy the benefits of being an early entrant into the product or service. Another consideration is our accessibility to new technology and the ease with which it can be absorbed and accepted in the environment in which we work. Trade fairs are a good source of technology exposition.

2.2.5 Competition

The enterprise faces competitive pressures from its suppliers if their number is small. Project ideas may emerge from the need to gain control over the supply of inputs for our enterprise. The strategy of gaining control over inputs is referred to as backward integration. An organization may resort to forward integration which implies gaining control over those facilities which use our outputs as their inputs and thus ensuring that our outputs have a captive user. For instance, Bata decided to take over the distribution of its products and set up stores to retail its products directly to customers. Such integrative strategies can give rise to ideas for projects. We often face competition from substitute products and from new entrants. Our strategic response to such competition is likely to throw up project ideas. For instance, when Bajaj scooters realized that motor cycles were becoming a popular substitute product, they set up a project to manufacture motor cycles themselves.

Strategic choices lead to ideas for projects. However, the firm's ability to implement the project is equally important. The firm can measure its strengths and weaknesses in different functional areas like finance, marketing, human resources, production and operations, research and development and so on to assess which ideas are capable of being implemented. The opportunities and threats offered by the external environment coupled with the internal strengths and weaknesses of the organization determine its business areas of activity.

2.3 OTHER SOURCES FOR PROJECT IDEAS

Project ideas can be obtained from a variety of sources. Some of these are:

(a) *Existing industries.* A careful study of existing industries especially with relation to their profitability and capacity utilization can throw focus on promising investment opportunities. The location of such industries should also be considered. It may be worthwhile to establish profit-making industries where they do not exist in order to cut down on transportation costs and so on.

(b) *Inputs and outputs of various industries.* An analysis of the inputs and outputs of various industries can help generate ides for projects. If the raw materials, components and sub-assemblies required are being produced by a few sources located far away, there is an opportunity to set up sources of such inputs close to the facility using them as it will reduce time delays and transportation costs. Often, it may be cheaper for a firm to outsource the supply of components to specialist units than to make them itself. Similarly, there may be scope for adding value to the outputs of existing industrial units and this may throw up business opportunities and ideas for projects.

(c) *Imports and exports.* A study of existing imports and exports can give ideas for projects. Import substitution is always welcome, as it helps in the balance of payments, provides employment opportunities and encourages the set-up of supporting industry and services. Similarly, existing exports and their potential for growth can generate project ideas.

(d) *Plan outlays and government guidelines.* The government lays down priorities for targets for various sectors as part of its plans for economic development. In India, the government's five-year plan lays down priorities and targets for industrial development and growth. It also gives incentives for development in backward areas. An analyzes of such guidelines helps to generate ideas in the priority sectors. Financial institutes and development agencies offer suggestions on investment opportunities. They offer prepared project reports and feasibility studies to assist the entrepreneur in selecting projects.

(e) *Local materials and resources.* Project ideas may originate from a study of local materials and local skills. One may consider different ways of adding value to local materials and employing local skills so that their potential can be fully realized. For instance, Pochampalli in Andhra Pradesh has skilled silk weavers who dye the yarn before weaving and yet produce beautiful patterns in the finished silk sarees that they produce. One may come up with the idea of using the skill not just for producing exclusive sarees but for weaving cloth and fabric for other uses. The traditional handloom may be replaced by a power loom to increase productivity and so on.

(f) *Technology watch.* Technology is changing at a rapid pace. Technology provides a competitive edge to the organization by reducing costs, improving quality and reducing the time for production. A close watch should be kept on technology so that early entrant advantage can be taken by identifying useful technology and innovating products using the same. Technological changes may generate project ideas for new products or improvements in the existing products and processes.

(g) *Revival of sick units.* This can prove to be another source for project ideas. Units are declared sick when their assets are reduced to half due to continuing losses. If the organization has the wherewithal to achieve a turnaround in such units, it may invest in acquiring them and then running them with or without changes to processes and products.

(h) *Trade and industrial fairs.* Items on display at such fairs may generate project ideas.

2.4 PRELIMINARY SCREENING

After generating a large number of ideas, a preliminary screening is carried out to shortlist those ideas that can be developed further for implementation. It is useful to screen competing project ideas by asking questions such as

(a) Does the project support the organization's mission?
(b) Is the project compatible with the organization's strategic plan?
(c) Is the cost of the project reasonable and is there an available source of funds?
(d) Does the project's cost–benefit analysis justify its initiation?

The following factors that may be considered for preliminary screening of project ideas.

Compatibility with promoter's interest

The project idea must be compatible with the promoter's interests and other business ventures. It should be within the capability of the promoter and should take into account the strengths and weaknesses of the organization.

Government policy

Project ideas must be in conformity with government policy. If the government does not permit the import of certain inputs, it would be futile to consider projects which are based on such inputs. Ideas should be in keeping with national interests and global priorities. The foreign exchange requirements and the availability of foreign exchange should be borne in mind while considering project ideas.

Availability of inputs

All inputs required for the project should be available or it should be possible to procure them. The inputs consist of raw materials, technology, skilled manpower, infrastructure, and services like electricity, power, fuel, water and so on.

Availability of market

The project idea should take into account the availability of suitable market for the product or service proposed to be set up. The potential market and the expected market share have a major impact on the profitability of the project.

Cost

An estimate of the costs involved in implementing a project is necessary. Projects that are within the budgetary constraints of the organization can be considered for further appraisal.

Risk

Projects are fraught with uncertainty and the risk associated with it. We should examine the level of risk involved in a project. Project ideas which fall within the risk level acceptable to us may be shortlisted for further consideration.

2.5 PROJECT RATING

The shortlisted projects are then ranked according to their desirability. They are rated comparatively. The process involves:

1. Identifying factors that are relevant to the projects.
2. Assigning a weightage to each factor. The weights assigned to each factor are such that the sum of the weights is 1.
3. Each project is then rated against each factor and a score out of 5 or 10 may be given.
4. The score is multiplied by the weightage of the factor and the total weighted score is obtained for each project. Projects are ranked according to this weighted score or rating index.

Let us understand the procedure with the help of an example. Let us consider four projects A, B, C and D. The critical factors identified for rating the projects are compatibility with promoter's interest, availability of inputs, availability of markets, cost and risk involved. The projects have been rated on a score of 5 for each factor and the weights assigned to the factor, the score and overall project rating are shown in Table 2.1.

Table 2.1 Weight, score and overall project rating

Factor	*Weight*	*Projects*			
		A	*B*	*C*	*D*
Compatibility	0.10	3	4	5	2
Availability of inputs	0.30	4	4	5	3
Availability of markets	0.25	3	4	3	2
Cost	0.20	3	4	5	3
Risk	0.15	4	2	1	4
Weighted score	1.00	3.45	3.70	3.90	2.80
Rank		3	2	1	4

The weighted score is calculated by multiplying the score for each factor with its weight and then taking the sum of all scores. For project A,

$$\text{Weighted score} = 3 \times 0.1 + 4 \times 0.3 + 3 \times 0.25 + 3 \times 0.20 + 4 \times 0.15 = 3.45$$

Sometimes it may be difficult to assign weights or scores and projects which are very closely competing may end up with the same ranking. In such cases, the forced decision matrix, which is based on paired comparisons, can be used. The method consists of making paired comparisons among the attributes and awarding 1 to the attribute rated higher and 0 to the attribute rated lower. The name 'forced decision' implies that the attributes being compared cannot be rated equal.

We shall first determine the attribute weights by paired comparisons. This is shown in Table 2.2.

Table 2.2 Attribute weightage

	Compatibility	*Inputs*	*Markets*	*Cost*	*Risk*	*Total*
Compatibility		0	0	0	0	
Inputs	1					
Markets	1					
Cost	1					
Risk	1					

The paired comparisons are carried out with the help of a matrix. The shaded cells show that a comparison is not possible. We start by comparing the attribute of compatibility of promoter's interest with others. Comparing it with inputs, we feel that availability of inputs is more important to us than compatibility. A score of 0 has been given to the cell (compatibility inputs) indicating that factor of inputs is preferred in importance to compatibility. At the same time, a score of 1 has been entered in the cell (inputs compatibility) indicating that the inputs has a higher preference than compatibility. Similarly, other paired comparisons for (compatibility) are completed and the scores are entered in the (compatibility) row and (compatibility) column. Then the next (inputs) is considered. It has already been compared with (compatibility). It cannot be compared with itself. It is next compared with (markets). If we feel inputs is more important to us than markets, we enter 1 in the cell (inputs markets) and a 0 in the cell (markets inputs). We can complete the matrix as shown in Table 2.3. The scores in each row are totalled up.

Table 2.3 Attribute weightage matrix

	Compatibility	*Inputs*	*Markets*	*Cost*	*Risk*	*Total*
Compatibility		0	0	0	0	0
Inputs	1		1	1	1	4
Markets	1	0		1	1	3
Cost	1	0	0		1	2
Risk	1	0	0	0		1

In the matrix shown above, we find that the factor 'Compatibility with promoter's interest' gets a score of 0. With a score of 0, it will not figure in our further considerations. At the outset, however, it was felt that it was an important factor. The situation is remedied by adding a dummy to the rows and columns of the matrix and assuming that all factors are more important than the dummy. This is shown in Table 2.4.

Table 2.4 Attribute weightage matrix

	Compatibility	*Inputs*	*Markets*	*Cost*	*Risk*	*Dummy*	*Total*
Compatibility		0	0	0	0	1	1
Inputs	1		1	1	1	1	5
Markets	1	0		1	1	1	4
Cost	1	0	0		1	1	3
Risk	1	0	0	0		1	2
Dummy	0	0	0	0	0		0

For getting the weightage, divide the score of each attribute by the total score. The weightage for the various attributes is shown in Table 2.5.

Table 2.5 Weightage for various attributes

Compatibility	1/15
Inputs	5/15
Markets	4/15
Cost	3/15
Risk	2/15

The next step is to carry out paired comparisons for the projects but considering one factor at a time. The same method of scoring and forcing a decision can be adopted. In this case, a dummy is not necessary even if a particular project gets a score of 0 for an attribute or factor. Let us first consider the factor Compatibility with promoter's interest (C). We shall now compare the four projects only on the basis of Compatibility with the promoter's interest and take no other factor into account.

Factor considered (compatibility): This is shown in Table 2.6.

Table 2.6 Compatibility factor

	A	*B*	*C*	*D*	*Total*
A		1	0	1	2
B	0		0	0	0
C	1	1		0	2
D	0	1	1		2

Similarly, consider the other factors.

Factor considered (inputs): This is shown in Table 2.7.

Table 2.7 Input factor

	A	*B*	*C*	*D*	*Total*
A		0	0	1	1
B	1		0	1	2
C	1	1		1	3
D	0	0	0		0

Factor considered (*markets*): This is shown in Table 2.8.

Table 2.8 Market factor

	A	*B*	*C*	*D*	*Total*
A		1	1	1	3
B	0		0	1	1
C	0	1		1	2
D	0	0	0		0

Factor considered (*cost*): This is shown in Table 2.9.

Table 2.9 Cost factor

	A	*B*	*C*	*D*	*Total*
A		0	0	0	0
B	1		0	1	2
C	1	1		1	3
D	1	0	0		1

Factor considered (*risk*): This is shown in Table 2.10.

Table 2.10 Risk factor

	A	*B*	*C*	*D*	*Total*
A		0	1	1	2
B	1		1	1	3
C	0	1		1	2
D	0	0	0		0

While carrying out paired comparisons, ensure that mathematical logic is followed, that is, if A is greater than B and B is greater than C, then A is greater than C.

Next a total weightage matrix is constructed as shown in Table 2.11.

Table 2.11 Total weightage matrix

Project	*Attribute Weightage*	*Compatibility* 1/15	*Inputs* 5/15	*Markets* 4/15	*Cost* 3/15	*Risk* 2/15	*Total*	*Rank*
A	Score	2	1	3	0	1		
	Wtd score	2/15	5/15	12/15	0/15	2/15	21/15	III
B	Score	0	2	1	2	3		
	Wtd score	0/15	10/15	4/15	6/15	6/15	26/15	II
C	Score	2	3	2	3	2		
	Wtd score	2/15	15/15	8/15	9/15	4/15	37/15	I
D	Score	2	0	0	1	0		
	Wtd score	2/15	0/15	0/15	3/15	0/15	5/15	IV

The weighted score (Wtd score) is obtained as the product of the score for the particular attribute and its weight. The projects are then ranked according to their overall scores. In the example shown above, project C is ranked first, B is ranked second, A is third and D is fourth. The best project is C. The ratings and comparisons are subjective. The subjectivity can be reduced by making a panel or a committee to consider the paired comparisons. The forced decision matrix technique is especially useful in case of closely competing alternatives as the method forces a choice of one over the other in a paired comparison.

The objective of rating projects is to identify and select those ideas which may be considered for further appraisal. The ability to undertake a number of projects simultaneously is limited by budgetary considerations and technical and administrative limitations. A feasibility study is carried out for the projects that are under consideration. The feasibility involves the following analyses.

Market analysis

The analysis is aimed at determining the potential market that exists for the product or service that would be produced by the project and the potential market share that the entrepreneur is likely to enjoy. It involves collection of information, carrying out a market survey and demand forecasting.

Technical analysis

This determines whether the project is technically feasible or not. Some of the considerations are availability of inputs, availability of compatible technology, issues related to location, layout and capacity of the facility and so on.

Ecological analysis

In recent years, society has become conscious of ecological degradation and its harmful effects on life on earth. In India, a ministry for environment has been set up which oversees that projects do not degrade the environment beyond permissible limits. The ecological analysis is aimed at determining the impact of the project on the environment and the measures necessary to reduce the impact to the minimum within acceptable limits.

Financial analysis

A financial analysis is carried out to determine the financial viability of the project. As projects involve large outlays, it is important that the project is financially profitable or has social benefits which outweigh the costs of the project. Measuring profitability of the project involves determining its costs and the stream of cash flows expected from it. A financial appraisal helps in selecting projects that should be undertaken.

Social cost–benefit analysis

The social benefits of a project must be determined especially for projects undertaken by the government or jointly by the public and private sectors. Often, very profitable projects may be rejected in favour of projects which benefit the society most. Entrepreneurs must understand their social responsibility. For instance, production and marketing of drugs may be financially profitable, but would hardly qualify for implementation because of its social implications. The social cost–benefit analysis becomes particularly important for underdeveloped and developing countries as they cannot afford to spend money on socially unproductive activities because of poverty and the lack of development of the masses. The social concerns have prompted United

Nations International Development Organization (UNIDO) to formalise and lay down guidelines for carrying out a social cost–benefit analysis.

The feasibility study assists in shortlisting and selecting projects for implementation.

SUMMARY

Most projects originate from a desire to solve problems or to satisfy an unfulfilled societal need. Projects may also originate from government policy directives and statutory requirements. An environmental scan dealing with political, economic, social and technological factors (PEST analysis) and competition highlights the opportunities and threats for business which may be exploited through projects. The opportunities and threats posed by the environment have to be matched with internal strengths and weaknesses to arrive at strategic choices for the firm. These strategic choices may need projects for their implementation and thus become a source for projects.

A study of existing industries, input and output requirements of various industries, imports and exports, plan outlays and government guidelines, local materials and resources, technology watch, revival of sick units and trade and industrial fairs are other sources of ideas for projects.

A preliminary screening is carried out to shortlist ideas for further study. Shortlisted projects should be compatible with the promoter's interests, should conform to government policies, should have a viable market and adequate availability of inputs, and should meet the cost and risk criteria of the organization. Projects can be rated by using a weighted rating score or a forced decision matrix. Shortlisted projects are then studied for their feasibility through a market analysis, technical analysis, financial analysis, ecological analysis, and social cost–benefit analysis.

QUESTIONS

1. Explain the sources of project ideas.
2. What factors would you consider while carrying out preliminary screening of projects?
3. Why is project rating carried out? Explain a method for project rating.
4. A firm has three projects A, B and C under consideration. It has identified critical factors as availability of inputs, availability of markets, cost, risk, compatibility with promoter's interest, and government policy. The company has rated the important factors for each project as follows:

Factors	*Weight*	*Scores (0 to 100)*		
		A	*B*	*C*
Availability of inputs	0.25	85	90	50
Availability of market	0.20	90	75	85
Cost	0.15	90	50	75
Risk	0.15	65	90	85
Compatibility	0.10	80	60	70
Government policy	0.15	85	90	75

Which project would you recommend?

CHAPTER 3

Project Feasibility

My personal philosophy is not to undertake a project unless it is manifestly important and nearly impossible.

—Edwin Land

LEARNING OBJECTIVES

After reading this chapter, you will be able to:

- Appreciate the need for feasibility study of projects.
- Understand the need for market analysis to establish demand and market share for the deliverables of the project.
- Study the issues involved in technical analysis and technology transfer.
- Examine the methodology for carrying out a financial analysis to determine the financial profitability of a project.
- Study the need for an environmental analysis and the requirements of an environmental impact statement.
- Examine the rational for a social cost–benefit analysis and study the methodologies for conducting a social cost–benefit analysis.
- Examine the use of various criteria for selection of a project portfolio.

3.1 INTRODUCTION

A project involves large capital outlays spread over time. An organization undertakes a project in the expectations of future returns. It is imperative that the returns or benefits of a project justify the costs involved. Before a project is undertaken, a feasibility study is carried out. The study examines the viability of a project from the financial profit or the social benefit point of view. The financial profitability of the project involves an examination of its costs and its profits. The costs of the project depend on the technology used, the choice of which is often dictated by the capacities desired. The capacity requirements are dependent on the demand for the product, service or other deliverable that is the end result of the project. The feasibility study involves a market analysis, a technical analysis, a financial analysis, an environmental analysis, and a social cost–benefit analysis.

3.2 MARKET ANALYSIS

A market analysis aims to identify the need or the potential demand for the product or service resulting from the project. The first step in carrying out a market analysis is to get a 'feel' of the market and the product. An informal interaction with customers, retailers, competitors and others gives a general 'feel' of the market situation. It is important to identify the market structure. We should examine the basis on which the market can be segmented. The basis of segmentation may be income levels, education levels, age levels, sex, size of the family, geographical division, and industry or a combination of some of these factors. This will help to determine the segment to be targeted.

The nature of demand should also be considered. The demand may be driven by seasonal requirements, regional requirements, fashion and current trends, price, disposable income and so on. The target market segment and the nature of demand help us to determine the size of the potential market. The potential market share can then be determined on the basis of our capacity and that of our competitors to fulfil the demand.

Objectives for the study are spelt out in question form and can be grouped under the four P's of marketing, namely, product, price, place and promotion. Let us consider a firm that plans a project to set up a unit to manufacture domestic air-conditioners. The objectives for the market and demand analysis may be expressed as follows:

(a) *Product*

(i) Who are the buyers of air-conditioners?
(ii) What is the current total demand?
(iii) How is the demand distributed (geographically as well as seasonally)?
(iv) What is the break-up of the demand (by sizes and models)?

(b) *Price*

(i) What price is the customer willing to pay?
(ii) What will be the cost of production?

(c) *Place*

(i) What should be the channels of distribution?
(ii) What should be the trade margins?

(d) *Promotion*

(i) How can customers be convinced of the superiority of the air-conditioner over those produced by competitors?
(ii) How should the customers be made aware of the attributes of the product?

The objectives determine the information that is required to be collected. Information may be gathered from secondary and/or primary sources. Secondary information is information that has already been collected in some other context and is readily available. Primary information is collected for the first time and is specific to the study on hand. A study of secondary information reveals the gaps in the information required by us and helps us to design our market research and survey. Secondary information may be available internally within the organization. Data such as past trends of sales and so on are invariably available. Some data may have been collected for some other purpose by the organization. Secondary data can be obtained from external sources like market research organizations such as Market Analysis and Research Group (MARG) which researches various markets and provides standard and customized reports, Centre for Monitoring Indian Economy (CMIE) which maintains specific industry databases and so on. It is available in the publications of trade associations like Federation of Indian Chambers of Commerce and Industry (FICCI) and through publications of various government research organizations like the Central Statistical Organization and so on which publish reports such as the census report, government plan documents, statistical surveys, industry-specific publications and so on. However, secondary information must be carefully evaluated. Some of the issues that must be considered are as follows:

(a) *Purpose.* What was the purpose of collecting the information? It is important to appreciate the purpose for which the information was collected. For instance, if we were to collect information about the requirements of air-conditioners from a study aimed at determining the preference of customers for air-conditioners vis-à-vis central air-conditioning, the conclusions may be totally misplaced.
(b) *Person.* Who collected it? It is relevant to know who collected the information. This reflects the experience and the interest of the researcher, which may be at cross purpose to our study.
(c) *Method.* How was it collected? The issue is relevant as the methodology of collecting the data can bring in biases in the data. For instance, if the data were collected through mailed questionnaires, then the number of non-respondents may not be reflected in the data and this may alter the conclusions drawn considerably.
(d) *Time.* When was it collected? This is an indicator of the currency of the data. If the data is too old or outdated, it may not serve our purpose.
(e) *Sample.* All research involves sampling. We draw inferences from the sample. It is necessary to know how the sample was determined both for its size and for its composition. How representative was it of the population group in which we are interested? Were some biases introduced in the sample? What is the degree of error that can be attributed to the sample? These issues can have far-reaching effect on our study.

Secondary data is easy to obtain and saves time. It is often more economical if obtained through public domain agencies, and is sometimes more accurate as it is a result of professional research. However, the quality of data and the data collection process cannot be accurately ascertained by the user. Information, to be useful, must be relevant, accurate, timely, and obtained at reasonable cost.

Primary data–based research involves collection of data by the researcher through a market survey. The market survey may be a census survey where every element of the population is considered or it may be a sample survey in which a representative sample is surveyed and inferences are drawn from it for the population. A census survey is useful only when the population is restricted in numbers. Generally, the more common form is a sample survey.

The methodology for conducting a market survey is well documented in books on market research and is beyond the scope of this text which is concerned primarily with project management.

Demand forecasts are made through the use of a suitable demand forecasting method. They may be qualitative or quantitative. The forecasts are the basis of computing pro forma (future) profit and loss accounts which help to determine the financial viability of the project.

3.3 TECHNICAL ANALYSIS

Technical analysis involves the technical areas of the project. These are manufacturing process and technology; material inputs and utilities; product mix; plant capacity, location and layout; machines and equipment; civil works and structures; and project charts, layouts and work schedules.

It is often felt that technology and matters related to technology are best left to technical experts. Nothing could be farther from the truth. While technical experts are well versed in technical matters, they are not conversant with the aspects of marketing products and managing enterprises. The choice of technology should be made in consultation with the technical experts but the responsibility for decision-making should rest fairly and squarely with the top management. A wrong technical decision can have far-reaching implications as technological decisions involve large capital outlays and are generally irreversible. They also directly affect the competitiveness of a firm. As managers are often unaware of the issues related to technology and technology transfer, these are being covered in some detail.

3.3.1 Selection of Technology

W. Skinner, a famous expert in technological matters, advocates that good decisions can be made by asking the following questions:

1. What will the technology do?
2. What will it not do?
3. What inputs will it require?
4. What will it cost?
5. How certain are the above?

3.3.2 Sources of Technology

Technology may be developed in-house by the firm or may be acquired from outside the organization either from abroad or indigenously. It is preferred to develop the technology in-house when the organization desires to keep the technology strictly confidential. Sometimes the cost of acquiring the technology is very high and the terms of agreement proposed by the collaborator may not be acceptable, or the technology may be closely held and may not be available easily. In such cases, the organization will be left with no alternative except to develop the technology in-house. A prerequisite for in-house development is the availability of time and resources within the organization.

It is preferable to acquire technology from outside when it is too expensive or takes too long to develop technology in-house. The lack of capability, resources and infrastructure required to develop technology may dictate its acquisition. Often, technology may be available at attractive terms. It may be profitable under such circumstances to acquire technology than to 'reinvent the wheel'.

3.3.3 Issues Involved in Technology Acquisition

Some of the important issues involved in technology acquisition and the technology acquisition process are described as follows:

(a) *Long-term relationship.* Technology acquisition is not similar to acquiring machinery or raw materials as it involves a long-time relationship and not a one-time relationship as in the case of machinery.

(b) *Components.* A technology package has many components like design parameters, operation process parameters, quality control, material specifications, training, research and development aspects and so on. Acquiring them as a package or otherwise involves complexities.

(c) *Uncertainty.* The changes in technology in the future are not known, but they need to be negotiated and decided upon at the present moment. This poses its own problems to the decision-maker.

(d) *Costs.* There are no standard price lists for technologies. The decision-maker has to judiciously assess the price that he is willing to pay for the technology.

(e) *Sources.* It is difficult to ascertain sources of technology and the quality of technology being supplied. There is always the risk of acquiring technology which is approaching obsolescence. Sources are generally unwilling to part with the latest technology or current technology.

3.3.4 Technology Acquisition Process

It involves the identification of the technology needed, evaluation of the technology and the sources of technology. The final stages of technology acquisition involve negotiations and technology transfer agreement.

Identification

The choice of technology is dictated by plant capacity, the principal inputs available, capital outlays, product mix and the ease of absorption.

Plant capacity influences the choice of technology as certain processes can be carried out economically only when performed at a certain scale. Inputs often dictate the choice of technology. For instance, the quality of limestone available for a cement plant determines whether to use the wet or the dry process. Capital availability and the cost of technology have to be matched. Technology must be viewed in terms of the total product mix that it can produce. The ease with which technology can be absorbed becomes an important factor for its selection.

The component of technology that is to be acquired also needs considerable thought. This will be largely influenced by the strengths and weaknesses of the company. For instance, if a company already has certain plant and machinery installed, it may desire to choose a technology that involves minimal addition of plant and equipment. A company that is already producing a product and merely wishes to enhance its size or some other attribute may only need drawings and designs for the necessary equipment rather than the whole range of equipment.

The company must decide whether to acquire technology through a licensing agreement or an outright purchase of technology or a joint venture with the supplier of technology.

Evaluation

The selected technology must be evaluated for its suitability and appropriateness. The selected technology should suit the local economic, social and cultural conditions. The following issues should be considered:

(a) Does it use local raw materials which are easily available?
(b) Can it be used by the local inhabitants? Does it conform to the knowledge and skills available locally, or will it require that highly skilled and trained man power be brought in from elsewhere to operate the technology?
(c) Will the products and services produced or facilitated by the technology meet the basic needs?
(d) Is the technology ecologically friendly and will it maintain environmental harmony?
(e) Is it in harmony with the local social and cultural norms?

Sources

The possible sources of technology are other manufacturers, research and development (R & D) organizations, technical institutes or experts. Technology sourced from R & D organizations or technical institutes is likely to be cheaper than that sourced from a manufacturing organization. This is because the technology from a manufacturer would be commercially proven, whereas technology from an R & D organization or an academic institute is likely to be at the laboratory or bench scale and will require considerable effort to scale up to commercial level. Despite this risk, the advantage of procuring technology through R & D organizations or academic organizations is that we will procure an evolving technology with sufficient growth potential.

Technology sourced from a manufacturer has the advantage of being commercially proven and would ensure successful commercial production. However, it is likely to be more expensive. It is unlikely that a manufacturing organization will part with the latest evolving technology as it would not like to create a potential competitor but would like to exploit the technology developed by it. Manufacturing organizations will generally part with technology that is nearing obsolescence.

All possible sources of technology should be identified as this will provide leverage in price negotiations. The standing of the supplier in terms of his integrity, reputation, rating, level of expertise in the concerned field, market share both national and international and so on should be ascertained. The package offered by the supplier should be given due consideration. This may cover features like guarantees offered, training support, marketing, buy-back arrangements, R & D support, intellectual property issues and so on.

Negotiations

The next stage of technology acquisition involves negotiations so that the technology can be acquired at the best terms possible. The negotiating team should include technical specialists and financial and legal experts. It should be borne in mind that technology payments are not restricted to licensing fee, engineering fee and royalties alone. They may also include other costs such as cost of machinery, components, raw materials, intermediates and catalysts which, a technology supplier insists, may be procured from him or from a specific source suggested by him. In fact, such payments are several times more than the payments for technology per se.

Technology transfer agreement

The final stage of technology transfer involves the drawing up of a technology transfer agreement. Some of the major clauses that should be included are:

(a) *Definition.* The technology, the process, the technical services and so on being transferred should be clearly defined and specified.
(b) *Technology package.* Details of the technology package should be clearly spelt out. The services to be provided by the technology supplier, such as process parameters, designs and drawings, quality assurance, training, specification of raw materials and so on, should be specified.
(c) *Payment.* The amount, manner, mode, currency and schedule of payments should be included. Milestones should be specified at which payments shall be released.
(d) *Duration.* The duration for which the agreement will be valid should be specified.
(e) *Access to improvements in technology.* The agreement should specify the availability or otherwise of any improvements in technology that may take place at the supplier's or the receiver's end during the period of the agreement.
(f) *Rights and obligations.* Rights and obligations of both the supplier and the buyer should be clearly spelt out in the agreement to avoid disputes and litigations at later stages.
(g) *Indemnification.* It is desirable to include an indemnification clause in the agreement by which the supplier indemnifies the buyer from any infringement of the third party's rights protected by a patent.
(h) *Exclusivity or non-exclusivity.* This refers to the extent of right for the use of technology. A technology transfer agreement may be exclusive, conditionally exclusive, exclusive for a region or non-exclusive. This aspect should be covered in the agreement.
(i) *Force majeure.* While both parties make genuine efforts to honour their commitments in terms of the agreement, there may be circumstances which render it difficult for either or both parties to fulfil their commitments. These may be acts of God, natural

disasters, riots, strikes, lockouts and so on. These should be included in the agreement and compensation payable, if any, under such circumstances must be specified.

(j) *Arbitration.* The agreement should include mechanism for quick and amicable solution of disputes or differences which may arise during the operation of the agreement. Arbitration is considered an appropriate method of settling such disputes.

(k) *Governing law.* It is important to specify the law that would be applicable in case of disputes.

3.3.5 Material Inputs

It is necessary to study the availability of material inputs required for a project. Raw materials may be available in natural form as deposits, when it becomes necessary to extract them, transport them and process them before use. The quality and quantity of raw material available should be assessed as it affects the viability of the project under consideration. Non-availability of material inputs will affect the project adversely or increase its cost. Materials may take the form of finished products or by-products from some other plants already in operation or the inputs may have to be imported from abroad. Technology decisions are influenced by the availability or otherwise of material inputs.

Other issues involved in a technical analysis are plant location and plant layout. These issues are adequately dealt with as part of operations management courses.

3.4 FINANCIAL ANALYSIS

Financial analysis aims at studying the financial viability of a project. It is concerned with the financial profitability of the project. This involves the estimation of the cost of the project and an estimation of cash flows that will result after the project is completed. Various criteria are used to determine the expected profitability of the project. Some of these are net present value, internal rate of return, return on investment and benefit–cost ratio.

3.4.1 Project Costs

These include cost of the following items.

Land and site development

The importance of location of a project is adequately dealt with during the technical analysis. However, some issues that need to be considered from the financial point of view are the availability of government subsidies and tax exemptions and relief. The government often offers subsidies for projects located in backward or tribal areas with a view to encouraging investments in such areas and developing them so as to bring them in the social mainstream. The subsidies are generally offered as a percentage of the total fixed capital investment or as concessional land rates and so on. The government may also offer tax exemption schemes for the first few years of a project or may offer schemes under which payment of taxes is deferred for the first few years. Such subsidies and schemes can considerably reduce the cost of the project. However, the savings through such schemes must be weighed against the extra expenses that would be incurred to develop the infrastructure needed for the project. The elements of cost which determine the cost of land and site development are basic cost of land, conveyance charges and other allied charges, levelling of the plot, laying of internal roads, laying of approach roads, construction of boundary wall, provisioning for water and electricity required during the construction and so on.

Buildings and civil works

The plinth areas required for the main plant building, administrative buildings, storage facilities and other buildings are worked out and the cost is estimated by multiplying the area with the prevailing cost per unit area for the type of construction that is being considered. As the project may have a long gestation period, the current costs of building materials and labour are suitably enhanced to cater for expected inflation of prices over time.

Plant and machinery

The plant and machinery costs should be estimated based on the latest quotations and costs. An escalation factor should be added in case of long delivery periods. The cost of plant and machinery also includes the cost of duties on imported equipment, taxes, excise and sales tax. The octroi, freight, transportation charges, handling and erection charges are also included in these estimates.

Miscellaneous fixed assets

Other items which do not form part of the manufacturing process are called miscellaneous fixed assets. These may include generating sets, boilers, air-conditioning equipment, plants like welding sets, erection of railway siding if required, effluent treatment plant or other equipment required to meet statutory environmental controls, fire fighting equipment, laboratory and testing equipment, transformers, furniture, office equipment and so on. Expenses incurred for patents, licenses, trademarks, copyrights and so on are also included under this head.

Pre-operative expenses

This head includes the expenses that are likely to be incurred before the project goes on stream and commercial production commences. These comprise establishment expenses; promotional expenses; organizational and training costs; rents, rates and taxes; travelling expenses; printing and stationery costs; postage and telephone charges; insurance during the currency of the project; interest during project period and so on. These are generally capitalized by apportioning them to depreciable fixed assets in the ratio of their book value. This implies that these costs instead of being offset against the operating income in the first year of operation itself are distributed over the operative life of the assets.

Preliminary expenses

These include expenses incurred for carrying out market survey, feasibility study, preparing project report, drafting the memorandum and articles of association and incorporating the company. These expenses are capitalized through amortization.

Capital issue expenses

These are expenses that are incurred for raising capital from the public. These include underwriting commission, brokerage, fees to managers and registrars of the issue, printing and postage expenses, advertising and publicity expenses, listing fees, stamp duty and so on. These expenses are capitalized through amortization.

Provision for contingencies

Price escalation is built into individual items of expenditure. However, escalation of costs may occur because of small delays in project execution or due to minor changes in specifications and the scope of the project. The project cost items are broken up into 'firm' and 'non-firm' cost items. Firm cost items are those which have already been acquired or for which definite arrangements have been made. The risk of price escalation on items that have not yet been firmed up is greater. Generally, provision for contingencies is made at 5% of costs for firm items and at 10% of costs for non-firm items.

Technical know-how fees

Sometimes it is necessary to engage technical experts and consultants to assist in various technical aspects of the project like preparation of the project report, choice of technology, selection of plant and machinery, design drawings and so on. The fees paid for such services are included under this item. However, royalties paid annually are included as operating expenses while preparing the profitability projections for a project.

Margin money for working capital

While working capital is arranged through short-term commercial borrowings and trade creditors, banks require that some portion of the working capital be provisioned through long-term finances. This portion is called margin money and must be catered for by the promoters.

3.4.2 Means of Finance

After the costs have been estimated, the means of providing for finance have to be considered. This is important as it affects the future cash flows which shall have to be computed in order to ascertain the profitability of the project or otherwise. There can be various means of long-term finance. The following are some of the important ones.

Equity capital

This represents the capital contributed by the owners of the enterprise. The equity shareholders are entitled to a share of the profits in the form of dividends that the company may declare from time to time. They also bear the risk of ownership and bear losses, if any. While the company does not have to pay any interest on this money, the dividend paid is taxable.

Preference capital

This represents the contribution of the preference shareholders. These shareholders are paid a fixed rate of dividend irrespective of whether the company declares a dividend or not. Even when the company declares a dividend higher than the preference rate of dividend, the preference shareholders get only the fixed rate of dividend.

Term loans

Financial institutes and commercial banks provide secured term loans to companies at fixed rates of interest. The loans may be rupee loans or foreign exchange loans. These form an important part of long-term finance for the company. The interest paid on these loans is not taxable to the company and results in tax savings for the company. However, a company cannot meet all its capital needs through such long-term borrowings as banks and financial institutes expect the owners to bring in their own share of capital too. The financial structure of a company is a mix of debt and equity and industries lay down norms for debt equity ratio of a firm.

Debentures

These are instruments for raising debt capital. Debentures carry a fixed rate of interest and are normally issued for a period of five to seven years after which they are redeemed. Debentures may be fully convertible, partially convertible or non-convertible. The convertible debentures are converted into equity shares as per the terms and conditions spelt out at the time of issue of the debentures. Debentures may be redeemed when they expire or their redemption may be spread over two or three years as may be laid down in the terms and conditions of issue. The interest paid on debentures is also non-taxable for the company.

Deferred credit

Suppliers of plant and machinery sometimes offer a deferred credit facility under which the payment can be made over a period of time.

Miscellaneous sources

Public deposits, unsecured loans and lease and hire purchase agreements are some other sources of finance. Incentive schemes in the form of 'seed capital assistance' where capital is provided to the company at very nominal rates to encourage investments in particular sectors, capital subsidy, tax deferment or exemption are some other sources of capital.

The cost of equity funds is more than the cost of debt funds because the interest paid on debt funds is a tax-deductible expense, whereas the dividend paid to equity shareholders is taxed. The financial structure of the company must also take risk into account. Debt carries greater risk because of its fixed financial burden in terms of interest. Equity shareholders may or may not be paid dividend at the discretion of the company. Another important consideration is the amount of control that the promoters like to exercise on the affairs of the company. Issue of additional equity reduces the control of the promoters as it affects their percentage holding of shares adversely.

3.4.3 Working Capital Requirements

An estimate of working capital requirements is required to compute the short-term bank borrowings that the company may seek. Interest has to be paid on these borrowings and this has to be taken into account while making pro forma profit and loss statements. Net working capital is defined as the difference between current assets and current liabilities of the firm. The current assets of the company consist mainly of raw materials (both indigenous and imported), stocks of finished goods, stock of work in process, and debtors or accounts receivable. The current liabilities consist chiefly of trade credits and other payables. In order to calculate working capital requirements an estimate of sales revenue and cost of production will have to be made. The sale revenue depends on demand forecasts and sale prices. The terms of credit have also to be taken into account in order to calculate receivables. The cost of production consists of the cost of raw materials, labour and overheads. This will help to determine the inventory requirement of raw materials, work in process and finished goods. This will also facilitate determination of trade credit and other payables. As explained earlier, commercial banks require that certain margin money be provided for working capital requirements by the company from its long-term capital assets. The working capital less the margin money is raised through short-term bank borrowings at rates of interest as laid down.

3.4.4 Profit and Loss Statements

The next step is to draw up estimated profit and loss statements covering the operative life of the facility resulting from the project. This may be computed as follows:

A. Revenue from sales and other income
B. Operating expenses
C. Gross profit (A – B)
D. Interest on term loans and short-term borrowings
E. Depreciation and amortization of preliminary expenses
F. Profit before tax (C – D – E)
G. Tax
H. Profit after tax (F – G)
I. Dividend on preference shares and equity shares
J. Repayment of loans
K. Retained profit
L. Net cash accrual (K + E)

The stream of cash flows is obtained from the profit and loss statements. In the final year of the life of the project, salvage value of assets, final settlement of all loans and working capital are also taken into account. The profitability of the project can now be determined by using any of the criteria such as net present value, internal rate of return, return on investment or benefit–cost ratio.

Net present value

The net present value (NPV) uses the management's minimum desired rate of return as a discounting rate to compute the present value of all net cash inflows. If the result is positive, the project meets the minimum desired rate of return and is eligible for further consideration. If the NPV is negative, the project is unprofitable from the management's point of view and is rejected.

The NPV is calculated as follows:

$$\text{NPV} = I_0 + \sum_{t=1}^{n} \frac{F_t}{(1+k)^t}$$

where

I_0 = Initial investment (since it is as outflow, it is negative)
F_t = Net cash flow for period t
k = Required rate of return

Microsoft Excel spreadsheet has a function NPV for making these calculations.

EXAMPLE 3.1 What will be the NPV of a project whose cash flows are shown in Table 3.1.

Table 3.1 Cash flows of a project

Year	*Cash flow (₹, lakh)*
0	–25
1	5
2	6
3	7
4	9
5	7
6	6
7	6

Solution Printout of the Excel spreadsheet is given as follows:

	A	*B*	*C*	*D*	*E*	*F*	*G*	*H*	*I*
1									
2		Years							
3		0	1	2	3	4	5	6	7
4	Outflows	–25							
5	Inflows		5	6	7	9	7	6	6
6	Desired rate of return	15%							
7	NPV	₹ 1.96							
8									
9	Formula in cell B7	= B4 + NPV(15%, C5, D5:15)							
10									

As the project has a positive NPV of ₹ 1.96 lakh, the project is profitable and can be undertaken.

Internal rate of return

The internal rate of return (IRR) of a project is the discount rate which makes its NPV equal to zero. It can be calculated as follows:

$$I_0 + \sum_{t=1}^{n} \frac{F_t}{(1+k)^t} = 0$$

where

I_0 = Initial investment (since it is as outflow, it is negative)
F_t = Net cash flow for period t
k = Internal rate of return

Microsoft Excel spreadsheet has a function which computes the IRR.

EXAMPLE 3.2 Let us consider the same project data as given in Example 3.1 and compute the IRR.

Solution Printout of the Excel spreadsheet is given as follows:

	A	*B*	*C*	*D*	*E*	*F*	*G*	*H*	*I*	*J*
1										
2						Years				
3			0	1	2	3	4	5	6	7
4	Outflows		–25							
5	Inflows		–25	5	6	7	9	7	6	6
6	Desired rate of return		15%							
7	IRR		₹ 0.17							
8										
9	Formula in cell C7		IRR = IRR(C5:J5, 15)							
10										

As the IRR of 17% is higher than the desired rate of return (15%), the project is profitable and can be undertaken.

Return on investment

It is the average return on investment and is also called the accounting rate of return. There can be many methods of computing the accounting rate of return. The commonly employed methods are as follows:

1. Average income after tax/Initial investment
2. Average income after tax/Average investment
3. Average income after tax but before interest/Initial investment
4. Average income after tax but before interest/Average investment
5. Average income before interest and tax/Initial investment
6. Average income before interest and tax/Average investment

If the accounting rate of return is higher than the expected accounting rate of return, the project is profitable and acceptable.

Benefit–cost ratio

It is the ratio between benefits and costs.

$$\text{Benefit–cost ratio} = \frac{\text{Present value of benefits}}{\text{Initial investment}}$$

A project which has a benefit–cost ratio of more than 1 is acceptable.

3.5 ENVIRONMENTAL ANALYSIS

Environmental concerns were unheard of till a few decades ago, particularly in India. Industries merely found some stream or water source and discharged their effluents into it with impunity. Social awakening towards the environment is a fairly recent phenomenon. Today, the world is concerned with the changing climate, depletion of the ozone layer, carbon emissions and so on. Green Peace activists protest against the disposal of waste in a manner which would be harmful to the environment. It has rightly been said that we have not inherited the world from our forefathers but have borrowed it from our descendants, and it is our social responsibility to ensure that we leave it fit for them to live in.

Technological advances have always been mixed blessings. They have brought about new problems in the disposal and handling of toxic industrial waste. Electronic waste, in the form of computer and electronic hardware, nuclear waste, debris from space and so on have added to the list of environmental pollutants.

The increasing awareness of our social responsibility towards the environment prompted the Government of India to make it mandatory for any project to obtain clearance from the Ministry of Environment and Forests before implementation.

Some definitions are as follows:

Environment: The environment of man consists of everything that is outside him. According to the Environment (Protection) Act, 1986, 'environment' includes water, air, land and the interrelationship that exists between water, air, land and human beings, other living creatures, plants, micro-organisms and property. The definition includes interaction between the non-life components and their interaction with living beings.

Environmental pollutant: The Act defines an environmental pollutant as 'any solid, liquid or gaseous substance present in such concentrations as may be, or tend to be injurious to environment.'

Environmental pollution: It is the presence in the environment of an environmental pollutant.

Environmental pollutions may occur from many sources. Major sources of pollution are discussed in the following paragraphs.

3.5.1 Sources of Pollution

Industries are the major source of pollution of air and water which are essential for all living creatures on earth. Smokestacks of factories pollute the air with suspended particles. All types of fuel used by the industry—be it coal, oil, natural gas, electricity or nuclear energy—cause air pollution of varying degrees. Thermal power plants, most of which are located near population centres, are a major source of pollution. Polluted air causes respiratory and other diseases. Vehicles and transportation of all forms—road, rail, ships and aircraft—contribute to air pollution.

Water pollution is more complex. Groundwater gets polluted through the dumping of industrial effluents on the ground. Human waste, sewage and decomposing organic matter also seep into the ground and affect the groundwater.

Water draining from fields into canals and so on carries with it pesticides used for agriculture. Even fertilizers cause water pollution. Direct discharge of industrial wastes into water bodies is a cause for major concern.

Some of the most polluting industries are tanneries, textile industry, distilleries, fertilizers, steel mills, oil refineries, drugs and pharmaceuticals, and sugar.

The Water (Prevention and Control of Pollution) Act, 1974, amended in 1989, the Air (Prevention and Control of Pollution) Act, 1981, amended in 1987 and the Environment (Protection) Act, 1986, amended in 1991, are relevant legislations which lay down rules and regulations for prevention and control of environmental pollution.

There are various methods of dealing with pollution. The costs of pollution control and treatment should be taken into account while carrying out a financial appraisal of the project.

3.5.2 Environmental Impact on Projects

Environmental Impact Assessment Notification (2006) of the Government of India spells out the type of projects that require environmental clearance and the authorities that will accord such clearance. Clearances are based on the environmental impact assessment. The assessment determines the impact of the project on the environment.

International Association for Impact Assessment (1999) defines environmental impact assessment as 'the process of identifying, predicting, evaluating and mitigating the biophysical, social, and other relevant effects of development proposals prior to major decisions being taken and commitments made'. The purpose of the assessment is to ensure that decision-makers consider environmental impacts before deciding whether to proceed with new projects.

Environmental Impact Assessment (EIA) is a tool used to identify the environmental, social and economic impacts of a project prior to decision-making. It aims to predict environmental impacts at an early stage in project planning and design, find ways and means to reduce adverse impacts, shape projects to suit the local environment and present the predictions and options to decision-makers.

An EIA study involves the following steps.

Scoping

Key issues and concerns of interested parties are identified. Scoping helps in site selection and in identifying possible alternatives. It sets the terms of reference to be addressed in the Environmental Impact Statement. Environmental impact is not restricted to a site of the project but covers a much larger area surrounding it.

Screening

It identifies the project and helps to decide whether the project needs environmental clearance or not. All projects which are likely to have a major impact on the environment need clearance.

Identifying and evaluating alternatives

Alternative sites for projects should be identified and evaluated so that the one with the least impact on the environment can be selected. In some cases, alternate sites may not be possible.

For instance, a project involving extraction of ore can only be set up where that ore is available. While alternatives may not be possible, mitigating measures that will help to reduce the impact on the environment will still have to be spelt out and implemented.

Mitigating measures

The process reviews the actions taken to prevent, avoid or minimize the actual or potential adverse impact of the project. The project may have to be abandoned or suitably modified to meet the requirements of pollution control. Various methods for reducing the harmful effects of the project can be adopted. These are discussed in a subsequent section. Uncertainties in the project proposal with regard to environmental degradation are studied and if necessary the project is deferred till the full impact of such uncertainties can be studied.

3.5.3 Environmental Impact Statement (EIS)

The aforementioned processes help in preparing the EIS. This is a comprehensive document that reports the findings of the EIA. This is the final stage of the EIA and the EIS is the document required to be submitted for obtaining clearance for the project from the Ministry of Environment and Forests, Government of India. An EIS must include the following:

1. A description of the project, its purpose, its location, its size, its design and technical details such as materials to be used and so on.
2. Description of the significant effects of the project. This should include the effect of the project on each component of the environment, describing the nature and severity of the impact. For government projects, the effect on plans for land usage and surrounding areas should also be included. Private projects which would affect land usage in surrounding areas are not permitted to be undertaken.
3. Possible alternatives should be spelt out in the EIS, in terms of both alternate sites and alternate projects which do not cause adverse effects to the same degree as foreseen in the project under review.
4. The report should list details of the possible remedial and mitigating measures that will be adopted to prevent, avoid and reduce the adverse effects and the extent to which these effects will be reduced.
5. The residual adverse effects of the project despite the mitigating measures adopted.
6. Evaluation of the commercial and social desirability of the project vis-à-vis the adverse impact on the environment caused by it.
7. Amount of resources that have to be committed irretrievably to the project.

3.5.4 Mitigating Measures

Some measures that can be taken to obviate the effects of environmental pollution are discussed in the following paragraphs.

Life cycle assessment

It is the process of evaluating the effects that a product has on the environment throughout its life cycle. It is also referred to as 'cradle to grave' assessment. It can be used for developing business strategy, purchasing decisions, product design and improvement and for eco-labelling and communicating about the environmental effects of the product. Examples of eco-labelling are products labelled as 'green' products or star ratings for energy consumption and so on. It identifies and quantifies the environmental loads involved, for example, the energy and raw materials consumed, the emissions and wastes generated; evaluates the potential environmental impacts of these loads; and assesses the options available for reducing these environmental impacts. The life cycle assessment of a product or function is shown in Figure 3.1.

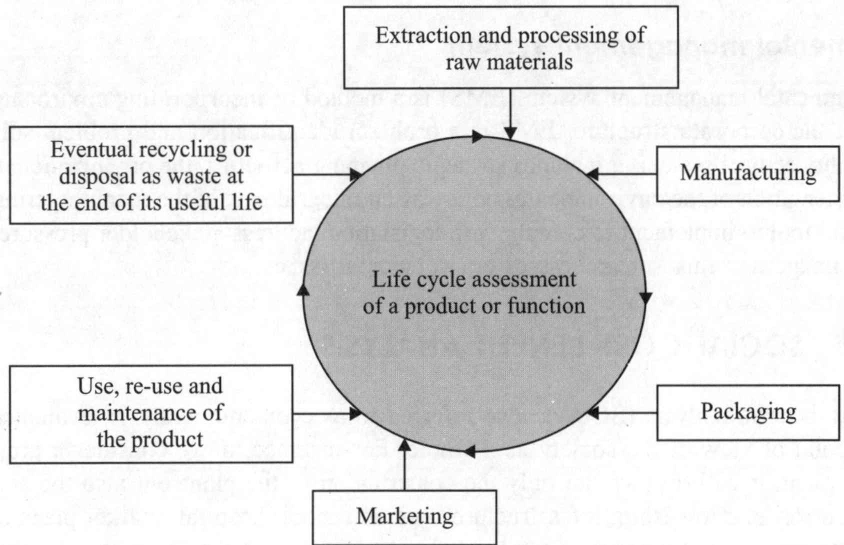

Figure 3.1 Life cycle assessment of a product or function.

Environmentally sound technologies

These technologies protect the environment, are less polluting, use all resources in a more sustainable manner, recycle more of their wastes and products, and handle residual wastes in a more acceptable manner than the technologies for which they were substitutes. Such technologies encompass a variety of cleaner production processes and are pollution preventing.

Cleaner production

It means 'the continuous application of an integrated preventive environmental strategy to processes, products and services to increase efficiency and reduce risks to humans and the environment'. It is a preventive approach and in the long run is the most effective way to design and operate industrial processes and to develop products and services that minimize the costs of wastes, emissions and negative environmental and health impacts.

Eco-design

It implies that the environmental aspects of the product are considered at all stages of the development process so that the environmental aspect is the lowest throughout the product life cycle. Eco-design also provides information on the environmental aspects of goods and semi-finished products.

Supply chain management

Environmental goals can be achieved by involving suppliers in environmental issues. The firm should screen suppliers for environmental performance. It should work collaboratively with them on green design initiatives and should train them to build their environmental management capacity.

Environmental management system

An environmental management system (EMS) is a method of incorporating environmental care throughout the corporate structure. EMS is a problem identification and problem-solving tool. Like a quality control system, it includes strategic planning activities, the organizational structure and implementation of the environmental policy as an integral part of the manufacturing process. It is a useful tool to implement to comply with legislation, address stakeholder pressure, improve corporate image and raise awareness of environmental issues.

3.6 SOCIAL COST–BENEFIT ANALYSIS

Social cost–benefit analysis (SCBA), also referred to as economic analysis, evaluates projects from the point of view of the society as a whole. For instance, if we consider a project to set up a steel plant, it will involve not only the construction of the plant but also the construction of approach roads, a township, infrastructure such as school, hospital, market place and so on. While these are primarily meant as facilities for the workers of the plant, they offer economic opportunities to the local population resulting in some benefits to society as a whole. Similarly, the pollution caused by the steel plant may result in destruction or degradation of the environment and increased health hazards for the local population. This may be considered as the cost or the price that the locals would have to pay for the economic benefits accruing because of the location of the steel plant. A financial analysis does not take the value of these benefits or costs into account.

The significance of economic development cannot be underplayed especially in the case of underdeveloped and developing countries. In such cases, the government makes heavy public investments in projects and it is imperative that contribution of such projects to the well-being of society is properly evaluated. The concern for economic development and the economic uplift and well-being of society led the United Nations International Development Organization (UNIDO) and a team of two economists—I.M.D. Little and J.A. Mirrlees—to develop methodologies in the late 60s and early 70s for carrying out SCBA. The methodologies are explained in detail in Appendix—Social Cost–benefit Analysis.

3.7 PROJECT APPRAISAL AND SELECTION

When an organization has a number of projects which meet the feasibility criteria but does not have enough resources to undertake all of them, a portfolio of projects will have to be selected based on some criteria. The criterion may be numeric or non-numeric. Non-numeric criteria have been discussed in Chapter 2. Amongst the numeric criteria, the net present value, the internal rate of return, the benefit–cost ratio, the accounting rate of return and the payback period are generally used to compare projects. Barring the payback period, the methods to calculate others have been described earlier in this chapter (Section 3.4). The financial analysis is further modified by taking into account costs that may be incurred on account of the environmental factors. The social cost–benefit analysis overrides the financial analysis, especially in the case of public investments in underdeveloped and developing countries.

The ***payback period*** is the time that would elapse before the initial investment is fully recovered. Let us consider the data given in Table 3.1.

The payback period can be calculated with the help of Table 3.1 by cumulating the benefits. See Table 3.2.

Table 3.2 Calculation of payback period

Year	*Cash flow* (₹, lakh)	*Cumulative inflows*
0	–25	
1	5	5
2	6	11
3	7	18
4	9	27
5	7	
6	6	
7	6	

The investment of ₹ 25 lakh will be recovered in 3.78 years. This is the payback period.

A complete discussion of these models can be found in any standard work on financial management and is beyond the scope of this text which concentrates on project management.

SUMMARY

All shortlisted projects are examined for their feasibility. The feasibility study examines whether the project is profitable in terms of its benefits or not. The study consists of the following:

1. Market analysis aimed at determining the need and the potential for the deliverables of the project. The analysis involves market segmentation, framing of objectives in the form of questions, collecting secondary data, and collecting primary data through a market survey. The data is then analyzed and various forecasting techniques are used to forecast the potential demand.
2. A technical analysis determines the most viable processes for production of the product. The technology may be available in-house or may have to be acquired. The acquisition of technology involves many issues which must be given due consideration. The technology selection also takes into account the availability of inputs. The capacity of the plant, its location and its layout are determined after a technical analysis.

3. A financial analysis is carried out to study the financial viability or the financial profitability of a project. This involves taking all project costs into consideration and then making projections of the stream of cash flows expected throughout the life of the project. Pro forma balance sheets and profit and loss account statements are prepared for each year. The project is evaluated on the basis of net present value, internal rate of return, average rate of return or benefit–cost ratio. The net present value is calculated by discounting cash flows at the expected rate of return desired by the sponsors of the project. Projects with a positive net present value are considered suitable for implementation. The internal rate of return and the average rate of return are also compared with the desired rate of return. Projects that yield a rate of return higher than the expected rate of return qualify for implementation.
4. In recent times, society has become very conscious of environmental protection and it is mandatory for most projects to obtain environmental clearances. An environmental analysis studies the impact of the project on the environment and results in an environmental impact statement. The statement covers the residual impact of the project on the environment despite the mitigating measures taken by the organization.
5. A social cost–benefit analysis is carried out to study the impact of the project on society at large. It differs from the financial analysis in that the financial analysis only considers direct costs and profits, whereas the social cost–benefit analysis considers the impact of the project on society and economy as a whole. For instance, the setting up of an industry in a backward area results in development of roads which bring in prosperity and development for the local residents. Similarly, there are social costs involved. For instance, while the establishment of an international airport may result in its attendant benefits, the noise pollution caused by taking off and landing aircraft may affect the local flora and fauna and pose a health hazard to the local population.

The most commonly used methods for selection of a project portfolio are net present value, payback period and the internal rate of return.

QUESTIONS

1. Why is a feasibility study carried out?
2. What is the basic purpose of carrying out a market analysis?
3. What do you understand by preliminary expenses and pre-operative expenses of a project? How do we capitalize the cost of preliminary and pre-operative expenses of a project?
4. What is the difference between financial analysis and economic analysis of a project?
5. Two new projects are under consideration by a company. Project A will cost ₹ 1,50,000 to develop and is expected to yield an annual net cash flow of ₹ 40,000. Project B will cost ₹ 2,20,000 to develop and is expected to result in an annual cash flow of ₹ 55,000. The company being cash strapped is very concerned with cash flows. Using the payback period, which project will you recommend?
6. A project which will cost ₹ 50,000 to implement has projected cash flows of ₹ 15,000, ₹ 20,000, ₹ 30,000, ₹ 25,000 and ₹ 15,000 over the next five years. The required rate of return is 20%. What is the NPV of the project? What is the IRR for the project?

7. What would happen to the NPV of the above project if the inflation rate is expected to be 3% in each of the next five years?
8. A company expects to earn at least 18% on its investments. The cash inflows and outflows of two projects are given in the following table. Which of the two projects would you recommend purely on financial considerations?

Project Alpha			*Project Beta*		
Year	*Inflow*	*Outflow*	*Year*	*Inflow*	*Outflow*
0	0	3,00,000	0	0	2,35,000
1	60,000	1,20,000	1	0	2,00,000
2	1,60,000	0	2	1,60,000	0
3	2,60,000	60,000	3	2,30,000	40,000
4	2,60,000	0	4	2,25,000	0
5	2,00,000	60,000	5	2,15,000	40,000
6	1,90,000	0	6	2,00,000	0
7	1,30,000	40,000	7	1,10,000	40,000

APPENDIX

Social Cost–Benefit Analysis

A.1 INTRODUCTION

Social cost–benefit analysis (SCBA), also referred to as economic analysis, examines the impact of a project on society at large or on the overall economy. It is especially useful for analyzing the benefits of public investments even though it can be employed to assess the usefulness or otherwise of private projects. It was given special emphasis in the 1960s and 1970s, particularly in the context of developing countries. The social disparities in these countries required vast public investments and it was imperative that the effects of such investments on the economy and the well-being of society be analyzed before making such heavy commitments. In planned economies, SCBA is a tool for analyzing individual projects keeping in view the national economic objectives and the resources allocated to various sectors as spelt out in the plan.

The concern for economic development and the economic uplift and well-being of society led the United Nations International Development Organization (UNIDO) and a team of two economists—I.M.D. Little and J.A. Mirrlees—to develop methodologies in the late 60s and early 70s for carrying out SCBA.

A.2 RATIONALE FOR SCBA

SCBA, as the name suggests, focuses on social costs and social benefits, which may be different from monetary costs and benefits. The main reasons for such discrepancies are discussed in the following.

A.2.1 Market Imperfections

The financial profitability of a project is based on market prices. These do not reflect social value unless the market operates under conditions of perfect competition. As we are aware such a condition rarely exists. The market price is generally an administered price and does not always conform to economic principles.

Some of the common market imperfections found in developing countries are on account of rationing, prescription of minimum wage rates and foreign exchange regulations. Rationing implies control over the price and distribution of commodities. The commodity may often be sold at prices which are much lower than what would prevail in a competitive market. For example, petroleum products are sold at highly subsidized rates in India. Similarly, 'fair price shops' sell food grains at cheaper rates to the economically weaker sections of society for whom they are meant. In a country where unemployment is high, labour may be willing to work at rates much lower than those prescribed as minimum wages. In developing countries which regulate the foreign exchange rate, the official rate of foreign exchange is less than the rate that would prevail if there were no regulations. Foreign exchange usually commands a premium in unofficial transactions.

A.2.2 Externalities

A project may have external effects which may be either beneficial or harmful. These are costs and benefits which will accrue to different people, groups in the society, locality or region, other than those targeted by the project as intended beneficiaries. These effects are not factored in while carrying out the financial analysis for the project. For instance, if a steel plant is built in some remote underdeveloped area, certain infrastructure beneficial to the residents of that area will be created. The steel plant may set up a township for its employees, which may include a commercial marketplace, school for children, a hospital and so on. These facilities will also become available to those living in the area and thus improve their lot. It would also provide employment to some of the local residents. At the same time, the steel plant may damage the environment because of the pollution that it would cause. While the financial costs and benefits do not take such effects into account, these are considered in SCBA. All costs and benefits, no matter to whom they accrue, and whether they are paid for or not, are relevant in SCBA.

A.2.3 Taxes and Subsidies

Taxes and subsidies constitute costs and benefits for the project owners. However, in the context of the overall economy, they merely represent book transfers. They are ignored while carrying out SCBA as they do not have an impact on the economy.

A.2.4 Concern for Savings

It is immaterial whether the benefits of a project lead to increased consumption or to increased savings, from a financial point of view. The project owners or sponsors are concerned only with the financial profitability of the project. From a social point of view, it is important to consider how the benefits of the project are divided between consumption and savings. Savings can be used for further investments and so a rupee of savings is considered more valuable than a rupee of consumption. This is especially applicable to economies of developing countries which face a scarcity of capital. SCBA takes into account this concern for savings. Savings are valued at a higher premium than consumption.

A.2.5 Concern for Redistribution

Private entrepreneurs are not concerned how their benefits are distributed across various groups in society. However, the society is concerned about the distribution of benefits to various groups. It considers a rupee of benefits to the economically weaker sections as more valuable than a rupee of benefits to the affluent groups. In developing countries, where the disparities between the rich and the poor are significantly large, this assumes greater importance and is considered in SCBA.

A.2.6 Merit Wants

Merit wants are those goals and objectives which are desirable from a social point of view even though they may be financially disadvantageous. For example, setting up of primary health centres in rural areas is much more desirable from a social point of view than setting up of a brewery even though the latter may yield much higher profits. Projects dealing with merit wants are given a higher value in SCBA.

A.3 UNIDO APPROACH

UNIDO laid down an elaborate framework for project appraisal and SCBA in a document called 'Guidelines for Project Evaluation' in 1972. The approach was later simplified and UNIDO published *Guide to Practical Project Appraisal* in 1978. The UNIDO approach to SCBA is based on these documents. As per the UNIDO approach, SCBA consists of the following stages:

1. Calculation of financial profitability of the project at market prices.
2. Obtaining the net benefit of the project measured in terms of economic prices, also referred to as shadow prices or 'efficiency' prices.
3. Adjustment for the impact of the project on savings and investment.
4. Adjustment for the impact of the project on income distribution.
5. Adjustment for the impact of the project on merit and demerit goods whose social value is different from the monetary value.

The first stage of determining the financial profitability of the project has been dealt with under financial analysis.

A.4 NET BENEFIT IN TERMS OF ECONOMIC/SHADOW/EFFICIENCY PRICES

Stage 2 of the UNIDO approach involves calculation of the net benefits of the project in terms of economic or shadow prices. Shadow prices and market prices are the same only in conditions of perfect competition. Since this is virtually impossible, shadow prices have to be developed. Before we deal with shadow prices of specific resources, let us examine some basic issues concerning shadow prices.

A.5 SHADOW PRICES—BASIC ISSUES

A.5.1 Choice of Numeraire

Numeraire is the unit of account to express or measure shadow prices.

Some basic questions that need to be answered are as follows:

1. What *unit of currency* should be used? Should we measure and express shadow prices in terms of domestic currency or foreign currency? The question is relevant as the currencies of most developing countries are not internationally accepted.
2. Should costs and benefits be measured in *current values* or *constant values*? Projects by nature take considerable time to complete and the benefits are spread over long periods. The issue of measuring in current or constant values is therefore relevant. Should we take the cost of an item to be what it was when we purchased it, or should we take its current value?
3. Should we measure all costs and benefits in terms of *net present value* or *future value*? The issue arises because of the long-term benefits of projects.
4. Will the benefits of the project be used for *consumption* or *investment*?
5. Should we measure the benefits in terms of *consumption* or *investment*?
6. With reference to which *group* should the benefits of the project be measured? The benefits of the project are not uniformly distributed amongst the various groups of society. As discussed earlier, a project benefiting the economically weaker section is socially more valuable than a project which benefits the affluent sections of society.

Considering the above issues, UNIDO's specifications for numeraire are:

Net present consumption in the hands of people at the base level of consumption in the private sector in terms of constant prices in domestic accounting currency (rupees in our case).

UNIDO approach measures social costs and benefits in terms of consumption because savings are only 'deferred consumption'. The amount saved can be reinvested giving rise to further income of which some portion shall certainly be used for consumption. UNIDO's definition of numeraire answers all the questions that were raised.

A.5.2 Concept of Tradability

A key issue in shadow pricing is whether a good is tradable or not. For a good that is tradable, the international price, also referred to as the 'border price', is a measure of its opportunity cost to the country because it is possible to substitute imports for domestic production and vice versa. Similarly, it is possible to substitute export for domestic consumption and vice versa. The border price or international price represents the true economic value of the item.

A.5.3 Sources of Shadow Pricing

Using imports and exports UNIDO suggests three sources of shadow pricing. These depend on the impact of the project to national economy. A project uses resources as inputs and produces products or another set of resources as outputs. The inputs and outputs may:

1. Increase or decrease the total consumption in the economy.
2. Increase or decrease production in the economy.
3. Increase or decrease imports.
4. Increase or decrease exports.

The impacts are explained in Table A.1:

Table A.1 Sources of shadow pricing

Impact	*Basis of shadow pricing*
On consumption in the economy	Consumer's willingness to pay
On production in the economy	Cost of production
On international trade	Foreign exchange value (border prices)

A.5.4 Taxes

Taxes usually pose difficulties in computation of shadow prices. UNIDO guidelines lay down the following:

1. Include taxes, when a project results in diversion of non-traded inputs, which are fixed in supply from other producers, or results in addition to non-traded consumer goods. Taxes form a part of the price others are willing to pay.
2. Exclude taxes, when a project augments domestic production by other producers.
3. Ignore taxes, for fully traded goods.

For example, if we are undertaking a construction project and the supply of cement was not to increase, then the cement for the project would be taken away from present users of cement. Obviously, they would be willing to pay extra so that their supply of cement is maintained. Their willingness to pay becomes the shadow price of the cement and taxes are included as they form the price that others are willing to pay.

If, on the other hand, the production of cement is increased, then the shadow price of cement becomes the cost of production and taxes are excluded.

A.5.5 Consumer's Willingness to Pay

As mentioned in the earlier example, if the impact of the project is on consumption in the economy, the basis of shadow price is the consumer's willingness to pay. This can best be explained with the help of Figure A.1.

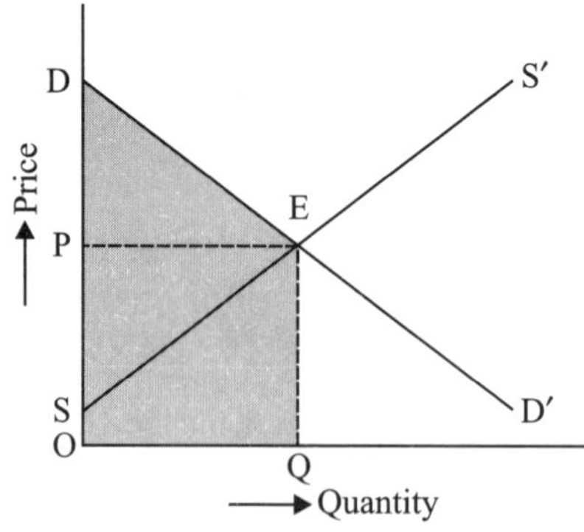

Figure A.1 Consumer's willingness to pay.

In Figure A.1, SS′ represents the supply schedule and DD′ represents the demand schedule. E represents the equilibrium point, OQ the quantity bought and OP the price per unit. In conditions of perfect competition, the person who buys the first unit is willing to pay OD, while the person who buys the last unit is willing to pay OP. The consumer's willingness to pay for various units is given by the schedule DE. The total amount that the consumers are willing to pay for the product is indicated by ODEQ. The actual amount paid by them is OPEQ. The difference between ODEQ and OPEQ, namely DEP, is called the consumer surplus. The concept of consumer's willingness to pay is important for computing shadow prices.

A.6 SHADOW PRICING OF SPECIFIC RESOURCES

A.6.1 Tradable Inputs and Outputs

The shadow price for fully traded goods is the border price expressed in domestic currency at the market exchange rate. The market exchange rate may be different than the official exchange rate.

Goods are fully traded when an increase in their production either increases the exports or decreases the imports as the extra production may substitute for imports. Similarly, an increase in their consumption results in an increase in imports or reduction in exports. This implies that the domestic changes in demand or supply only affect the level of import or export. In practice, tradable inputs are regarded as fully tradable even if these conditions are not fully met.

Goods may not be traded even though they are tradable for various reasons. These could be due to government policies and restrictive quotas; inelasticity of import supply and export demand; surplus domestic capacity and so on. Tradable goods that are not traded are treated in the same manner as non-tradable goods.

EXAMPLE A.1 A project X uses 800 tons of steel whose price is ₹ 10,000 per ton. Steel is a tradable commodity whose border price is $200 per ton. The official exchange rate is ₹ 40 per dollar. The market price of a dollar is ₹ 45. Find the market and social cost of steel.

Solution

Market cost	*Social cost*
800 × 10,000 = ₹ 80,00,000	800 × 200 × 45 = ₹ 72,00,000

A.6.2 Non-tradable Inputs and Outputs

A good is non-tradable when its import price (CIF) is greater than its domestic cost of production, or when its export price (FOB) is greater than its domestic cost of production in the destination country. CIF means cost, insurance and freight. The importer has to pay the cost of the item to the exporter, the insurance cost during transit and the freight cost of transporting the item where it is required by the importer. FOB means 'free on board' and includes the cost of the item, insurance cost if any and the cost of transportation up to placing it on board, the carrier which is to transport it to its final destination. FOB and CIF costs are borne by the exporter and the importer, respectively.

If the non-tradable inputs are taken away from others resulting in reduced consumption by others, the shadow price is others' willingness to pay. If the inputs are obtained through increased production, the shadow price is the marginal cost of production. For instance, if cement was required for a construction project and its production did not increase; the requirement would have to be met by depriving other construction agencies of it. Clearly, its shadow price will be the others' willingness to pay for the cement. On the contrary, if the additional demand were met through additional production, the marginal cost of production will be the shadow price.

If non-tradable outputs increase consumption, the shadow price is the marginal consumer's willingness to pay. If production of non-tradable outputs results in substituting or replacing existing production, that is, it results in decreased production by others, the shadow price is the saving in the cost of production. For instance, let us consider a cement plant project. If the additional quantity of cement produced by this plant is purchased due to increased demand of cement, its shadow price will be the marginal consumer's willingness to pay. On the other hand, if the overall demand does not increase, the plant will be able to sell the cement produced by it only if it is priced cheaper (assuming all other factors like quality and so on to be the same), which will be possible only if it is produced at lesser cost than the competitors' cement. In such a situation, the competitors will have no option but to cut back on their production. The shadow price will be the saving in the cost of production, that is, the alternative production costs avoided. Table A.2 summarizes the shadow prices for non-tradable goods.

Table A.2 Shadow price of non-tradable goods

Inputs	
Impact	*Shadow price*
Project reduces the availability of the input to others	User's willingness to pay
Project's input requirement is met by its additional production	Marginal cost of production
Outputs	
Impact	*Shadow price*
Project increases the consumption of the output in the economy	Marginal consumer's willingness to pay
Substitutes or replaces other production of the same non-tradable output in the economy	Saving in the cost of production

EXAMPLE A.2 Project X uses 1,20,000 tons of cement, a non-tradable commodity, whose market price is ₹ 1000 per ton. 60% of the requirement is met by reducing the availability to others and 40% requirement is met through additional production. The cost of production is ₹ 700 per ton, while others are willing to pay ₹ 1300 per ton. Find its cost from the project control board's and economic point of view.

Solution

Project control board cost	*Social cost*
1,20,000 × 1000 = ₹ 12,00,00,000	60% requirement met through reducing availability to others. Cost is the others' willingness to pay for it. 1,20,000 × 0.60 × 1300 = ₹ 9,36,00,000 40% requirement met through additional production. Cost is the cost of production. 1,20,000 × 0.40 × 700 = ₹ 3,36,00,000 Total cost = ₹ 12,72,00,000

A.6.3 Externalities

Externalities are the costs and benefits that accrue to groups not targeted as beneficiaries of the project. They are not deliberately created by the project sponsor but are an incidental outcome of legitimate economic activity. They are beyond the control of the persons who are affected by it, for better or for worse, and they are not traded in the marketplace. Let us consider some examples.

1. A multi-purpose river valley project may result in preventing flooding of areas. This benefit is incidental to the project.
2. The approach roads made by a company may improve the transport system of an area.
3. Training of employees may enhance their skills.
4. A school set up by a company may provide education for the children of the locals.
5. A river valley project results in the submergence of farmlands.
6. A new airport in the vicinity causes noise pollution.
7. A river valley project may cause formation of mosquito breeding grounds.

As may be seen from the above examples, it is difficult to compute benefits or costs in monetary terms directly. Externalities are measured indirectly. If we consider the examples given above, then we may use the following as measures of benefits or costs:

1. The value of flood prevention may be gauged in terms of the money saved by the government that was earlier spent on flood relief every year.
2. The improvement of the transport system may result in saving of travelling time which can be valued according to the hourly wages of the beneficiaries.
3. The benefit of training may be measured in terms of the increased wages that the trained employee may get in alternative employment because of his improved skills.
4. The measure of the educational benefit to children may be measured in terms of their increased earning capability.
5. The submergence of farmland may be measured in terms of the yield lost per annum.
6. The fall in rental value of buildings in the vicinity of the airport because of the noise caused by the airport may be used as a measure for the cost of noise pollution.
7. The value of the increase in the inflow of anti-malarial drugs into the area may be a measure of the cost of the mosquito breeding grounds caused by the river valley project.

The effects of externalities are difficult to measure, but these should not be ignored because of this. As far as possible, some indirect method to assign a value to such effects should be devised and the effects of externalities should be taken into account while performing SCBA.

A.6.4 Labour Inputs

The principles applied to estimate shadow prices for goods may be applied to labour, even though it is a service. When a project hires labour, it may have the following impacts on the rest of the economy:

1. The project may take labour away from other employment.
2. The project may induce the 'production' of additional labour.
3. It may employ foreign labour.

When the project takes labour away from other employment, the shadow price of labour is what the others are willing to pay for it. For instance, if there are some workers with a particular skill available in an industry and are presently fully employed, and the project requires such workers, they will have to be weaned away from their present employment. In such a case, it is obvious that those who are likely to lose their skilled workers will try and retain them by offering higher wages. The shadow price of labour in this case will be their willingness to pay for it.

The 'production' of additional labour may involve offering employment to unemployed or partially employed workers, offering urban employment to rural workers or relocating workers from one area to another, or offering skilled employment to previously unskilled workers by retraining them. The shadow price of such labour consists of the following:

1. The marginal product (the wage earned at the margin) earned by the worker in his previous employment. In case of unemployed workers now being offered work, the marginal product in previous employment will be zero.
2. The value assigned by him to the leisure that he may have to forego to take up employment. This is reflected in his 'reservation wage', which depends on the income he enjoys through transfer payments, his perception of what job is acceptable to him, and his preference for work and leisure.
3. The additional consumption of food when a worker is fully employed as against his consumption of food when he is partially employed or unemployed.
4. The cost of transporting and rehabilitation when the worker is relocated. For example, during the harvest season in Punjab, a lot of farm labour is transported from Bihar.
5. The cost of training a worker to improve his existing skills or to acquire new skills.
6. The increased consumption by the worker and its negative impact on savings and investments when the worker is paid market wage rate by the project.

The shadow price of foreign labour is the wage they command. However, a premium is added on account of the foreign exchange that they may remit abroad from their wages. The shadow price of labour is shown in Table A.3.

Table A.3 Shadow price of labour

Impact	*Shadow price*
Project reduces the availability of labour to others	Others' willingness to pay
Project induces additional labour through (i) Improvement of productivity of underutilized workers (ii) Relocation of labour (iii) Offering skilled employment to unskilled labour	(i) The marginal product (or wage) earned by the worker in his previous employment (ii) The value assigned by him to the leisure that he may have to forego to take up employment (iii) The additional consumption of food when a worker is fully employed (iv) The cost of transportation and rehabilitation when the worker is relocated (v) The cost of training a worker to improve his existing skills (vi) The increased consumption by the worker and its negative impact on savings and investments
Project employs foreign labour	Wages paid to foreign labour and a premium added on account of foreign exchange remitted abroad

EXAMPLE A.3 **The project employs 1000 unskilled labourers for 300 days at a wage of ₹ 80 per day. The workers are willing to work for ₹ 40 per day. It employs 500 skilled workers at a wage of ₹ 200 per day. Others are willing to pay ₹ 250 per day for skilled workers. It also employs 50 foreign workers who are paid ₹ 8000 per day for 200 days of which 40% can be repatriated. The official exchange rate is ₹ 40 per dollar and the shadow price is ₹ 45 per dollar. What are the costs from the project control board's point of view and from the social point of view?**

Solution

Project board's view	*Social cost*
Unskilled labour 1000 × 300 × 80 = ₹ 2,40,00,000	Worker's willingness to work for ₹ 40 per day 1000 × 300 × 40 = ₹ 1,20,00,000
Skilled labour 500 × 300 × 200 = ₹ 3,00,00,000	Others' willingness to pay 500 × 300 × 250 = ₹ 3,75,00,000
Foreign labour 50 × 200 × 8000 = ₹ 8,00,00,000	60% non-repatriable 50 × 200 × 8000 × 0.60 = ₹ 4,80,00,000 40% repatriable (convert to dollars and then convert to rupees at shadow price) $50 \times 200 \times 8000 \times 0.40 \times \frac{45}{40} =$ ₹ 3,60,00,000 Total ₹ 8,40,00,000

A.6.5 Capital Inputs

Capital investments made in a project can be viewed from two angles. Firstly, the capital resources are converted into physical assets, and secondly, the commitment of financial resources to the project denies their allocation to other projects. The shadow price of capital resources involves the following issues:

1. How should we evaluate the value of physical assets?
2. What is the opportunity cost of capital (value of the opportunity foregone by sacrificing alternative projects)?

The shadow price of physical assets is calculated in the same way as the shadow prices for other resources. If the resource is a fully traded good, its shadow price is the border price. If it is a non-tradable good and the project induces additional domestic production, it is the cost of production, and if the resource is taken away from others then its shadow price is the others' willingness to pay for it. The value of labour involved in the construction of the physical facilities is also calculated at its shadow price as discussed in the preceding sub-section. The net present value of capital investments at shadow prices is calculated.

The aspect of opportunity cost of capital depends on how the capital requirement is generated. The capital may come from additional savings. Additional savings imply consumption foregone by the saver, for which he expects a certain rate of return, known as the *consumption rate of interest*. Alternatively, the capital may come from an already existing pool of financial resources. Since the commitment of this capital denies the availability of it to alternate projects, the project undertaken must earn a rate of return which is at least equal to the rate of return that would have accrued if the capital inputs were utilized on the alternate project. This is called the *investment rate of interest*. Table A.4 summarizes the shadow price of capital inputs. In practice, the consumption rate of interest is used as the discount rate for computing the net present value as in stage 3 of the UNIDO analysis all inputs and outputs are expressed as consumption equivalents. This is also in keeping with the numeraire chosen (*net present consumption* in the hands of people at the base level of consumption in the private sector in terms of constant prices in domestic accounting rupees).

Table A.4 Shadow price of capital inputs

Impact	*Shadow price*
Converted into physical assets	
Fully traded good	Border price
Induces additional production	Marginal cost of production
Reduces availability to others	Other's willingness to pay
Opportunity cost	
Sourced from additional savings	Consumption rate of interest
Sourced from already existing pool	Investment rate of interest

The computation of the consumption rate of interest poses some problems. Two approaches can be used to simplify the problem. The analyst can compute the internal rate of return of the project and present it to the decision or policy makers. If they accept the project using this as the discount rate, the analyst may assume that the policy makers perceive the consumption rate of interest to be lower than the internal rate of return. Through an iterative process of suggesting various rates of return, the range can be narrowed sufficiently for practical use. For instance, if the project is acceptable to the planner at a discount rate of 15% but unacceptable at a discount rate of 12%, the analyst may assume that the consumption rate of interest lies between 15% and 12%.

The second approach is to use the discount rate as a budgetary device. If the discount rate used indicates more projects are acceptable than the resources available, the discount rate can be increased. (Projects with a positive net present value are acceptable. An increase in the discount rate lowers the net present value.) Conversely, if fewer projects qualify (those with positive net present value) leaving resources available for further investment, the discount rate can be lowered.

A.6.6 Foreign Exchange

The UNIDO method uses domestic currency as the numeraire. Foreign exchange in developing and underdeveloped countries is at a premium and is more valuable than indicated by the exchange rate. The impact of foreign exchange on the project must be identified and a premium added to the project's net present value to make an adjustment for this impact. This will increase those values that were measured in border rupees (where the foreign exchange component was converted to domestic rupees at official exchange rate).

The shadow price of foreign exchange, as suggested by the UNIDO guidelines, is determined on the basis of the consumer's willingness to pay for goods imported at the margin. For instance, we know that in our country we are willing to pay more than the dollar price converted to rupees at the official exchange rate for imported goods that we wish to possess. The shadow price of a unit of foreign exchange is equal to:

$$\sum_{i=1}^{n} F_i Q_i P_i$$

where

F_i = The foreign exchange, at the margin spent on importing commodity i

Q_i = The quantity of commodity that can be bought with one unit of foreign exchange (1/CIF value of the commodity in question)

P_i = The domestic market clearing price of commodity i

EXAMPLE A.4 Commodities A, B, C and D have been imported at the margin for a total of \$10,000. The official exchange rate is ₹ 45 per dollar. The proportion of foreign exchange spent on them, the quantities that can be bought with \$1 and the domestic clearing price of the commodities per unit are as follows:

$$\begin{array}{lll} F_A = 0.1 & Q_A = 0.6 & P_A = 40 \\ F_B = 0.2 & Q_B = 1.2 & P_B = 60 \\ F_C = 0.3 & Q_C = 0.4 & P_C = 50 \\ F_D = 0.4 & Q_D = 1.8 & P_D = 40 \end{array}$$

The value of foreign exchange is:

$$0.1 \times 0.6 \times 40 + 0.2 \times 1.2 \times 60 + 0.3 \times 0.4 \times 50 + 0.4 \times 1.8 \times 40 = 51.6$$

This implies that the shadow price of a dollar is ₹ 51.6, whereas its official exchange rate is ₹ 45. We should use the shadow price of the dollar when converting border prices to domestic rupees. Alternatively, we shall multiply the values obtained of border prices expressed in terms of rupees at the official exchange rate by 1.147 (51.6/45) to add the value of premium to foreign exchange.

EXAMPLE A.5 A project needs imported equipment worth $10,00,000. A gift of $10,00,000 has been given by a foreign organization. However, the gift is not tied to this project. If the shadow price of a dollar is ₹ 45, what is the financial and social cost of the imported equipment?

Solution

Financial cost	*Social cost*
As the equipment is purchased through gifted capital, the financial cost incurred for the equipment is zero.	The gifted capital is not tied to the project. It could have been used for alternative purposes. It thus has an opportunity cost equal to its shadow price expressed in rupees. 10,00,000 × 45 = ₹ 4,50,00,000

The calculation of shadow price based on consumer's willingness to pay is based on the assumption that the foreign exchange is being met by a sacrifice from others. We could also have raised foreign exchange through increased exports or reduced imports (by import substitution). In such a case, the shadow price of foreign exchange should be related to the cost of producing foreign exchange and not to the consumer's willingness to pay. (This is in keeping with the principle explained earlier.) Michael Bruno's domestic resource cost method is one of the best known approaches to determine the cost of producing foreign exchange. (The discussion is beyond the scope of this text.)

It may be argued that all goods, whether tradable or not, may contain some element of foreign exchange (tradable component), labour and capital inputs. However, the foreign exchange component included in non-tradable goods is already valued at a premium which is included in the domestic cost of the particular good. It is only necessary to consider foreign exchange of border prices for the purpose of applying shadow price of foreign exchange.

Let us understand the application of shadow prices with the help of an example.

EXAMPLE A.6 The Government of Fantasia is considering making a bridge over River Sargana at Fakir Ghat. Presently, a ferry is used at the crossing. The ferry operates for 300 days in a year. During the monsoons the ferry does not operate due to heavy current. The ferry carries the following loads:

1. Cars 200 per day (with two passengers each).
2. Passengers not in cars 175 per day.
3. The ferry currently charges ₹ 150 per car and ₹ 4 per passenger.

The proposed bridge will require the following:

1. 2000 tons of steel. Market price is ₹ 25,000 per ton. The FOB price of steel which is a tradable item is $500 per ton.

2. 15,000 tons of cement. Market price is ₹ 1200 per ton. 25% of the requirement is met by taking cement from other users who are willing to pay ₹ 1500 per ton for it. The balance requirement is met through additional production. Cost of production is ₹ 1000 per ton.
3. Other construction material worth ₹ 5 million.
4. 0.1 million man days of unskilled labour at a daily wage of ₹ 80. Workers are willing to work for ₹ 60.
5. Skilled labour costing ₹ 5 million. This also represents others' willingness to pay for the skilled labour.
6. Imported equipment worth $0.2 million.
7. The official exchange rate is ₹ 40 per dollar. The shadow price of a dollar is ₹ 45.

Once the bridge is constructed, the ferry will close down. The boat can be sold for ₹ 40,00,000. The annual operating cost of the ferry is ₹ 3,70,000 including ₹ 45,000 towards depreciation.

In addition to the present traffic, the bridge is expected to carry the following additional loads:

1. Cars 100 per day (with two passengers each).
2. Pedestrians 75 per day.
3. A toll tax of ₹ 40 per car is proposed.
4. No charge will be recovered from pedestrians.

The bridge will remain open throughout the year (360 days for ease of calculations). The annual maintenance cost of the bridge will be ₹ 10,00,000. It will cut down the travel time by half an hour. The average value of a person's time is ₹ 8 per hour. The bridge will result in increased economic activity in the area and this will increase the annual income of 5000 families in this area by an average of ₹ 1000. The life of the bridge is 50 years (assume perpetuity). Identify the social costs and benefits of the project. Find the net present value of the project. Social discount rate is 10%.

Solution

Cost of bridge (one time)

The one time cost is shown in Table A.5.

Table A.5 One time cost of bridge

Item	*Social value (₹, million)*	*Total (₹, million)*
(a) Steel (tradable, shadow price is border price)	2000 × 500 × 45 = 45	45.000
(b) Cement (non-tradable)		
(i) Obtained from others	15,000 × 0.25 × 1500 = 5.625	
(ii) From additional production	15,000 × 0.75 × 1000 = 11.25	16.875
(c) Other construction material	5	5.000
(d) Unskilled labour	0.1 × 60 = 6	6.000
(e) Skilled labour	5	5.000
(f) Imported equipment	0.2 × 45 = 9	9.000
Total cost (one time)		**86.875**
Maintenance cost (annual)	1	1.000

Benefits

Sale of ferry (one time) = ₹ 4 million

Operation and maintenance (annually) = 3,70,000 – 45,000 = ₹ 3,25,000

(Depreciation must be subtracted as it is not a cash flow.)

Cars

Presently number of cars = 200 × 300 = 60,000

On the bridge number of cars = 300 × 360 = 1,08,000

The cars were paying ₹ 150 on the ferry, that is, the 60,000th car was willing to pay ₹ 150. The cars will be required to pay a toll of ₹ 40 per car. The last car, that is, the 10,800th car will be willing to pay ₹ 40. Therefore, consumer's willingness to pay is the shaded area shown in Figure A.2.

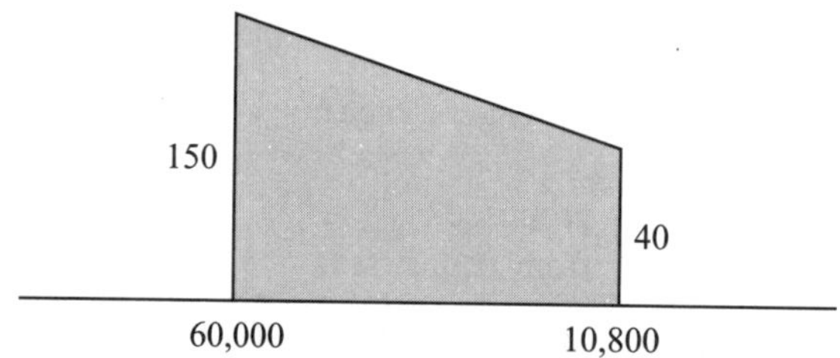

Figure A.2 Consumer's willingness to pay for cars.

$$\text{Consumer's willingness to pay} = 48,000 \times 40 + \frac{1}{2} \times 48,000 \times 110 = 45,60,000$$

Pedestrians

Number of persons crossing by ferry = 175 × 300 = 52,500

Number of persons crossing on the bridge = 250 × 360 = 90,000

The ferry was charging ₹ 4 per person. The 52,500th person was willing to pay ₹ 4. Persons on the bridge are not charged anything. The 90,000th person is willing to pay zero.

Consumer's willingness to pay is given by the shaded area as shown in Figure A.3.

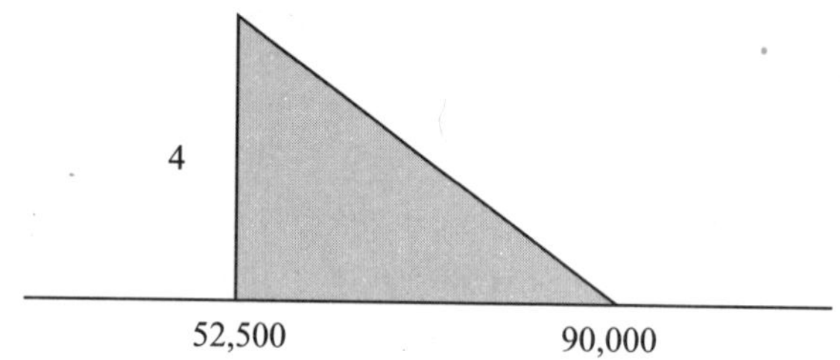

Figure A.3 Consumer's willingness to pay for pedestrians.

$$\text{Consumer's willingness to pay} = \frac{1}{2} \times 37,500 \times 4 = 75,000$$

Value of time saved

The benefit of saved time accrues only to those who were earlier using the ferry and taking longer time. Those who will now use the bridge and were earlier not travelling do not save any time.

$$\text{Number of persons using the ferry annually} = [2 \times 200(\text{people in cars}) + 175] \times 300 = 1{,}72{,}500$$

$$\text{Value of time saved} = 1{,}72{,}500 \times \frac{1}{2} \times 8 = 6{,}90{,}000$$

$$\text{Benefit of additional income to families} = 5000 \times 1000 = 50{,}00{,}000$$

The benefits are shown in Table A.6.

Table A.6 Benefits

Benefits	*Social vlaue (₹, million)*	*Total (₹, million)*
Sale of boat (one time)	4	4.000
Operation and maintenance (annually)	0.325	0.325
Cars (annually)	4.56	4.560
Pedestrians (annually)	0.075	0.075
Value of time saved (annually)	0.69	0.690
Additional income	5	5.000
Total annual benefits		**10.65**

Net investment (one time) = 86.875 – 4.00 = 82.875 million

Net benefits (annually) = 10.65 – 1.000 (maintenance cost of bridge) = 9.65 million

$$\text{Net present value} = -82.875 + 9.65\left(\frac{1}{0.10}\right) = ₹\,13.625 \text{ million}$$

(Net present value of an annuity of ₹ 1 for perpetuity is $\left(\frac{1}{k}\right)$, where k is the discount rate.)

A.7 IMPACT OF SAVINGS

Stages 3 and 4 of the UNIDO approach deal with the impact of savings and the impact of income distribution on the project. The prerequisite for calculating this impact is to determine the income accrued to different groups in society from the project. Society may be divided into any number of groups for the purpose. However, the UNIDO approach seeks to measure the gains and losses by the following groups:

1. Project
2. Other private business
3. Government
4. Workers
5. Consumers
6. External sectors

The gains and losses to groups are measured as the difference between shadow prices and market prices for each input and output in the case of physical resources, and in the case of financial transactions it is the difference between the value received and the price paid. For instance, if a labourer is willing to work at ₹ 50 per day but is paid ₹ 80 per day as the minimum wage, then the labourer gains an income of ₹ 30 per day. If the project requires 5000 labourers, the income gained by the group is ₹ 1,50,000 per day.

Most underdeveloped and developing countries face a resource crunch and hence attach a premium to savings as these can provide resources for further investment. How does the project impact savings? The UNIDO approach addresses two issues:

1. Given the impact of income distribution of the project, what is its impact on savings?
2. What is the value of these savings to society?

A.7.1 Impact on Savings

Each group saves according to its marginal propensity to save (MPS). In case the project results in a loss of income for a group, it is obvious that that particular group will save less than what it was saving earlier, and the effect on overall savings will be negative. The savings impact of a project is:

$$\Sigma \Delta Y_i \text{ MPS}_i$$

where

ΔY_i = the change in income of group i because of the project

MPS_i = the marginal propensity to save of group i

EXAMPLE A.7 The income gained/lost by four groups as a result of the project and the marginal propensity to save of each group are as follows:

Change of income for group 1 = ₹ 7,00,000, MPS for group 1 = 0.2
Change of income for group 2 = ₹ 3,00,000, MPS for group 2 = 0.1
Change of income for group 3 = ₹ – 2,00,000, MPS for group 3 = 0.3
Change of income for group 4 = ₹ – 1,00,000, MPS for group 4 = 0.4

Net savings = 7,00,000 × 0.2 + 3,00,000 × 0.1 – 2,00,000 × 0.3 – 1,00,000 × 0.4 = 70,000

A.7.2 Value of Savings

The numeraire measures the impact as the net present consumption (*Net present consumption* in the hands of people at the base level of consumption in the private sector in terms of constant prices in domestic accounting rupees). The value of ₹ 1 of savings is the net present value of the additional consumption stream produced when that rupee of saving is invested at the margin. Let us assume that the invested rupee will have a marginal productivity r, that is to say that the investment of ₹ 1 at the margin will produce a return of ₹ r. Of this return of ₹ r, let us assume that we shall reinvest a proportion a, the balance being used in consumption. The consumption at the end of the first year will be $(r - ar)$, and the investment at the beginning of the second year will be $1 + ar$, as ar is the additional amount committed to investment. The stream of cash flows is shown in Table A.7.

Table A.7 Stream of cash flows

Year	1	2	3	n
Investment at beginning of the year	1	$(1 + ar)$	$(1 + ar)^2$	$(1 + ar)^{n-1}$
Income (end of the year)	r	$r(1 + ar)$	$r(1 + ar)^2$	$r(1 + ar)^{n-1}$
Additional investment	ar	$ar(1+ ar)$	$ar(1 + ar)^2$	$ar(1 + ar)^{n-1}$
Consumption	$r(1 - a)$	$r(1 - a)(1 + ar)$	$r(1 - a)(1 + ar)^2$	$r(1 - a)(1 + ar)^{n-1}$

The net present value of the consumption stream discounted at the social discount rate k is:

$$I = \frac{r(1-a)}{(1+k)} + \frac{r(1-a)(1+ar)}{(1+k)^2} + \frac{r(1-a)(1+ar)^2}{(1+k)^3} + \cdots + \frac{r(1-a)(1+ar)^{n-1}}{(1+k)^n} + \cdots$$

$$= \frac{\dfrac{r(1-a)}{(1+k)}}{1-\dfrac{(1+ar)}{(1+k)}} = \frac{r(1-a)}{(k-ar)}$$

where

I = Social value of a rupee of savings
r = Marginal productivity of capital
a = Reinvestment rate on additional income arising from investment
k = Social discount rate

The social value of savings is also called the shadow price of investment. The formula given earlier is valid when the following conditions are satisfied:

1. The marginal productivity of capital and the reinvestment rate on additional income are constant over time.
2. Savings rate in society will not become optimal in the foreseeable future.

The net savings computed are then multiplied by the social value of savings and the amount is added to the net present value of the project computed in stage 2.

Assuming that the value of r is 0.15, the value of a is 0.20 and the value of k is 0.08, the value of I is:

$$I = \frac{r(1-a)}{(k-ar)} = \frac{0.15(1-0.20)}{(0.08-0.20\times 0.15)} = 2.4$$

Let us apply this to the savings calculated in Example A.7.

Net value of savings = 2.4 × 70,000 = 1,68,000

An amount of ₹ 1,68,000 will be added to the net present value of the project computed in stage 2.

EXAMPLE A.8 Let us continue our discussions with the help of the data given in Example A.6. It was mentioned that because of the construction of the bridge, there was an increase in economic activity in the area and the income of 5000 families increased by ₹ 1000 per year on an average. The 5000 families belong to three groups as given in Table A.8.

Table A.8 Increase in income by groups

Group	*Present income*	*Number of families*	*Increase in income*	*MPS*
A	Above ₹ 1,50,000	500	2000	0.2
B	Between ₹ 5000 and ₹ 10,000	2500	1200	0.3
C	Below ₹ 5000	2000	500	0.1

Compute the impact of savings if $r = 0.15$, $a = 0.30$ and $k = 0.10$.

Solution

$$\text{Savings of group A} = 500 \times 2000 \times 0.2 = 2{,}00{,}000$$
$$\text{Savings of group B} = 2500 \times 1200 \times 0.3 = 9{,}00{,}000$$
$$\text{Savings of group C} = 2000 \times 500 \times 0.1 = 1{,}00{,}000$$
$$\text{Total savings annually} = 12{,}00{,}000$$
$$\text{Social value of ₹ 1 of savings} = \frac{r(1-a)}{(k-ar)} = \frac{0.15(1-0.30)}{(0.10-0.30\times 0.15)} = 1.91$$
$$\text{Social value of savings annually} = 1.2 \times 1.91 = ₹\ 2.292 \text{ million}$$
$$\text{Net present value of savings} = 2.292 \times \frac{1}{0.10} = 22.92$$

This should be added to the net present value calculated in Example A.6.
Net present value of the project after adjusting for the impact of savings is

$$13.625 + 22.920 = ₹\ 36.545 \text{ million}$$

A.8 IMPACT OF INCOME DISTRIBUTION

The disparities in different sections of the society are large in developing and underdeveloped countries. Governments try to reduce these disparities through economic policy measures such as taxes and subsidies. However, when these measures are not enough, it is necessary to evaluate the impact of a project on income distribution and suitably adjust the net present value of the project for this impact. A premium is generally attached to projects which favour income distribution to the economically weaker sections of society.

The calculation of impact of income distribution is facilitated as the net income gain or loss for different groups has already been computed at the beginning of stage 3. Suitable weights must now be assigned to reflect the relative value of income in the hands of various groups. After adjustment of income of each group separately, by multiplying the income of the group with the weight assigned to it, and expressing this income flow in terms of net present value, this is added to the net present value of the project as computed at the end of stage 3.

The UNIDO guidelines suggest that the weights be arrived at through an iterative process between the analyst and the planners. The analyst determines the weights by seeking the preference of planners for projects with different net present values and distribution impacts. Let us study the process with the help of an example.

Let us consider a project that has a net present value of –₹ 2 million. Only two income groups have been identified—those earning less than ₹ 12,000 per annum and those with higher incomes. Let us also assume that over its life the project would generate income flows to the lower income group whose net present value is ₹ 10 million. If the planner accepts this project despite its negative net present value, it implies that the planner is attaching a premium worth ₹ 2 million to the income of the lower income group, or a premium of 20% is being added to the lower income group's earnings. This will make the net present value of the project zero, and hence worth accepting. However, if this project is rejected and another project whose net present value is –₹ 1.5 million is accepted, the analyst can say that the weightage factor given to the lower income group's earnings lies between 15% and 20%. Through an iterative process, the range can be sufficiently narrowed for practical use. This methodology would work well if there were only two groups involved. But in actual practice, the number of groups involved may be more than two. We then need to find a slightly more sophisticated method which focuses on a single factor to determine the weights to be assigned to the incomes of different groups.

The single factor used for calculating weights is the elasticity of marginal utility of income. The utility of income falls as the income rises (Law of diminishing utility). The elasticity of marginal utility of income is the rate of change of marginal utility of income vis-à-vis the rate of change of income, or the rate at which the marginal utility of income declines for a unit increase in income. The marginal utility of income is negative but by convention the minus sign is dropped. If the marginal utility drops by 5% for a 5% increase in income then the elasticity of marginal utility of income is 1. Similarly, if the marginal utility of income drops by 10% for a 5% increase in income, the elasticity of marginal utility of income is 2. Let us consider the case where the elasticity of marginal utility of income is 1. In such a case, a 1% increase in the income of a person earning ₹ 1000 is socially as valuable as a 1% increase in the income of a person earning ₹ 10,000, or a 1% increase in income of a person earning ₹ 1,00,000, or a 1% increase in income of a person earning ₹ 500. To express it numerically:

₹ 10 increase for a person earning ₹ 1000 is equal to
₹ 100 increase for a person earning ₹ 10,000 is equal to
₹ 1000 increase for a person earning ₹ 1,00,000 is equal to
₹ 5 increase for a person earning ₹ 500.

If we consider the base level of income to be ₹ 1000, then the weight assigned to this income is 1. In order to make the incomes earned equal, we shall have to assign:

weight of 1/10 to the income of the group earning ₹ 10,000,
weight of 1/100 to the income of the group earning ₹ 1,00,000,
weight of 2 to the income of the group earning ₹ 500.

The general relationship to calculate weights is:

$$w_i = \left(\frac{b}{c_i}\right)^n$$

where

w_i = the weight attached to income at c_i level

b = base level of income that has a weight of 1
n = the elasticity of marginal utility of income

EXAMPLE A.9 Let us consider the same data given in Table A.8 and Example A.6. What is the impact of income distribution if group C is the base income group and elasticity of marginal utility of income is 0.6?

Solution

$$w_i = \left(\frac{b}{c_i}\right)^n$$

$$\text{Weightage factor for group A} = \left(\frac{5000}{15,000}\right)^{0.6} = 0.52$$

$$\text{Weightage factor for group B} = \left(\frac{5000}{10,000}\right)^{0.6} = 0.66$$

Weighted income for group A = 500 + 2000 × 0.52 = 5,20,000
Weighted income for group B = 2500 + 1200 × 0.66 = 19,80,000
Weighted income for group C = 2000 + 500 × 1 = 10,00,000
Total annual income = 35,00,000 or 3.5 million

The net present value of the project was worked out in Example A.6 with an annual income of ₹ 5 million. A negative adjustment of ₹ 1.5 million annually needs to be made (5 – 3.5 = 1.5) as the weighted income is only ₹ 3.5 million.

Net present value of ₹ 1.5 million received for perpetuity at 10% discount is

$$\text{Net present value} = 1.5 \times \frac{1}{0.10} = ₹\,15 \text{ million}$$

Net present value of the project = NPV as computed in step 3 (Example A.8) – 15
= 36.545 – 15 = ₹ 21.545 million

A.9 ADJUSTMENT FOR MERIT AND DEMERIT GOODS

Stage 5 of the UNIDO method involves making adjustments for merit goods and demerit goods. A merit good is one whose social value is more than its economic value. For example, a project to supply clean drinking water to an area is socially more desirable than a project to set up a brewery which may have a much better return on investment. The clean drinking water is a merit good, whereas the liquor produced by the brewery is a demerit good. Stage 5 adds a premium to the net present value of the project for merit goods.

The methodology is as follows:

1. Estimate the economic value.
2. Estimate the social value.
3. The adjustment factor is the difference between the ratio of social value to economic value and unity, i.e.

$$\frac{\text{Social value}}{\text{Economic value}} - 1$$

4. Multiply the economic value by the adjustment factor to obtain the adjustment.
5. Add the adjustment to the net present value of the project.

Let us study this with the help of an example.

EXAMPLE A.10 Consider a brewery whose net present economic value is ₹ 10 million in terms of consumer's willingness to pay. It is estimated that the social value of the liquor is no more than its cost of production (assumed to be 55% of the market price).

$$\text{Adjusment factor} = \frac{55}{100} - 1 = -0.45$$

$$\text{Adjustment} = 10 \times (-0.45) = -4.5 \text{ million}$$

Add this to the net present value.

$$\text{Net present value} = 10 - 4.5 = 5.5 \text{ million.}$$

As liquor is a demerit good, the adjustment is negative and the net present value of the project is reduced.

If the socially valuable output does not appear as an output in the economic analysis of the project, it is treated as an externality. For example, a project may create employment for people. This may not figure in the economic analysis. It can be treated as an externality and its valuation in social terms is the adjustment.

While the adjustment for merit and demerit goods is desirable, it is unfortunately amenable to abuse. Projects which are economically unattractive may be made to appear attractive after adjustments for merit and demerit goods. There is a very thin line between the 'political' and 'social' benefit. Often, this adjustment is used to push political agendas and undertake projects which though economically unviable are politically expedient. The UNIDO stage-by-stage approach highlights the adjustments attributed to this factor and this may act as a deterrent for large scale misuse.

To sum up, the five-stage UNIDO method computes the net present value of the project in terms of its social costs and benefits and provides a methodology to select projects on the basis of their value to society rather than on their financial merit alone.

A.10 LITTLE–MIRRLEES APPROACH

The approach to social cost–benefit analysis developed by Little and Mirrlees is quite similar to the UNIDO approach. Some of the similarities are:

1. Calculation of shadow prices, particularly for foreign exchange savings and unskilled labour
2. Consideration of equity
3. Use of discounted cash flow analysis

However, it differs from the UNIDO approach in that:

1. It measures costs and benefits in terms of international or border prices, whereas the UNIDO approach measures costs and benefits in domestic accounting rupees.

2. It measures costs and benefits in terms of uncommitted social income, whereas the UNIDO approach measures costs and benefits in terms of consumption.
3. The UNIDO method is a stage-by-stage approach which considers efficiency (shadow prices), impact of savings and redistribution of income in different stages. The Little–Mirrlees (L–M) approach tends to view these considerations together.

A.11 SHADOW PRICES (L–M APPROACH)

The inputs and outputs of a project are classified into traded goods and services, non-traded goods and services, and labour.

A.11.1 Traded Goods

The shadow price of traded goods is the border price of those goods. If the good is exported, its FOB price is the shadow price, and if it is imported, the CIF price is its shadow price. In case foreign demand and supply are not perfectly elastic, the border price is substituted by the marginal export revenue or the marginal import cost as applicable. The rationale behind using border prices is that these prices represent the correct social opportunity costs or benefits of using or producing a tradable good.

A.11.2 Non-traded Goods

Since non-traded goods do not have a border price, their shadow prices are determined in terms of marginal social cost and marginal social benefit.

The marginal social cost of a good is the value in terms of shadow prices of the resources required to produce an additional unit of that good. The marginal social cost of producing an additional ferry trip is the cost of the material inputs like fuel and oil, and wear and tear of the ferry expressed in terms of border prices and the social wage of the ferry operators.

The marginal social benefit is the social value of an extra unit of the good. When a good is consumed only by one income group and is not taxed, its marginal social value benefit is equal to the market price multiplied by a factor which represents the value assigned to an increase in the income of that group vis-à-vis an equal increase in the uncommitted social income. The L–M method measures costs and benefits in terms of uncommitted social income (savings), unlike the UNIDO method which measures costs and benefits in terms of consumption.

The shadow price of a non-tradable good is based on the proportion in which the requirement is met by increased production and decrease in consumption by others. (Compare this to the UNIDO method, which also spoke of meeting requirements through increase in production or decrease in consumption. See Example A.2.) If we assume that the proportion of requirement met through increased production is 3/4 and that met through decrease in consumption by others is 1/4, then the shadow price is:

$$\frac{3}{4}\text{(marginal social cost)} + \frac{1}{4}\text{(marginal social benefit)}$$

A.11.3 Conversion Factors

In practice, it is difficult to calculate the marginal social cost and the marginal social benefit. The L–M method suggests that for computing the shadow price of non-tradable goods, the cost should be broken down into tradable, labour and residual components. The tradable and residual components are converted into social costs by applying social conversion factors, and the labour component is converted to social cost by using social wage rate.

A.11.4 Social Wage Rate

The social wage rate or the shadow wage rate (SWR) is difficult to determine, but nevertheless an important element of social cost–benefit analysis. The shadow wage rate is dependent upon the marginal productivity of labour, the cost of urbanization and the cost of having an additional amount committed to consumption when the consumption of the worker increases with the increase of income that he enjoys in urban employment. It is assumed that urban employment will offer labour a much better and higher wage than what he commands in rural employment. The L–M method suggest the following formula for calculating the shadow wage rate:

$$\text{SWR} = c' - \frac{1}{s}(c - m)$$

where

SWR = The shadow wage rate

c' = The additional resource devoted to consumption

$\frac{1}{s}$ = The value of a unit of committed resources

c = The consumption of the wage earner

m = The marginal productivity of labour (previous wage of labour at the margin)

The equation may be rewritten as follows:

$$\text{SWR} = m + (c' - c) + \left(1 - \frac{1}{s}\right)(c - m)$$

The equation in this form clearly explains the relationship. m is the marginal productivity of the worker, $(c' - c)$ represents the cost of urbanization and $(1 - 1/s)$ is the value of uncommitted resources, that is, savings. (The L–M method measures costs and benefits in terms of savings.)

The concept can be better understood by modifying the terms slightly. Let c' be the actual wage (in the urban employment), and m be the wage and the marginal productivity of the labour in the rural sector from which it is assumed that the worker is drawn. c is the urban wage expressed in a way comparable, from the worker's point of view with m, so that $c - m$ is the benefit to the worker from moving to the new urban job. c' is higher than c, as the benefit perceived by the worker would be net of the extra cost of living in the urban area in terms of higher rentals for accommodation, higher transportation costs, higher cost of food and so on. Therefore, $(c' - c)$ represents the cost of urbanization. s is the ratio of the value of the money in the hands of the government to that of the extra money gained by the worker, that is, $c - m$. Or, we can say that s is the value of a unit of money with the government (akin to the value of ₹ 1 of savings). Since governments of developing and underdeveloped nations are cash strapped, the value (social value) of one unit of money with the government may be more than 1, as this money can be invested for developmental purposes. Values of c, c' and m are all expressed in terms of foreign exchange.

EXAMPLE A.11 Let us assume that a worker is presently earning ₹ 150 in urban employment. His wage in rural employment was ₹ 60. ₹ 50 is the cost of urbanization and the value of s is 1.50. Then the shadow wage rate is:

$$\text{SWR} = c' - \frac{1}{s}(c - m)$$

$$\text{SWR} = 150 - \frac{1}{1.5}(100 - 60) = ₹\,123.33$$

A.12 L–M ACCOUNTING RATE OF RETURN (SOCIAL DISCOUNT RATE)

The L–M method refers to the social discount rate as accounting rate of return and is, therefore, quite different from the accounting rate of return as normally understood in financial accounting. While determining the social rate of discount, the following considerations should be kept in mind:

1. The same rate should be used for discounting the future social profits of all projects.
2. The rate chosen should be such that all projects compatible with each other yield a positive net present value and can be accepted.
3. The selected rate should help to maintain a balance between the possible investments and the funds available. If the funds are more and the projects qualifying for investment are less, the discounting rate can be lowered and vice versa.
4. The current rate of return is a good guide to selecting the social discount rate provided that indirect taxes are fairly uniform with little discrimination between imported and exported commodities, and the social wage rate is close to the actual wages.
5. The rate selected should be such that only a few of the best projects undertaken in the past would qualify for investment, that is, they would have a positive net present value when discounted at the selected rate.

A.13 SCBA BY FINANCIAL INSTITUTIONS

Financial institutes appraise projects mostly from the financial point of view. However, they also scrutinize projects from the social point of view. The method generally used is a modified form of the L–M method. Let us examine the method used for project appraisal from the social point of view by IDBI. It considers three main aspects: economic rate of return, effective rate of protection and the domestic resource cost.

A.13.1 Economic Rate of Return

IDBI uses a partial L–M method. The main features are as follows:

1. International prices are substituted for market prices for all non-labour inputs.
2. For tradable goods whose international prices are directly available, use the CIF price for imported goods and the FOB price for exported goods.
3. For tradable goods whose international price is not directly available and for non-tradable goods, social conversion factors (SCF) are used. Either the actual rupee cost is multiplied directly by the social conversion factor or the actual rupee cost is broken into tradable component, labour component and residual component and these components are valued in social terms. The social conversion factor/break-up into components as used by IDBI are shown in Table A.9.

Table A.9 Social conversion factors

Item	*SCF or proportion*
Tradable component (T)	1/1.5
Labour component (L)	0.5
Residual component (R)	0.5
Land	1/1.5
Buildings and construction	$T = 0.5$; $L = 0.25$; $R = 0.25$
Indigenous equipment	0.70
Transportation	$T = 0.65$; $L = 0.25$; $R = 0.10$
Engineering and know-how fees	1.50
Bank charges	0.02
Pre-operative expenses	1.00
Labour	0.50
Salaries	0.80
Repairs and maintenance	1/1.5
Water, fuel, etc.	$T = 0.5$; $L = 0.25$; $R = 0.25$
Electricity	$T = 0.71$; $L = 0.13$; $R = 0.16$
Domestic stores	0.80
Other overheads	1/1.5

EXAMPLE A.12 A company is appraising a project which will result in import substitution of a product. The life of the project is expected to be 10 years. The capital expenditure estimates for the project are given in Table A.10.

Table A.10 Capital expenditure estimates

	₹, million
Land	0.75
Buildings	12.00
Plant and machinery (imported) (CIF value is ₹ 10 million)	8.00

(Contd...)

Table A.10 Capital expenditure estimates (*Contd...*)

	₹, million
Plant and machinery (indigenous) (CIF value of similar equipment is ₹ 40 million)	50.00
Transportation costs	4.00
Technical know-how fee	5.00
Pre-operative expenses	6.00
Bank charges	0.50

The project profitability statement of the company is shown in Table A.11.

Table A.11 Project profitability statement

	₹, million
Income	
Net sales (10,000 tons at ₹ 10,000 per ton; CIF value is ₹ 7500 per ton)	100.00
Expenditure	
Imported raw material (CIF value is ₹ 8 million)	10.00
Indigenous raw material and stores	35.00
Labour	8.00
Salaries	4.00
Repair and maintenance	1.00
Water, fuel, etc.	5.00
Electricity (Rate 3; Duty 2)	5.00
Depreciation	4.00
Other overheads	6.00
Taxable profit	22.00

Working capital estimated to be ₹ 20 million (CIF value is ₹ 15 million).

Solution Let us calculate the social cost of initial outlay. All figures are in millions of rupees. The data is shown in Table A.12.

Table A.12 Social cost of initial outlay

Item	*Financial cost*	*Basis of conversion*	*Tradable value ab initio*	*T*	*L*	*R*
Land	0.75	1/1.5	0.5			
Buildings	12.00	$T = 0.5$ $L = 0.25$ $R = 0.25$		6.00	3.00	3.00
Plant and machinery	8.00	CIF value	10.00			
Plant and machinery indigenous	50.00	CIF value	40.00			

(*Contd...*)

Table A.12 Social cost of initial outlay (*Contd...*)

Item	*Financial cost*	*Basis of conversion*	*Tradable value ab initio*	*T*	*L*	*R*
Transportation costs	4.00	$T = 0.65$ $L = 0.25$ $R = 0.10$		2.60	1.00	0.40
Technical know-how fee	5.00	1.50	7.50			
Pre-operative expenses	6.00	1.00	1.00			
Bank charges	0.50	0.02	0.01			
Working capital	20.00	CIF value	15.00			
Total			74.01	8.60	4.00	3.40

Social cost of initial outlay

Tradable value ab initio	74.01
Social cost of tradable components (8.60 × 1/1.5)	5.73
Social cost of labour component (4 × 0.50)	2.00
Social cost of residual component (3.40 × 0.50)	1.70
Total	**83.44**

Let us calculate the social cost of other inputs. The data is shown in Table A.13.

Table A.13 Social cost of other inputs

Item	*Financial cost*	*Basis of conversion*	*Tradable value ab initio*	*T*	*L*	*R*
Imported raw material	10.00	CIF value	8.00			
Indigenous raw materials and stores	35.00	0.80	28.00			
Labour	8.00	0.50	4.00			
Salaries	4.00	0.80	3.20			
Repair and maintenance	1.00	1/1.5	0.67			
Water, fuel, etc.	5.00	$T = 0.5$ $L = 0.25$ $R = 0.25$		2.50	1.25	1.25
Electricity (**Ignore duties and taxes**)	3.00	$T = 0.71$ $L = 0.13$ $R = 0.16$		2.13	0.39	0.48
Other overheads	6.00	1/1.5	4.00			
Total			47.87	4.63	1.64	1.73

Social cost of other inputs

Tradable value ab initio	47.87
Social cost of tradable components (4.63 × 1/1.5)	3.09
Social cost of labour component (1.64 × 0.50)	0.82
Social cost of residual component (1.73 × 0.50)	0.87
Total	**52.65**

(Depreciation is ignored as it is not a cash flow)

Social value of output (CIF value) (10,000 × 7500)	75.00
Net social benefit per annum = 75 – 52.65 = 22.35	

If we assume that the working capital received at the end of the life of the project (eight years) is ₹ 15 million and the salvage value is ₹ 3 million, then the cash flows will be as follows:

Year 0	– 83.44
Years 1 to 7	22.35
Year 8 (22.35 + 25.00 + 3.00)	50.35

We can now calculate the IRR (internal rate of return) of the project or estimate its net present value by discounting it at the social rate of discount. The acceptance of the project will depend on whether the project has a positive net present value or not, or alternatively, whether the IRR is greater than the social discount rate or not.

A.13.2 Effective Rate of Protection

Governments try and protect domestic industry from international competition through a system of taxes, duties, import restrictions and so on. This is specially true of developing and underdeveloped countries who encourage development of domestic industrial capability even though in the initial stages it may be costlier to produce than to import goods. The degree to which protection is provided to domestic industry is measured by the effective rate of protection (ERP). It is calculated as follows:

$$\text{ERP} = \frac{\text{Value added at domestic prices} - \text{Value added at world prices}}{\text{Value added at world prices}} \times 100$$

ERP is expressed as a percentage.

$$\text{Value added} = \text{Selling price} - \text{Input costs}$$

Selling price is net of taxes and excise duties but includes selling commission. The input cost of tradable goods is valued at both domestic and world prices, and for non-tradable goods at domestic prices only. Traded and non-tradable goods are segregated as follows:

Raw materials and stores

These are generally treated as traded items and their values at domestic and world prices are estimated. However, in case of items which are generally not traded or are non-tradable, only the domestic cost is considered.

Power, fuel and water

These are generally treated as non-tradable items. When a large part of the fuel consists of oil or coal and has significant cost, the coal and oil are treated as tradable items and their value is determined at both domestic and world prices.

Repairs and maintenance

This is treated as a non-tradable item. However, if it involves substantial consumption of spares and chemicals (not included in raw materials), it is treated as a tradable item.

Selling expenses

This is treated as a non-tradable item.

Administrative overheads and expenses

These can be broken down into labour and other expenses like rentals, insurance charges and so on. As the labour costs are part of value added, only the non-labour costs are included and treated as a non-tradable item.

EXAMPLE A.13 The following are the values at domestic and international prices of inputs and outputs of a project (Table A.14). Determine the effective rate of protection.

Table A.14 Values of inputs and outputs at domestic and international prices

	Domestic prices		World prices	
Tradable inputs				
Raw materials		400		300
Consumable stores		60		40
Total		*460*		*340*
Non-tradable inputs				
Power, fuel and water		30		
Repairs and maintenance		20		
Administrative overheads		40		
Selling expenses		25		
Total		*115*		*115*
Total input costs		**575**		**455**
Output				
Sales realization		725		575
Value added	(725 – 575)	150	(575 – 455)	120

Solution

$$\text{ERP} = \frac{150 - 120}{120} \times 100 = 25\%$$

If ERP = 0 then the domestic industry enjoys no protection and if ERP is negative, the domestic industry is more competitive than the foreign industry.

A.13.3 Domestic Resource Cost

It is the amount of spending required in terms of domestic currency to save one unit of foreign currency. The foreign currency generally used as a reference is the US dollar. It is the ratio of the value added at domestic prices to value added at world prices multiplied by the exchange rate. However, while computing the value added, capital costs in terms of charge on capital employed and depreciation are also taken into account. The annual charge on capital is taken as 10% and the depreciation on assets exclusive of land and working capital requirements is taken as 8%. Financial institutes use the following relationship to calculate domestic resource cost (DRC):

$$\text{DRC} = \frac{A+B+C}{P-(Q+R+S+T)} \times \text{Exchange rate}$$

where

A = the annual charge on domestic capital at 10%
B = the annual depreciation on domestic capital assets (less land and working capital requirements) at 8%
C = the cost of domestically procured non-tradable inputs
P = the sale realization at world prices
Q = the annual charge on imported capital assets at 10%
R = the annual depreciation on imported capital assets (lessland and working capital requirements) at 8%
S = the annual cost of imported inputs
T = the annual cost of domestically procured but tradable inputs

Domestic resource cost can be segregated as follows:

Domestic capital

It consists of the following:

1. Cost of domestically procured plant, machinery and other fixed assets less duties and taxes.
2. Preliminary and pre-operative expenses excluding interest paid during construction period.
3. Clearing and local transportation cost of imported machinery.
4. Working capital investment other than investment in imported and tradable raw material inventory.

Imported capital

Items to be included are:

1. Cost of imported plant, machinery and other fixed assets. Duties are excluded.
2. Working capital investment in imported and tradable raw material inventory less all taxes and duties.

Cost of domestically procured operating inputs

These include:

1. Tradable inputs, which are priced at border prices.
2. Non-tradable inputs are valued at domestic costs. All taxes, duties and subsidies are ignored.

Cost of imported operating inputs

These are valued at the actual price paid for them. Duties are not considered. Transportation costs are treated as domestic costs.

Sales realization at international prices

CIF price for an imported/importable or import substitute good and FOB price for an exported/exportable good.

EXAMPLE A.14 Details of a project are given in Table A.15 (all figures are in millions of rupees):

Table A.15 Details of project

S. No.	*Item*	*Total cost (excluding taxes and duties)*	*Domestic capital*	*Imported capital*
1.	Land	20	20	
2.	Buildings	12	12	
3.	Plant and machinery			
	(i) Imported	80		80
	(ii) Indigenous	50	50	
4.	Transportation	5	5	
5.	Other fixed assets	30	20	10
6.	Preliminary and pre-operative expenses	30	30	
7.	Contingencies	20	10	10
8.	Working capital requirement	50	40	10
9.	Total capital employed	297	187	110
10.	Charge on capital at 10%		18.7	11.0
11.	Depreciation on capital at 8% (excluding land and working capital requirements)		10.16	8.0

The output of the projected value at border prices is expected to be ₹ 240 million.

The costs are expected to be as given in Table A.16.

Table A.16 Expected cost

S. No.	*Item*	*Total cost*	*Non-tradable component*	*Tradable component*	*Imported component*
1.	Raw materials	140	30	90	20
2.	Utilities (power, fuel, etc.)	25	20	5	
3.	Repairs and maintenance	10	10		
4.	Wages and salaries	25	25		
5.	Rent and insurance	5	5		
6.	Administrative expenses	5	5		
7.	Selling expenses	5	5		
8.	Total	215	100	95	20

The present exchange rate is ₹ 40 per dollar.

$$\text{DRC} = \frac{18.7 + 10.16 + 100}{240 - (11 + 8 + 20 + 95)} \times 40 = ₹\ 48.63$$

The domestic resource cost is ₹ 48.63 per dollar.

Part II Project Planning

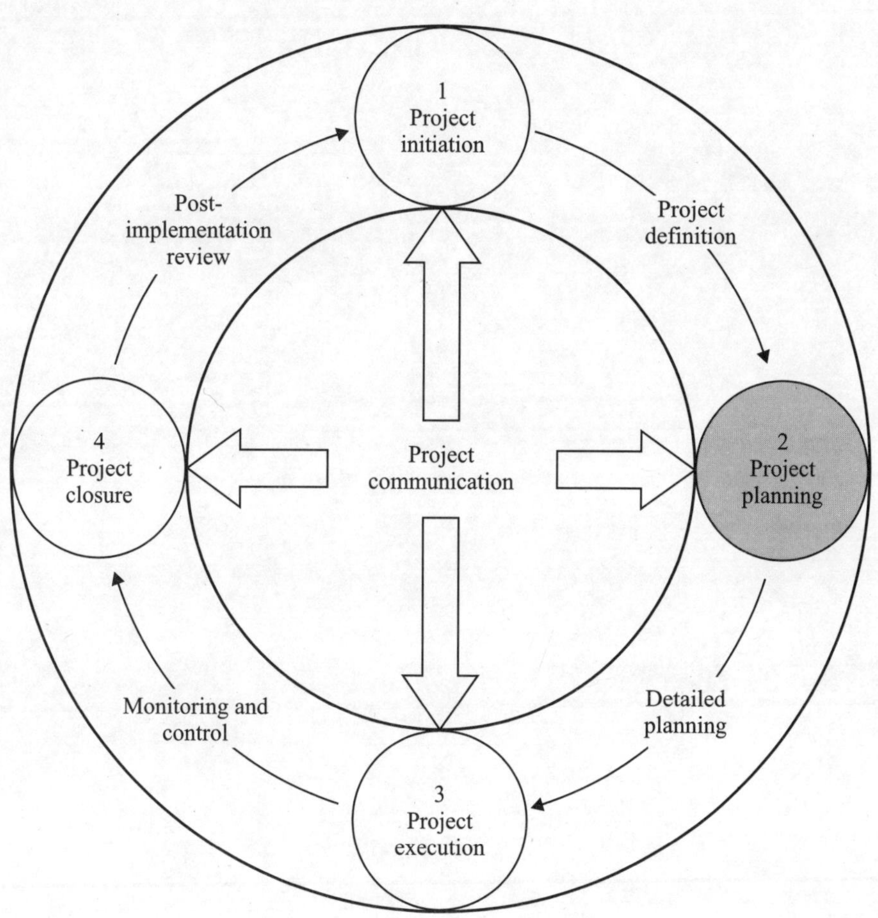

CHAPTER 4

Project Definition

Running a project without a WBS is like going to a strange land without a roadmap.
—J. Phillips

LEARNING OBJECTIVES

After reading this chapter, you will be able to:

- Understand the planning process for a project.
- Defining the project scope.
- Study the methodology for developing a work breakdown structure (WBS).
- Integrating the WBS with the organization to develop an organizational breakdown structure (OBS).
- Understand project roll up.

4.1 INTRODUCTION

A well-executed stage performance by a ballet group enthrals an audience. It almost appears spontaneous as the director would have us believe. However, we know that perfection of the coordinated and harmonized movements is achieved through countless hours of practice. The ballet group is more into operations than project management. Projects are one-time activities producing unique outcomes. The project manager can ill-afford to make mistakes and learn by practice. Project management does not give a 'second chance'. It is, therefore, imperative that projects are executed without hitches as far as possible. Good execution can be achieved only by good planning. A plan answers the what, when, how and who issues of a project.

It provides answers to the following questions:

1. What does the project involve? What tasks have to be carried out for completing the project?
2. When do these activities have to be carried out—that is, the schedule of the project?
3. How are these tasks to be carried out—that is, the resources required for the tasks?
4. Who is responsible for each task?

Planning and controlling are two facets of the same coin. Control aims at measuring current status against a laid down standard and then taking corrective action to reduce the deviations. The plan lays down the required standards. We can control only what we plan. The first step in planning is to define the project scope.

4.2 PROJECT SCOPE

A project scope is a definition of the end results of the project—a product or service for the client or customer. It clearly defines the deliverables for the end user. Though this appears elementary, it is often ignored. A clear definition of the deliverables ensures a proper understanding between the client and the project manager. The client knows precisely what to expect from the project, while the project manager knows what is expected of him by the client. An ill-defined scope leads to changes being made as the project progresses resulting in scope creep, delays and consequent time and cost overruns.

The project scope is developed by the project manager and the customer or end user. Discussion with end users may throw up a large number of requirements. An attempt should be made to keep the project simple by breaking it up into multiple phases or into multiple projects. Requirements are often conflicting, and the scope should be restricted to what is 'doable'. The owner and the project manager must agree on the project objectives and on the deliverables at each stage of the project. For instance, in the early stages, the deliverable may be specifications and design drawings, at the next stage it may be two prototypes of the product and so on.

The project scope definition is a document that is used by the project owner and the project participants for planning the project and measuring its success. The following aspects must be carefully considered while formulating project scope.

4.2.1 Project Objective

This defines the overall objective to meet the client's needs. For example, if the organization decides on the basis of extensive market survey that it needs to enhance its car production capacity, it may specify its objective as: to enhance the production capacity from 1,20,000 cars per year to 1,50,000 cars per year in the next six months at a cost not exceeding ₹ 3 crores. The project objective provides answers to what, when and how much.

4.2.2 Deliverables

The next step is to define the major deliverables—the outputs required at various stages of the project. For instance, in the early stages of the car manufacturer's example the deliverable may be identification of suitable plant which can be integrated with the existing facility. At a later stage, it may be identification of suitable vendor. Later still, the deliverable may be physical procurement of the plant, its erection, testing and so on.

4.2.3 Milestones

A milestone is a significant event that occurs at a point of time during the course of a project. A milestone indicates the completion of a major element of work and is the basis of a rough estimate of cost and time. For instance, milestones in the project for the car manufacturer could be: plant identification completed by 10 September; plant physically procured by 30 October; foundations for machines completed by 20 November and so on. Milestones should be easily identifiable by every one working on the project. They must be tangible. They form important control points in the project.

4.2.4 Limits and Exclusions

The limits and boundaries of the scope must be clearly defined. If this is not done, the client's expectations may differ from what is actually intended. Resources may be needlessly spent on solving the wrong problem. Some examples of limits may be: the vendor shall deliver machinery only at the rail head; the cost of transportation of the machinery beyond the rail head will have to be borne by the company. Boundaries of the project are further defined by the exclusions. For instance, a two bedroom, hall and kitchen flat will be constructed, but no electronic security devices will be provided.

4.2.5 Review with the Client/Customer

Finally, a review with the client or customer, whether internal or external, must be carried out. This will ensure that there is no ambiguity in the understanding between the project manager and the client in terms of project deliverables, key accomplishments, budgets, schedules and so on. The scope limits and boundaries are clearly defined and understood by both the client and the project manager. A clear understanding at this stage will facilitate better planning and execution and avoid the need for incorporating changes at later stages as these can be dysfunctional and can result in cost and time overruns or in poor quality.

An example of project scope is given in the following box. The project was initiated by the Delhi Police and was part of the projects for the Commonwealth Games held at Delhi in 2010.

INTELLIGENT TRAFFIC SYSTEM

(Excerpts from document inviting 'Expression of Intent')

In view of the forthcoming Commonwealth Games 2010, Delhi Traffic Police proposes to provide IT Solutions for traffic management particularly on the important roads and at the intersections numbering about 200 to start with. ITS must carry the following:

1. Day and night **On Line** monitoring of traffic at the intersections and on the roads on 24 × 7 × 365 basis. This includes installation of IP based cameras (either PTZ or fixed).

INTELLIGENT TRAFFIC SYSTEM
(Excerpts from document inviting 'Expression of Intent')

2. Analytical software for analyzing video receipt from the camera for definite incident detection and help in its management.
3. The camera should be intelligent and should have the capacity of reading the registration (APNR) number in Indian conditions.
4. Capability of enforcement of traffic laws and rules which may include enforcement against speeding, red light jumping, lane violations, stop line violations, etc.
5. Communication of useful messages information to the motorists through installation of VMS, GSM, Internet, etc.
6. Identification of disaster/road emergencies and response thereon.
7. Digitalized location of the Traffic Police and other resources to deal with such emergencies.
8. Setting up of centralized command and control centre with facility of **On Line** real time display on **Video Wall** slides.
9. Generation of various statistics and incident management reports.
10. Integration of existing sub-system, i.e. ATC, TMS, VMS, RL and SC.
11. The video wall should be able to indicate:
    (a) Volume of traffic on the roads.
    (b) Flagging of accidents, etc.
    (c) Availability of traffic police vehicles on GPS and vehicle tracking system.
    (d) Any other information of traffic violation.
12. Red Light Speed Cameras.

Broadly, Delhi Traffic Police expects/requires this ITS to deliver the following:

1. On line seemless monitoring of the traffic on roads and intersections.
2. Detailed incident detection and its management.
3. Enforcement of traffic laws/rules such as speed, Red Light Violation, etc.
4. Automatic Plate Number Reader.
5. Outprint through Variable Message Signs.
6. Integration of existing sub-system/system.
7. Centralized Command and Control Centre.
8. Other by-products of the system.
9. Location of response/resources on GIS Map.
10. Volume of traffic on the roads.
11. Red Light Speed Cameras.

The project envisages:

1. A study of the existing processes and pilots.
2. Creation of an ITS blueprint and road map.
3. Mapping international best practices in ITS with local requirements and customization.
4. Selection and customization of global ITS technologies.
5. Setting up of ITS infrastructure and applications.
6. Support and management of ITS systems.
7. Growth of ITS systems aligned with traffic police requirements and plans.
8. Integration of existing sub-systems to proposed system.

A well-defined project scope goes a long way to avoid scope creep and its accompanying delays and cost overruns. The project manager should also lay down priorities amongst cost, time and performance or scope of the project. Some of these factors may be constraining. For instance, a prestigious project which is scheduled to be inaugurated by the President on the Republic Day may have time as a constraining factor. We may accept increases in the cost of the project to fulfil this requirement or may accept a lower quality or scope in order to meet the inaugural deadline. While a factor may be constraining, another one may be enhanced or changes accepted in a trade-off between them to ensure fulfilment of the goals.

4.3 PLANNING MODEL

Once the project scope has been properly defined, planning of the project can be undertaken. Figure 4.1 explains the planning model diagrammatically. The steps involved in planning are:

Step 1 *Develop a work breakdown structure.* The project scope statement defines the deliverables of the project. The work breakdown structure identifies all the tasks that have to be completed to build the required deliverables.

Step 2 *Estimate work packages.* An estimate of resources required for each of the tasks identified in the work breakdown structure is made. The estimate covers resources like labour, materials, machines and plant, time and cost.

Step 3 *Identify task relationships.* The work packages are placed in a proper sequence. Some activities can be carried out simultaneously, while others must follow one another sequentially.

Step 4 *Work out an initial schedule.* After estimating the duration of work packages and arranging them according to their relationship, an initial schedule is worked out. Networks can be used as a tool for this purpose. Project management software packages can also be used. The initial schedule may have to be revised and updated as the project progresses.

Step 5 *Allocate and level resources.* The schedule is adjusted to account for resource constraints. The project schedule must optimize the use of resources.

Step 6 *Develop the budget.* The costs of labour, materials, equipment and services are combined to prepare a budget and cash flow projections.

The aforementioned steps will yield all the information necessary to understand how to execute the project. The steps are systematic but a number of iterations of the planning process may be required to come with an optimal balance between cost, schedule and quality.

4.4 WORK BREAKDOWN STRUCTURE

After the scope and the deliverables of a project have been identified, the next logical step is to prepare a work breakdown structure (WBS). It is a tool for breaking up the project into its component parts and is the foundation of project planning. It is an outline of the project showing different levels of detail. The WBS is a task list and helps in understanding the project. It turns

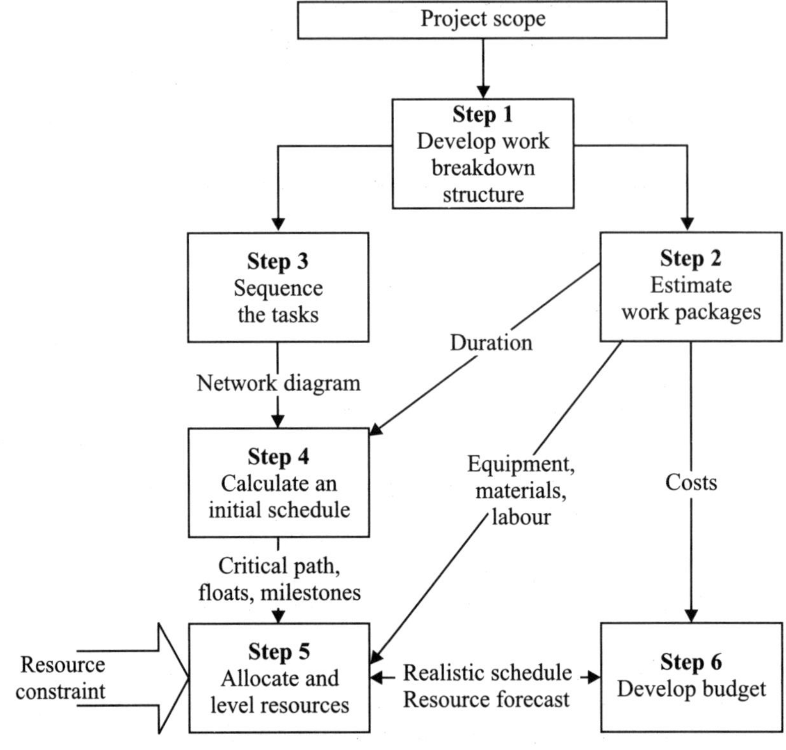

Figure 4.1 Planning model.

a large, unique project into many small manageable tasks. For instance, if we were to consider the construction of a three-storey building for housing a school, we could break the task on the basis of various floors. If we assume that the top floor has to house two classrooms, a computer laboratory and toilet facilities, then each of these would involve different tasks. For instance, the construction of the computer laboratory would not only involve civil works but also involve electrification as per the layout, installation of computer hardware, installation of computer software, testing, audio-visual projection systems, teaching aids like whiteboards, network connections and so on.

The WBS begins with the project as a deliverable. It then lists out the deliverables required to complete the project. The deliverables are broken into sub-deliverables. These are in turn broken down to summary tasks, tasks and sub-tasks involved and so on till the task can be managed and an individual can be assigned the responsibility for it. The task is further divided into work packages which are generally grouped by type of work—for instance, hardware installation, software installation, testing and so on. The work packages become the units for cost accounting and for monitoring the progress of the project by work, cost and responsibility.

Work packages should have the following characteristics:

1. They should be capable of being executed independently without dependence or linkages to other elements.

2. They should be identifiable with specific level of authority and should be so designed that responsibility for successful completion can be assigned to the person with the relevant authority. They promote a match between authority and responsibility.
3. Work packages should be tangible, specific and measurable. It should be possible to measure the progress of a work package at each stage.
4. We should be able to integrate them with other elements after all elements are completed.
5. Work packages facilitate the preparation of the scope of work. They are the level at which line managers operate.

The WBS may be shown graphically or in outline form. Each work package is coded and identified and this coding forms the basis of reporting and consolidating costs. The project may be considered as a large package broken up into smaller and smaller sub-packages. The total project is a summation of all the smaller work packages. The WBS facilitates evaluation of costs, time and performance at all levels of the organization.

The resources required and the cost estimates are worked out in detail for each task and these are then consolidated in a bottom-up approach. This helps to plan and budget resources and to monitor the same during execution of the project. The WBS also provides a framework for developing management information and control systems.

Since individual responsibilities are assigned during the development of the WBS, it integrates the work and the organizational structure. This process is sometimes called the organizational breakdown structure (OBS).

4.4.1 Development of WBS

The first step in the development of a WBS is to define the scope of the project. At the next level, the main deliverables are listed. Each deliverable is further broken into sub-deliverables. The sub-deliverables are broken into work packages and the work packages are further subdivided into tasks and work elements. A sub-deliverable may consist of a number of work packages and include the outcomes of more than one department. Therefore, a sub-deliverable does not consume time and resources directly; it consumes the sum total of resources of the work packages that go into producing it. We should be able to plan, schedule, monitor and control a work package individually, without relying on any other element at the same or different level.

A detailed work description is prepared for each work element listing the inputs required, the technical specifications, the stipulations laid down by the client, if any, and the end result or deliverable. The manpower, equipment, funds, materials required in terms of both quantity and quality, and the facilities required for each work element are identified. Personnel who are to carry out different activities are identified and authority and responsibility relationships are spelt out. A sequence of activities is developed.

The next stage involves a review of the WBS by the persons entrusted the responsibility of executing tasks. They review the schedule, the scope of work and the cost and resource estimates. The resources requirement and schedules are aggregated upwards to arrive at the work elements and resources required at that level. At the top level, we get the total plan for the project in terms of work elements, schedules and resource budgets.

The question that often troubles project mangers is: what should be the size of a work package? If the work package is too large, it will become a mini-project in itself. On the other hand, if the work packages are broken down to very fine detail, the exercise might become dysfunctional. Some thumb rules that are generally followed as guidelines are:

(a) *The* 8/80 *rule.* No task should be less than 8 labour hours or more than 80 labour hours. Tasks should be between 1 and 10 labour days. This is just a guideline and not a rule. (In India where we work for six days a week, we may modify this to read 8/96 rule so that tasks are not more than 12 labour days.)
(b) *The reporting period rule.* No task should be longer than the interval between two reporting periods. This implies that if weekly reports are obtained, the task should not be longer than a week. This avoids receiving confusing status reports such as 40% complete or 60% complete and so on. The task is either complete, or started (if progress is 50%), or not yet started (if progress is 0%). No scheduled task should be reported as started for two consecutive reporting periods.
(c) *The 'if it is useful' rule.* Tasks are broken down into smaller elements so that:
   (i) *Estimation becomes easier.* Smaller tasks have less uncertainty and are easier to estimate.
   (ii) *Assignment of the task becomes easier.* Smaller task can be assigned to an individual and he or she can be given responsibility for the same. He or she can also be held accountable. Larger tasks assigned to many people result in poor accountability. (Each one thinks someone else will do it.)
   (iii) *Tracking becomes easier.* Smaller tasks are easier to track and easier to report on. This is very similar to the 'reporting period' rule.

If breaking down a task into smaller elements does not make it easier to estimate, assign or track, the task should not be broken down any further. Projects which are to be completed in very short spans of time may have tasks broken down into very small elements. The level of detail should be compatible with the nature of the project in hand and the degree of control required at various levels.

To sum up, each work package in the WBS defines the work to be done (what), the time required to complete it, the cost and resources in terms of men and material required to execute it, the individual responsible and accountable for it, and the stages at which it will be monitored for progress.

Creating a WBS from scratch is a difficult task. The organization should draw on its past experience in handling similar projects or refer to other relevant projects for help. The details can be worked out by the people responsible for the specific work. The information can then be aggregated into a WBS. The WBS is approved by the relevant stakeholders and the client after they arrive at an agreement of its contents. The WBS should be end-item or output oriented. It should aim towards deliverables rather than on functions.

Let us understand the WBS with the help of an example. Let us consider a construction company involved in various types of projects. We shall focus our attention to the construction of a single-storey house for residential purposes. The house consists of a hall, two bedrooms, kitchen, two toilets and a garage. We are assuming that land and materials required have been procured. We shall only consider some activities for this illustration and shall use the same example in our further discussions.

At the top level, we can list the company itself—Apsara Construction—as it has a number of projects running concurrently. At the next level, we can list the projects as shown in Figure 4.2.

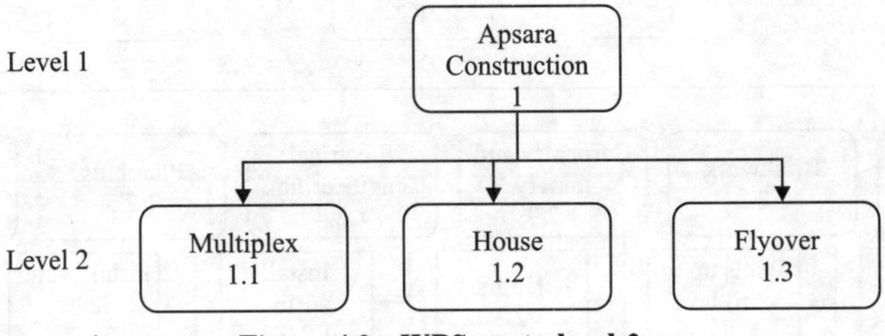

Figure 4.2 WBS up to level 2.

The main deliverable for each project has been listed at level 2. Let us now add some of the deliverables for the house project at level 3 (Figure 4.3).

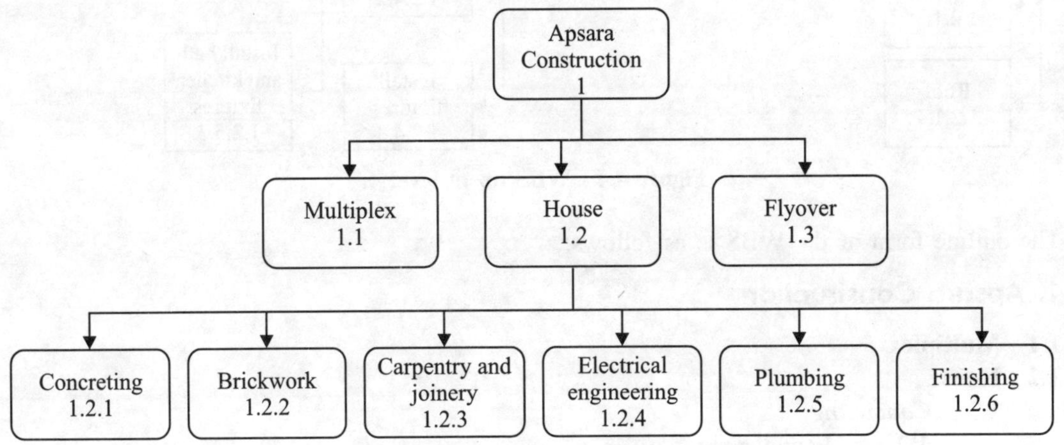

Figure 4.3 WBS up to level 3.

Notice the numbering system used for the projects and their sub-components. We can add further levels of details as required. We have added another level to the WBS for some of the activities to give an idea of how a WBS is developed. The WBS developed to the fourth level is shown in Figure 4.4.

The WBS can also be represented in an outline form instead of a diagram. It must be remembered that though the WBS looks like an organization chart, it is not an organization chart. It merely lists the tasks that have to be performed to complete the project.

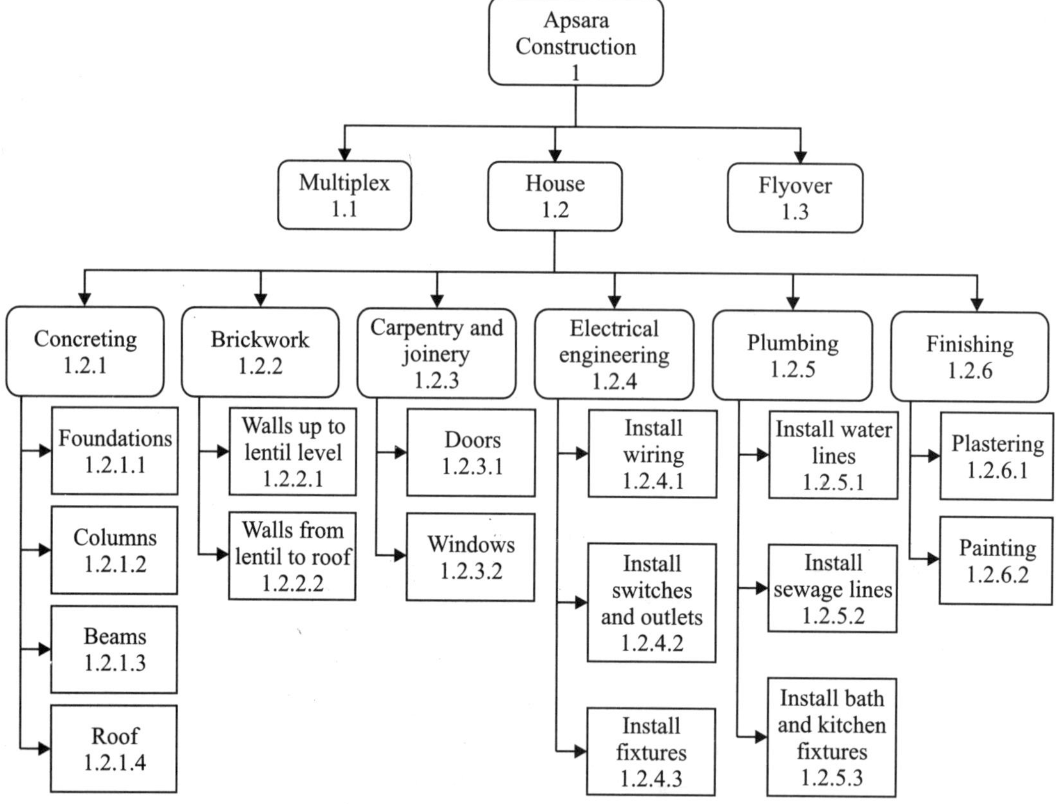

Figure 4.4 WBS up to level 4.

The outline form of the WBS is as follows:

1. Apsara Construction

1.1 Multiplex

1.2 House

1.2.1 *Concreting*

1.2.1.1 Foundations
1.2.1.2 Columns
1.2.1.3 Beams
1.2.1.4 Roof

1.2.2 *Brickwork*

1.2.2.1 Walls up to lentil level
1.2.2.2 Walls from lentil to roof

1.2.3 *Carpentry and joinery*

1.2.3.1 Fabrication of panelled doors and door frames
1.2.3.2 Fabrication of window frames and windows

1.2.4 *Electrical engineering*

1.2.4.1 Install wiring

1.2.4.2 Install switches and outlets
1.2.4.3 Install fixtures

1.2.5 *Plumbing*

1.2.5.1 Install water lines
1.2.5.2 Install sewage lines
1.2.5.3 Install bath and kitchen fixtures

1.2.6 *Finishing*

1.2.6.1 Plastering of walls
1.2.6.2 Painting of walls

1.3 Flyover

Once the WBS is complete, we develop the WBS dictionary. The WBS dictionary is a narrative documentation of the effort needed to accomplish all the tasks in the WBS. It is developed only for the lowest level elements in the WBS. If we were to draw an analogy, the WBS is like the table of contents of a book, and the WBS dictionary is the book itself. The WBS dictionary helps us to develop statements of work (SOW) for the project.

4.5 ORGANIZATIONAL BREAKDOWN STRUCTURE

An integral part of the WBS is to assign responsibility for the work packages to individuals. The outcome of this process is the organizational breakdown structure (OBS). The OBS indicates the organizational relationship. It is structured on the basis of responsible department and at the lowest level by the performing department. A part of the Apsara Constructions organization for the construction of the house is shown in Figure 4.5.

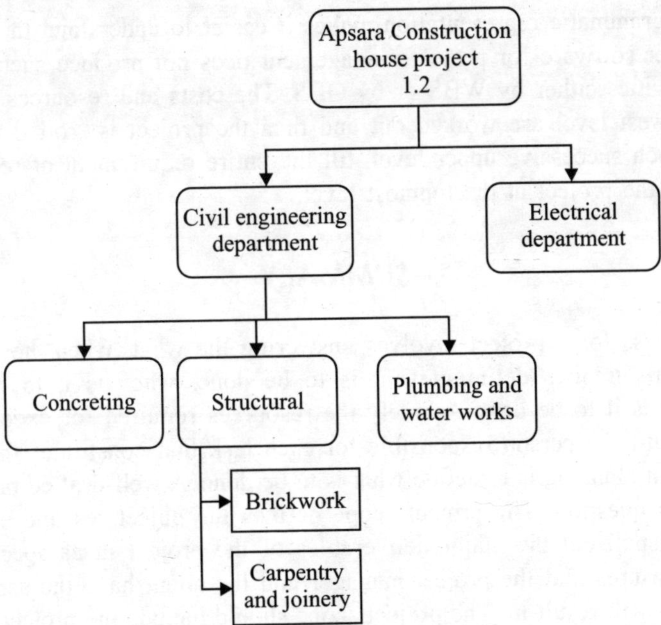

Figure 4.5 Apsara Construction organization for the construction of house.

The organizational structure and the WBS can now be combined as a responsibility assignment matrix as shown in Figure 4.6.

Tasks	*Civil engineering department*				*Electrical*
	Concreting	*Structural*		*Plumbing*	
		Carpentry and joinery	*Brickwork*		
Foundation 1.2.1.1	X				
Columns 1.2.1.2	X				
Beams 1.2.1.3	X				
Roof 1.2.1.4	X				
Walls 1.2.2.1			X		
Walls 1.2.2.2			X		
Doors 1.2.3.1		X			
Windows 1.2.3.2		X			
Install wiring 1.2.4.1					X
Install switches and outlets 1.2.4.2					X
Install fixtures 1.2.4.3					X
Install water lines 1.2.5.1				X	
Install sewage lines 1.2.5.2				X	
Install bath and kitchen fixtures 1.2.5.3				X	
Plastering of walls 1.2.6.1			X		
Painting of walls 1.2.6.2			X		

Figure 4.6 Organizational structure and the WBS as a responsibility assignment matrix.

Though a diagrammatic representation makes it easier to understand the concept of OBS, available computer software for project management does not produce such diagrams. It can only sort out activities either by WBS or by OBS. The costs and resources required for each activity at the lowest level are worked out and then the project is 'rolled up'—that is, it is consolidated at each successive upper level, till the entire requirement of resources and costs are arrived at for the project at the topmost level.

SUMMARY

The planning process for a project involves answering the what, when, how and who issues of the project. This implies defining what is to be done, when is it to be done—that is, the schedule, how is it to be done—namely the resources required for executing the project, and who is to do it—the person responsible for each task that constitutes the project.

The first step in planning is to define what is to be done. A well-drafted project scope gives the answer to this question. The project scope defines the objectives and end results of the project. It should spell out the major deliverables of the project in as specific a manner as possible. It also ensures that the project manager and the client have the same understanding of what the project will result in. The project scope should include the project objectives, a list of deliverables, milestones of the project, technical requirements and limits and exclusions.

A well-defined project scope will ensure that the client or customer expectations are met, and scope creep, which results in delays and subsequent time and cost overruns, is avoided.

The major deliverables identified in the project scope are successively divided into smaller and smaller deliverables and work elements. This is called the work breakdown structure (WBS). The WBS is an outline of the project with different levels of detail at different hierarchical levels. The work package defines the work to be done (what), the time required to complete it, the cost and resources in terms of men and material required to execute it, the individual responsible and accountable for it, and the stages at which it will be monitored for progress. The project is 'rolled up' from the work package level. The resources and time required for work packages are consolidated at the next higher hierarchical level, and the topmost level yields a budget for resources for the project.

The WBS is integrated with the organization resulting in an organizational breakdown structure and a responsibility assignment matrix.

The WBS is the basis of project planning and a well-defined WBS ensures the success of the project at the implementation stage. We can control only what we plan and the WBS is the cornerstone of project planning.

QUESTIONS

1. What do you understand by a project objective? What should a project objective statement contain? Give an example of a good project objective.
2. What do you understand by a work package? What should the description of a work package contain?
3. What is the difference between a project limitation and a project exclusion?
4. What is project roll up and how would a project manager use this information?

CHAPTER 5

Estimating Time and Costs

To estimate a project, work out how long it would take one person to do it then multiply that by the number of people on the project. —Stephen Seay

LEARNING OBJECTIVES

After reading this chapter, you will be able to:

- Understand the importance of estimation.
- Study the factors that affect estimates.
- Study the guidelines for better estimates.
- Understand the nuances of cost estimation.

5.1 INTRODUCTION

Estimating the duration and cost of a project is an important part of planning. It helps to establish a baseline for the project. While it may appear as an elementary requirement, a majority of projects flounder because of inaccurate and overly optimistic estimates. Estimating processes are unique to an organization and cannot be bought off the shelf. Organizations generally use a top-down or a bottom-up approach. Sometimes both the methods are used and the differences are reconciled to come to workable estimates.

Accurate estimates reduce the gap between client expectations and 'actuals' delivered. However, it must be appreciated that there is a fair amount of uncertainty in projects and this can affect estimates. Estimating accuracy improves with the time and effort put in. Estimating effort is costly in terms of data collection and analysis and a balance must be drawn between the costs and accuracy necessary for the project.

Project estimates form the basis of project control. The estimates form the baseline against which the progress of the project is measured during execution. The estimates form an input for calculating variances and then taking corrective action. If the estimates are unrealistic, the project will fail to live up to expectations and will not deliver to the required standards of cost, time and quality.

Estimating time and costs is important because estimates are required to schedule work; determine how long a project will take and what it would cost; decide whether the project is worth undertaking; develop cash flows and time-phased budgets; and track the progress of the project. Estimates are an essential support for good decision-making.

5.2 FACTORS AFFECTING QUALITY OF ESTIMATES

Estimates are generally based on past experience. However, past experience must be suitably modified to bring it in consonance with the present situation. Projects are unique and the uniqueness will have a strong influence on the accuracy of estimates. Let us consider the case of a bridge construction project. The time standards achieved at the last construction site may be totally awry when applied to the current site as the soil conditions or the river bed conditions may be totally different. We must consider the uniqueness of the project, the people and the external factors to improve the quality of time and cost estimates.

5.2.1 Project Definition

If the project scope is not properly understood, the estimates will be inaccurate. It is important that the project is well defined and the WBS contains all the work packages needed to be completed for the 'deliverables' of the project. The quality of estimates is also dependent on the duration of the project. The longer the project, the greater the uncertainty attached with it. Estimates for a short planning horizon are much more accurate than estimates spanning a longer period.

5.2.2 People

The people factor can also affect the quality of estimates. The accuracy of estimates depends on the people making the estimates and their experience and skills. It is not only their individual skills that matter but also their ability to work and gel as a team. If people have not worked together earlier, they will spend more time communicating and tasks are likely to take a longer time than anticipated based purely on the work content. A close match between the task and people skills influences productivity and learning time.

5.2.3 Project Structure and Organization

The project structure adopted by the organization affects the estimates of time and cost. If a project is handled by a dedicated team which has the necessary authority to take decisions, it will be able to work faster than complex matrix organizations where decision-making gets delayed because of the divided attention and coordination required. Government projects invariably suffer because of the delays in taking decisions as the decision-making authority is vested in high level steering committees, which more often than not fail to meet as often as required. The delay involved in decision-making is rarely taken into account while making estimates. To illustrate, if we were asked how long it would take to paint a room in the house, our estimate would not include the weeks that may be spent on deciding what colour and shade to use that would be agreeable to the inmates of the house.

5.2.4 Padding/Understating Estimates

People tend to pad estimates. For instance, if you were asked how long it would take you to drive to the railway station, you might give an average time of 30 minutes, implying that you have a 50% chance of reaching the station in 30 minutes or less. If you were asked how long it would take you to drive to the railway station and be sure of catching a particular train, it is likely that you would increase your estimate to 50 minutes to ensure not being late. Similarly, when we make time and cost estimates in work situations, we tend to pad the estimate to be on the safe side. However, the padding at each stage inflates the estimates excessively, resulting in the estimates being seriously overstated. This tendency affects the quality and accuracy of the estimate.

On other occasions, estimates are understated because estimating authorities want the project to be approved. Understatement may also be because of failure to allow for change; foresee contingencies; allow for management activities and so on.

5.2.5 Other Factors

Finally, 'non-project' factors also tend to affect estimates. For instance, equipment failures and breakdowns; project prioritization for scarce resources—a crane may be required at two projects at the same time and only one may be available. In such a case, the lower priority project may get delayed while it waits for availability of the crane. National holidays, unforeseen natural calamities and so on can have an influence on the estimates.

Estimating is a complex process and managers must take all factors that impact the situation into account to arrive at reasonably accurate estimates. The estimates form the basis of time-phased budgets and a good estimation is the key to good control.

5.3 ESTIMATING GUIDELINES

Good estimates involve a detailed project definition. The project should be broken into its deliverables, sub-deliverables and down to work packages. The work packages should include as much detail as possible. This helps in estimation as smaller elements are easier to estimate than larger pieces of work. It is easier to estimate the time that plumbing of a bathroom including the fittings would take, than to estimate the time the entire building would take. Some guidelines that can help estimation are given in the following paragraphs:

(a) *Who should estimate?* Estimates for work packages should be drawn up preferably by the person or persons responsible for executing the particular work package.

The person is likely to have experience in carrying out the particular task and is, therefore, likely to make a realistic estimate of the time and costs. Since those actually performing the task are first line supervisors or technicians, they are unlikely to have any preconceived imposed duration for a deliverable in mind. Since they will also be executing the task, their estimates will not only be realistic but will also carry their commitment towards meeting the estimates at the execution stage. As far as possible, estimates should be obtained from multiple sources so that individual biases that may occur due to experience in particular work environments can be eliminated.

(b) *Normal working conditions.* Estimates of time, cost and resources are based on certain assumptions. Estimates should be based on normal working conditions, efficient methods and normal level of resources. Normal working conditions are often difficult to specify but a consensus in the organization must exist as to what normal conditions mean. For instance, a company may work only one eight-hour shift a day, five days a week instead of six, then the estimate should be based on 40 man hours per week of labour. Similarly, if the organization has two bull dozers available to it, the plan should be based on the availability of two dozers only. Often space restrictions impose levels of normality. For instance, one may estimate that it would require eight man hours to paint a particular wall. This does not imply that by employing eight painters we will be able to paint the wall in one hour. The wall may be a monolith which does not permit more than one painter at a time to work on it. At the estimation stage, we should not attempt to resolve any conflicts in the demands for scarce resources. These would be resolved at the stage of resource allocation. A thumb rule often followed is the square root rule. According to this thumb rule, if a task is estimated to take nine man days, then it would be normally possible to complete it in three days using three men (square root of nine is three). Estimates must be based on normal conditions, even though it may be possible to reduce time taken for a task by increasing the resources used. Obviously, this will result in additional direct costs because of the employment of additional resources.

(c) *Time units.* All estimates should be made in consistent time units. These may be work hours, work days, calendar weeks, work weeks and so on. The same units should be used throughout the project. The choice of units depends on the nature of the project. While work weeks may be a suitable unit for a multi-purpose hydroelectric project, work minutes may be more appropriate for a project involving the scheduling of a heart transplant surgery.

(d) *Estimate independently.* Tasks must be estimated as if they were to be carried out independently and then integrated by the WBS. Estimates by first line managers usually follow this dictum. Top managers tend to aggregate many tasks into a single time estimate and then try and make the individual task estimates total up to the aggregate estimate arrived at earlier. Even when tasks follow each other in a sequence, it is best to estimate each task separately and then aggregate them rather than doing it the other way round. The tendency to look at the whole sequence as a single task and then to try and adjust estimates for the individual tasks to conform to some arbitrary imposed schedule or 'guesstimate' must be avoided. More often than not, this results in the uncertainties in individual tasks being ignored and the estimate is too optimistic. A realistic estimate can be made when tasks are considered independently.

(e) *Contingencies.* Work package estimates should not consider or include allowances for contingencies. An allowance for contingencies should be built into the estimates after they have been aggregated by the management at the top level. The contingency allowance will cover unforeseen circumstances. If contingencies are included at each work package level, the estimate will be grossly overstated as it is unlikely that contingencies will affect every work package. The tendency to have built in reserves of time and funds at each level only inflates the estimates.

(f) *Risk.* Some activities carry higher degree of risk than others. For example, new technology always carries high risk. It may or may not work. The risk associated with cost helps decision-makers to decide whether to undertake a project or select an alternative. The risk in time element is often taken into account by having an optimistic, most likely and a pessimistic time estimates. Three time estimates are used in Programme Evaluation and Review Technique (PERT) and shall be dealt with in detail in later chapters.

Estimates may be made at the macro or the micro level. Estimates that are made bottom-up are likely to be more accurate. Good estimates will come from persons experienced in handling a particular task, and since bottom-up estimating starts at the work package level with estimates being made by front line supervisors who will ultimately execute the task, these estimates are bound to be more realistic and accurate than estimates made by top management. Past data can help in estimation. If the project in hand is similar to an earlier project, the data collected on the earlier project can act as a start point for making estimates for the project in hand. The changes from the earlier project must be carefully assessed and included in the estimate. Suitable cost escalation factors may be added to the cost estimates, while the learning curve must be accounted for in the time estimates. Often ratio method and parametric techniques are used. For instance, if the current construction yardstick is ₹ 1000 per square foot, then the macro cost of a 2500 square feet building can be estimated as ₹ 2,500,000 at the macro level. At the micro level, parametric standards are often available. For example, we may have data that a painter can paint 50 square feet of a wall in an hour. This can help us estimate the time required for painting walls for the building. Such data is collected and is available with organizations engaged in this type of work. For instance, construction planning data is available in the Standard Schedule of Rates maintained by the Military Engineering Service (MES), the largest construction agency in India. Similar data is also available with Central Public Works Department (CPWD) and other such organizations. An organization which deals with projects may develop its own database over time. The use of templates and planning data help in estimation of time and costs for projects.

5.4 COST ESTIMATES

There are three types of costs involved in a project—direct costs, project overhead costs, and general and administrative overhead costs. The direct costs include the cost of labour, materials, equipment and other costs. These costs can be attributed and charged to a specific work package. They represent real cash outflows and must be paid as the project progresses. Lower level project roll-ups generally include only the direct costs.

Project overhead costs are the overheads that can be directly attributed to the project. For example, the salary of the project manager is a direct project overhead cost. The direct overheads are charged as percentages of direct labour expenses, material expenses, equipment expenses and so on. While estimating the direct project overheads must be included.

The general and administrative expenses are the organization costs not directly linked to a specific project but spanning the entire range of projects that the organization may be undertaking. They could be corporate expenses like the salary of top management above the project level, advertising and promotion expenses, expenses on maintaining a legal department and so on. Every organization follows its own systems of allocating these costs to the projects. They may be allocated in the ratio of the overall costs of the projects or as percentages over and above the direct and project overhead costs.

The cost estimates should include all the costs. If a bid is being made for a project contract, the profit margin should also be added to these estimates.

Estimates obtained through the process of rolling up from the work package level and including the overheads need to be adjusted for contingencies and risk factors. These are dependent on the uncertainty associated with the project. Some of the reasons why cost estimates need adjustment are as follows:

(a) *Interaction costs.* At the work package level, it is assumed that the work is being done independently of other tasks. This is really not so. Even though the task can be performed independently, it is still a part of the whole and needs to be integrated. The integration involves coordination and interaction between different sections of the organization. This takes up time which needs to be included in our estimates. There is also a cost involved and the estimates must be adjusted to cater for these activities.

(b) *Normal conditions.* The estimates assume that normal conditions will prevail. For instance, we may normally be having four dozers available to us and may have estimated that a task would take 15 days with four dozers. In case one dozer goes off road due to a major fault, we shall have to work with three and the task may take 22 days instead of 15. Alternatively, we may decide to hire an additional dozer so that our time schedule is met. The cost of hiring will add to the cost of the project. While normal condition is a good start point, resource shortages in terms of people, materials and equipment will invariably occur. Estimates must be modified to cater for such contingencies.

(c) *Things go wrong.* While it is everyone's endeavour to see that things go as per plan, certain things do go wrong. Remember Murphy's law—what can go wrong, will go wrong. Accidents, natural calamities, strikes, political unrest and so on are beyond the planner's control. While one should not plan for these risks, their impact should be considered.

(d) *Scope creep.* This is one of the biggest causes of estimates going haywire. The project scope tends to change as we go along and get a better understanding of what needs to be done to accomplish the project objective. In today's world, the advent of information technology has made everything faster. Product life cycles as well as development cycles are becoming shorter and only the organization which can keep pace with the rapidly changing demands of society can be competitive enough to survive. The scope of the project may undergo changes as it is being implemented because of new technology, new client needs and the rapid changes taking place in the environment. This results in time and cost overruns and cannot be fully visualized at the planning stage.

Despite our best efforts, all the information needed for estimation is not available, nor can we predict the future. The longer the duration of the project, the more the uncertainty connected with it. Yet estimates need to be reasonably accurate for them to be meaningful. Time and cost overruns are commonly seen in projects. Organizations deal with the challenge of making meaningful estimates by adjusting estimates, providing contingency funds and time buffers and revising and changing baseline budgets and schedules, if required.

Organizations adjust estimates derived from a roll-up of the WBS for risks, resource constraints and abnormal conditions. For instance, if the organization feels that only three dozers would be available instead of four at the time when the activity which uses them is due, then it will adjust the estimate accordingly. Similarly, if the construction falls in a seismic zone, the estimates for the foundations are suitably altered.

Contingency funds are also provided for activities that are identified as risky. An overall fund for contingencies may also be provisioned for at the project level. However, if contingency funds have been included in the estimate for a particular activity and the contingency has not occurred, it should be ensured that the fund is not spent nevertheless on the activity. The tendency to spend up to budgeted amount should be curbed, especially when it is not necessary.

Sometimes a complete revision of the baseline budget and schedule may be required. This may occur due to major changes in the project scope or design of the deliverable. It is prudent, in such cases, to revise the entire budget and schedule and get the approval of the stakeholders for the change rather than to stick to an unworkable plan and an unachievable baseline.

Meaningful estimates are vital to the success of a project and the organization must devote every effort to improve its capability in this regard. A database should be created from projects executed in the past and the information should be used to help make estimates for current projects by suitable escalations and modifications in keeping with the prevailing technology and environment.

SUMMARY

Estimates are the basis of planning. We must estimate the time and the cost of the project with reasonable accuracy to reduce the gap between the expectations of the client and the 'actuals' delivered. Estimates form the baseline of the project and help us to track progress and take corrective action for deviations.

Estimates are affected by the project definition. An unclear project definition results in inaccurate estimates. Often an unclear project definition results in project scope creep which negates the estimates. The people making the estimate affect the quality of the estimate. As far as possible, we should break down the project to its basic activities or work packages and let the person responsible for the task carry out an estimate. This will result in the benefit of having an experienced person make an estimate. There will also be commitment towards meeting the estimate when it is made by the person who is to execute the task. Project organization structure is another factor which affects estimates. When authority, responsibility and accountability are not properly assigned, decision-making gets delayed resulting in longer time and increased costs. There is also a tendency to pad up estimates so that one can play safe. Padding up at every stage results in overestimation. Sometimes there is a tendency to underestimate, especially when the sponsor wants the project to be approved. Other factors like natural calamities, breakdowns and so on also affect the quality of estimates.

Estimates can be improved by following a bottom-up approach. Estimates for tasks should be prepared by those who are responsible for their execution. Estimates should be based on normal working conditions and should conform to a consistent time unit. We should estimate tasks as if they were to be executed independently. Allowances for contingencies and risk must be made only at the higher level of planning when integrating the estimates for individual tasks, that is, at project roll-up stage. Estimates based on past experience should be suitably modified to meet the current situation.

QUESTIONS

1. Why are accurate estimates essential to effective project management?
2. How does the person making the estimate affect its quality?
3. Why is there a tendency to overestimate?
4. Describe some guidelines which can be followed to improve estimation.
5. Mr. and Mrs. Malhotra are planning to build their own house in the suburbs of Bangalore. The plan shows the house as having a covered area of 280 square metres. The average cost of construction for the specifications desired by the Malhotras is ₹ 10,000 per square metre. Mrs. Malhotra is an accomplished interior designer and proposes to do the interior decoration work herself to save on cost. The following information regarding the various tasks involved in terms of their cost percentage is available:

   28% Excavation, foundations and walls
   8% Roof
   18% Windows, doors and plastering
   6% Flooring
   10% Interior and exterior finishes
   12% Plumbing and fixtures
   12% Electric wiring, fittings and fixtures
   6% Interior decoration

   (a) What is the complete estimate for the house if Mr. Malhotra uses a contractor to complete it?
   (b) How much would be the saving if Mrs. Malhotra did the interior decoration work herself?

CHAPTER 6

Scheduling

Each completed task establishes certain parameters and imposes constraints on the next task.

—Louis Fried

LEARNING OBJECTIVES

After reading this chapter, you will be able to:

- Understand the importance of activity scheduling and importance of networks.
- Study the techniques of drawing AOA and AON networks.
- Study the critical path method.
- Understand the computation of earliest and latest start and finish times and calculation of floats or slacks.
- Appreciate the importance of critical activities and the managerial implications of slacks.
- Study time–cost trade-off and cost crashing.
- Study the programme evaluation and review technique.

6.1 INTRODUCTION

The duration required to complete each task is derived from the estimates. The next important step in planning is to schedule the tasks. The schedule answers the 'when' issue of the project. We plan on when to start and finish each activity. The scheduling of activities helps us to allocate resources accordingly and to plan for any conflicts that may arise due to competing requirements. Scheduling also helps us to plan our cash requirements. The schedule, resources and cash requirements and availability have a direct bearing on one another.

Tasks do not necessarily follow one another. Some tasks can commence only when others have been finished, while some can be carried out simultaneously and independently of each other. For example, the construction of walls can only commence once the foundations have been completed (at least for the portion of the buildings where walls are being erected). Similarly, work on the roof can commence only when the load bearing walls or columns are completed (we are considering a brick, mortar and concrete building). However, the carpentry and joinery work for making doors and windows can commence independently of these tasks. The relationship that one task has to the other plays an important part in its scheduling. Networks are extensively used to plan and manage projects. With the advent of high speed computers and software, planning hundreds of activities and keeping track of them have become relatively easy.

The network techniques most commonly used are the critical path method (CPM) and the programme evaluation and review technique (PERT). Both techniques are essentially the same in their approach. CPM is based on certainty, while PERT deals with probabilistic completion times for activities.

CPM and PERT originated at about the same time. PERT was developed to control the Polaris missile project in 1957 by the U.S. Navy Special Projects Office, Lockheed Aircraft Corporation and the management consulting firm of Booz, Allen and Hamilton. The Polaris missile programme was a massive project. It involved 250 major contractors and over 9000 sub-contractors. Hundreds of thousands of individual tasks had to be coordinated and monitored for its success, and the use of PERT ensured that the project was completed two years ahead of its original scheduled date. Since the activities involved in development of the Polaris missile had not been performed earlier, there was an element of uncertainty in the time that each activity would take. PERT addresses this uncertainty and gives estimates of the probability of meeting specified schedule dates at various stages of the project.

CPM grew out of a joint effort initiated in 1957 by Dupont and Remington Rand Univac. Their objective was to determine how best to reduce the time required to perform plant overhaul, maintenance and construction work. They were interested in determining optimum trade-off time (project duration) and total project cost. The activities involved in these types of projects were subject to very small amounts of variations. CPM treats the activity performance time in a deterministic manner and its main feature is to arrive at a project schedule which minimizes the total project costs.

The pioneering PERT and CPM groups were unaware of each other's existence until early 1959 when papers were published on the two techniques. Essentially the basis of PERT and CPM was network diagrams and network analysis.

A network is a schematic representation of work to be done (activities) drawn in such a way that relationships between work items are logically defined. The network shows a complete picture of the relationship which exists between different activities, as all the operations necessary to complete the project are represented on the network.

6.2 CRITICAL PATH METHOD

Let us study the critical path method for activity scheduling with the help of an example.

EXAMPLE 6.1 Rasoi Appliances is a white goods manufacturer. It manufactures kitchen appliances like food processors, food warmers, ovens, toasters, grills, refrigerators and other household goods. It has recently designed and tested a new microwave oven specially for Indian conditions in which Indian dishes can be prepared. The company feels that the product has distinct advantages over the conventional microwave ovens as it preserves the essence of spices so typical of the Indian cooking. Mr. Kapoor, the president of the company, is very keen that the product is launched after a proper promotion scheme, as it will give him a competitive edge and will help him to capture the major market share in the microwave oven field. He has held various meetings with the marketing manager and the advertising agency head. The company plans an extensive promotion campaign involving specially prepared promotion literature, TV and radio advertisements, training of field force, special demonstrations at select stores and various ladies clubs and social organizations, and proper point of purchase displays throughout the country. Mr. Kapoor realizes that all activities must be properly coordinated to ensure a simultaneous nationwide launch of the product. He wants to finalize the date of launch and must decide when each activity must start and finish. He would like to monitor critical activities himself. Should he have contingency plans to cater for delays in the execution of the activities affecting the launch of the product? Will he be able to shift resources from one activity to another to speed up those that may have got delayed? How should he plan his finances? Mr. Kapoor is besieged by a host of such questions. Are there methods available to help him plan, monitor and control the launch of this product?

Solution Let us consider Mr. Kapoor's problem. The first step is to list out all the activities involved in the promotional campaign for the new microwave. Mr. Kapoor's marketing manager came up with the list given below:

1. Develop the training plan (the design of the training programme that the stores representatives will be put through before the final in-store introduction of the product).
2. Develop promotion and training materials plan (a detailed study of the material that will be required for training stores representatives).
3. Select stores representatives who will undergo training.
4. Conduct the training programme.
5. Develop the advertising plan (a detailed plan of projected radio, TV and print media advertising).
6. Develop the advertising copy that will be required.
7. Schedule the radio, TV and print advertisements that will appear prior to the launch of the product.
8. Prepare promotion material which will be used during the in-store introduction.
9. Prepare material which will be used in the training of stores representatives.
10. Conduct the pre-advertising campaign.
11. Final in-store introduction of the product.

The next step is to rearrange the activities in their logical sequence and identify immediate predecessors (activities immediately preceding a particular activity) for each activity. The duration required for each activity was determined through estimates based on past experience. The result of this exercise for Mr. Kapoor's product launch are given in Table 6.1.

The next step is to draw a network diagram representing the relationship of the activities shown in the table. Networks may be drawn as 'activity on arrow' (AOA) or as 'activity on node' (AON). Most computer programmes for project management draw activity on node networks. We shall study both the methods. Let us first examine how to draw an activity on arrow network. It would be useful at this juncture to introduce some definitions of terms that are used in network analysis.

Table 6.1 List of activities showing relationship and duration

Activity symbol	*Activity description*	*Predecessor*	*Time (days)*
A	Develop advertising plan	—	6
B	Develop promotion and training materials plan	—	7
C	Develop training plan	—	8
D	Schedule radio, TV and print media advertising	A	20
E	Develop advertising copy	A	18
F	Prepare promotional material for in-store introduction	B	9
G	Prepare material for training of stores representatives	B	8
H	Conduct pre-introduction advertising campaign	D, E	7
I	Select stores representatives for training	C	2
J	Conduct training	G, I	14
K	Final in-store launch of product	F, H, J	10

6.3 DEFINITIONS

(a) *Activity.* The work content required to be achieved to accomplish an event. It is a clearly defined project element, a job or a task which requires the consumption of resources including time. The word activity has been adopted in preference to work content as it also includes non-work actions like waiting (for instance, curing of a roof slab before shuttering can be removed), whereas work signifies action or motion in time. It is denoted by an arrow.

(b) *Merge activity.* An activity which is dependent on two or more preceding activities.

(c) *Burst activity.* An activity that is followed by two or more activities.

(d) *Event.* The nodes or events represent points in time when certain activities have been started or completed. In other words, an event describes the start or completion of an activity. It is denoted by a numbered circle.

(e) *Path.* A path is an unbroken chain of activities from the initiating node to some other node, generally to the last node indicating the end or completion of the project.

(f) *Dummy activity* (*only used in AOA networks*). A dummy activity is that activity which has a logical function only and consumes no time or resources. It is denoted by a dotted arrow. There are two types of dummies:

  (i) *Identity dummy.* It helps to keep the designation of each activity unique or different from another.

  (ii) *Dependency dummy.* It helps to keep the logic correct.

6.4 RULES AND CONVENTIONS

While drawing AOA networks certain rules and conventions are followed. These are:

1. Activity arrows should be drawn from left to right indicating progressive approach towards the ultimate objective or the final event.

2. Crossing of activity arrows should be avoided. Arrows should be drawn as straight or bent lines but not curved lines.
3. Avoid use of unnecessary dummies.
4. Activities are set in the order of their execution. Events are set in the order of their occurrence.
5. Head event number should be greater than tail event number. No event is numbered until the tail event of each activity arrow ending into that event has been numbered.
6. There should be no danglers or loops. Danglers are activities which lead no where. All activities must be connected to events and the finishing activities must be connected to the finish event of the project.

Let us now see the application of these rules by drawing the network for Mr. Kapoor.

6.5 DRAWING A NETWORK (AOA)

Start with the event 'start of project' and draw the activities that can be started simultaneously, and have no predecessors. These are activities A, B and C. The network diagram is not a scaled diagram. It is merely showing logical relationship of activities (Figure 6.1).

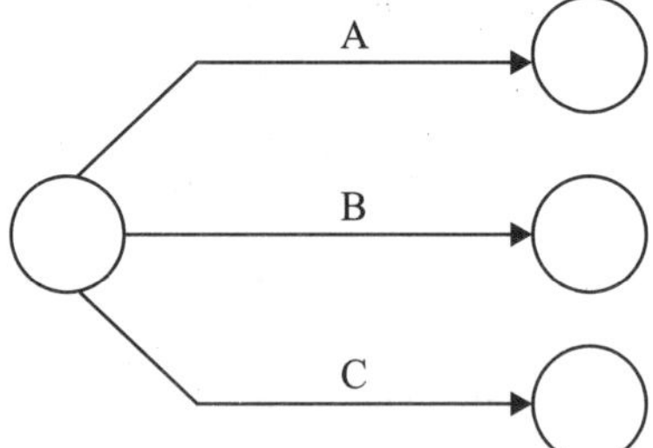

Figure 6.1 Drawing a network—Stage 1.

Next consider the activities which can follow only A or B or C since these have been completed. From Table 6.1, we know that D and E follow A; F and G follow B; and I follows C. Let us add these activities to the network as shown in Figure 6.2.

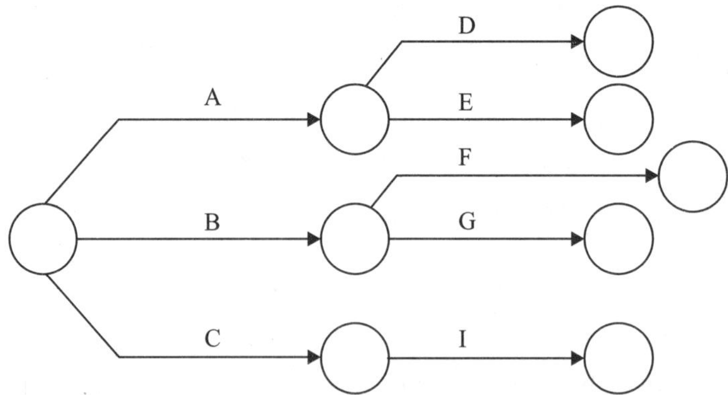

Figure 6.2 Drawing a network—Stage 2.

Activity H is dependent on the completion of activities D and E. Activity J is dependent on completion of activities G and I. Let us add these activities to the network as shown in Figure 6.3.

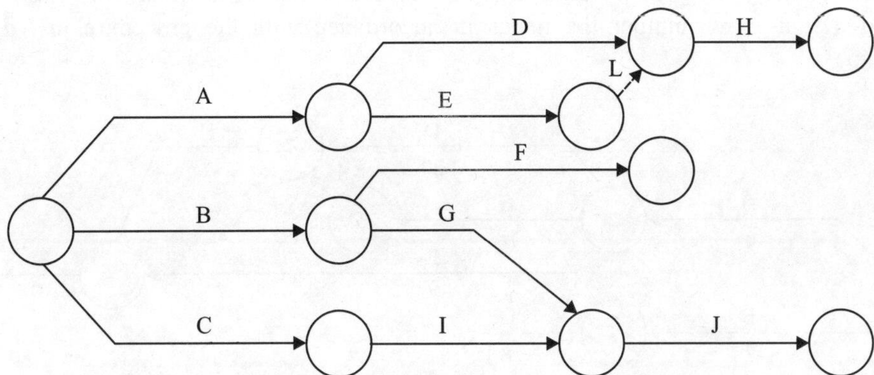

Figure 6.3 Drawing a network—Stage 3.

We notice that a dummy activity L has been drawn connecting the finish of activity E to the finish of activity D. This is an identity dummy. The logic would still be maintained if the finish point of D and E was the same, but reference to these activities through the node numbers would not be possible as both would have the same node/event numbers. In order to avoid this confusion of identity, a dummy activity has been added. There is no need of a dummy between G and I as the activities can be uniquely identified by the node numbers. This will become evident when we number the nodes/events. J can start only when G and I are completed and H can start only when D and E are completed. The logic is shown on the network. Now let us add activity K which can start only when activities H, F and J are completed (Figure 6.4). An identity dummy is required only when the two or more activities start from a single node and end at a single node.

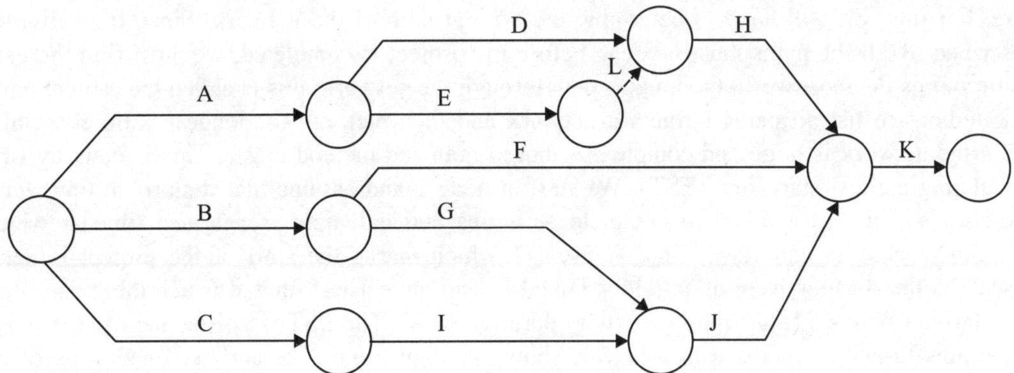

Figure 6.4 Completed network.

Now that all activities have been represented on the network, we must number the nodes. A simple way of ensuring that all rules are followed is to start from the left and number the nodes as we move to the right of the network in the order of their appearance. If two or more nodes are on the same line, number from top to bottom. This simple procedure will ensure that the number of the head event is always greater than the number of the tail event and that tails of all events joining at a common head event are numbered before the head event is numbered. Let us now number the nodes in accordance with the procedure just described (Figure 6.5).

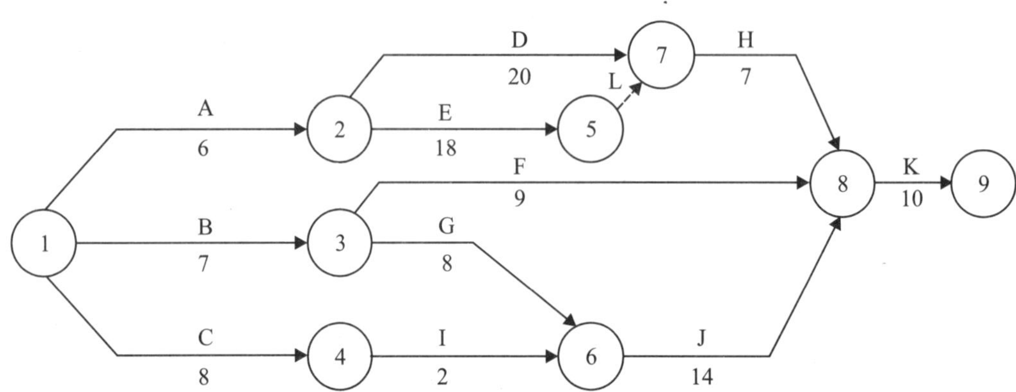

Figure 6.5 Numbering of nodes.

It may now be appreciated that had the dummy L not been put, then node 5 would have been eliminated and activity E also would have ended at node 7. In that case, a reference to activity between nodes 2 and 7 would refer to both D and E causing problems of unique reference. We have also added the time required for completion of each activity below the activity symbol.

6.6 CALCULATING EARLIEST START TIME

How much time will this project take? The next step is to calculate the time that the project will take. For this, we will have to determine the critical path of the network. Since the activities described by all the paths must be done before the project is completed, we must find the path that requires the most work, the longest path through the network; this is called the critical path. It is tedious to list all paths through a network and then pick out the longest path, especially when the network is large and complex. A more organized method exists. This is done by first calculating earliest start time (EST). We start at node 1 and assume that it starts at time zero. We then add the time taken to complete activities and calculate the earliest time at which subsequent activity can start. Time at event 1 which marks the start of the project is zero. Node 2 is the starting event of activities D and E, and the earliest time at which these activities can start is 0 + 6 = 6 (Start time + Activity duration of A). The EST is written next to the event it pertains to and is enclosed in a box as shown in Figure 6.6. The earliest finish time of an activity, which is also the earliest start time of the following activity, can be calculated from the relationship as follows:

Earliest finish time = Earliest start time + Activity duration (Time taken for activity)

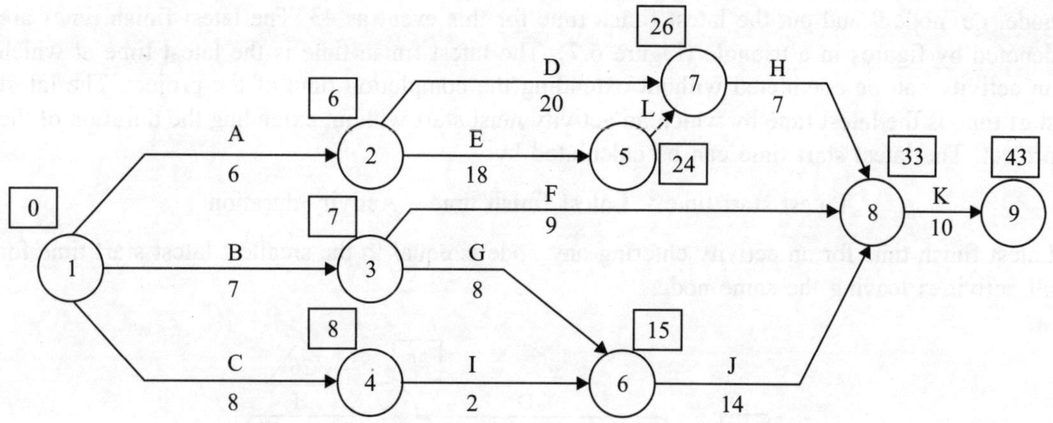

Figure 6.6 Network showing EST enclosed in a box.

At node 3, EST = EST at node 1 + Activity duration of B = 0 + 7 = 7
At node 4, EST = EST at node 1 + Activity duration of C = 0 + 8 = 8
At node 5, EST = EST at node 2 + Activity duration of E = 6 + 18 = 24

Node 6 is the starting event for activity J. Activity J can start only when activities I and G are completed. Activity I can be completed earliest by 8 + 2 = 10 days, as it can start earliest at the end of the eighth day. Similarly, activity G can end earliest on the 15th day as it can start earliest at the end of day seven and takes eight days. Hence, the earliest that J can start is the end of the 15th day. Since no activity can begin until all its predecessor activities are complete, the earliest start time for an activity leaving any node is equal to the largest earliest finish time of all activities entering the same node.

At node 6, we have (from 4 to 6) 8 + 2 = 10, and (from 3 to 6) 7 + 8 = 15. Take the larger of the values on the forward pass as the subsequent activity can start only when both G and I are completed.

Activity L is a dummy activity and takes zero time.

At node 7, EST = EST at node 2 + Activity duration of D = 6 + 20 = 26, and (from node 5 to node 7) 24 + 0 = 24. Earliest H can start is 26 days.

At node 8, we get
From 7 to 8, 26 + 7 = 33
From 3 to 8, 7 + 9 = 16
From 6 to 8, 15 + 14 = 29. Earliest K can start is 33 days.

At node 9, we get 33 + 10 = 43.

The earliest that node (event) 9 can occur is at the end of 43 days. Since node (event) 9 marks the end of the project, the least time required to complete the project is 43 days.

6.7 CALCULATING LATEST FINISH TIME

The second step in finding the critical path is to compute latest finish time (LFT) and latest start time (LST) for each activity. This is done by using a 'backward pass'. We start at the finish node, i.e. node 9 and put the latest finish time for this event as 43. The latest finish times are denoted by figures in a triangle (Figure 6.7). The latest finish time is the latest time at which an activity can be completed without extending the completion time of the project. The latest start time is the latest time by which an activity must start without extending the duration of the project. The latest start time can be calculated by:

$$\text{Latest start time} = \text{Latest finish time} - \text{Activity duration}$$

Latest finish time for an activity entering any node is equal to the smallest latest start time for all activities leaving the same node.

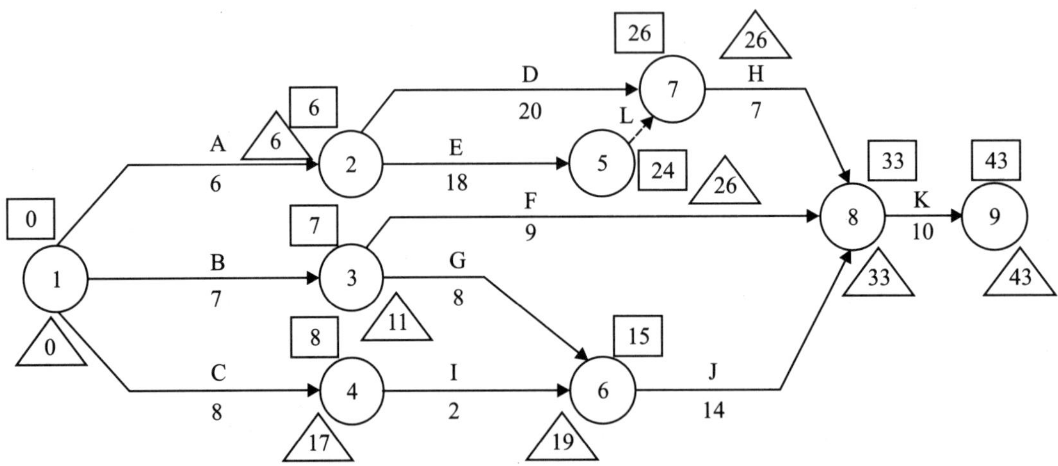

Figure 6.7 Network showing LFT in a triangle.

At node 8, LFT = LFT at node 9 – Activity duration of K
= 43 – 10 = 33

At node 7, LFT = LFT at node 8 – Activity duration of H
= 33 – 7 = 26

At node 6, LFT = LFT at node 8 – Activity duration of J
= 43 – 14 = 19

At node 5, LFT = LFT at node 7 (duration of activity L = 0 as it is a dummy)
= 26

At node 4, LFT = LFT at node 6 – Activity duration of I
= 19 – 2 = 17

At node 3, LFT = LFT at node 6 – Activity duration of G or LFT at node 8 – Activity duration of F
= 19 – 8 = 11 or 33 – 9 = 24

Take the smallest value, because if event 3 occurs at 24 then the project will get delayed.

At node 3, LFT = 11

Similarly, at node 2, we have LFT at node 5 – Activity duration of E or LFT at node 7 – Activity duration of D. Take the smallest value.

At node 2, LFT = 6
At node 1, LFT = 0

Examine the activities or nodes where the earliest start time and the latest finish time is the same. These nodes are 1, 2, 7, 8 and 9. The critical activities are the activities on this path—A, D, H and K. The critical path is written as A–D–H–K or 1–2–7–8–9.

6.8 FLOATS (SLACKS), CRITICAL ACTIVITIES AND CRITICAL PATH

The spare time in an activity is called *float*. It is used to economize on resources without affecting the overall duration of the project. Floats are of different types.

Total float

It is the spare time available on any given activity if the tail event occurred at its earliest time and the head event at its latest time. It can be calculated as:

Total float = Time latest at head – Time earliest at tail – Activity duration

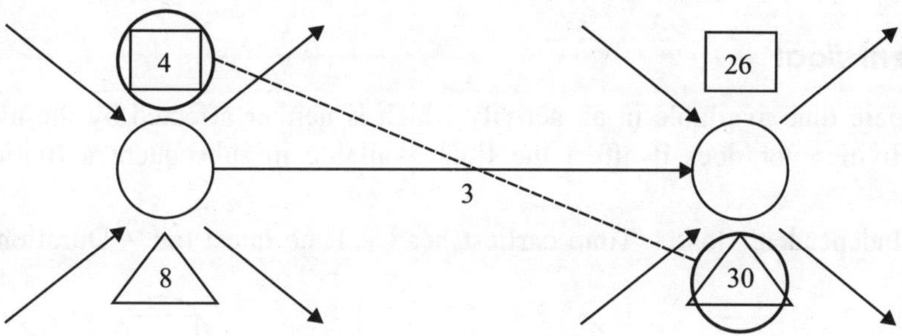

Figure 6.8 Total float.

From Figure 6.8, we get

Total float = 30 – 4 – 3 = 23

Free float

It is the spare time available on an activity if both the tail and the head events occurred at their earliest time. If this spare time is used up during the execution of this activity, it will have no effect on subsequent activities. It can be calculated thus:

Free float = Time earliest head – Time earliest tail – Activity duration

From Figure 6.9, we get

$$\text{Free float} = 26 - 4 - 3 = 19$$

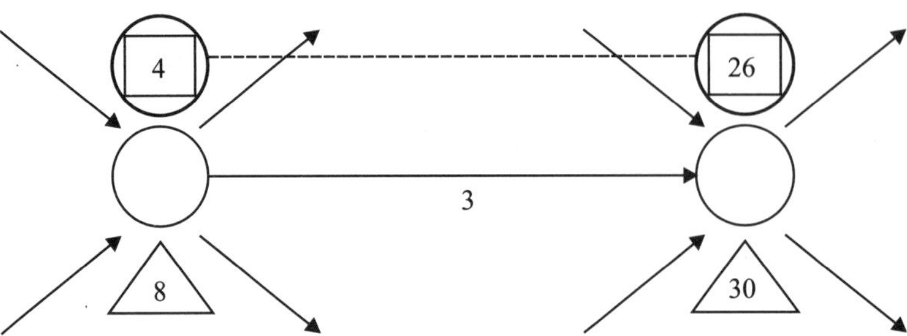

Figure 6.9 Free float.

Interference float

Interference float is equal to total float less free float. As the name suggests, if this float is used up in an activity, it will interfere with the availability of floats available for subsequent activities.

$$\text{Interference float} = \text{Total float} - \text{Free float}$$
$$= 23 - 19 = 4$$

Independent float

This is the spare time available in an activity which is neither affected by the use of float by preceding activities nor does it affect the float available in subsequent activities. It can be calculated as:

$$\text{Independent float} = \text{Time earliest head} - \text{Time latest tail} - \text{Duration}$$

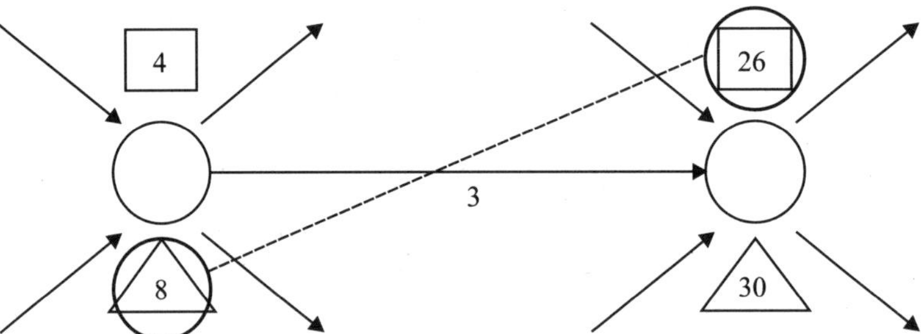

Figure 6.10 Independent float.

From Figure 6.10, we get

$$\text{Independent float} = 26 - 8 - 3 = 15$$

Let us calculate floats for Mr. Kapoor's problem and see their implications using the network shown in Figure 6.7. The calculation of floats is shown in Table 6.2.

Table 6.2 Calculation of floats

Activity	*Total float (TL head – TE tail – Duration)*	*Free float (TE head – TE tail – Duration)*	*Interference float (Total float – Free float)*	*Independent float (TE head – TL tail – Duration)*
A	6 – 0 – 6 = 0			
B	11 – 0 – 7 = 4	7 – 0 – 7 = 0	4 – 0 = 4	7 – 0 – 7 = 0
C	17 – 0 – 8 = 9	8 – 0 – 8 = 0	9 – 0 = 9	8 – 0 – 8 = 0
D	26 – 6 – 20 = 0			
E	26 – 6 – 18 = 2	24 – 6 – 18 = 0	2 – 0 = 2	24 – 6 – 18 = 0
F	33 – 7 – 9 = 17	33 – 7 – 9 = 17	17 – 17 = 0	33 – 11 – 9 = 13
G	19 – 7 – 8 = 4	15 – 7 – 8 = 0	4 – 0 = 4	15 – 11 – 8 (0)
H	33 – 26 – 7 = 0			
I	19 – 8 – 2 = 9	15 – 8 – 2 = 5	9 – 5 = 4	15 – 17 – 2 (0)
J	33 – 15 – 14 = 4	33 – 15 – 14 = 4	4 – 4 = 0	33 – 19 – 14 = 0
K	43 – 33 – 10 = 0			

Let us examine the entries in Table 6.2. Activities A, D, H and K have no float available. These are called *critical activities* and the *critical path* is the path joining these activities. As these activities have no slack time available, management must monitor them carefully and ensure that these are completed in time. Any delay in their completion will affect the overall duration of the project.

Activity B has a total float of four days. It can finish earliest on day seven, but must not finish later than day 11. In case resources are at a premium, management can delay this activity by a total of four days. However, it must be noted that activity B has no free float. The float of four days is interference float. This implies that if any part of this float is used in activity B it will affect the float available for remaining activities. For instance, if the complete float of four days is used up in activity B then its earliest finish time will become 11 instead of seven. Consequently, the total float in activity G will become 19 –11 – 8 = 0. The float available for activity G presently is four days (from the table above) and this is an interference float. Use of interference float affects the float available for subsequent activities.

The floats in activity C are similar to the floats in activities B and G.

Consider activity F. It has a total float of 17 days. This is also the free float, which implies that if activity F starts at its earliest time of eight days and the entire 17 days of float are used up, the subsequent activity K will not be affected. However, it has an independent float of only 13 days. If we trace the path B–F and use up the four days of float available in activity B, the earliest start time of activity F will become 11. It will then have a total float of 33 – 11 – 9 = 13 days. As we can see, interference float affects the float available in subsequent activities on the path, but the independent float is neither affected by the use of float in earlier activities nor does it affect the float of the subsequent activities.

Negative floats are meaningless as we cannot have negative time, and hence are ignored. (See independent float values for activities G and I is Table 6.2.)

To summarize, total float is the total slack available in an activity; free float is the spare time which will get affected by use of floats in earlier activities on the path but its use will not affect subsequent activities; interference float interferes with the float of subsequent activities on the path if it is used; and independent float is neither affected by the use of floats in preceding activities and nor does it affect the float available for subsequent activities if used.

Floats help in the shifting and planning of use of resources. For instance, consider a network in which two activities A and B can start simultaneously and each requires the services of a bulldozer for the first four days. If activity B has a float of four days available and there is only one bulldozer available, we can avoid hiring another one by starting the work on activity A first with the bulldozer and start work on activity B after four days with the same bulldozer. This may or may not affect floats in other activities depending on the type of float available in B that we use up.

Activities with no floats in them are critical activities and the path joining such activities is the critical path. Top management can now concentrate on the critical activities which have no leeway for delays.

6.9 ACTIVITY ON NODE (AON) NETWORK

As most computer packages draw activity on node networks, it is important for us to understand how to draw an AON network and the method of doing the calculations of EST and LFT for the same. The methodology for calculations remains the same. Different packages represent the network differently. However, for ease of understanding we shall use a standard format while drawing the network. We shall later see how the network can be drawn with the help of MS Project or the WinQSB 2.0 package. We shall use the same data as for Example 6.1.

Some of the rules used in the activity on arrow network get modified. In an activity on node network, the nodes represent the activities and the arrows merely show their logical relationship. Nodes representing activities which start the project may be connected to a milestone 'start' if desired. Dummy activities are not used. Arrows may cross each other. For our purpose, the node shall be drawn as Figure 6.11.

Earliest start time	Identity	Earliest finish time
Total float	Description	
Latest start time	Duration	Latest finish time

Figure 6.11 Format for node drawing.

Let us draw the network. Activities A, B and C start the project. This is shown in Figure 6.12.

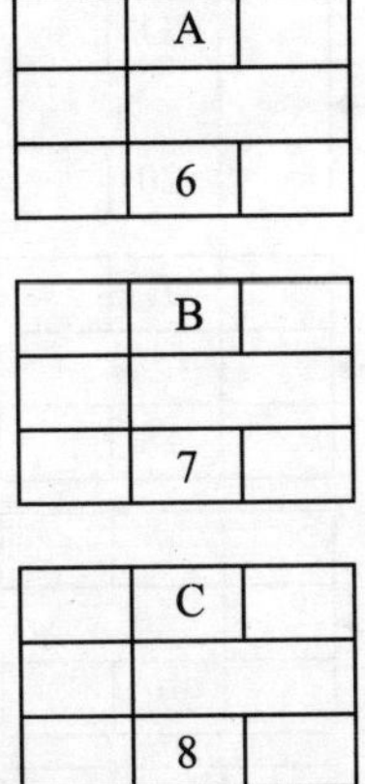

Figure 6.12 Network for activities A, B and C.

Activities D and E follow A; F and G follow B; and I follows C. Let us add these to the network as shown in Figure 6.13.

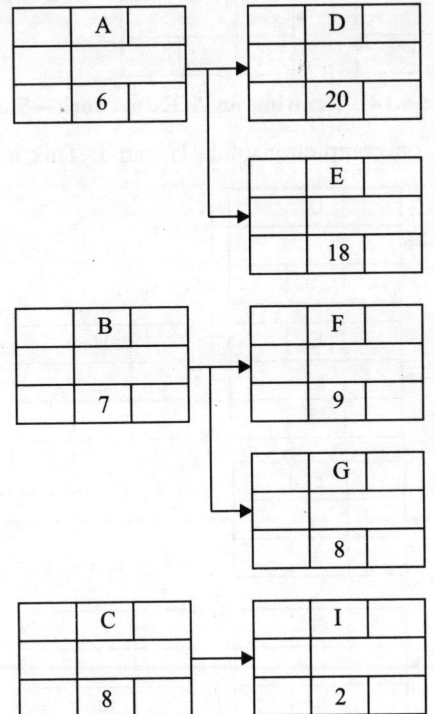

Figure 6.13 Drawing a network—Stage 2.

Activity H is dependent on completion of D and E, and J is dependent on completion of G and I. Let us add these to the network as shown in Figure 6.14.

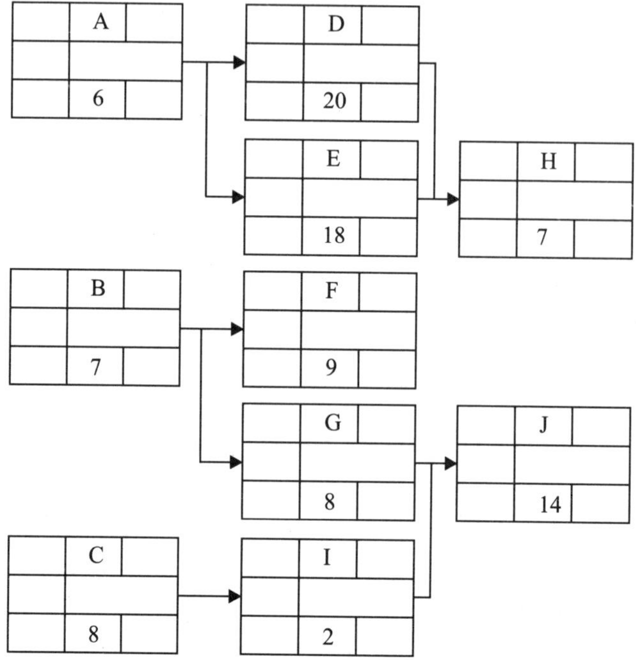

Figure 6.14 Drawing on AON network—Stage 3.

Activity K is dependent on completion of F, H and J. This is shown in Figure 6.15.

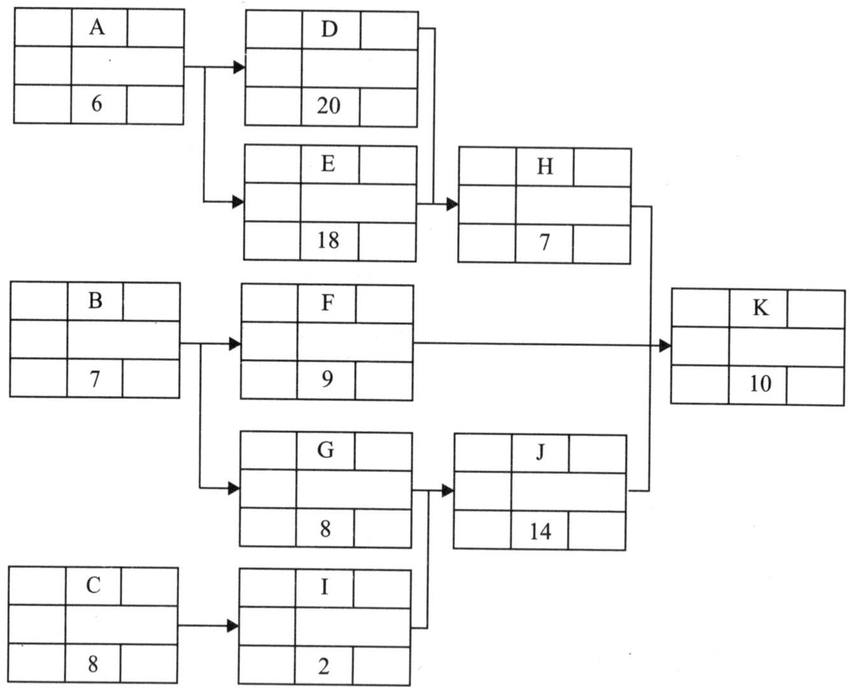

Figure 6.15 Completed network.

The complete network is as shown in Figure 6.15. Now let us compute the earliest start times by a forward pass. The earliest finish time is obtained by adding the activity duration to the earliest start time (EFT = EST + Duration). The earliest finish time of the preceding activity is the earliest start time of the succeeding activity, except when an activity is dependent on the completion of two or more activities (also called *merge* activity as two or more activities merge into it). In such a case, its earliest start time is the largest of the earliest finish times of all the immediate preceding activities. This is shown in Figure 6.16.

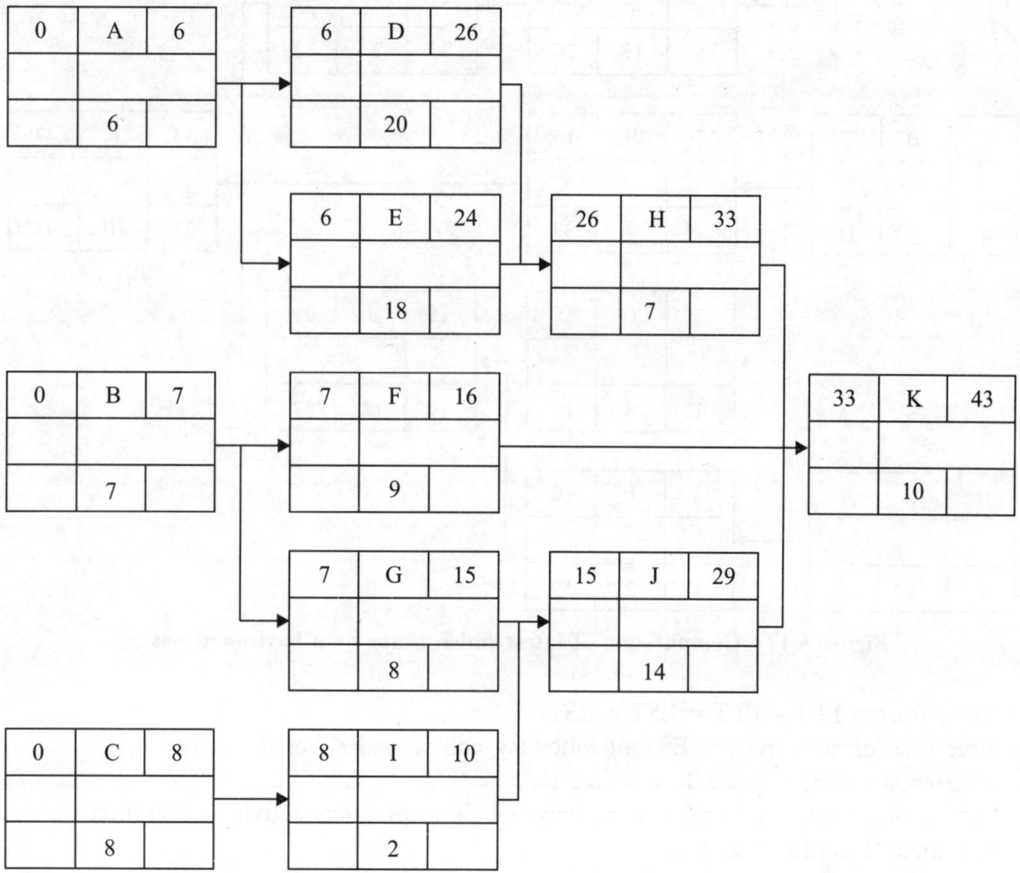

Figure 6.16 Computation of earliest start times by a forward pass.

Now let us compute the latest finish times by a backward pass. The latest start time is obtained by subtracting the activity duration from the latest finish time (LST = LFT – Duration). The latest start time of the following activity is the latest finish time of the preceding activity, except when an activity is followed by two or more activities (*burst* activity). In such a case, its latest finish time is the smallest of the latest start times of its immediate following activities. This is shown in Figure 6.17.

Now let us compute the total float.

The total float is the difference between the latest start time and the earliest start time or the latest finish time and the earliest finish time.

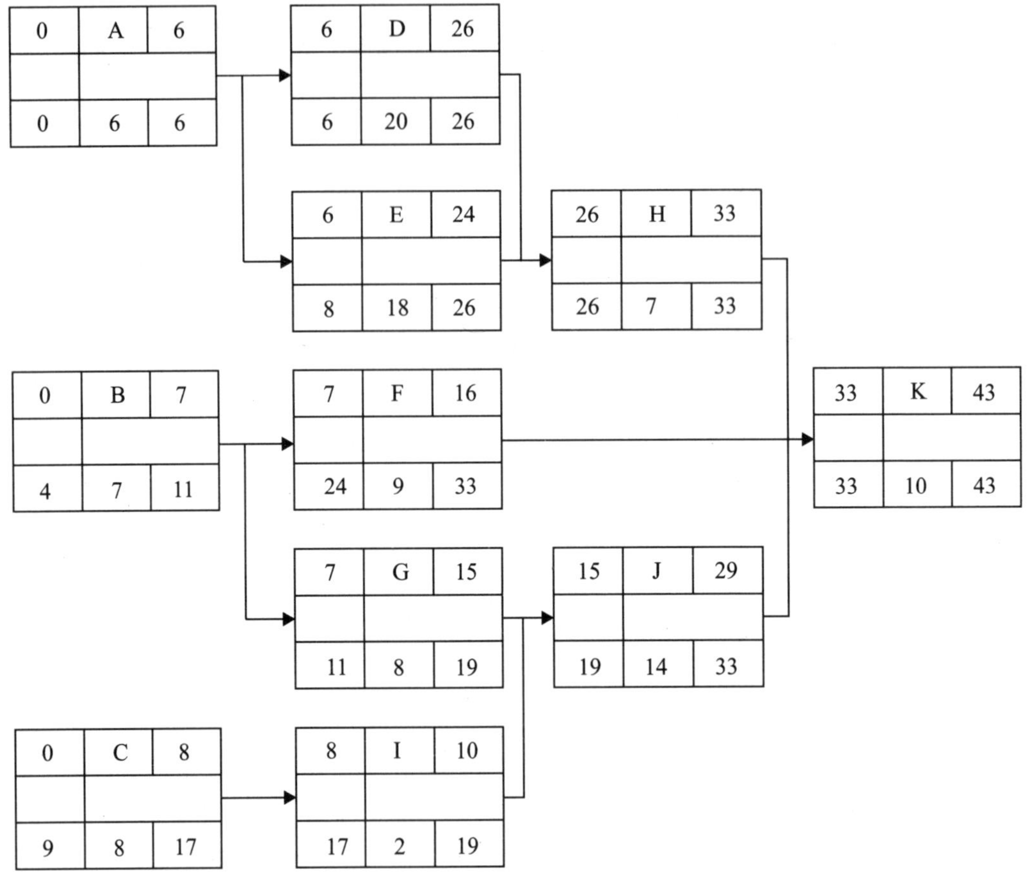

Figure 6.17 Computation of latest finish times by a backward pass.

Total float = LFT – EFT = LST – EST
Free float of an activity = EST of following activity – EFT of the activity
Interference float = Total float – Free float
Independent float = EST of next activity – LFT of previous activity – Duration
Calculate floats for activity F.
Total float = 33 – 16 = 24 – 7 = 17 days
Free float = 33 – 16 = 17 days
Interference float = 17 – 17 = 0 day
Independent float = 33 – 11 – 9 = 13 days

As can be seen from Figure 6.18, activities A, D, H and K have zero float and are critical. The critical path is A–D–H–K, and the project will take 43 days. The critical activities must be carefully monitored if the project is to be completed in 43 days.

The critical activities, the critical path and floats or slacks have the same implications as discussed earlier in Section 6.8. Floats play a major role in allocation of scarce resources.

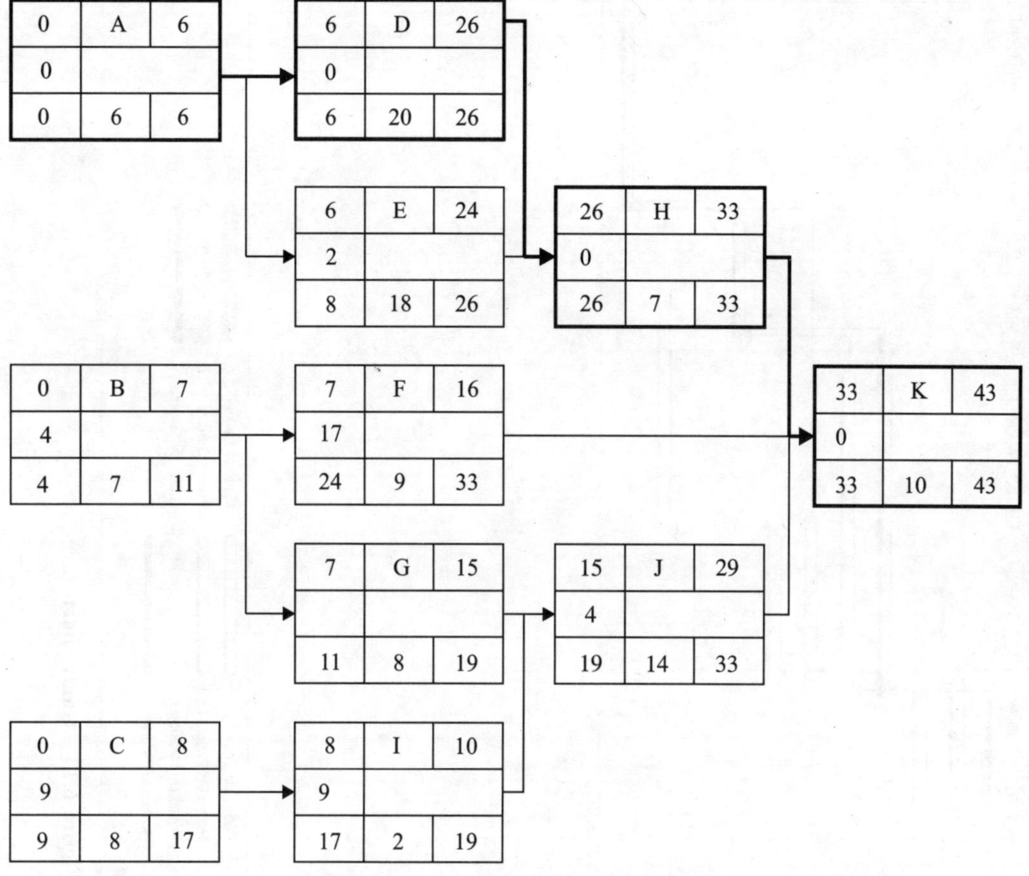

Figure 6.18 Computation of floats.

6.10 DEVELOPING NETWORKS THROUGH COMPUTERS

As mentioned earlier, computers can be used to develop and maintain networks. Most computer packages draw an activity on node network. Ultimately, the activities will have to be scheduled as per calendar dates. Computer packages do all computations based on calendar dates. Let us examine the use of computers for developing a network with the help of Microsoft Project 2007 software. We shall use the same data as given in Example 6.1. We are assuming that the project will start on 15 December 2010 and work will be carried out for five days in a week. We have also assumed that there are no other holidays during this period. Printouts of the Gantt chart and the network are shown in Figures 6.19 and 6.20.

6.11 LAGS

Consider a case where an underground cable has to be laid for five kilometres. The main activities are digging, laying cable, and filling and have to be necessarily so carried out in this

ID	Task Name	Duration	Start	Finish	Predecessors
1	A	6 days	Wed 15-12-10	Mon 20-12-10	
2	B	7 days	Wed 15-12-10	Tue 21-12-10	
3	C	8 days	Wed 15-12-10	Wed 22-12-10	
4	D	20 days	Tue 21-12-10	Sun 09-01-11	1
5	E	18 days	Tue 21-12-10	Fri 07-01-11	1
6	F	9 days	Wed 22-12-10	Thu 30-12-10	2
7	G	8 days	Wed 22-12-10	Wed 29-12-10	2
8	H	7 days	Mon 10-01-11	Sun 16-01-11	4,5
9	I	2 days	Thu 23-12-10	Fri 24-12-10	3
10	J	14 days	Thu 30-12-10	Wed 12-01-11	7,9
11	K	10 days	Mon 17-01-11	Wed 26-01-11	6,8,10

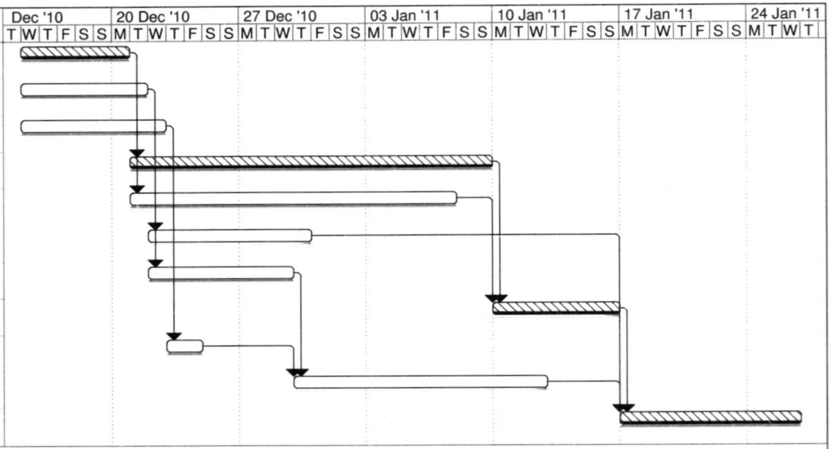

Project: Project6
Date: Fri 18-03-11

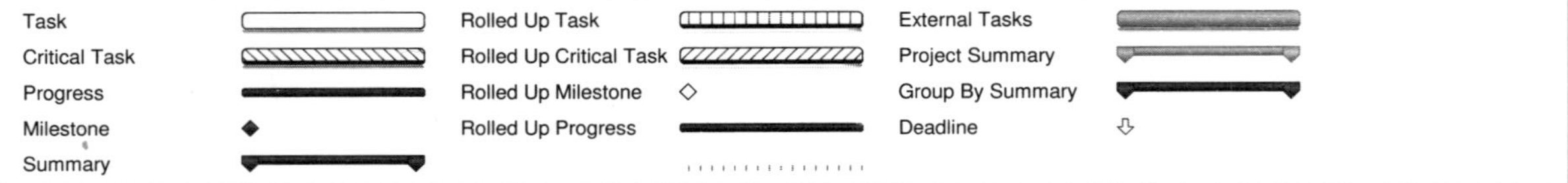

Figure 6.19 Gantt chart.

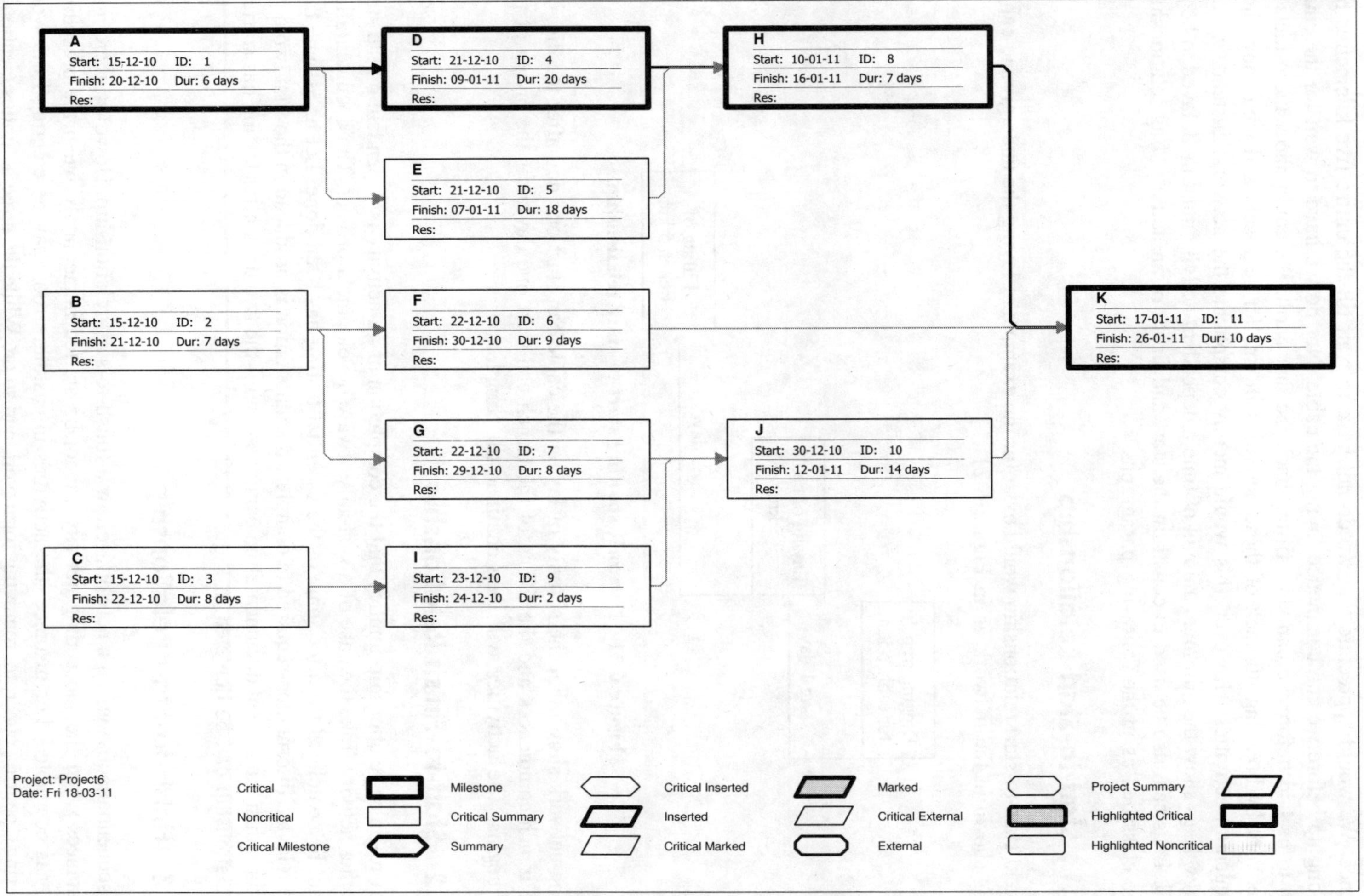

Figure 6.20 Gantt network.

sequence. We would appreciate that we do not have to wait till the entire five kilometres has been dug up before we can commence laying the cable. Nor do we have to wait for the entire length to be laid before we can start filling back the dug earth. We could show these facts in the network by breaking up each of these activities in smaller segments and then show them as sequential activities. However, this would merely complicate the network. Instead, we can use *lags*. Lags show the minimum amount of time a dependent activity must be delayed to begin or end. Lags can also be used to constrain the start and finish of an activity. Lag relationships can be classified as in the following paragraphs.

6.11.1 Start-to-Start Relationship

A typical start-to-start relationship would exist for the example of laying the underground cable. This is shown in the network as in Figure 6.21.

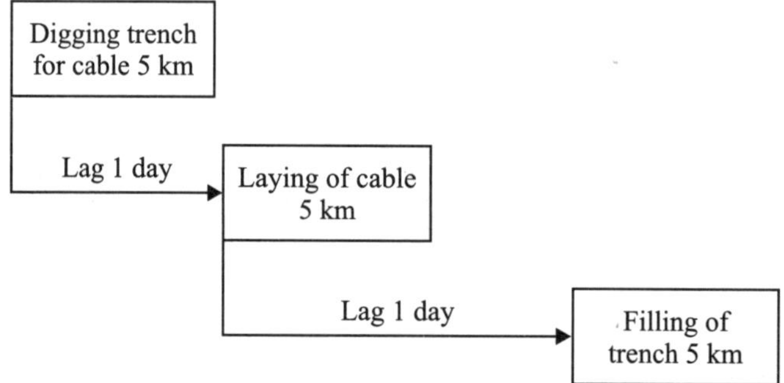

Figure 6.21 Network showing start-to-start relationship.

The network shows that the activity of laying the cable can start one day after the digging of the trench commences and the filling of the trench can start one day after the laying of the cable begins. The activities will then continue till completion.

6.11.2 Start-to-Finish Relationship

A start-to-finish relationship implies that the completion of an activity is dependent on the start of another activity. Take the case of a system software development project. The documentation may not be completed till after some of the essential testing has been done. Let us assume that all the relevant information required to complete documentation is produced in the first two days of testing, then the system documentation cannot end until the two days after testing has started. The relationship can be depicted in Figure 6.22.

6.11.3 Finish-to-Start Relationship

Most sequential activities on a network follow a finish-to-start relationship. However, there may be instances when the succeeding activity cannot be started immediately when the preceding activity is completed. For instance, the activities in casting a roof may be erecting form work (shuttering), pouring concrete, removing form work and so on. While the three activities mentioned

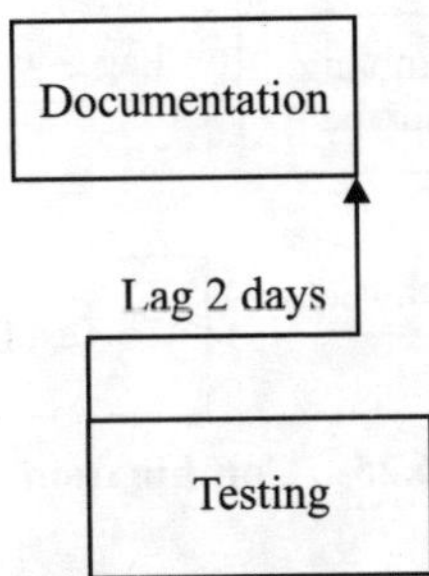

Figure 6.22 Network showing start-to-finish relationship.

follow one another sequentially, form work cannot be removed for at least two weeks after the concrete has been poured. This is depicted in Figure 6.23.

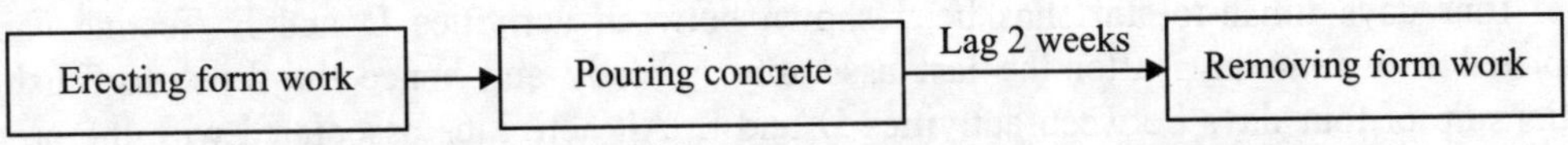

Figure 6.23 Network showing finish-to-start relationship.

6.11.4 Finish-to-Finish Relationship

When the finish of an activity depends on the finish of another activity we use a finish-to-finish relationship. If we consider the testing of a prototype of a new car model, the testing cannot be completed till the prototype is fully ready. However, this does not mean that testing cannot commence till the prototype model is ready. Testing of components and sub-assemblies may be in progress while the prototype is being assembled. This would represent a finish-to-finish relationship and is depicted in Figure 6.24.

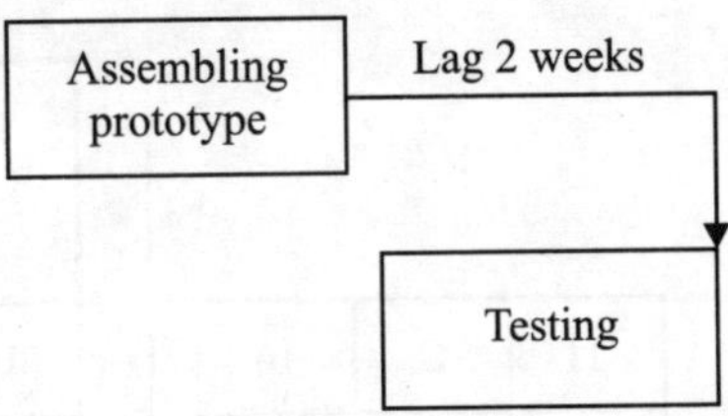

Figure 6.24 Network showing finish-to-finish relationship.

A combination of lags may also be used. For instance, in the example of the prototype car model, we may not be able to begin testing till some components or sub-assemblies are ready. We may depict this by a start-to-start lag as shown in Figure 6.25.

The procedure for calculating earliest start time and latest finish time by the forward and backward pass remains the same as explained earlier, except that we should check the lags to see if there are any changes in the timings. Let us illustrate this with an example. Consider the network shown in Figure 6.26. The network depicts the launch of a new prototype in the market

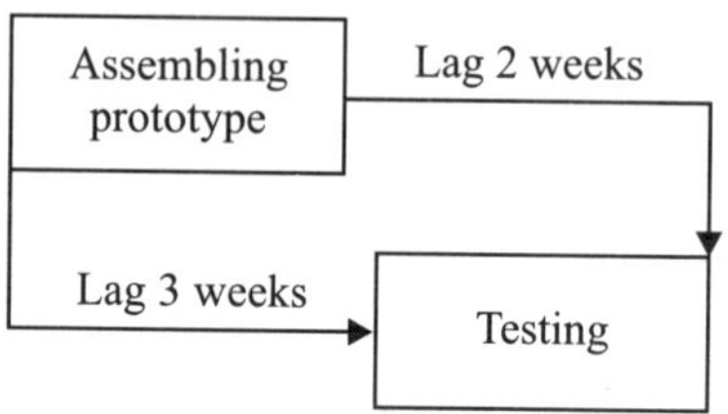

Figure 6.25 Combination of lags.

for market testing before finalizing the product. The order for components can be placed only after four days have elapsed into designing the product. This is shown by a start-to-start lag of four days between activities A and B. There is a finish-to-start lag of four days between activities B and C as the making of sub-assemblies can be started only after components are received. The testing of assemblies can only commence after some of them are ready and so a lag of four days finish-to-start has been shown between activities D and E. Testing can be completed only four days after the last assembly is ready and hence the finish-to-finish lag relationship of four days between activities D and E. All activities associated with the product launch can be completed only after testing is over and hence the finish-to-finish relationship between activities E and F.

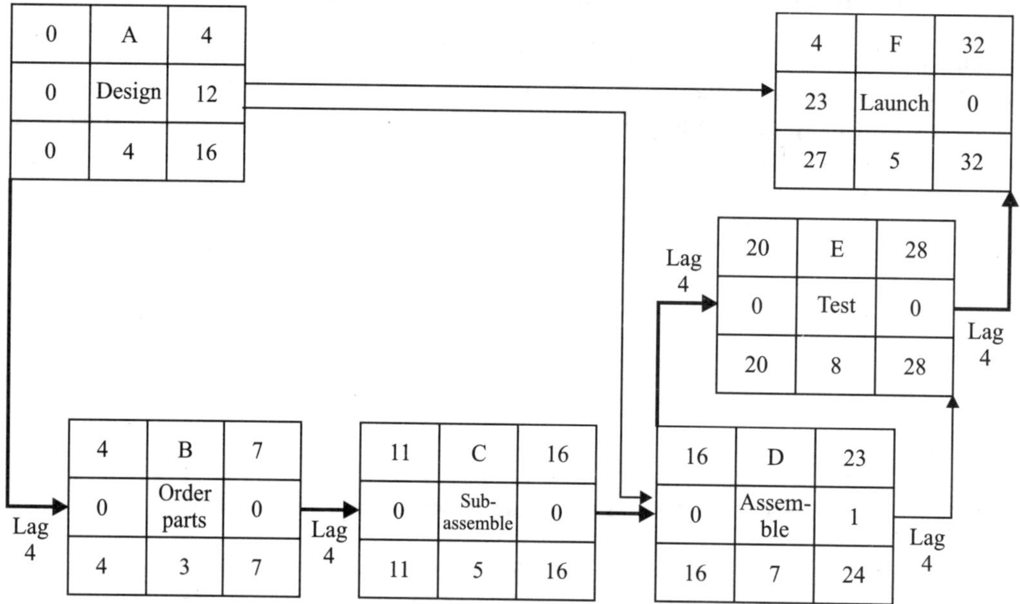

Figure 6.26 Computation of earliest start times and latest finish times.

As can be seen from the calculations shown above some activities are critical in their start but not in their finish, for example, activity A and activity D. Activity F is not critical as far as its start is concerned but is critical in its finish. The critical path is shown by the bold lines.

6.12 AON OR AOA NETWORK

The choice of method of drawing a network depends on the importance of the various advantages and disadvantages of each method.

It is easier to trace the path in an AOA network as this is simplified by activity/event numbering scheme. An AOA network is easier to draw when the dependencies are intense. However, the use of dummy activities complicates matters.

In an AON network, no dummies are used. Since events are not used, multiple starts and multiple finishes are depicted on the network almost giving the impression of being dangler activities. This can be offset by including the milestone nodes for start and finish. It is easier to draw when the dependencies are not intense. It is difficult to trace paths by activity numbers. If the network is not available, computer printouts must list dependencies for each activity. It is more difficult to understand the network drawing when there are complex dependencies. Most computer packages draw AON networks.

6.13 TIME AND COST TRADE-OFF

Project managers are often required to reduce the time of the project. There may be instances when after the project has been scheduled it is found that it is well beyond the date already committed to the client; or the project may be running behind schedule and it is important to finish it on time. Sometimes there are penalties involved for delays beyond the agreed date. The project is planned for being executed under 'normal conditions'. The project overall time can be reduced by trying to reduce the time taken by activities on the critical path, that is, the critical activities.

We can reduce time by adding more resources. However, it should be appreciated that doubling the resources will not necessarily result in halving the time. Sometime reduction will be possible but the relationship will rarely be linear. Additional resources will result in additional direct costs. Direct costs are the costs of material, labour, equipment and so on used in performing an activity. The indirect costs, that is, cost of overheads and general expenses, will be reduced if the duration of the project is reduced. A trade-off has to be made between time and costs. It is generally assumed that the increase in direct cost is linear over time. The reduced time is referred to as *crash time* and the cost of the activity when it is completed is referred to as *crash cost.* The additional cost per unit time is worked out. Let us understand this with the help of an example.

EXAMPLE 6.2 Consider a project with the following activities. The normal duration and cost, crash duration and cost and the precedence of activities are given in Table 6.3.

Table 6.3 Data for Example 6.2

Activity	*Dependency*	*Normal time*	*Crash time*	*Normal cost*	*Crash cost (increase per day)*
A	Start	4	4	4000	—
B	Start	8	6	8000	1500

(Contd...)

Table 6.3 Data for Example 6.2 (Contd...)

Activity	*Dependency*	*Normal time*	*Crash time*	*Normal cost*	*Crash cost (increase per day)*
C	F, D, Finish	3	3	600	—
D	B	6	5	900	150
E	Start	7	5	350	100
F	A	15	12	9000	900
G	B	12	10	1200	200
H	G, Finish	10	8	1000	150
J	L, Finish	5	4	1000	300
K	E	9	7	900	150
L	G and K	11	8	2200	350

Fixed overhead costs per day ₹ 500.

Solution Let us first draw the network. We shall draw an activity on arrow (AOA) network. Activities A, B and E can start simultaneously. This is depicted in Figure 6.27.

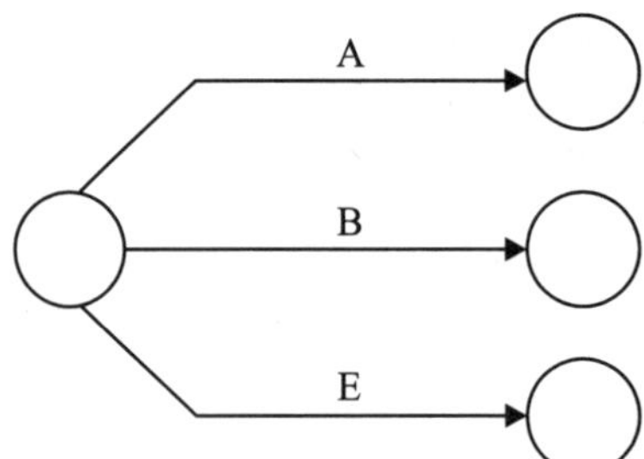

Figure 6.27 Drawing the network—Stage 1.

F follows A. D and G follow B and K follows E. This is shown in Figure 6.28.

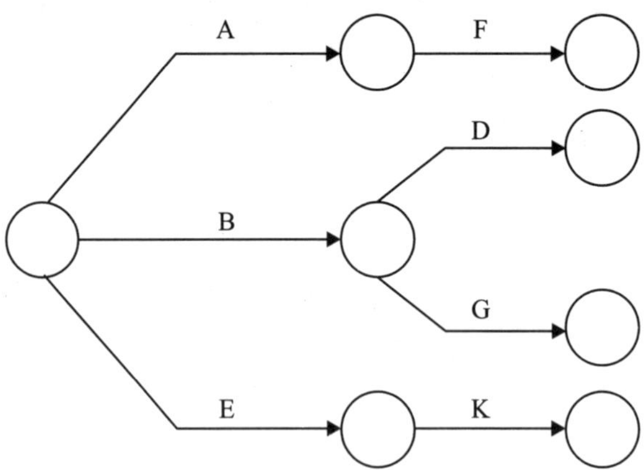

Figure 6.28 Drawing the network—Stage 2.

C follows F and D and finishes the project. H follows G and finishes the project. L is dependent on K and G and is followed by J which finishes the project. I is a dummy activity and reflects the logical relationship of L being dependent on K and G. This is shown in Figure 6.29.

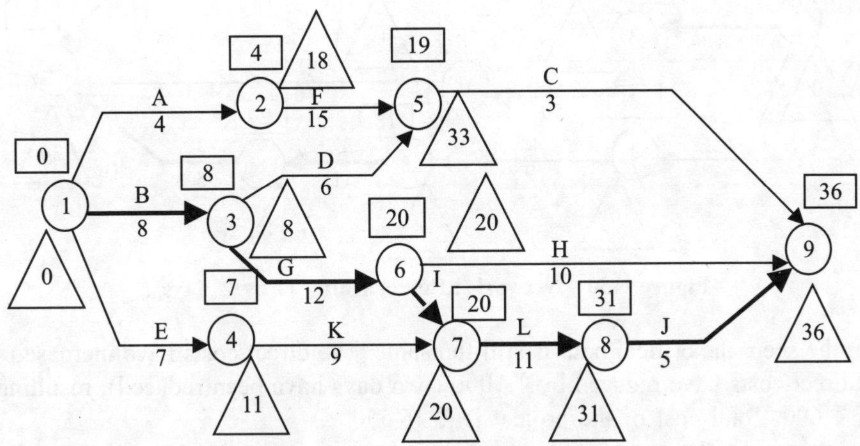

Figure 6.29 Complete network.

The complete network is shown above. The earliest start times and the latest finish times are also shown. Activities B, G, I, L and J are critical activities and the critical path is B–G–I–L–J.

The total cost of the project is the cost of all activities and overhead costs for a period of 36 days, that is, ₹ 47,150 (₹ 29,150 as direct cost of activities and ₹ 18,000 as cost of overheads).

In order to reduce the overall time of the project, we should attempt to crash critical activities. The duration of the project cannot be reduced otherwise. The choice of the activity to crash first is determined by the cost per day of crashing, the activity that is cheapest to crash is considered first. Table 6.4 below gives the duration and the cost of crashing per day for the critical activities.

Table 6.4 Duration and cost of crashing per day

Activity	*Crash by days*	*Cost of crashing per day*
B	2	1500
G	2	200
L	3	350
J	1	300

As can be seen from the table above, activity G can be crashed by two days at an additional cost of ₹ 400. The new duration of G is 10 days. Let us recalculate the earliest start times and latest finish times and determine the critical activities and critical path. This is shown in Figure 6.30.

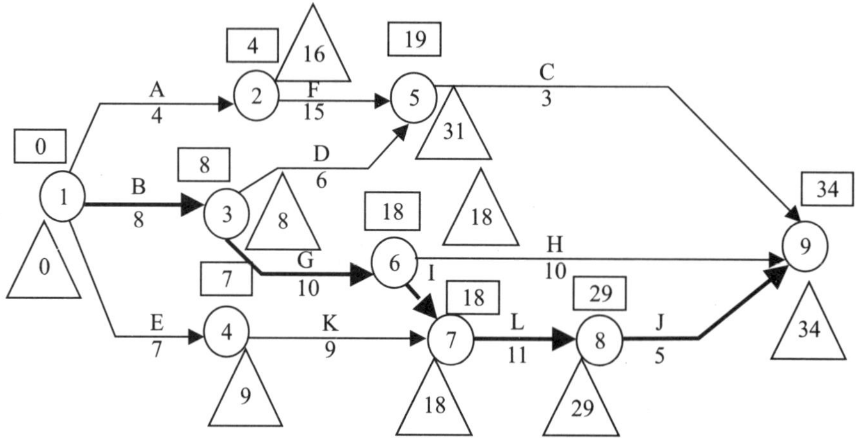

Figure 6.30 Network after crashing G by 2 days.

As can be seen, the critical path is still the same. The direct costs have increased by ₹ 400 but the indirect costs have reduced by ₹ 1000 (two days have been reduced), resulting in a net saving of ₹ 600. Total cost of the project is ₹ 46,550.

We can now consider crashing the next cheapest activity, i.e. J. Activity J can be crashed by one day at a cost of ₹ 350. Let us recompute the critical activities and the critical path. This is shown in Figure 6.31.

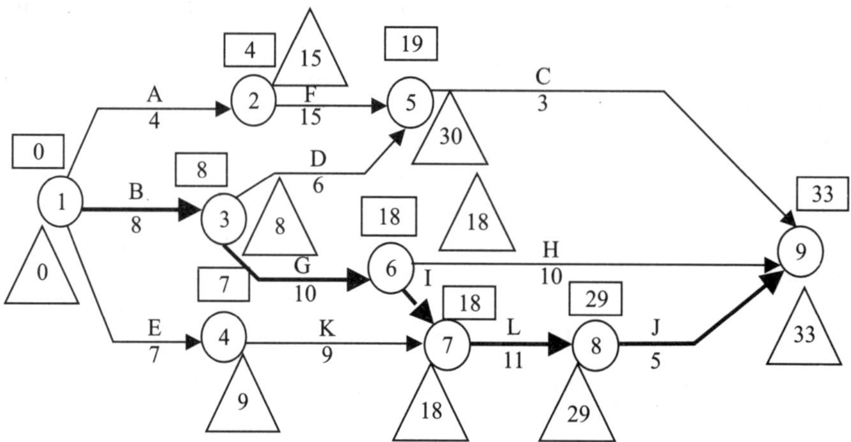

Figure 6.31 Network after crashing J by 1 day.

The critical path is still unchanged. The project can now be completed in 33 days. While crashing J has resulted in an additional cost of ₹ 350, there is a saving of ₹ 500 in overhead costs. The total cost of the project is now ₹ 46,400.

We can now consider crashing the next activity in order of its costs, that is, L. This activity can be crashed by three days at a cost of ₹ 350 per day. Let us recompute the critical path. This is shown in Figure 6.32.

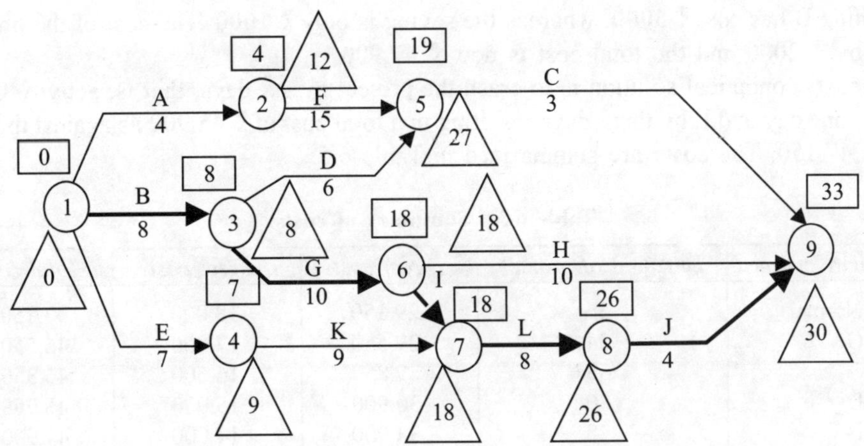

Figure 6.32 Network after crashing L by 3 days.

The critical path has still not changed. The project can now be completed in 30 days. The additional cost of crashing L by three days is ₹ 1050 while the saving in overheads is ₹ 1500, that is, a net saving of ₹ 450. The total cost of the project is ₹ 45,950.

Now let us consider the activity B which is the only uncrashed activity on the current critical path. B can be crashed by two days at a cost of ₹ 3000. Let us recompute the critical path. This is shown in Figure 6.33.

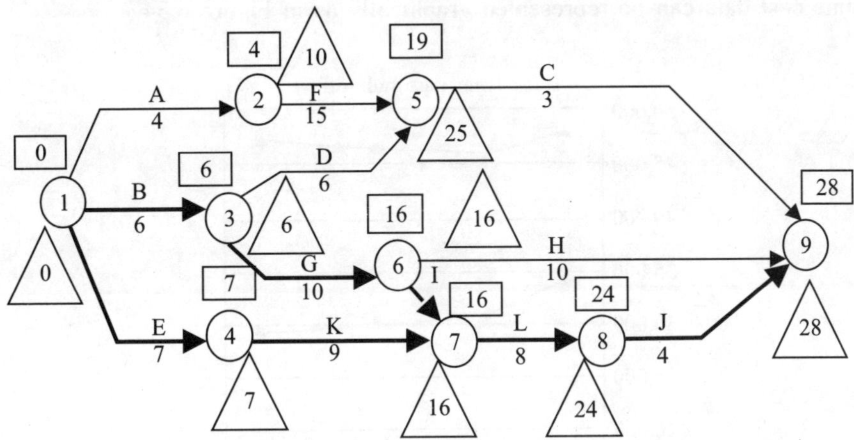

Figure 6.33 Network after crashing B by 2 days.

It can now be seen that there are two critical paths, B–G–L–J and E–K–L–J. Since all activities have been crashed on the path B–G–L–J, crashing activities E or K will not reduce the overall time of the project. While some other activities like C, D and H can be crashed, the overall time of the project will not be reduced and hence crashing these activities will only add to the costs with no benefit.

Crashing B has cost ₹ 3000, whereas the saving is only ₹ 1000. The cost of the project has gone up by ₹ 2000 and the total cost is now ₹ 47,900.

The most economical solution is to crash the project by six days, that is, activity G by two days, J by one day and L by three days resulting in a total cost of ₹ 45,900 as against the original cost of ₹ 47,150. The costs are summarized in Table 6.5.

Table 6.5 Summary of costs

Activity crashed	*Duration of project*	*Direct costs*	*Indirect costs*	*Total cost*
Normal	36	29,150	18,000	47,150
G	34	29,550	17,000	46,550
J	33	29,850	16,500	46,350
L	30	30,900	15,000	**45,900**
B	28	33,900	14,000	47,900

Crashing should only be resorted to when it affords some advantage. This may be in the form of a trade-off either between direct costs and indirect costs (like overheads) or between direct costs and *utility* costs, such as penalties for being late or bonuses for early finish. For instance, in the above problem, if the contractor knows that he is likely to exceed the time given for the project and will incur a penalty for delays, he should consider crashing activities only if the costs of crashing are less than the penalty that he will have to pay. Similarly, if there is a bonus for finishing before schedule, activities should only be crashed if they result in an overall gain for him. The least time required for the project is 28 days, but the cost will increase by ₹ 750.

The time cost data can be represented graphically as in Figure 6.34.

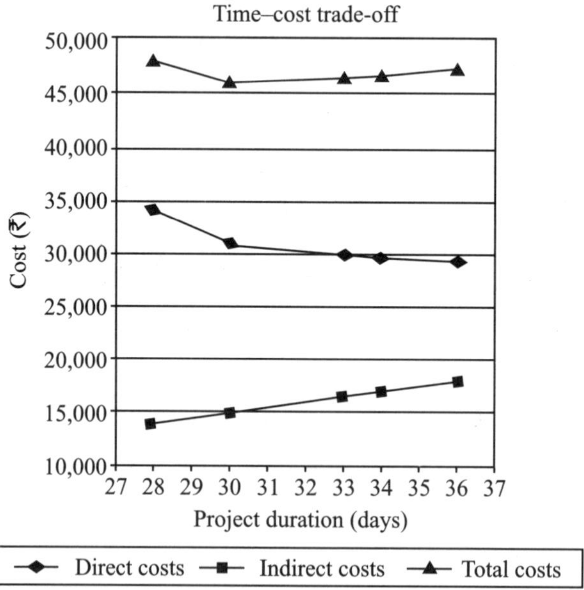

Figure 6.34 Time cost data.

Microsoft Project 2007 cannot perform cost crash analysis. WinQSB 2.0, a package designed for quantitative systems, performs cash analysis. The package being American in origin adds the $ symbol to the values instead of ₹. The data is fed in a simple spreadsheet format as shown in Figure 6.35.

Activity Number	Activity Name	Immediate Predecessor (list number/name, separated by ',')	Normal Time	Crash Time	Normal Cost	Crash Cost
1	A		4	4	$4,000	$4,000
2	B		8	6	$8,000	$11,000
3	C	D,F	3	3	$600	$600
4	D	B	6	5	$900	$1,050
5	E		7	5	$350	$550
6	F	A	15	12	$9,000	$11,700
7	G	B	12	10	$1,200	$1,600
8	H	G	10	8	$1,000	$1,300
9	J	L	5	4	$1,000	$1,300
10	K	E	9	7	$900	$1,200
11	L	G,K	11	8	$2,200	$3,250

Figure 6.35 Data input screen.

The network analysis using normal times is presented in Figure 6.36.

04-12-2009 15:33:55	Activity Name	On Critical Path	Activity Time	Earliest Start	Earliest Finish	Latest Start	Latest Finish	Slack (LS-ES)
1	A	no	4	0	4	14	18	14
2	B	Yes	8	0	8	0	8	0
3	C	no	3	19	22	33	36	14
4	D	no	6	8	14	27	33	19
5	E	no	7	0	7	4	11	4
6	F	no	15	4	19	18	33	14
7	G	Yes	12	8	20	8	20	0
8	H	no	10	20	30	26	36	6
9	J	Yes	5	31	36	31	36	0
10	K	no	9	7	16	11	20	4
11	L	Yes	11	20	31	20	31	0
	Project	Completion	Time	=	36	weeks		
	Total	Cost of	Project	=	$29,150	(Cost on	CP =	$12,400)
	Number of	Critical	Path(s)	=	1			

Figure 6.36 Solution using normal times.

The crash analysis is performed by the package. The input screen is shown in Figure 6.37.

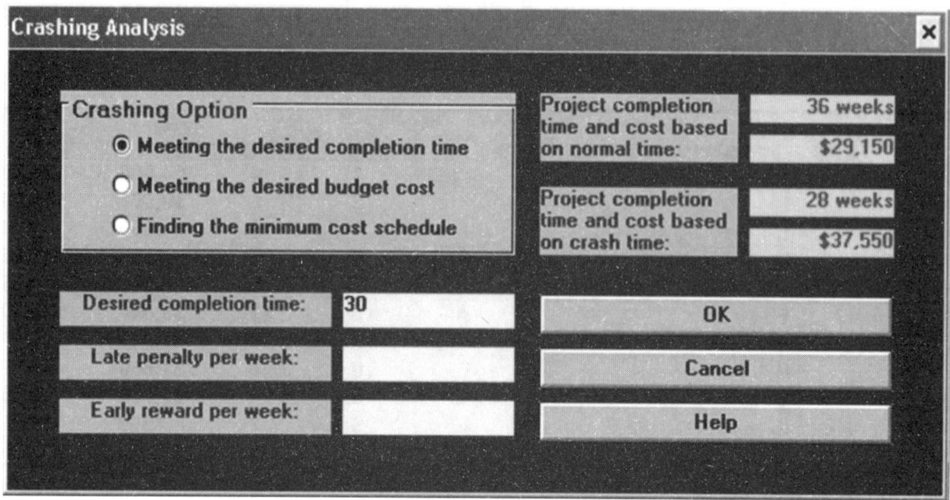

Figure 6.37 Input screen for crash analysis.

The solution is shown in Figure 6.38.

01-30-2010 16:58:31	Activity Name	Critical Path	Normal Time	Crash Time	Suggested Time	Additional Cost	Normal Cost	Suggested Cost
1	A	no	4	4	4	0	$4,000	$4,000
2	B	Yes	8	6	8	0	$8,000	$8,000
3	C	no	3	3	3	0	$600	$600
4	D	no	6	5	6	0	$900	$900
5	E	no	7	5	7	0	$350	$350
6	F	no	15	12	15	0	$9,000	$9,000
7	G	Yes	12	10	10	$400	$1,200	$1,600
8	H	no	10	8	10	0	$1,000	$1,000
9	I	Yes	5	4	4	$300	$1,000	$1,300
10	J	no	9	7	9	0	$900	$900
11	K	Yes	11	8	8	$1,050	$2,200	$3,250
	Overall	Project:			30	$1,750	$29,150	$30,900

Figure 6.38 Crashing analysis solution.

The programme does not take fixed costs into account. The programme also draws the network diagram. The network after crashing is shown in Figure 6.39.

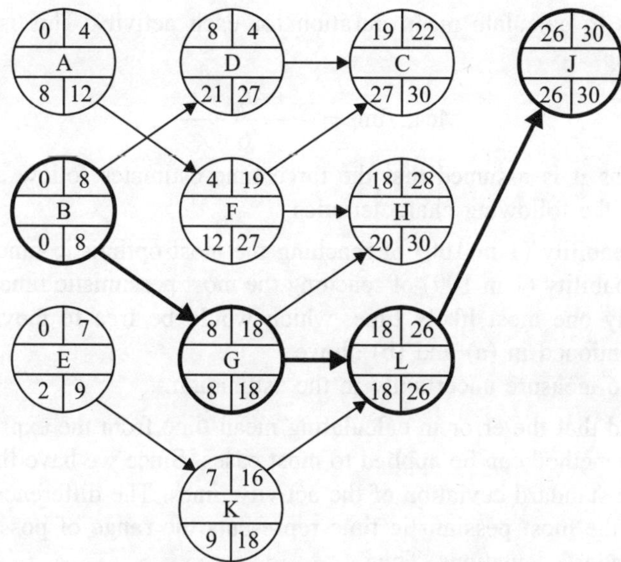

Figure 6.39 Network after crashing.

6.14 PERT (PROGRAMME EVALUATION AND REVIEW TECHNIQUE)

The PERT network is similar to CPM, but since it deals with activities whose duration is not exactly known, it relies on three time estimates of activity duration—pessimistic time, optimistic time and most likely time. A mean time for the activity is then worked out and the network is drawn as in the case of CPM. The critical path is determined and the variance on the path is calculated. The probability of completing the project by a certain date can then be determined. Let us study the technique with the help of an example.

EXAMPLE 6.3 Table 6.6 gives the activities, their precedence and the three time estimates for each in weeks.

Table 6.6 Data for Example 6.3

Activity	*Predecessor*	*Optimistic time*(t_o)	*Most likely time*(t_m)	*Pessimistic time* (t_p)
A	—	1	2	3
B	—	1	2	3
C	—	1	2	3
D	A	1	2	9
E	A	2	3	10
F	B	3	6	15
G	B	2	5	14
H	D and E	1	4	7
J	C	4	9	20
K	J and G	1	2	9
L	H, F, K and Finish	4	4	4

The first step is to calculate mean duration for each activity. This is calculated by the following relationship:

$$\text{Mean time} = \frac{t_o + 4t_m + t_p}{6}$$

The above is valid as it is assumed that the three time estimates follow a Beta distribution. The distribution has the following characteristics:

1. A small probability (1 in 100) of reaching the most optimistic time (shortest time).
2. A small probability (1 in 100) of reaching the most pessimistic time (the longest time).
3. One and only one most likely time, which would be free to move between the two extremes mentioned in (a) and (b) above.
4. The ability to measure uncertainty in the estimation.

It has been found that the error in calculating mean time from the expression given above is negligible and the method can be applied to most cases. Since we have three time estimates, we can calculate the standard deviation of the activity times. The difference between the most optimistic time and the most pessimistic time represents the range of possible activity times. The range is ±3 standard deviations. Thus,

$$\text{Standard deviation} = \frac{t_p - t_o}{6}$$

Mean time and standard deviation for each activity are shown in Table 6.7.

Table 6.7 Mean time and standard deviation for each activity

Activity	*Optimistic time (t_o)*	*Most likely time (t_m)*	*Pessimistic time (t_p)*	*Mean time*	*Standard deviation*
A	1	2	3	2	0.33
B	1	2	3	2	0.33
C	1	2	3	2	0.33
D	1	2	9	3	1.33
E	2	3	10	4	1.33
F	3	6	15	7	2.00
G	2	5	14	6	2.00
H	1	4	7	4	1.00
J	4	9	20	10	2.67
K	1	2	9	3	1.33
L	4	4	4	4	0

Now draw the network following the same rules as for the CPM network. Also compute earliest start times and latest finish times as done in the case of CPM. This is shown in Figure 6.40.

The mean duration of the project is 19 weeks, that is, there is a 50% chance that the project will finish in 19 weeks. The critical activities are C, J, K and L.

With 84% level of confidence how much time would the project take?

We know that the mean duration of the project is 19 weeks. We should now calculate the standard deviation of the critical path of the project. It must be remembered that standard

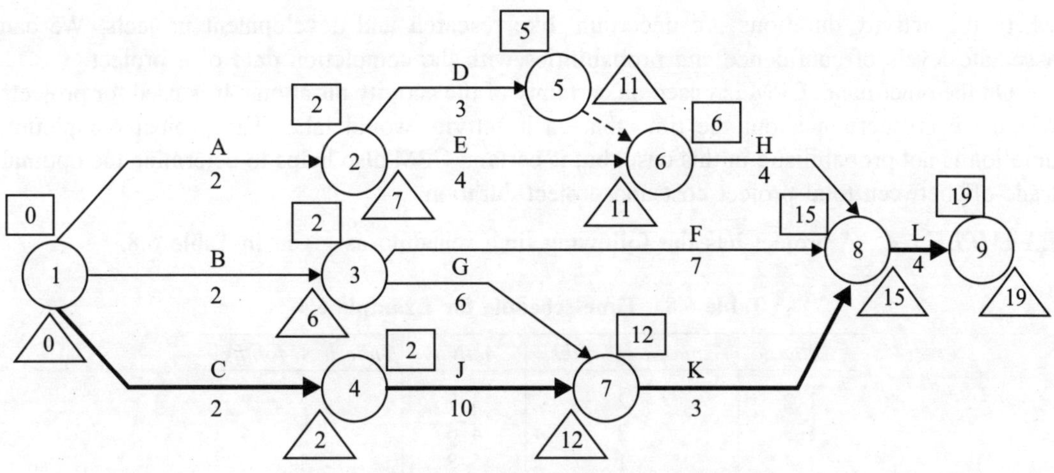

Figure 6.40 Network showing critical path.

deviation cannot be added, only variance (square of standard deviation) can be added, and the standard deviation is found by taking the square root.

Standard deviation of the finish time on the network with activities C, J, K and L on the critical path

$$= \sqrt{(\text{SD of C})^2 + (\text{SD of J})^2 + (\text{SD of K})^2 + (\text{SD of L})^2}$$

$$= \sqrt{(0.33)^2 + (2.67)^2 + (1.33)^2 + 0}$$

$$= 3.00$$

PERT assumes that the distribution of the total project completion time is normal. We know that 84% represents mean + 1 standard deviation. Hence, we can say with 84% level of confidence that the project will finish in 22 weeks.

What are the chances that the project will finish in 20 weeks?

$$z = \frac{x - \mu}{\sigma}$$

$$= \frac{20 - 19}{3} = 0.33$$

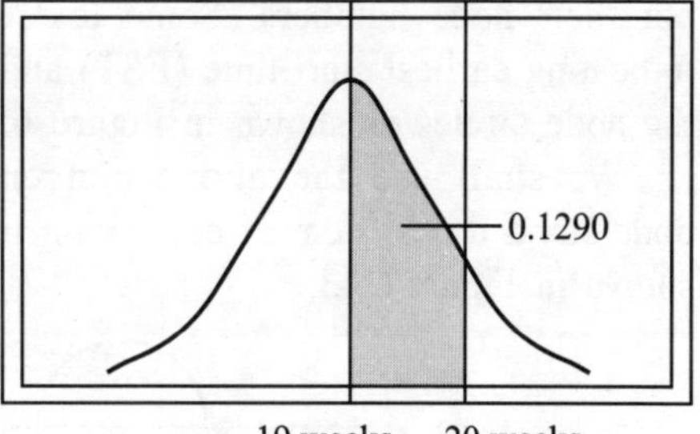

Figure 6.41 Area under normal distribution curve for $z = 0.33$.

This is shown in Figure 6.41.

From normal distribution tables the probability when $z = 0.33$ is 0.6290.

Hence, there is a 63% chance that the project will finish in 20 weeks.

6.15 DIFFERENCE BETWEEN PERT AND CPM

PERT is a probabilistic model and is based on three time estimates. It is used mainly for projects where the activity durations are uncertain, like research and development projects. We can associate levels of confidence and probabilities with the completion date of a project.

On the other hand, CPM is based on certainty of the activity durations. It is used for projects where we are certain about the time that each activity would take. The project completion duration is not probabilistic in this case, but is certain. CPM also helps to determine the optimal trade-off between total project cost and project duration.

EXAMPLE 6.4 A project has the following time schedule as given in Table 6.8.

Table 6.8 Time schedule for Example 6.4

Activity	*Time in (Months)*	*Activity*	*Time in (Months)*
1–2	2	3–7	5
1–3	2	4–6	3
1–4	1	5–8	1
2–5	4	6–9	5
3–6	8	7–8	4
		8–9	3

Draw a network and compute

1. Critical path and its duration.
2. Total float for each activity.

Also find the minimum number of cranes the project must have for its activities 2–5, 3–7, and 8–9 without delaying the project. Is any change required in the network? If so, indicate the same.

Solution The activities for the network have been referred to as per their node numbers. Some texts also use a convention of indicating earliest start time (EST) and latest finish time (LFT) in the node circles as shown in Figure 6.42.

We shall use the above convention for this problem to understand this system of conveying information. The network is shown in Figure 6.43.

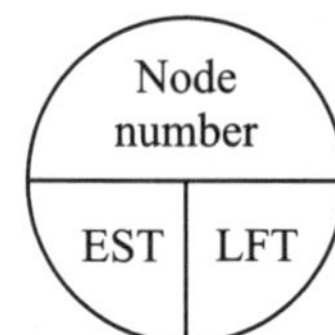

Figure 6.42 Node circle format.

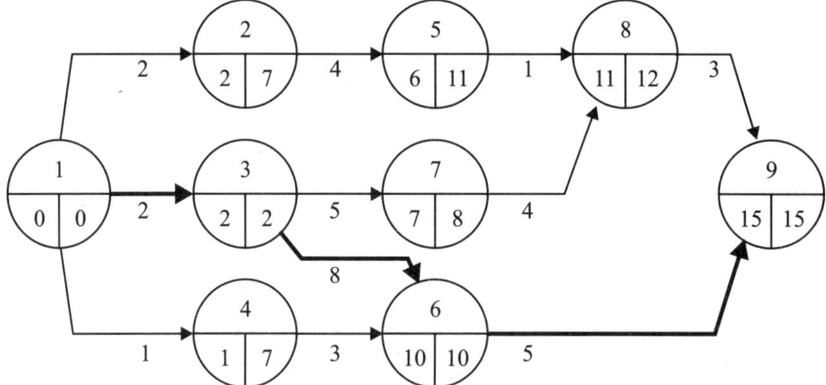

Figure 6.43 Network.

1. Critical path is 1–3–6–9. Duration of project is 15 months.
2. Total floats for non-critical activities are shown in Table 6.9.

Table 6.9 Total floats for non-critical activities

Activity	*Total float = Time latest head – Time earliest tail – Duration*
1–2	7 – 0 – 2 = 5
1–4	7 – 0 – 1 = 6
2–5	11 – 2 – 4 = 5
3–7	8 – 2 – 5 = 1
4–6	10 – 1 – 3 = 6
5–8	12 – 6 – 1 = 5
7–8	12 – 7 – 4 = 1
8–9	15 – 11 – 3 = 1

3. Crane is required for activity 2–5, 3–7 and 8–9. It is shown in Table 6.10.

Table 6.10 Crane required

Activity	*Duration*	*EST*	*LFT*	*Float*
2–5	4	2	11	5
3–7	5	2	8	1
8–9	3	11	15	1

Activity 2–5 and 3–7 can both start earliest at end of month two. As 3–7 has a float of only 1 month, allocate the crane to 3–7. The crane will be free at the end of month 7. Allocate it now to Activity 2–5. The work will commence at end of month 7 and finish at end of month 11 which is the latest time by which it must finish. The crane can now be allotted to Activity 8–9 which can start earliest at end of month 11.

Only one crane is required and should be employed as given below:

Activity 3–7 Months 3–7 (5 months)
Activity 2–5 Months 8–11 (4 months)
Activity 8–9 Months 12–14 (3 months)

EXAMPLE 6.5 For the data given in Table 6.11, draw the network. Crash the activities and determine the optimal cost of the project and the optimal duration.

Table 6.11 Data for Example 6.5

Activity	*Normal*		*Crash*	
	Duration	*Cost*	*Duration*	*Cost*
1–2	8	1000	6	2000
1–3	4	1500	2	3500
2–4	2	500	1	900
2–5	10	1000	5	4000
3–4	5	1000	1	2000
4–5	3	800	1	1000

Indirect cost is ₹ 700 per day.

Solution The network with normal times is shown in Figure 6.44.

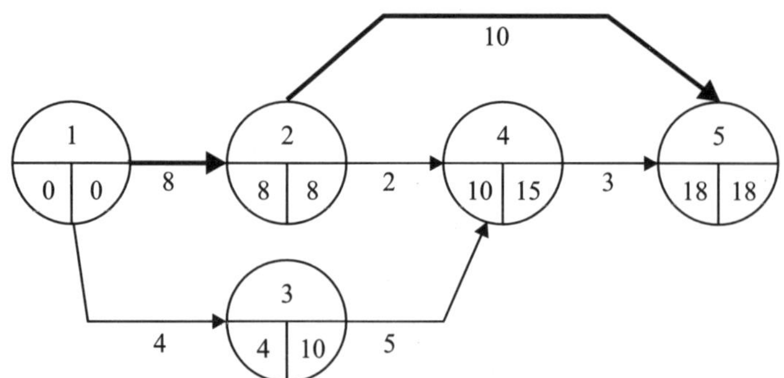

Figure 6.44 Network with normal times.

The critical path is 1–2–5.
Crash data is given in Table 6.12.

Table 6.12 Crash data

Activity	*Number of days by which it can be crashed*	*Additional crash cost*	*Crash cost per day*
1–2	2	1000	500
1–3	2	2000	1000
2–4	1	400	400
2–5	5	3000	600
3–4	4	1000	250
4–5	2	200	100

Cost of project without crashing. Direct cost ₹ 5800, indirect cost ₹ 12,600, total cost ₹ 18,400.

Critical activities are 1–2 and 2–5. Crash cost of 1–2 being less crash 1–2 by two days. The new network is shown in Figure 6.45.

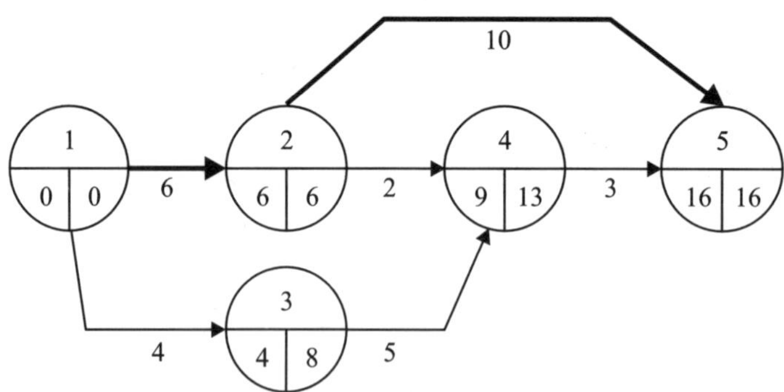

Figure 6.45 Network after crashing 1–2 by 2 days.

Change in cost: Direct cost ₹ 6800, indirect cost ₹ 11,200, total cost ₹ 18,000.

As critical activities are still 1–2 and 2–5, and since 1–2 has already been crashed now crash 2–5 by 5 days. The new network is shown in Figure 6.46.

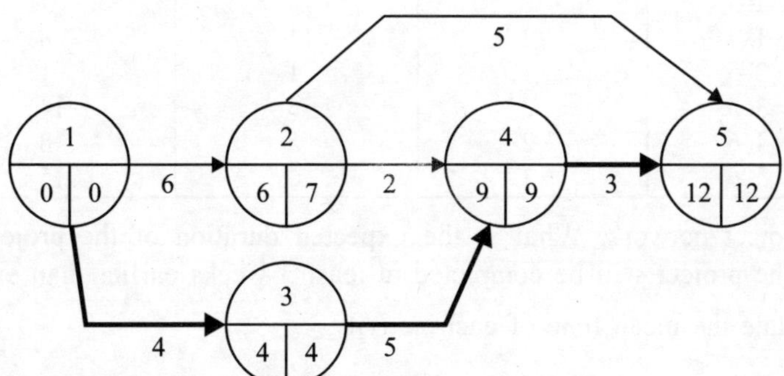

Figure 6.46 Network after crashing 2–5 by 5 days.

Change in cost: Direct cost ₹ 9800, indirect cost ₹ 8400, total cost ₹ 18,200.

Critical activities are 1–3, 3–4 and 4–5. The duration of the project is 12 days. Since the path 1–2–5 has already been crashed and takes 11 days, we should now crash the network by only one day. The cheapest activity that we can crash is activity 4–5. Crash this activity by one day. The new network is shown in Figure 6.47.

Critical activities are 1–2, 2–5, and 1–3, 3–4 and 4–5. Duration of the project is 11 days.

Cost: Direct cost ₹ 9900, indirect cost ₹ 7700, total cost ₹ 17,600.

Crashing any other activity will not reduce the time any further and will only result in increase in cost.

Optimal duration of the project is 11 days. Crash 1–2 by 2 days, 2–5 by 5 days and activity 4–5 by 1 day. Optimal cost of project is ₹ 17,600.

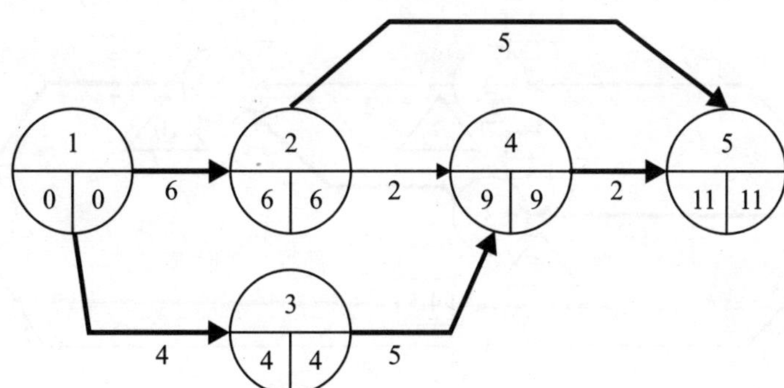

Figure 6.47

EXAMPLE 6.6 A project consists of 7 activities as given below in Table 6.13.

Table 6.13 Data for Example 6.6

Activity	*Optimistic time*	*Most likely time*	*Pessimistic time*
1–2	1	1	7
1–3	1	4	7
1–4	2	4	8
2–5	1	1	1
3–5	2	5	14
4–6	2	5	8
5–6	3	6	15

Draw the project network. What is the expected duration of the project? What is the probability that the project will be completed at least 3 weeks earlier than expected?

Solution Calculate the mean time of each activity.

$$\text{Mean time} = \frac{t_o + 4t_m + t_p}{6}$$

Activity	*Optimistic time*	*Most likely time*	*Pessimistic time*	*Mean time*	*S.D.*
1–2	1	1	7	2	
1–3	1	4	7	4	1
1–4	2	4	8	4.5	
2–5	1	1	1	1	
3–5	2	5	14	6	2
4–6	2	5	8	5	
5–6	3	6	15	7	2

Find the critical path and the critical activities with mean time. The network is shown in Figure 6.48.

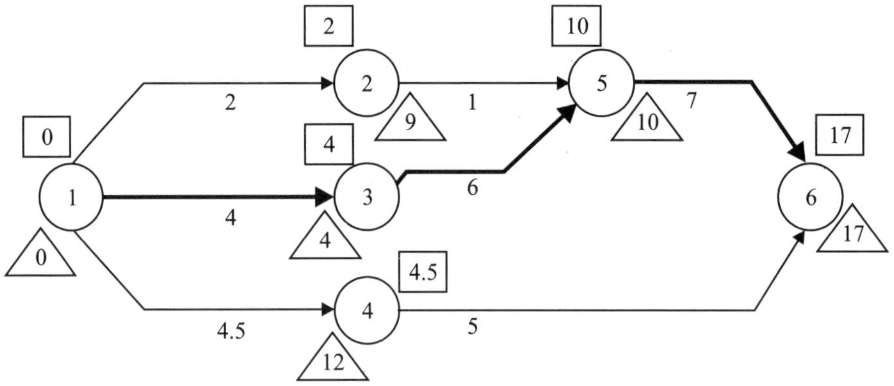

Figure 6.48 Network for Example 6.6.

The critical path is 1–3–5–6. Mean duration of the project is 17 weeks.
Variance on the path = 1 + 4 + 4 = 9. Standard deviation is three weeks.

Probability that the project will be completed at least three weeks earlier than expected:

$$z = \frac{(x-\mu)}{\sigma} = \frac{3}{3} = 1$$

For $z = 1$, the probability of the project being completed at least three weeks earlier is 0.16.

Expected duration of the project is 17 weeks. There is a 0.16 probability of the project being completed at least three weeks earlier than expected. It is shown in Figure 6.49.

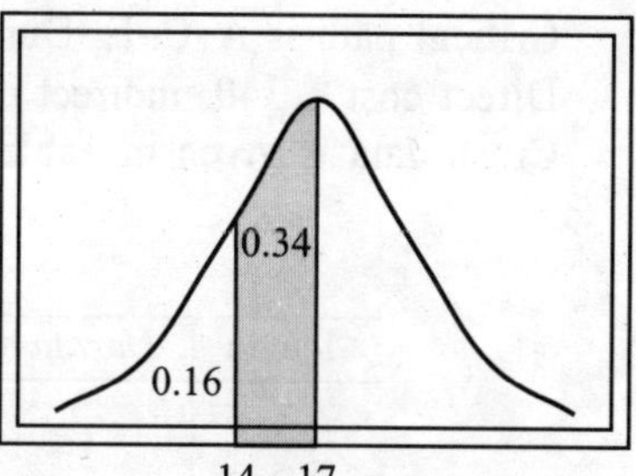

Figure 6.49 Area under the normal probability distribution curve for $z = 1$

EXAMPLE 6.7 A maintenance project has following estimates of times in hours and cost in rupees for jobs as given in Table 6.14. Assume that the jobs can be done either at normal or at fast pace but not at any other pace in between. Assuming a relationship between the job duration and job cost and with overhead cost of ₹ 25 per hour, what is the minimum duration of the project and its cost?

Table 6.14 Data for Example 6.7

Jobs	*Predecessor*	*Normal*		*Crash*	
		Time (Hours)	*Cost (₹)*	*Time (Hours)*	*Cost (₹)*
A	—	8	80	6	100
B	A	7	40	4	94
C	A	12	100	5	184
D	A	9	70	5	102
E	B, C, D	6	50	6	50
	Total		340		530

Solution The network is drawn with normal time as shown in Figure 6.50.

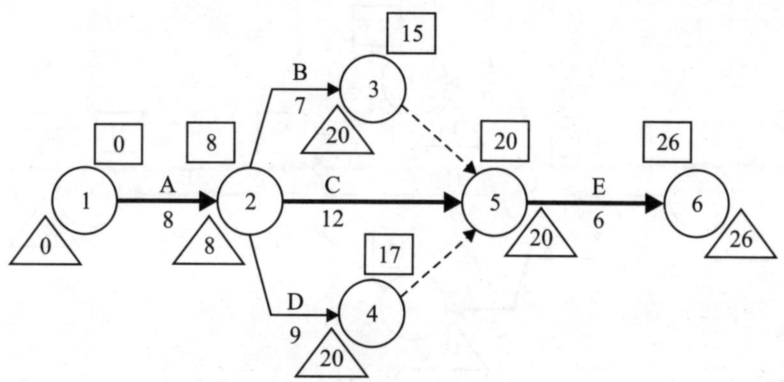

Figure 6.50 Network with normal time.

Critical path is A–C–E. Duration is 26 hours.
Direct cost ₹ 340, indirect cost ₹ 650, total cost ₹ 990.
Crash data is given in Table 6.15.

Table 6.15 Crash data

Activity	*Duration by which it can be crashed*	*Crash cost per hour*
A	2	10
B	3	18
C	7	12
D	4	8

As E cannot be crashed, consider crashing A or C. Since A costs less than C to crash, A should be crashed by 2 hours. The revised network is shown in Figure 6.51.

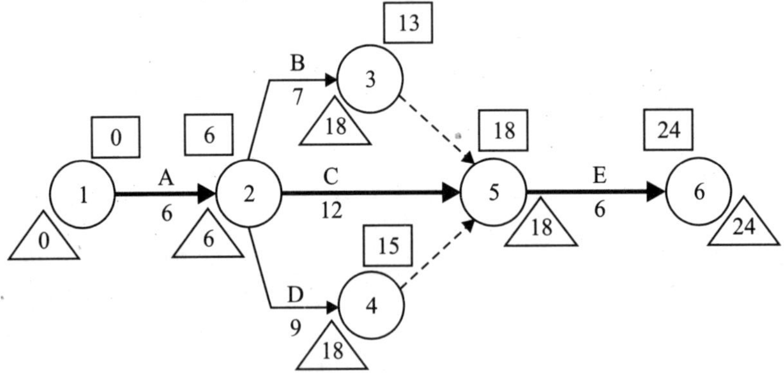

Figure 6.51 Revised network.

Critical path is A–C–E. Duration is 24 hours.
Revised cost: Direct cost ₹ 360, indirect cost ₹ 600, total cost ₹ 960.

As there is no change in the critical path, now crash C by 7 hours. Revised network is given in Figure 6.52.

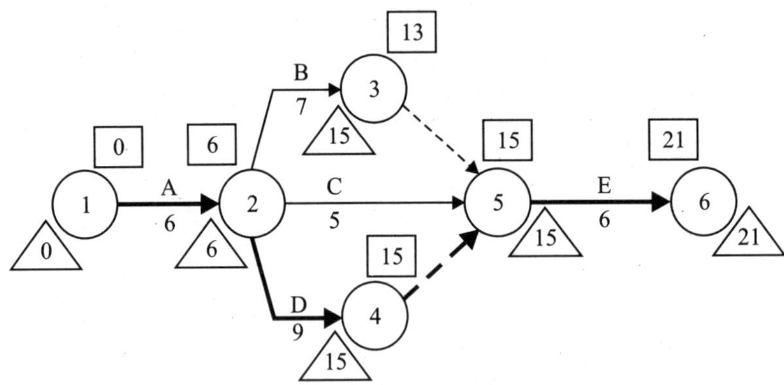

Figure 6.52 Revised network.

Critical path is A–D–E. Duration is 21 hours.
Revised cost: Direct cost ₹ 444, indirect cost ₹ 525, total cost ₹ 969.
Crash D by four days. Revised network is given in Figure 6.53.

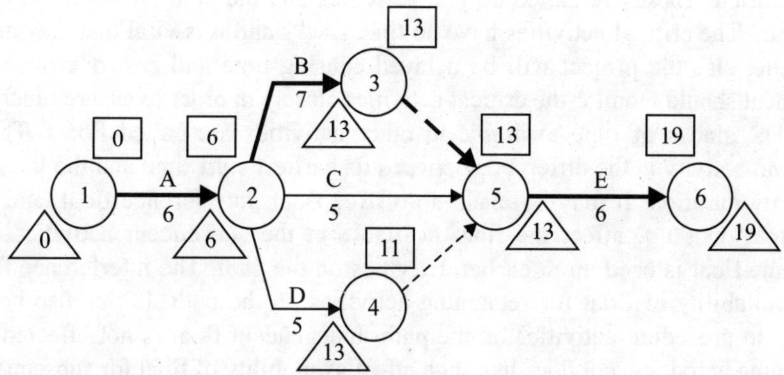

Figure 6.53 Revised network.

Critical path is A–B–E. Duration is 19 hours.
Revised cost: Direct cost ₹ 476, indirect cost ₹ 475, total cost ₹ 951.
Crash B by two days. Revised network is given in Figure 6.54.

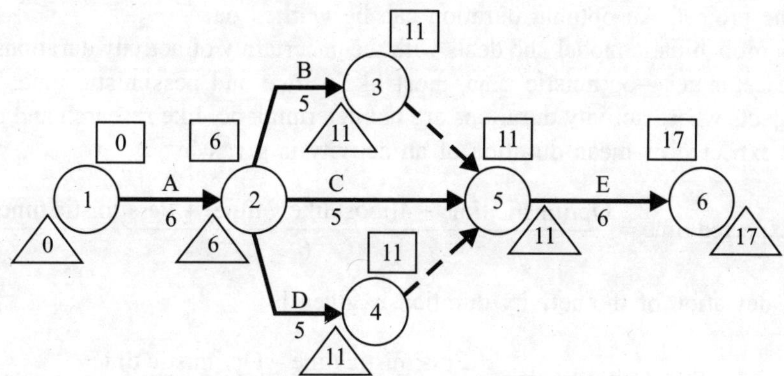

Figure 6.54 Revised network.

All activities are critical. Duration is 17 hours.
Revised cost: Direct cost ₹ 530, indirect cost ₹ 425, total cost ₹ 955.
Minimum duration of project is 17 hours and the cost is ₹ 955.

SUMMARY

PERT and CPM are network analysis techniques that help in planning, monitoring and controlling projects.

CPM is a deterministic technique and activity duration is known with certainty. Both techniques involve the drawing of a network, which is a graphical representation of activities in their logical order and relationship. Networks may be drawn as 'activity on arrow' or 'activity on node'. Computer packages generally draw networks as activity on node. Earliest start times and latest finish times are calculated for each activity and activities which have no slack are identified. These are called critical activities and the path on which they lie is called the critical path. The critical activities have no time slacks and it is vital that they are completed as per schedule, else the project will be delayed causing time and cost overruns.

Management should monitor the critical activities closely in order to ensure timely completion of projects. The slacks of time available in other activities are called floats. The total float available for an activity is the difference between its earliest start time and the latest finish time less the activity duration. It may be made up of free float, interference float, and independent float. Free float does not affect the float available in the subsequent activities but may get affected if some float is used up in earlier activities on the path. The interference float, if used, affects the availability of float for remaining activities on the path. It can also be affected by usage of float in preceding activities on the path. Independent float is not affected by usage of float in preceding activities, nor does its usage affect availability of float for subsequent activities. Critical activities have no float available in them. Lags may also be used in networks to show relationships such as start-to-start, start-to-finish, finish-to-start and finish-to-finish.

A time–cost trade-off can be calculated for a network. Some activities can be completed earlier than their normal times by the employment of extra resources. These result in increases in cost. However, the fixed costs or overheads reduce because of the overall reduction in the duration of the project. An optimal duration can be worked out.

PERT is a probabilistic model and deals with the uncertainty of activity durations. It is based on three time estimates—optimistic time, most likely time and pessimistic time. It is ideally suited for projects where activity durations are not deterministic, like research and development projects. The expected or mean duration of an activity is given by:

$$\text{Expected time} = \frac{\text{Optimistic time} + 4(\text{most likely time}) + \text{Pessimistic time}}{6}$$

The standard deviation of the activity duration is given by:

$$\text{Standard deviation} = \frac{\text{Pessimistic time} - \text{Optimistic time}}{6}$$

Networks are a useful tool not only for planning but also for monitoring and controlling. In subsequent chapters we shall study the use of network analysis for resource scheduling and for monitoring and controlling a project in its execution phase.

QUESTIONS

1. How does network analysis help in project management?
2. What do you understand by floats? Describe the different types of floats and their implications. What are the managerial implications of floats? Explain with the help of an example.

3. What are the three time estimates needed for drawing a PERT network? Show how you would use these estimates to compute the expected activity duration and variance.
4. Explain the use of float.
5. What is the purpose of dummy activities?
6. A project has the following time schedule:

Activity	*Time (Months)*	*Activity*	*Time (Months)*
1–2	2	3–7	5
1–3	2	4–6	3
1–4	1	5–8	1
2–5	4	6–9	5
3–6	8	7–8	4
		8–9	3

Draw a network and compute
1. Critical path and its duration.
2. Total float for each activity.

Also find the minimum number of cranes the project must have for its activities 2–5, 3–7, and 8–9 without delaying the project. Is any change required in the network? If so, indicate the same.

7. The following information is known for a project. Draw the network and find the critical path. Capital letters denote activities and numbers in brackets denote activity times.

This must be completed	*Before this can start*
A(30)	C
B(7)	D
B	G.
B	K
C(10)	D
C	G
D(14)	E
E(10)	F
F(7)	H
F	I
F	L
G(21)	I
G	L
H(7)	J(15)
I(12)	J
K(30)	L(15)
K	I

8. A firm is planning to manufacture a wall decorative fixture, consisting of three plates, X, Y and Z made individually and then put together. The design of X and Y takes 3 and 5 days, respectively. The design of Z takes only 2 days but cannot be completed till design of Y is finished. The procurement of material for X, Y and Z takes 7, 5 and 3 days, respectively. The pressing and grooving of Z has to be done first, then that of Y and last of all of X. Each takes 3 days. The polishing of plates takes 2 days each, and the assembly takes 1 day. Draw a CPM network, determine the critical path and the duration of the project.

9. The following table gives the list of various activities involved in the production of a wireless equipment, their immediate predecessor and their normal time in months. Find the critical path and the least duration of the project.

Activity	*Predecessor*	*Time*
A – Systems calculations	—	3
B – Release of drawings	—	3
C – Selection of PSU	A, B	10
D – Purchase of raw material	A, B	7
E – Production documentation	A, B	5
F – Time study/shop order	E	3
G – PCB manufacture	D, F	5
H – Mechanical parts manufacture	D, F	8
I – Electronic assembly	C, G, H	2
J – Testing	I	4

10. The following table gives the list of the activities involved in the publication of a book, their immediate predecessor and their normal times in weeks. Find the critical path and the earliest time when the book will be ready for distribution.

Activity	*Predecessor*	*Time*
A – Appraisal of book	—	9
B – Initial pricing	—	2
C – Marketability assessment	A, B	2
D – Revision by the author	A	7
E – Editing of final draft	C, D	5
F – Type setting of text	E	4
G – Plates for art work	E	2
H – Designing, printing of jacket	C, D	5
I – Printing and binding	F, G	6
J – Inspection and final assembly	I, H	1

11. The following table gives the list of various activities involved in a project, their immediate predecessor and their normal time in days. Find the critical path and the least duration of the project.

Activity	Predecessor	Time
A	—	9
B	—	4
C	—	7
D	B, C	8
E	A	7
F	C	5
G	E	10
H	E	8
I	D, F, H	6
J	E	9
K	I, J	10
L	G	2

12. The following table gives the list of various activities involved in the running of a Management Development Programme along with their immediate predecessors, and their normal time in weeks. Find the critical path and the earliest time when the programme can be run.

Activity	Predecessor	Time
A – Design programme theme	—	8
B – Design brochure	A	4
C – Compile list of speakers	A	2
D – Finalize and print brochure	B, C	8
E – Make travel arrangements	D	4
F – Dispatch brochures	D	3
G – Receive nominations	F	4
H – Conduct programme	E, G	6
I – Print proceedings	I	8

13. A project consists of eight activities denoted by A, B, C, D, E, F, G and H. Relationship between the activities is as follows:

(a) The project starts with activity A.
(b) When A is completed, activities E and B may be started.
(c) Activity F may be started when E is completed.
(d) Activity C depends for its start on the completion of F and B.
(e) When F is completed, activity G may begin.
(f) When C is completed, D may begin.
(g) H may begin when G and D are completed and is the final activity.

Expected time for the activities in days is given below:

Activity	A	B	C	D	E	F	G	H
Time	10	9	3	15	5	17	8	7

Draw the network and find the critical path.

14. A team of chemists is planning to undertake an applied research project to test a formula for a new synthetic material. The project can be separated into 12 distinct activities. The relationship amongst the activities and the time estimates in weeks are given as follows:

Activity	*Predecessor*	*Optimistic time*	*Most likely time*	*Pessimistic time*
A	—	2	2	2
B	—	1	3	7
C	A	4	7	8
D	A	3	5	7
E	B	2	6	9
F	B	5	9	11
G	C, D	3	6	8
H	E	2	6	9
I	C, D	3	5	8
J	G, H	1	3	4
K	F	4	8	11
L	J, K	2	5	7

Draw a network. What is the expected time to complete the project? What is the probability of completing the project in 26 weeks? In 23 weeks or less? In 25 weeks or more? What is the time estimate for project completion at 95% confidence level?

15. A project consists of eight independent activities as shown below. What is the expected time to complete the project? What is the probability of completing the project in 20 weeks or less? Time estimates are given as follows:

Activity	*Predecessor*	*Optimistic time*	*Most likely time*	*Pessimistic time*
A	—	1	3	5
B	—	2	3	4
C	—	3	4	5
D	A	2	9	10
E	C	4	5	6
F	B, D, E	5	6	13
G	A	2	4	6
H	C	1	3	6

16. A project consists of seven activities as given as follows:

Activity	*Optimistic time*	*Most likely time*	*Pessimistic time*
1–2	1	1	7
1–3	1	4	7
1–4	2	4	8
2–5	1	1	1
3–5	2	5	14
4–6	2	5	8
5–6	3	6	15

Draw the project network. What is the expected duration of the project? What is the probability that the project will be completed at least three weeks earlier than expected?

17. For the data given in the following table, draw the network. Crash the activities and determine the optimal cost of the project and the optimal duration.

Activity	*Normal*		*Crash*	
	Duration	*Cost*	*Duration*	*Cost*
1–2	8	1000	6	2000
1–3	4	1500	2	3500
2–4	2	500	1	900
2–5	10	1000	5	4000
3–4	5	1000	1	2000
4–5	3	800	1	1000

Indirect cost is ₹ 700 per day.

18. The estimate of a project to be completed at the shortest possible time is urgently required. Make use of the following information and answer the questions given as follows:

Activity	*Predecessor*	*Normal time*	*Crash time*	*Normal cost*	*Crash cost*
A	—	20	16	9000	12,600
B	—	25	25	1900	1900
C	A	10	7	4500	7200
D	A	12	8	4000	8400
E	B, C	5	2	4400	6200
F	D, E	10	6	4500	6500

(a) Draw the network and determine the critical path with normal time.
(b) What is the shortest duration by which the project can be completed?
(c) If the indirect costs are ₹ 850 per day, what is the optimal duration of the project?

19. An electronic firm has signed a contract to install an instrument landing device at the local airport. The complete installation can be broken down into activities as shown in the following table. The contract specifies that the installation will be completed within 18 days. There is a penalty of ₹ 1000 per day beyond the specified time.

Activity	*Predecessor*	*Normal time*	*Crash time*	*Normal cost*	*Crash cost*
A	—	3	2	3200	3600
B	—	5	4	5500	6000
C	—	6	4	5750	7000
D	A	7	5	7500	8500
E	A	4	3	4200	4700
F	B, D	2	2	1800	1800

(Contd...)

(Contd...)

Activity	Predecessor	Normal time	Crash time	Normal cost	Crash cost
G	C	4	3	4250	4850
H	A	8	5	8500	9600
I	C	5	4	4750	5350
J	C	7	5	6750	7350
K	E, F, G	4	3	4000	4400
L	H, I	6	4	6500	7500
M	L	3	2	2800	3350
N	J, K	5	4	5250	5750

(a) What is the normal time to complete the installation?
(b) What is the shortest possible time for completing the installation?
(c) What is the most economical period of time in which to schedule the installation?
(d) What is the minimum total cost (installation plus penalty)?

20. A project has nine activities. Their precedence, normal and crash duration (in days) and costs (₹ 000s) are given in the following table:

Activity	Precedence	Normal		Crash	
		Duration	Cost	Duration	Cost
A	—	2	3	1	5
B	—	4	5	3	7
C	—	4	4	2	10
D	A, B	4	3.5	4	3.5
E	B, C	8	7.5	6	15
F	C	2	6	1	9
G	D	6	4	4	9
H	G, E, F	12	16	7	26
I	H	6	10	4	20

Fixed cost is ₹ 4000 per day.
Determine the optimal duration and cost of the project.

21. Following table gives the list of activities involved in the launch of a new Credit Card service by a company, their immediate predecessors and their expected durations (in days):

Activity	Description	Predecessors	T_o	T_m	T_p
A	Conduct market research to determine size, potential and competition in the market	—	10	12	14
B	Define market strategy in terms of positioning and product features	A	14	15	17

(Contd...)

(Contd...)

Activity	*Description*	*Predecessors*	T_o	T_m	T_p
C	Estimate expected volumes	B	2	3	4
D	Estimate additional manpower required	C	4	6	8
E	Identify modifications required to the present computer system based on expected volumes	C	10	12	14
F	Implement computer system modification	E	20	25	27
G	Update physical facilities	C	10	17	20
H	Prepare instructional manuals	F	5	6	7
I	Hire additional sales force and operational staff	D	7	12	14
J	Train sales force and operational staff	H, I	14	17	20
K	Advertise for suppliers	C	1	2	3
L	Check supplier samples	K	10	15	20
M	Identify key suppliers and define quality standards	L	3	5	7
N	Roll out basic product to a few employees as a method of pre-testing	M, J	13	15	17
O	Generate and assess feedback	N	20	21	22
P	Modify and make changes where necessary	O	7	9	14
Q	Update procedures manual	P	2	3	4
R	Retrain concerned staff	Q	2	2	2
S	Design communications to prospective card holders	P	7	10	13
T	Design advertising schedule	S	5	7	9
U	Roll out final product – Launch	T, R, G	4	8	12

(a) Draw a network for the project.
(b) Find the expected project completion time.
(c) Determine the probability of completing the project in 165 days.

22. A sociologist plans a questionnaire survey consisting of the following tasks:

Activity	*Predecessor*	T_m	T_o	T_p
A – Design of questionnaire	—	5	4	6
B – Sampling design	—	12	8	16
C – Testing of questionnaire and refinements	A	5	4	12
D – Recruiting for interviewers	B	3	1	5
E – Training of interviewers	D, A	2	2	2
F – Allocation of areas to interviewers	B	5	4	6
G – Conducting interviews	C, E, F	14	10	18
H – Evaluation of results	G	20	18	34

(a) What are the expected task durations and the variances of task durations?
(b) Draw a network for the project and find the critical path. What is the expected duration of the project?
(c) What is the probability that the project will not exceed 60 days?

23. A promoter is organizing a sports meeting. The relationship among the activities and time estimates in days are shown in the following table:

Activity	*Predecessor*	T_o	T_m	T_p
A – Prepare draft programme	—	3	7	11
B – Send to sports organization and get comments	A	14	21	28
C – Obtain promoters	A	11	14	17
D – Prepare and sign documents for stadium hire	A, C	2	2	2
E – Redraft programme and request entries	B	2	7/2	8
F – Enlist officials	D, E	10	14	21
G – Arrange accommodation for touring teams	E	3	4	5
H – Prepare detailed programme	E, F	4	9/2	8
I – Make last minute arrangements	G, H	1	2	4

(a) Find the expected activity durations and their variances.

(b) Draw a network and find the critical path. What is the expected duration of the project and what is its variance?

(c) What is the probability that the project will be completed in 56 days?

24. Jaipur is planning a large parking lot in Ram Niwas Garden to cater to the ever-increasing traffic. The PWD executive engineer must design the parking lot and put up a proposal before the Jaipur Development Authority. He has identified the following activities. The times are shown against them, and the precedence amongst them has been arrived at in consultation with his engineers.

ID	*Description*	*Predecessor*	*Time*
A	Survey	None	4
B	Soil analysis report	A	18
C	Traffic design	A	25
D	Layout	A	4
E	Design approval	B, C, D	60
F	Lighting	E	15
G	Drainage	E	25
H	Landscaping	E	25
I	Sign posting	E	15
J	Project proposal	F, G, H, I	10

Prepare an AON network for the project with the activity early, late and slack times. Mark the critical path.

25. From the following information, draw the AON project network. Compute the early, late and slack times for each activity. Identify the critical path.

ID	*Duration*	*Finish-to-start Predecessor*	*Finish-to-start lag*	*Additional lag relationships*	*Lag*
A	5	None	0	None	0
B	12	A	0	None	0

(Contd...)

(Contd...)

ID	*Duration*	*Finish-to-start Predecessor*	*Finish-to-start lag*	*Additional lag relationships*	*Lag*
C	17	A	0	Start-finish C to D	18
D	7	B	5	Start-start D to E	6
				Finish-finish D to E	25
E	22	B	0	Finish-finish E to F	1
F	15	D	0	None	0
G	8	C	8	Finish-finish G to F	8
H	18	F	0	None	0

26. A new version of a popular spreadsheet software is due to be released in a year. However, the preliminary project team has not been able to come up with an expected completion date. But, as the table that follows show, they have been able to estimate durations for each activity involved. Because disagreements arose, three time estimates are given: optimistic, most likely and pessimistic. Analyze this situation addressing the following questions:

(a) Construct a network for the project.
(b) Compute the mean time of each activity.
(c) Compute the expected project completion time.
(d) Compute the standard deviation of the project completion time.
(e) Determine the likelihood that the project will be completed in 52 weeks.
(f) Determine the likelihood that the project will be completed in 65 weeks.
(g) Determine the probability that the project will not be ready within 70 weeks.

Activity	*Predecessor*	T_o	T_m	T_p
A – Complaints review	—	2	4	8
B – Suggestions review	—	1	2	3
C – Initial specifications	A, B	3	5	8
D – Team completion	C	2	2	3
E – Clarification requests	A, B	3	4	7
F – Detailed specifications	D, E	4	6	9
G – First coding phase	F	8	12	20
H – Preliminary testing	G	2	3	5
I – First press release	G	2	2	3
J – External alpha testing	H	5	8	12
K – Second coding phase	H	6	9	14
L – Commercial response	I, J	3	4	7
M – Consolidation review	K, L	3	4	6
N – Secondary testing	K	2	3	5
O – External beta testing	N	4	6	9
P – Second press release	M	2	2	3
Q – Final revision coding	M, O	3	5	10
R – Final testing	Q	2	4	6
S – Package design	O, P	4	7	12
T – Production completion	R, S	2	3	4

APPENDIX

Critical Chain Scheduling and Buffer Management

A.1 INTRODUCTION

Critical chain project management (CCPM) was developed by Eliyahu M. Goldratt based on his 'Theory of Constraints' in 1997. Application of CCPM has resulted in projects being completed 10–50% faster and/or cheaper than traditional methods like CPM and PERT. While CPM and PERT lay emphasis on technical scheduling, CCPM emphasizes technical scheduling as modified by resource levelling.

Studies show that for projects managed by traditional CPM and PERT networks, only 44% of the projects get completed on time. Projects usually get completed in 222% of their estimated time and 189% of estimated costs (studies by Standish Group and others, 1998).

A.2 RATIONALE FOR CCPM

Projects are fraught with uncertainty and risk. Traditionally, estimates of duration or costs are made conservatively so that they have a 90–95% chance of success. CCPM advocates a more aggressive approach to estimating and obtains estimates which have a 50% chance of success. The rationale behind this thinking is that statistically 50% activities will be completed earlier than the estimated time and 50% activities shall take longer, with the overall variance becoming zero in the end. If this rationale is to be believed, then why do most conventionally planned projects end up with time and cost overruns even though every activity has a 95% chance of being completed in time? Let us analyze some of the common practices followed in conventional CPM or PERT planning.

Schedules are normally derived from deadlines for component tasks and from estimates of various activities. Estimates are usually arrived at by line persons who give a 'realistic', safe estimate. Estimates are not single values but are a set of values, each associated with a statistical level of confidence of being achieved. Line persons tend to make estimates with 90 or 95% level of confidence. A safety margin is added to take care of Murphy's law—'What can go wrong, will go wrong'. This is especially so as line persons making the estimate may have to live up to their promises. It is only human to add 'safety' time to the estimate. Confidence level of aggressive and conservative estimates is shown in Figure A.1.

Unfortunately, after having added 'safety' to the estimate, complacency seems to set in. Parkinson's law—'Work expands to fill the time available'—takes over. Traditional techniques like the CPM lay too much emphasis on start and finish dates for activities. When a line person knows that the average time to complete a task is 10 days and 16 days have been allocated for it, there is a tendency to become complacent ('we still have time to do it'). The line person initially tends to spend time on other tasks, which are perceived to be 'urgent' or more important,

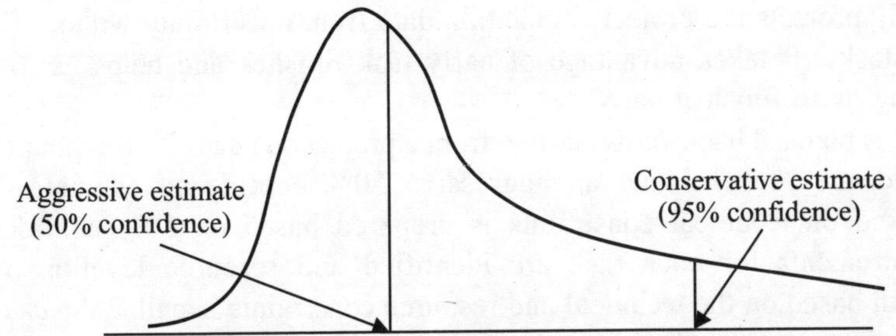

Figure A.1 Confidence level of aggressive and conservative estimates.

and starts work on the project scheduled task when it is already too late. Even the average time required to complete the task is not available. There is a tendency to rush to meet the schedule, which more often than not, is not met. As this happens on various activities, the entire project ends up with time and cost overruns. We are all the time looking at the due date of the deliverable and become victims of Parkinson's law. We protect our project due date by building safety into our estimates for individual tasks and then fritter it away because of the comfort that the built-in safety provides. Goldratt contends that projects fall behind schedule despite 'safe' estimates because of the following:

(a) *Parkinson's law*. As stated above.
(b) *Self-protection*. Participants fail to report early finish of activities out of fear that management will modify their standards and demand more next time.
(c) *Dropped baton*. Early finishes may not lead to the start of the next activity as the persons or resources which are to execute it may not be ready to start work early. The time gained is, therefore, lost. Goldratt compares a project to a relay race. Just as in a relay race, a runner's time is lost if the next runner is not ready to receive the baton, the time gained from completing a task early is lost if the next group of people are not ready to receive the project task.
(d) *Excessive multi-tasking*. This adds time to the completion of tasks.
(e) *Resource bottlenecks*. Delays are caused by limited availability of critical resources.
(f) *Student syndrome*. There is a tendency to delay the start of tasks until you absolutely have to.

CCPM lays emphasis on only one date—that is, the completion date of the project. There are no schedule dates for every activity. Each activity must start as soon as possible and finish earliest. If an activity finishes before schedule, the successor activity must start and not wait for its start date as laid down in the conventional schedule. Scheduling is based on aggressive (50% confidence) estimates. Buffer times are added to counter Murphy's law and build in some 'safety'.

A.3 PLANNING

CCPM aims at managing and scheduling projects without task due dates and the accompanying undesirable behaviour that the dates instigate (complacency and Parkinson's law syndrome).

It systematically protects the project completion date from uncertainty without fixing deadlines for individual tasks. It takes advantage of early task finishes and helps us to accelerate the project allowing us to finish it early.

The project is planned backwards starting from a project due date. Two estimates—a 'realistic' 90–95% confidence estimate and an aggressive 50% confidence estimate—are obtained. A network based on technical constraints is prepared based on 50% confidence estimates. Resource requirements for each task are identified and resource levelling is carried out. The longest path based on the technical and resource constraints is called the *critical chain*. No start and finish dates are specified for activities. Since the schedule is based on 50% estimates, it would be incorrect to expect all activities to meet this schedule. The uncertainties are taken care of by providing time buffers. A time buffer is added to the project duration on the critical chain and is called a *project buffer*. However, this buffer is not an aggregate of the buffers in each activity on the critical chain which would have been included if we were basing our schedule on 90–95% confidence estimates. The buffer can be considerably reduced (say up to 50%). As far as chains of non-critical activities are concerned, a time buffer is added where the chain merges with the critical chain. This buffer is known as *feeder buffer*. Time buffers are also added where scarce resources are involved. This is known as *resource buffer*.

CCPM also takes advantage of early finishes. The problem faced is, how do we know when the resources will be required, if there are no scheduled finish or start dates? There are two types of resources: resources that perform critical tasks and resources that perform non-critical tasks. We are concerned about the ones used on critical tasks as they directly determine how long the project will take. We must ensure that the resources required for critical tasks are available when the preceding task is completed without relying on fixed due dates.

This is achieved by determining how much of warning resources need to finish what they are engaged on and shift to another task, so that when the preceding task is complete, they can drop what they are doing and shift to the critical task. The resources must also provide regular updates of the current estimate of time remaining to complete the task in hand. This will ensure that the resources required for the next activity are available. Let us understand this with an example. Suppose A and B are two successive critical activities in the chain and activity A is currently being undertaken. Let us assume that a resource X currently employed on activity C is required for activity B and needs five days warning to wind up its work on C and shift to B. When resources employed on activity A report that it will be completed in five days, resource X employed on activity C will be informed that work on activity B is to start and it should be ready to take it on after five days. There is a significant shift from traditional monitoring of projects where a track is kept of 'percentage of work completed'. We are now keeping track of how much more time is required to complete a task, rather than on how much has been finished. By following this process we ensure availability of resources in case of early finishes without having calendar date schedules. We are no longer tied down to calendar due dates, and can move up activity as its predecessors finish early, and we can avoid the effects of Parkinson's law.

Work on the non-critical activities is started as soon as possible, but they are not micro-managed like the critical activities. It is hoped that the slack in them will be enough to cater for any delays that may occur. However, the feed buffer ensures that the non-critical activities do not impinge on the critical chain. 'Work coming alerts' are not used for non-critical activities.

Even if the feeder buffer is totally used up, it would perhaps only result in some project buffers being used up. Critical chain scheduling is shown in Figure A.2.

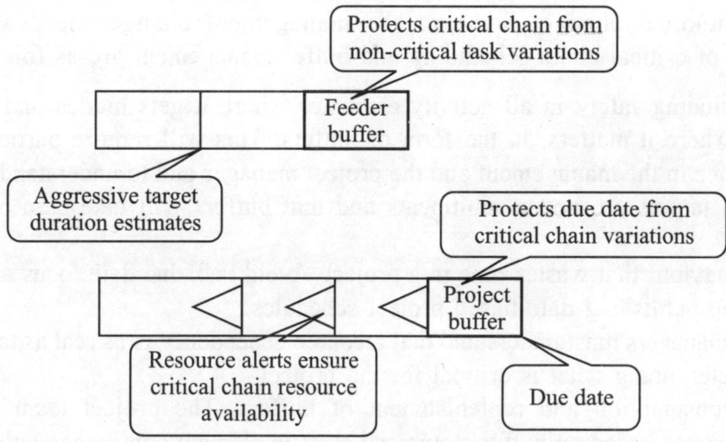

Figure A.2 Critical chain scheduling.

A.4 EXECUTION AND MONITORING

When the plan is complete, the project network is fixed and the buffer size is 'locked', that is, their planned duration may not be altered during the project, because the buffers are used to monitor the project.

As the schedule is based on 50% confidence estimates, there is pressure on the participants to perform and complete critical chain activities at the earliest overcoming Student's syndrome and Parkinson's law.

Since there are no completion dates to track, the progress of the project is monitored through 'buffer management'. As tasks are completed, we know how much they have eaten into or replenished the buffer. We are getting estimates of time-to-completion of all current activities on a regular basis and this helps us to keep track of buffer usage on an ongoing basis. We can set warning signals when an activity consumes a certain amount of buffer and could have contingency plans drawn up for the eventuality that the buffer usage goes beyond a certain point. We could then implement the contingency plans.

This permits us to stay out of the way of project resources if things are on track, build contingency plan in other than a crisis situation and implement it only if necessary.

SUMMARY

CCPM plans a network based on aggressive 50% confidence estimates incorporating both technical and resource constraints. It eliminates task due dates and minimizes the impact of Parkinson's law. Project buffer, feeder buffer and resource buffer efficiently protect against things going wrong (Murphy's law). Project participants can work without task due date distraction. Resource alerts and effective prioritization allow managers to take advantage of early task finishes. The focus shifts to buffer management.

CCPM is not a simple technical change of how we plan and monitor projects but needs a managerial attitudinal change. Some of the management changes needed for effective implementation of critical chain scheduling and buffer management are as follows:

1. Stop including safety in all activity estimates where it gets hidden and wasted. Build safety, where it matters, in the form of buffers. This will require participants to have confidence in the management and the project manager and to understand that their task duration targets are not commitments and that buffers will take care of any slips on targets.
2. Stop behaviour that wastes time in a project. Avoid task due date focus and Parkinson's law. Stop publishing date-based project schedules.
3. Project managers must understand that resource dependency is as real as task dependency when determining what is critical for the project.
4. Track consumption and replenishment of buffers. The project team must plan for contingencies based on buffer status and must implement contingency plans only if and when required.

CCPM is a relatively new technique but results in early project completion. It has distinct advantages over traditional methods and is well worth the effort involved in managing project with CCPM. Organizations which value efficiency will have to change and adopt the critical chain approach making the necessary changes in the organizational attitude.

CHAPTER 7

Resource Allocation

No major project is ever installed on time, within budget, with the same staff that started it.
—Edwards, Butler, Hill and Russell

LEARNING OBJECTIVES
After reading this chapter, you will be able to: • Appreciate the need for resource scheduling. • Understand the type of constraints imposed on a project. • Study the methodology for resource levelling for time constrained projects. • Study the methodology for levelling resources for a resource constrained project. • Appreciate the use of computer software for resource levelling.

7.1 INTRODUCTION

Network techniques give a schedule for carrying out various activities. However, the network assumes that resources needed to carry out an activity will be available when they are required. This may not always be the case. There may be restrictions due to availability of resources or due to competing requirements for different activities or on different projects. Even when adequate resources are available, their demand may vary widely over the life of the project. It may be desirable to smoothen out resource demand by delaying or rescheduling non-critical activities so that peaks and troughs in demand are evened out. This process is called *resource levelling*. There may be other occasions when the resource availability is restricted; this may result in the delay in start of certain activities and a consequent delay in the completion of the project. Such scheduling is referred to as *resource constrained scheduling*.

The cost of failing to consider use of resources and their availability is generally hidden and is not so obvious. More often than not, resource scheduling does not get the attention it deserves. A failure to schedule resources at the planning stage leads to project delays which manifest themselves at the execution stage and are difficult to correct. The problem becomes compounded in organizations which deal with a number of projects. The major resources are shared across the organization and unless properly scheduled can cause project time and cost overruns.

7.2 TYPES OF PROJECT CONSTRAINTS

Project constraints affect the start of activities. This may reduce the slack available in the network, or reduce the flexibility in scheduling. This may also cause a reduction in the number of parallel activities and a delay in the completion of the project. The constraints may be technical, physical or due to resources.

Technical constraints dictate the sequence in which activities must be executed. For instance, filling of foundations can take place only after excavation of foundations is completed. The project network depicts the technical constraints. It shows whether activities are sequential or can be undertaken in parallel. The predecessor and successor activity relationship is based on technical constraints. Technical constraints are also referred to as logical constraints.

In certain cases, environmental conditions may restrict activities that may otherwise be performed in parallel. For instance, space restrictions may permit only a limited number of workers to work at a time. Consider the renovation of a small office cabin which involves painting of two walls and decorative fittings on a third wall. While the paint work and the work on decorative fittings are independent of each other and may be executed in parallel, the space in the cabin may not be sufficient to permit both the work teams to work at the same time. The tasks will then perforce have to be executed one after the other. The procedure for handling physical constraints is the same as for handling resource constraints.

Resource constraints—the absence or shortage of resources—can drastically alter technical constraints. For example, it may be theoretically possible to level the area required for a multi-storey housing complex and build an approach road at the same time or in parallel. However, if we require a bulldozer for both the tasks and have only one bulldozer available, we shall be able to carry out only one activity at a time, resulting in overall delay on the path. The concept is explained diagrammatically in Figures 7.1(a) and 7.1(b).

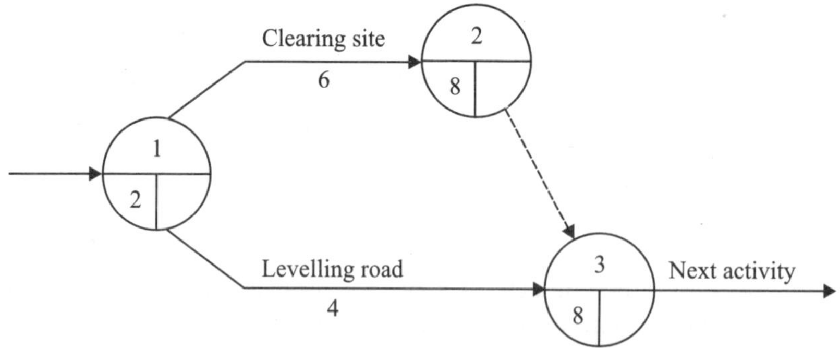

Figure 7.1(a) Network without taking dozer availability into account.

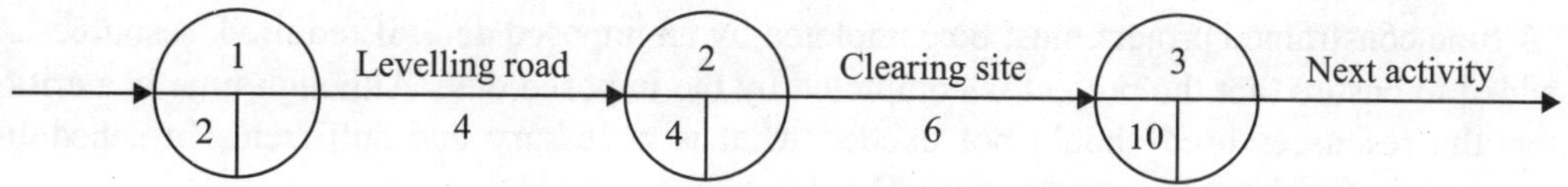

Figure 7.1(b) Network after taking dozer availability into account.

As can be seen, the availability of only one dozer affects the network relationships and the following activities get delayed. We should note that the resource dependency takes priority over the technical dependency but does not violate the technical dependency. This implies that while levelling work on the road and the clearing of the site are done sequentially, they must both be completed before the next activity can start.

The interrelationships between time and resource constraints are very complex, even for a small project. They become doubly so when a number of projects have to be managed. It is important to understand the implications of resource constraints at the planning stage so that realistic time schedules can be worked out. Computer software programmes for project management can carry out resource scheduling and require only resource needs for every activity and resource availability information to schedule resources.

The major resources that project managers have to schedule and manage on an almost daily basis are people, materials, equipment, and working capital. Human resources are required not only by numbers but also by skills. The many different skills that are required on the project add to the complexity of scheduling human resources.

Project materials cover a large spectrum. They may vary from steel and cement for a building project to bitumen and aggregate for a road project or even survey data for a marketing project. Material non-availability and shortages are the cause of project delays. Whenever material is critical, it should be included in the resource schedule. For instance, availability of nuclear fuel, which may be an imported item, is critical to the completion of a nuclear power plant. The cost of the material may dictate that it is procured just in time to avoid storage and other inventory-related costs. The nature of the material may also impose restrictions. If the material has a very short life span, it must be ensured that it is available on time.

Equipment is usually described by type, size and quantity. It is generally reusable and a pool is maintained by the organization for its needs on various projects. It is often assumed that the pool of equipment would suffice and scheduling is not necessary. Nothing is farther from the truth. A project may require a crane for two weeks, six months from now. We may assume that this should pose no problem as the organization has a pool of four cranes. However, it may so transpire that all four cranes are employed elsewhere at the time when required by our project. It is prudent to schedule equipment at the planning stage to avoid high crash costs or delays in the project.

Working capital should be treated as a resource as the availability of funds will determine the amount of activities on which we can work concurrently. Shortage of funds restricts the usage of labour, equipment and materials. The requirements should be planned and cash flows should be arranged accordingly or conversely the activities should be planned according to the availability of funds.

Projects may be resource constrained or time constrained. A resource constrained project is one that assumes that the level of available resources cannot be increased. If the resources are inadequate, delay in the project will be accepted, but it will be kept to the minimum.

A time constrained project must be completed by an imposed date. If required, resources can be added to ensure that the project is completed by the imposed date. Although time is a critical factor, the resources used should not exceed what is necessary and sufficient. In scheduling terms, time is fixed while resources are flexible.

We shall now study the methods of resource allocation. We shall assume that an activity cannot be split. This means that once an activity is started it will not be stopped till its completion. This assumption may not be valid in real life. It may be possible to split an activity and stop and commence it later. It should, however, be remembered that some time shall be spent in the stoppage and resumption of the activity. This may be due to physical shifting of resources or attitudinal adjustment required when a worker shifts midway from one activity to another. We shall make this assumption for ease of understanding the methods of resource allocation. We shall also assume that the level of resources used for an activity cannot be changed.

7.3 TIME CONSTRAINED PROJECTS: RESOURCE LEVELLING

The focus in case of time constrained projects is on resource utilization. An attempt is made to level the utilization of resources by evening out the peaks and troughs of resource demand. This is necessary because it is difficult to manage resources with heavy fluctuations in demand over the project life. In the case of human resources, a policy of hiring and firing will always prove costlier in the long run. The risk of non-availability of manpower with the required skill increases. Extra costs are incurred in hiring and training new manpower as well as on laying off manpower whenever we resort to such measures. Resource levelling is done by delaying activities that have slack available in them. Let us understand the procedure with the help of an example.

EXAMPLE 7.1 Table 7.1 gives a list of activities involved in a project, their duration, their precedence and the requirement of resources. For the sake of simplicity, we are considering only one resource, that is, labour.

Table 7.1 Data for Example 7.1

Activity	*Preceded by*	*Duration*	*Manpower required*
A	Start	3	3
B	Start	2	2
C	B	2	3
D	A	4	2
E	B	3	3
F	D, C	3	3
G	F, E, finish	4	3
H	Start, finish	8	1
I	D, C	6	2

Let us first draw the network, calculate the earliest and latest start and finish times and find the critical activities and the critical path. The network is shown in Figure 7.2. As can be seen, the activities A, D, F and G are critical. The project will take 14 days to complete.

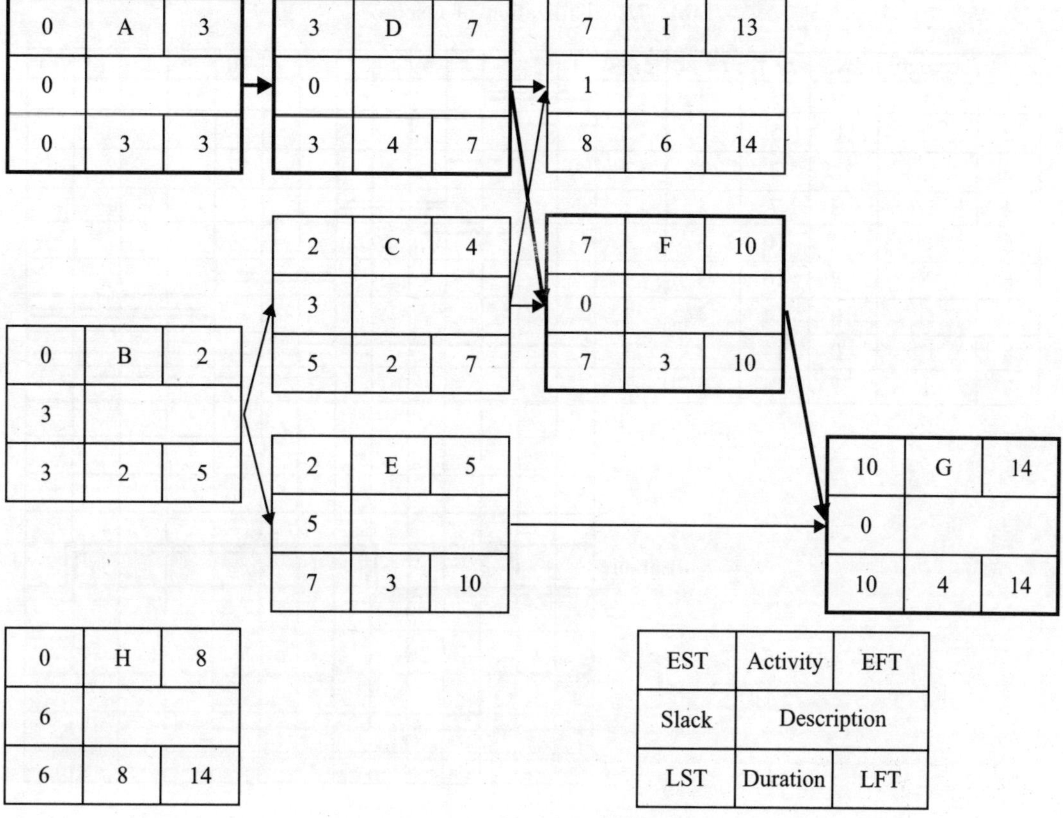

Figure 7.2 Network for Example 7.1.

Now let us tabulate the activities in the descending order of their latest finish times.

The left part of Table 7.2 shows the details of the activities. The right part of the table is a chart showing the number of days. The thick continuous line in the top part of the right side of the table shows the latest finish time of each activity. The critical activities are first filled in. As they have no floats, they start at the earliest start time and finish at the latest finish time. For example, activity A starts on Day 1 and finishes on Day 3. Similarly, activity D starts on Day 4 and finishes on Day 7.

The critical activities are shown by a double line.

The other activities are shown starting at the earliest start time by a thick dashed line. For example, activity H can start on Day 1 earliest and finish on Day 8. Similarly, activity E can start earliest on Day 2 and finish on Day 5.

The lower part of Table 7.2 shows the daily requirement of labour. The first step is to plot the labour requirements for the critical activities, as there is no scope of adjusting these. As activity A takes three days and requires three men, the lower portion of the table shaded in dark grey shows three men being employed for three days. The activity D starts on Day 4 and requires four days to complete. It requires two men. This is also shown in the lower part of the table.

Table 7.2 Utilization of resources

ID	*Activity*	*EST*	*LFT*	*Days*	*Men*	1	2	3	4	5	6	7	8	9	10	11	12	13	14
1	**A**	0	3	3	3														
2	B	0	5	2	2														
3	C	2	7	2	3														
4	**D**	3	7	4	2														
5	E	2	10	3	3														
6	**F**	7	10	3	3														
7	G	10	14	4	3														
8	H	0	14	8	1														
9	I	7	14	6	2														

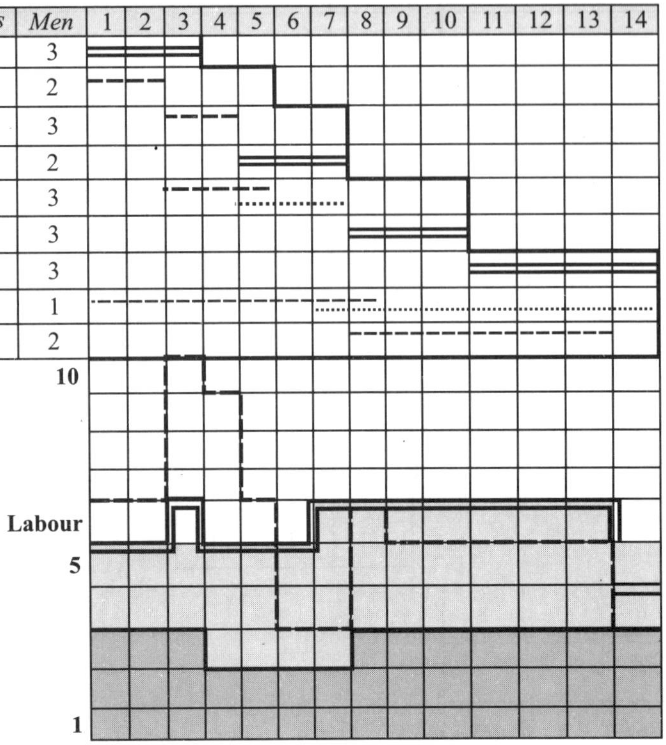

10

Labour

5

1

The daily labour requirement, if all activities start at the earliest start time, is plotted in the single dashed line. For instance, on Day 1, activities A, B and H can be started. A requires three men, B requires two men and H requires one man—a total of six men on Day 1. Similarly, on Day 3, the requirement is 10 men; three for activity A, three for activity C, three for activity E and one for activity H. It may be noted that there are peaks and troughs in the requirement of labour. For instance, six men are required for the first two days, 10 on Day 3, nine on Day 4, six on Day 5, four on Days 6 and 7, six on Day 8, five from Day 9 to Day 13 and three on Day 14.

An attempt must be made to level out the requirement of labour by shifting activities which have some available float in them. If we shift activity E to start on Day 5 and finish on Day 7, and shift activity H to start on Day 7 and finish on Day 14, the requirements of labour are depicted by the continuous double line on the table. It may be noted that the peak requirement of 10 has been reduced to six. If six men are employed continuously, the project can be completed on time with seven man days going idle.

It may be possible to make such 'trial and error' adjustments in a very small project. When projects are large and involve a number of resources, such manual adjustments may not be possible. The optimal combination can be found on the basis of 'least sum of squares'. This implies that the sum of squares of the number of men required per day should be the least. Even with computers it is generally impossible to enumerate all answers and arrive at the sum of least squares. A heuristic approach is followed. Software packages which can handle resource levelling are available today.

Computer printouts of the same example as solved by Microsoft Project 2007 are given in Figures 7.3(a) to (f). Figures 7.3(a) and (b) show the Gantt charts before and after levelling. It may be noticed that the schedule of activities E and H have been shifted. Though the earliest start time for activity E is 17 December, in the levelled network it has been shifted to start on 19 December. Two days of float available in the activity have been utilized. Similarly, though the earliest start time for activity H is 15 December, the activity is scheduled to start on 18 December. Three days of the available slack have been utilized. Figures. 7.3(c) and (d) show the network before and after levelling. Figures 7.3(e) and (f) show the utilization of resources before and after levelling. It may be noticed that the peak requirement of Days 3 and 4 has been reduced and the troughs of demand on Days 6 and 7 have been filled up. Compare the graph of resource utilization in Figures 7.3(e) and (f) with Table 7.2. There is no difference in the utilization of resources before levelling, but the solutions for the resource utilization after levelling are different. This is because there can be many feasible solutions to the problem. Activity E has been shifted by two days in both cases but in the manual solution activity H has been shifted by six days, whereas in the computer solution it has been shifted by three days. Even a computer does not carry out full enumeration and uses heuristics to solve the problem. Heuristic solutions are 'quick and dirty' methods following 'rules of thumb' approach to get a 'good' workable solution even though it may not be the optimal solution. For example, in this case, if the 'sum of least squares' criteria is applied to both the solutions, the sum of squares for the manual solution is lesser than that of the solution worked out by the computer by four units. This is not of much consequence. It may be noticed that in both cases when only six people are employed, there is an underutilization of seven man days. The problem becomes more complex when the number of resources increases and when levelling has to be done across a number of projects. Tackling large problems manually becomes infeasible and computer software is used to provide solutions.

7.4 RESOURCE CONSTRAINED PROJECTS

When the resources—people, material, equipment or working capital—are not adequate, the situation is resource constrained and levelling has to be done with constraints on the resources. The project is likely to be delayed but we should ensure that the delay is minimal. The resource scheduling problem offers a large number of combinations and permutations and a mathematical solution is impractical because of the massive data requirements. Heuristics offers the best approach. Since the objective is to minimize project delay, activities are prioritized heuristically when the resources are inadequate. The following priority rules to schedule activities consistently minimize project delays and are widely used by computer software:

1. Schedule activities with minimum slack.
2. If activities have the same slack, schedule activities according to their duration with the smaller duration activity being scheduled before the one with a longer duration.
3. In case the activities have the same slack and the same duration, schedule them according to their identification number.

ID		Task Name	Duration	Start	Finish	Predecessors
1		A	3 days	Wed 15-12-10	Fri 17-12-10	
2		B	2 days	Wed 15-12-10	Thu 16-12-10	
3		C	2 days	Fri 17-12-10	Sat 18-12-10	2
4		D	4 days	Sat 18-12-10	Tue 21-12-10	1
5		E	3 days	Fri 17-12-10	Sun 19-12-10	2
6		F	3 days	Wed 22-12-10	Fri 24-12-10	3,4
7		G	4 days	Sat 25-12-10	Tue 28-12-10	5,6
8		H	8 days	Wed 15-12-10	Wed 22-12-10	
9		I	6 days	Wed 22-12-10	Mon 27-12-10	3,4

'10 | 20 Dec '10 | 27 Dec '10
T W T F S S M T W T F S S M T W T

LABOUR[3]
LABOUR[2]
LABOUR[3]
LABOUR[2]
LABOUR[3]
LABOUR[3]
LABOUR[3]
LABOUR
LABOUR[2]

Project: Project1
Date: Thu 09-12-10

Task
Critical Task
Progress
Milestone
Summary
Rolled Up Task
Rolled Up Critical Task
Rolled Up Milestone
Rolled Up Progress
Split
External Tasks
Project Summary
Group By Summary
Deadline

Figure 7.3(a) Gantt chart before levelling.

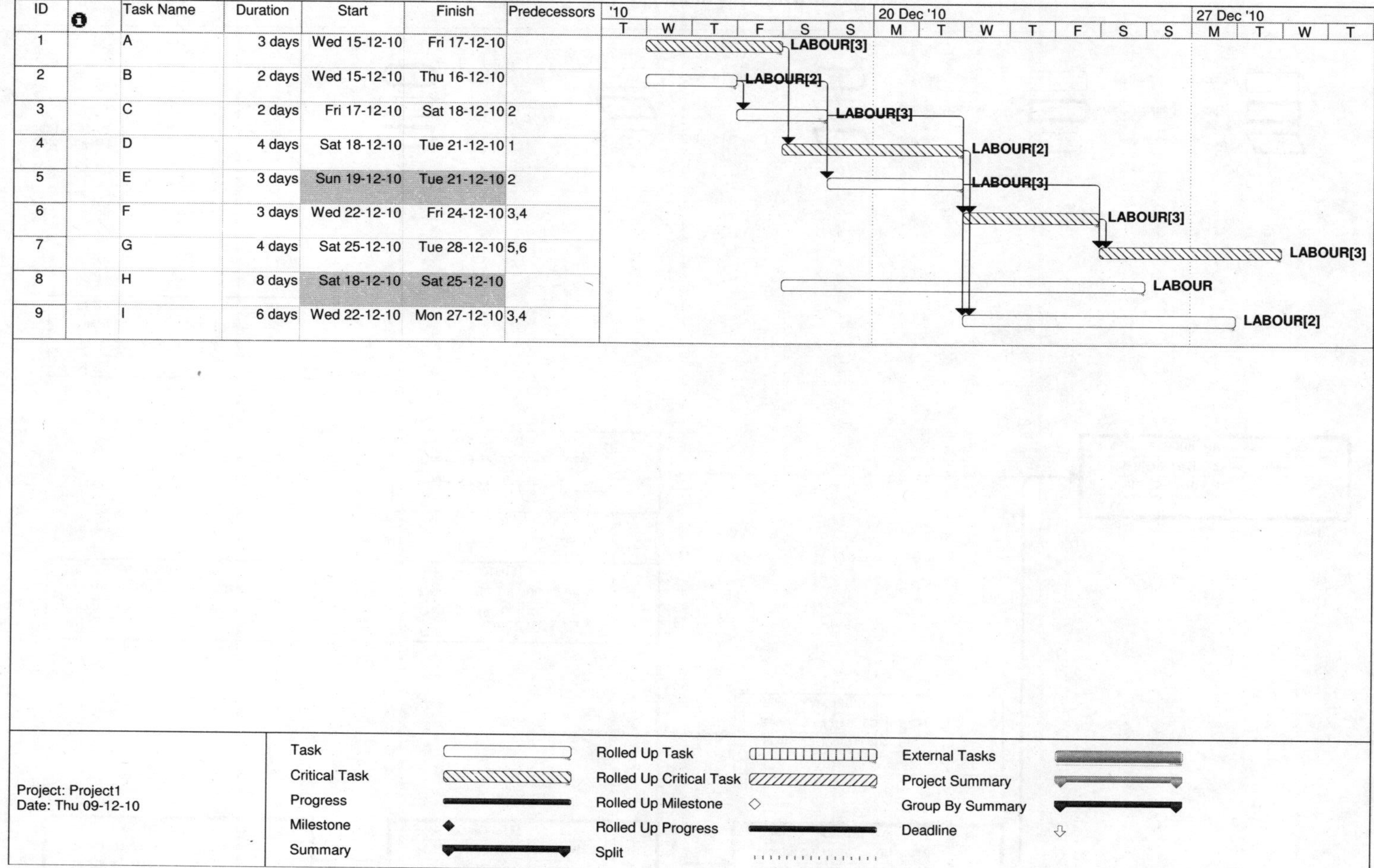

ID	Task Name	Duration	Start	Finish	Predecessors
1	A	3 days	Wed 15-12-10	Fri 17-12-10	
2	B	2 days	Wed 15-12-10	Thu 16-12-10	
3	C	2 days	Fri 17-12-10	Sat 18-12-10	2
4	D	4 days	Sat 18-12-10	Tue 21-12-10	1
5	E	3 days	Sun 19-12-10	Tue 21-12-10	2
6	F	3 days	Wed 22-12-10	Fri 24-12-10	3,4
7	G	4 days	Sat 25-12-10	Tue 28-12-10	5,6
8	H	8 days	Sat 18-12-10	Sat 25-12-10	
9	I	6 days	Wed 22-12-10	Mon 27-12-10	3,4

Figure 7.3(b) Gantt chart after levelling.

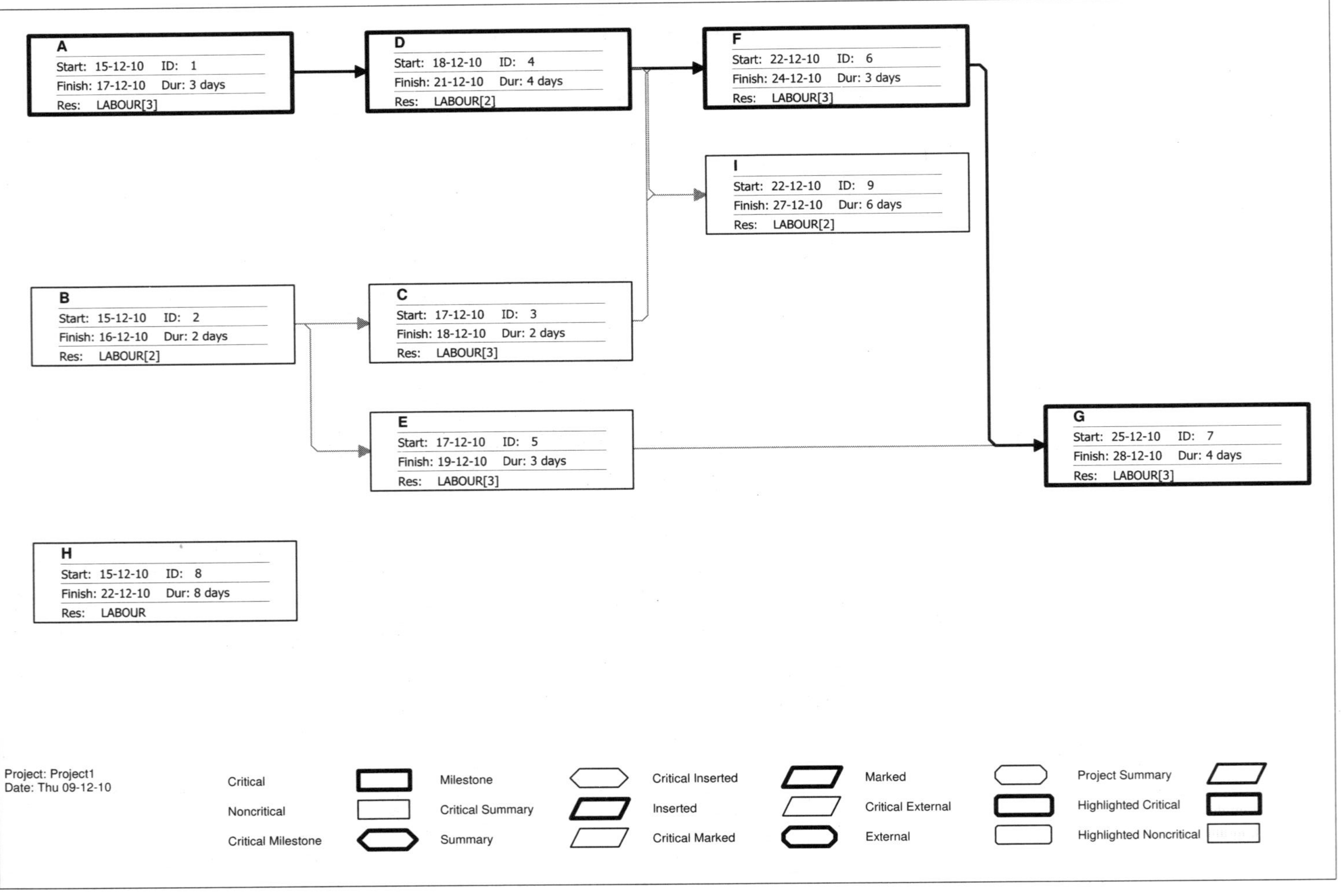

Figure 7.3(c) Network before levelling.

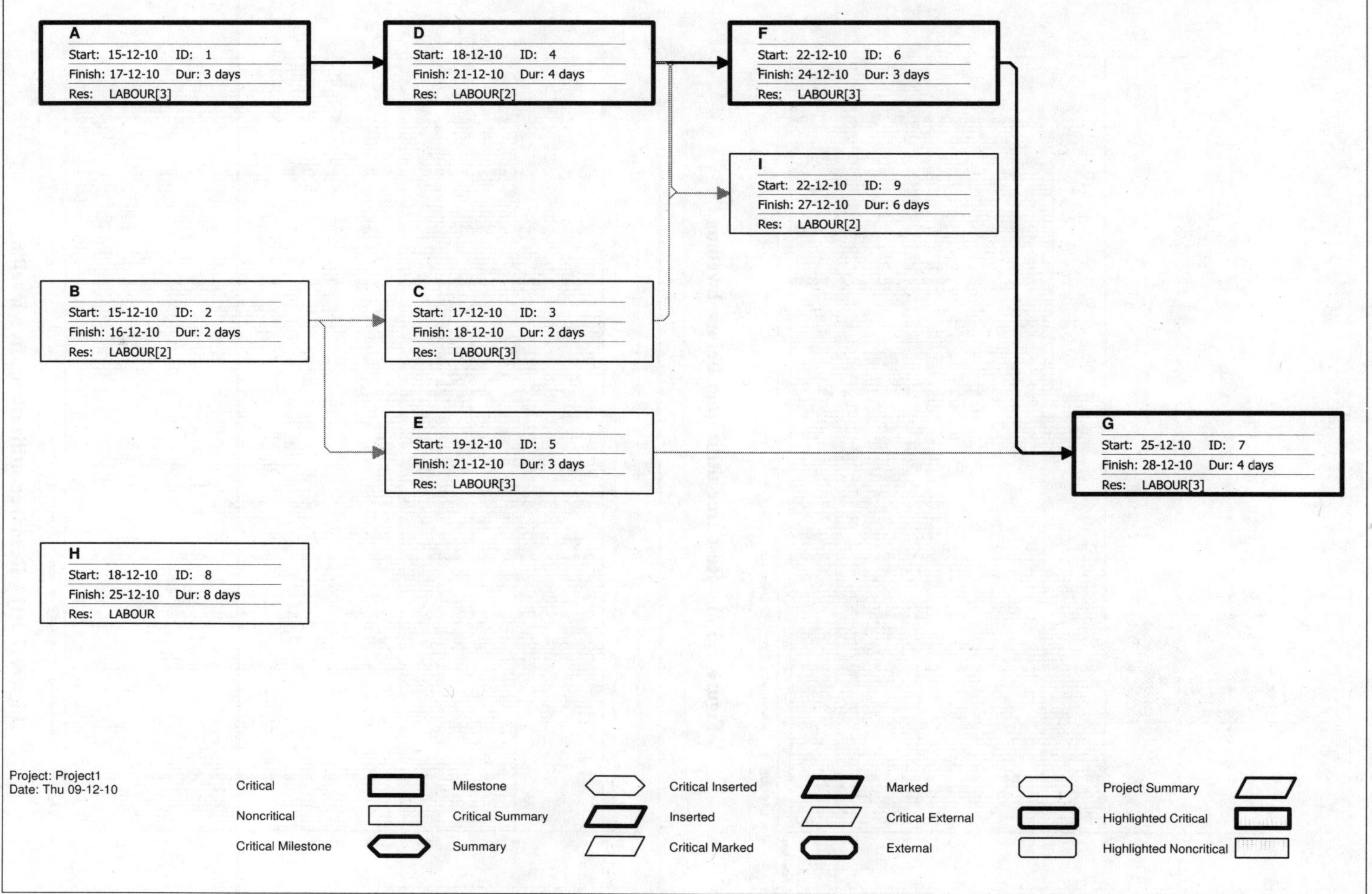

Figure 7.3(d) Network after levelling.

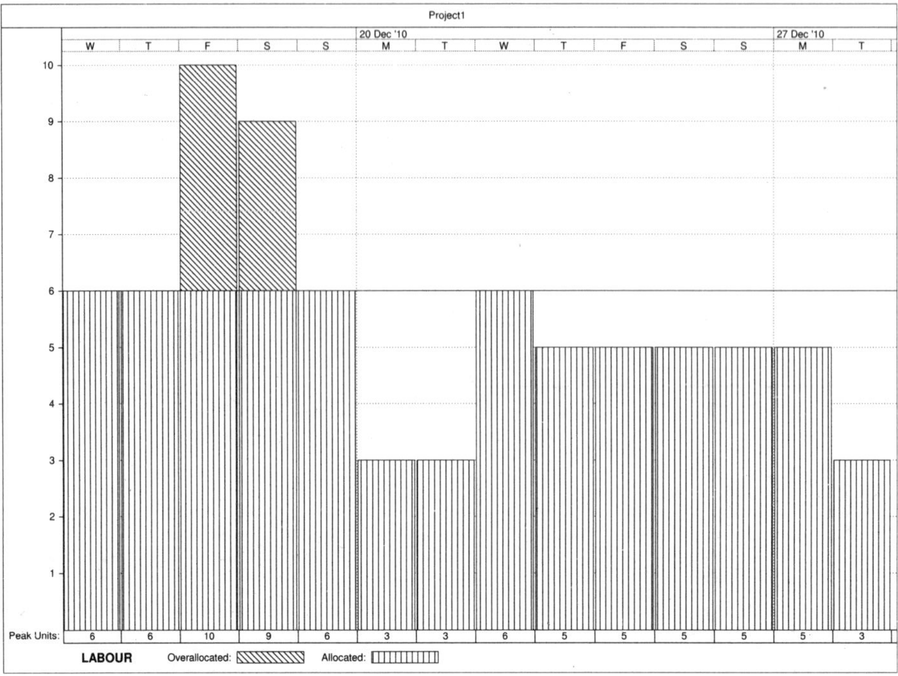

Figure 7.3(e) Resource utilization before levelling.

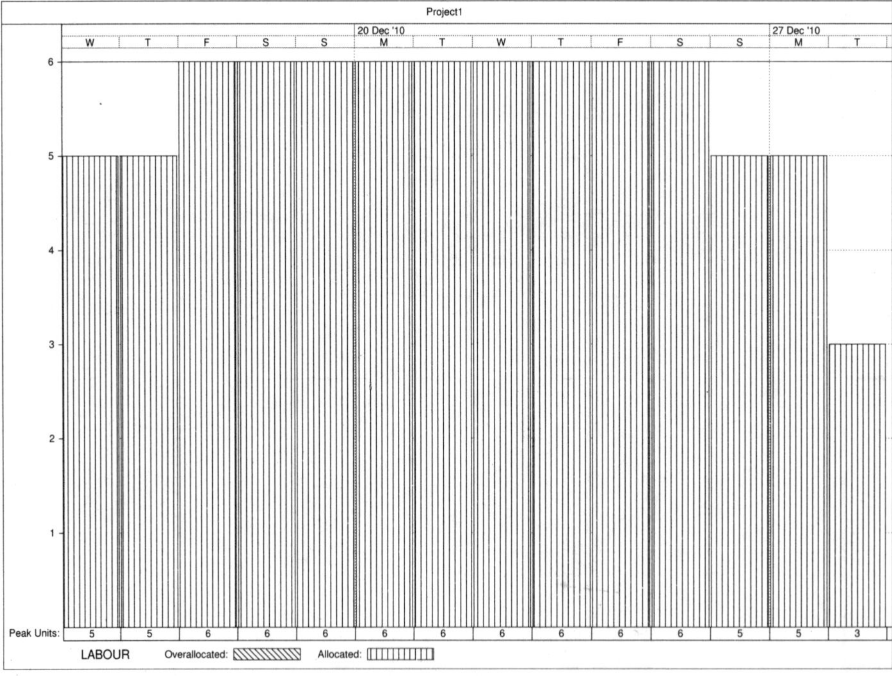

Figure 7.3(f) Resource utilization after levelling.

The most widely used method to apply heuristics is the parallel method. The iterative process starts with the first time period and schedules activities that are eligible to start, period by period. When two or more activities require resources in the same period, the priority rules are applied. Let us understand the methodology with the help of an example. We shall use the data given in Example 7.1 with the added information that only five persons are available for employment on the project. Table 7.3 shows the resource allocation with the resource constraint of only five persons available. Table 7.4 is self-explanatory and shows how allocation is made each day and the delay that occurs. As may be seen, the project is completed in 19 days instead of 14 days as per the earlier schedule without resource constraints.

Table 7.3 Resource allocation with resource constraints

ID	*EST*	*LFT*	*Dn*	*Men*	*Slack*	1	2	3	4	5	6	7	8	9	10	11	12	13	14	15	16	17	18	19
A	0	3	3	3	0	3	3	3																
B	0	5	2	2	3	2	2																	
C	2	7	2	3	3			X	X	X	X	X	**3**	**3**										
D	3	7	4	2	0				2	2	2	2												
E	2	10	3	3	5			X	X	X	X	X	X	X	X	X	X	**3**	**3**	**3**				
F	7	10	3	3	0								X	X	3	**3**	**3**							
G	10	14	4	3	0											X	X	X	X	X	**3**	**3**	**3**	**3**
H	0	14	8	1	6	X	X	1	1	1	1	1	1	**1**	**1**									
I	7	14	6	2	1								X	X	X	2	2	2	2	2	2			
Total resource load						5	5	4	3	3	3	3	4	4	4	5	5	5	5	5	5	3	3	3
Total resource available						5	5	5	5	5	5	5	5	5	5	5	5	5	5	5	5	5	5	5

Earliest start time schedule   Slack available   Delay

Table 7.4 Iterative process for resource allocation

Day	*Activity that can be scheduled*			*Action*		*Remarks*
	ID	*Resource requirement*	*Slack*	*Scheduled or delayed*	*Balance slack*	
1	A	3	0	S		
	B	2	3	S		
	H	1	6	D	5	
2	A	3	0	S		
	B	2	*	S		Work started
	H	1	5	D	4	
3	A	3	0	S		
	C	3	3	D	2	Availability exceeded
	E	3	5	D	4	
	H	1	4	S		
4	C	3	2	D	1	
	D	2	0	S		

* Since the work is started the slack is immaterial.

(*Contd...*)

Table 7.4 Iterative process for resource allocation (*Contd...*)

Day	*Activity that can be scheduled*			*Action*		*Remarks*
	ID	*Resource requirement*	*Slack*	*Scheduled or delayed*	*Balance slack*	
	E	3	4	D	3	
	H	1	*	S		
5	C	3	1	D	0	
	D	2	*	S		
	E	3	3	D	2	
	H	1	*	S		
6	C	3	0	D	0	
	D	2	*	S		
	E	3	2	D	1	
	H	1	*	S		
7	C	3	0	D	0	
	D	2	*	S		
	E	3	1	D	0	
	H	1	*	S		
8	C	3	0	S	0	
	E	3	0	D	–1	
	F	3	0	D	–1	F depends on C and D
	H	1	*	S		
	I	2	1	D	0	
9	C	3	0	S	0	
	E	3	–1	D	–2	
	F	3	–1	D	–2	F depends on C and D
	H	1	*	S		
	I	2	0	D	–1	
10	E	3	–2	D	–3	
	F	3	–2	S		
	H	1	*	S		
	I	2	–1	D	–2	
11	E	3	–3	D	–4	
	F	3	0	S		
	G	3	0	D	–1	G depends on E and F
	I	2	–2	S		
12	E	3	–4	D	–5	
	F	3	0	S		
	G	3	0	D	–2	G depends on E and F
	I	2	–2	S		
13	E	3	–5	S		
	G	3	–2	D	–3	G depends on E and F
	I	2	–2	S		
14	E	3	–5	S		
	G	3	–3	D	–4	G depends on E and F
	I	2	–2	S		

(*Contd...*)

Table 7.4 Iterative process for resource allocation (*Contd*...)

Day	*Activity that can be scheduled*			*Action*		*Remarks*
	ID	*Resource requirement*	*Slack*	*Scheduled or delayed*	*Balance slack*	
15	E	3	–5	S		
	G	3	–4	D	–5	G depends on E and F
	I	2	–2	S		
16	G	3	–5	S		
	I	2	–2	S		
17	G	3	–5	S		
18	G	3	–5	S		
19	G	3	–5	S		

* denotes that slack is immaterial since the work has started.

The resource scheduling graph and network as drawn by MS Project after resource utilization are as shown in Figure 7.4(a) and Figure 7.4(b) respectively. The solution is the same as the manual allocations.

It may be noted that the critical activities have changed because of the resource constraints. Activities B, E and G are now critical. The technical or logical constraints are maintained and modified due to the resource constraints.

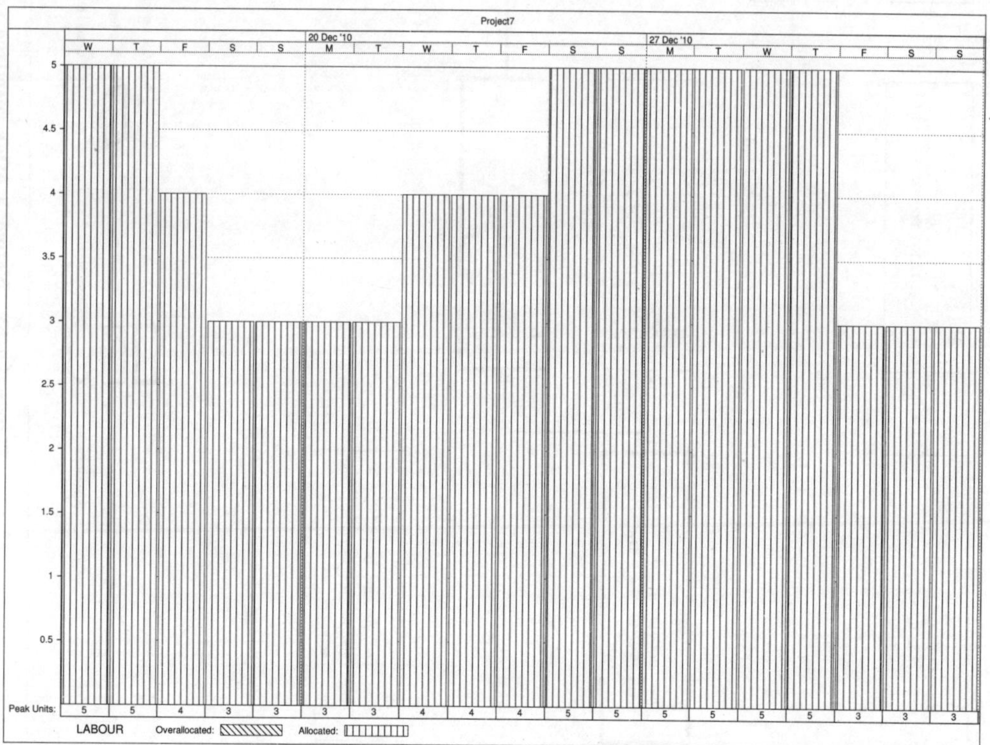

Figure 7.4(a) Resource utilization.

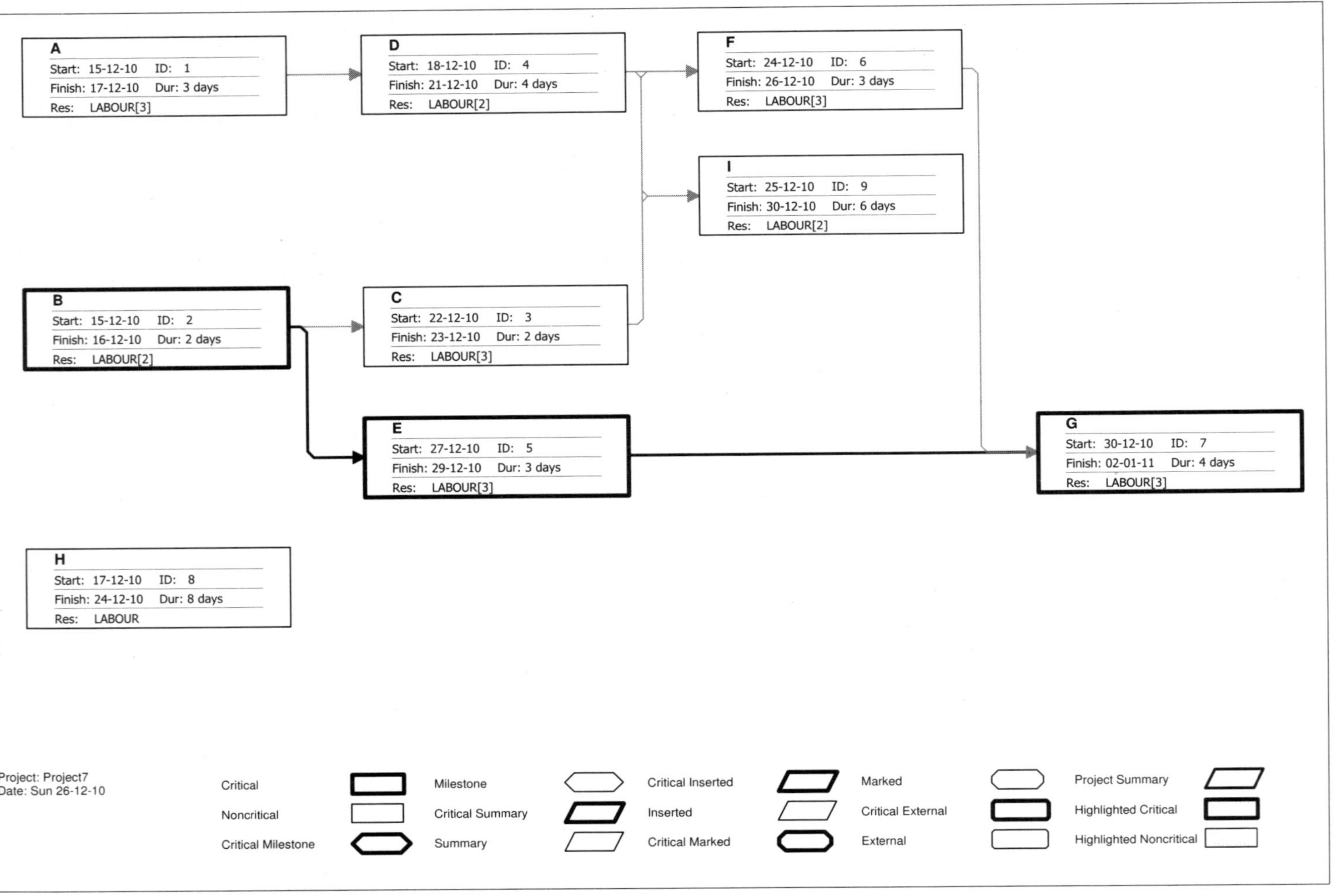

Figure 7.4(b) Network after resource scheduling (five persons available).

7.5 WORKING CAPITAL MANAGEMENT

Just as we considered delaying activities to achieve resource levelling, the project manager has the option of starting all activities at their earliest start times at one extreme and starting them at their latest start times at the other extreme. This will afford the manager flexibility in planning cash flows. Let us consider the above example and add costs for each activity to our original list as shown in Table 7.5.

Table 7.5

Activity	*Preceded by*	*Duration*	*Manpower required*	*Cost per day*
A	Start	3	3	3000
B	Start	2	2	2000
C	B	2	3	3000
D	A	4	2	2000
E	B	3	3	3000
F	D, C	3	3	3000
G	F, E, finish	4	3	3000
H	Start, finish	8	1	1000
I	D, C	6	2	2000

We have already calculated earliest start times and latest start times. Table 7.6 shows the earliest schedule. The daily costs and cumulative costs (000s) are shown at the bottom of the table.

Table 7.6 Daily costs and cumulative costs with earliest schedule

S. No.	*Activity*	*EST*	*LFT*	*Cost/day*	1	2	3	4	5	6	7	8	9	10	11	12	13	14
1	A	0	3	3000														
2	B	0	5	2000														
3	C	2	7	3000														
4	D	3	7	2000														
5	E	2	10	3000														
6	F	7	10	3000														
7	G	10	14	3000														
8	H	0	14	1000														
9	I	7	14	2000														
Daily costs					6	6	10 0	9	6	3	3	6	5	5	5	5	5	3
Cumulative costs					6	12	22	31	33	40	43	49	54	59	64	69	74	77

If we were now to start all activities at the latest time possible, we would get the profile as shown in Table 7.7.

Table 7.7 Daily costs and cumulative costs with latest time schedule

S. No.	Activity	*EST*	*LFT*	*Cost/day*	1	2	3	4	5	6	7	8	9	10	11	12	13	14
1	A	0	3	3000														
2	B	0	5	2000														
3	C	2	7	3000														
4	D	3	7	2000														
5	E	2	10	3000														
6	F	7	10	3000														
7	G	10	14	3000														
8	H	0	14	1000														
9	I	7	14	2000														
Daily costs					3	3	3	4	4	5	6	7	9	9	6	6	6	6
Cumulative costs					3	6	9	13	17	22	28	35	44	53	59	65	71	77

Let us now prepare the cost profiles. The cumulative cost at the end of Day 6 is ₹ 40,000 if the earliest schedule is followed and only ₹ 22,000 if the latest schedule is followed. Figure 7.5 gives the accumulated costs for early start of activities and late start of activities.

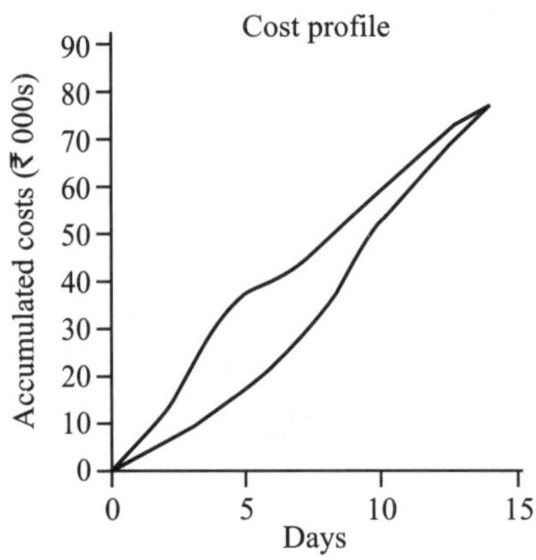

Figure 7.5 Accumulated costs for early start and late start of activities.

The graph permits us to plan our activities according to our cash flows or manage our cash flows according to our schedules. This is also referred to as PERT/Cost analysis. The WinQSB software carries out PERT/Cost analysis and can generate the PERT/Cost graph. The graph for this data is in Figure 7.6.

Resource scheduling attempts to level resources or work within constrained resources. This often reduces slacks in order to minimize delays and may increase the number of critical activities. Complexities increase when the technical constraints are combined with resource

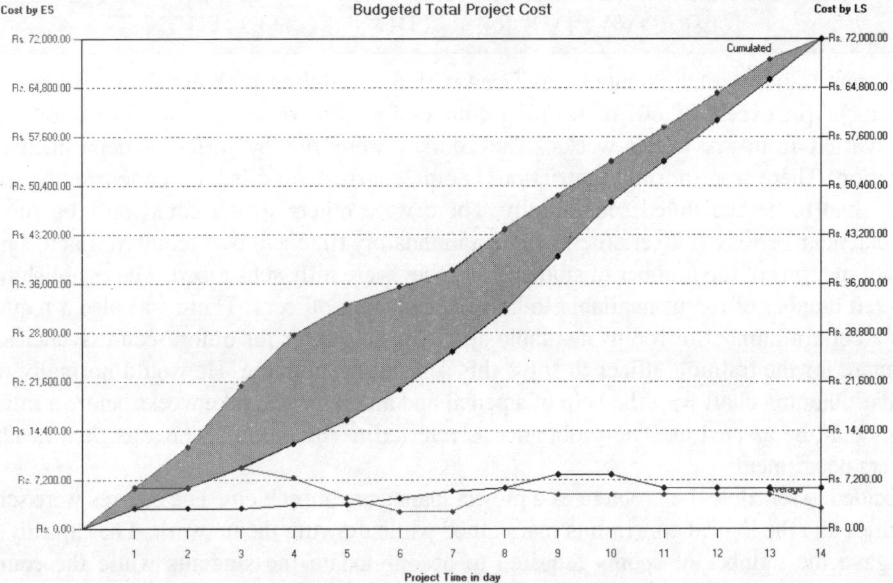

Figure 7.6 PERT/Cost graph.

constraints. If resources are truly limited and activity time estimates are reasonably accurate, a resource constrained schedule will materialize as the project progresses rather than a time constrained schedule. If resource scheduling is done before the start of the project, we can consider suitable alternatives if delay is unacceptable. Cost–time trade-offs can be considered or in some cases priorities may undergo changes.

Resource scheduling across multi-projects increases the complexity of the problem. While the principles illustrated in the foregoing discussion apply to the multi-project environment, the task of allocating and reallocating resources poses a managerial challenge. Interdependencies amongst projects will have to be established and kept in mind while scheduling resources. The most commonly encountered problems are slippages in overall schedule, inefficient utilization of resources and resource bottlenecks.

SUMMARY

Allocation of resources is a major planning activity. Projects are affected by technical constraints, physical constraints and resource constraints. The technical or logical constraints are taken care of while scheduling activities with the help of CPM or PERT networks. Physical constraints are dealt with in the same manner as resource constraints. Resources pose a problem as they may not be adequate or they may not be available when required.

A project in which time delays are not acceptable is a time constrained project. In such projects, resource levelling aims at smoothening out the peaks and troughs of resource demand, by rescheduling some non-critical activities within the slacks that exist in them.

A project where resources are limited is a resource constrained project. Resource scheduling aims to complete the project within the available resources with as little delay as possible.

INNOVATIVE RESOURCE SCHEDULING

A large army training establishment was faced with a scheduling problem. It was running a very large number (in excess of 60) of training courses for officers every year. The duration of the courses varied from six to 10 weeks. The courses were run by different departments in the organization. There were normal restrictions. Some courses could be run concurrently; others of necessity had to be scheduled sequentially. There were others which could only be run during certain calendar periods and yet others where a mandatory time gap was required. Each course had a capacity in terms of the number of students and they were fully subscribed. The establishment had a restricted number of rooms available to house the student officers. There was also a requirement to keep a certain number of rooms available at all times to cater for unforeseen exigencies. It was a nightmare for the training officer to solve this scheduling problem. He would normally work on a calendar planning chart with the help of a pencil and an eraser and take weeks before a satisfactory solution could be arrived at. The problem was referred to the author, who was then heading the computers department.

I decided to schedule the problem as a project management problem. The courses were scheduled as activities and the logical constraints maintained while drawing the network. The capacity of each course gave the number of rooms required to accommodate the students while the course was running. I treated the number of rooms required for each course as a resource and then carried out resource levelling as the total number of rooms available was known. Computer software 'Prism' (a DOS-based project management software from Tata Consultancy Service) was used and a schedule was produced in less than an hour. The schedule was better than any produced earlier as it left more spare rooms throughout the year than had ever been achieved through manual programming.

The example just reiterates that operations research is a problem-solving approach limited only by the ingenuity of the user, and not just a set of techniques.

Computer software packages designed for project management solve resource levelling problems through heuristic methods.

A failure to schedule resources can lead to project time and cost overruns. If resource scheduling is done at the project planning stage, it gives the project manager an opportunity to consider alternate solutions and reduces the uncertainty faced by him/her. The problem is compounded if resources have to be managed over multiple projects.

We have so far discussed the network approach to planning using conventional network techniques such as CPM and PERT. In 1997, Eliyahu Goldratt advocated the 'critical chain approach' to project management based on his 'theory of constraints'. For a brief introduction to the critical chain approach, readers may refer to the appendix 'Critical Chain Scheduling and Buffer Management' given at the end of Chapter 6.

QUESTIONS

1. Explain why resource scheduling is an important task.
2. How does resource scheduling reduce flexibility in managing a project?
3. What is the difference between a time constrained project and a resource constrained project?

4. How do the objectives of resource scheduling differ in the case of a time constrained project and a resource constrained project?
5. The table below gives the details of project activities, their precedence, duration and labour requirements.

Activity	*Predecessor*	*Duration*	*Resource*
A	—	3	Carpenter
B	—	5	Carpenter
C	—	4	Electrician
D	A	2	Carpenter
E	D	7	Electrician
F	B	3	Electrician
G	C	5	Carpenter

(a) Draw the project network and find the duration of the project and critical activities.
(b) Assume only one carpenter and one electrician are available. Give the resources schedule, compute early, late and slack times for your project. What is the new project duration and what are the project activities?

6. Details of a project are as follows:

Activity	*Predecessor*	*Duration*	*Labour*
A	—	5	1
B	—	6	2
C	A	5	2
D	A, B	6	1
E	B	4	2
F	C, D, E	3	2

Three labourers are available. Develop a resource schedule using the parallel method and the heuristic rules given in Section 7.4.

7. Details of a project are given as follows:

Activity	*Predecessor*	*Duration (months)*	*Bulldozer*
A	—	1	1
B	—	2	1
C	—	3	1
D	A, B	2	1
E	B, C	4	2
F	D, E	2	2

You have three bulldozers available with you. You receive a call from your corporate office that one dozer is urgently required for another project. You must complete your project in 11 months. Is it possible for you to complete the project in 11 months with two dozers? Prepare a resources schedule.

CHAPTER 8

Risk Management

If you don't attack the risks, the risks will attack you. —Stephan Seay

LEARNING OBJECTIVES

After reading this chapter, you will be able to:

- Understand risks inherent in projects.
- Explain the steps in risk management.
- Study the methods employed for risk identification and risk analysis.
- Study strategies for risk response.
- Examine the need for risk monitoring and control and management of change.

8.1 INTRODUCTION

Risks are inherent in projects and no amount of planning can completely eliminate them. Risk is due to the uncertainty present in projects. A project risk is an uncertain event or condition that, if occurs, has a positive or negative effect on at least one aspect of the project, that is, time, cost, scope or quality. Risks may be foreseeable such as equipment failures or entirely beyond control such as natural calamities, man-made events like a terrorist strike and so on. Risk management identifies as many potential risks as possible (what can go wrong), minimizes their impact by doing whatever can be done before they occur to mitigate their effect and makes contingency plans to deal with risks that actually occur, so that time and cost overruns on projects are avoided.

Risks are more likely to occur in the initial phases of a project. For instance, the risk of a faulty design, incorrect estimates, incorrect scheduling and so on will occur at the planning and initiation phases. The cost of dealing with these risks, if detected and responded at these early stages, is low. However, if the same risks are not foreseen earlier and the event actually occurs at a later stage, the cost of dealing with them increases considerably. Consider a situation where design flaws are detected after a prototype is ready. The rectification of the design at such a late stage will involve considerable costs and delays in the overall project. Figure 8.1 shows the relationship between risks, costs and time. It is imperative that risks are managed properly.

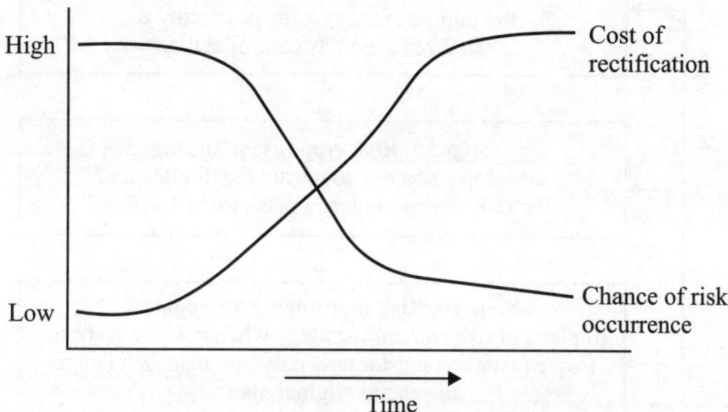

Figure 8.1 Risk and cost relationship.

The sources of risk may be external or internal. External risks such as inflation, fluctuations in demand, exchange rates and so on are normally taken into account when selecting a project for implementation. The external risks are also referred to as threats. Some contingency provisions are made to deal with such risks.

Risk management is a proactive approach rather than a reactive approach. It aims at preventing the negative effects of risks. It also prepares the management to take risks when advantageous fleeting opportunities present themselves. Successful management of risk gives the project manager better control over the project enabling him to achieve the project goals within the time frame and budget allotted while conforming to the qualitative requirements.

8.2 RISK MANAGEMENT PROCESS

The risk management process involves risk identification, risk analysis (both qualitative and quantitative), risk response planning and risk monitoring and control. Figure 8.2 shows the risk management process schematically.

8.3 RISK IDENTIFICATION

The first step in the risk management process is risk identification. It aims at determining which risks may affect the project and documents their characteristics. A list is made of all the possible risks in the project. Typically a risk management team is formed consisting of members from each core group and the stakeholders. The team first identifies the risks which will affect the overall project. The team must be encouraged to keep an open mind and identify as many risks

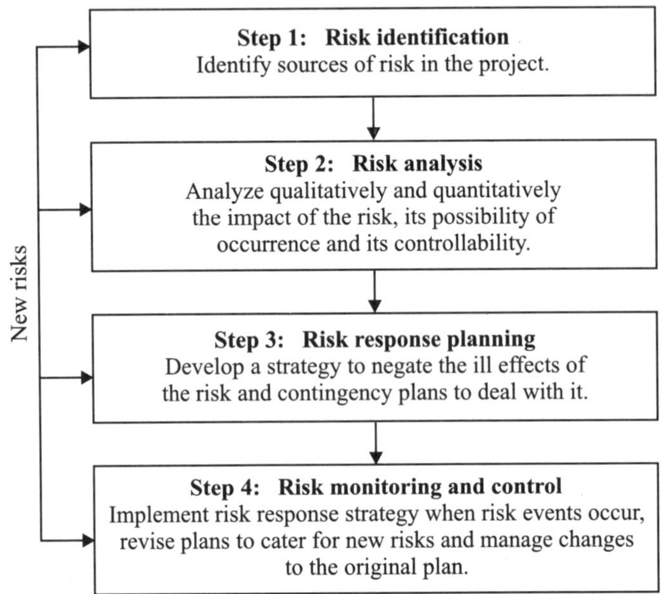

Figure 8.2 Risk management process.

as possible. Attitudinally, the team should believe in the Murphy's law—"What can go wrong, will go wrong." At this stage, the team should avoid being judgemental and should list all risks no matter how preposterous they may appear or how unlikely to occur they may appear. Some of the methods that the team can use to help them with their task are given in the following paragraphs.

Documentation reviews

The team should review all documents. It should study the project definition in detail and also the assumptions made for the project. The assumptions may or may not be valid and may be a source of risk for the project.

Information gathering techniques

The team can resort to information gathering techniques like brainstorming, Delphi technique, interviewing, root cause identification and SWOT analysis. A common mistake in risk identification is to focus on consequences and not on the events that produce these consequences. For instance, the team may identify failure to meet a particular deadline as a risk. They need to focus on the events which will cause a delay in meeting the deadline—inadequate working capital, or inadequate availability of a seasonal raw material input and so on. A focus on such events will result in potential solutions to the risk.

Checklist analysis

A checklist is a list of questions regarding the traditional areas of uncertainty on a project. The checklists can be developed based on historical data or knowledge that has been accumulated from previous experience on similar projects. It may even be obtained from other sources like project consultancy services and so on. It should also be appreciated that the checklist for all projects will not be the same. A checklist prepared for a software development project will be quite different from one prepared for a new car project. The risks associated with projects vary according to the nature of the project.

Assumptions analysis

All projects are based on a set of hypotheses, scenarios and assumptions. Assumptions analysis aims at studying the validity of the assumptions and the risk they offer because of their inaccuracy, incompleteness and inconsistency.

Diagramming techniques

The team may also use diagramming techniques like the cause and effect diagram, system and process flow charts and influence diagrams.

After the overall risks are identified, the risks associated with various activities can be studied in detail. The work breakdown structure (WBS) can form the basis of carrying out risk identification at the micro level, so that at the planning stage no risks are overlooked.

8.4 RISK ANALYSIS

Risk identification produces a list of all possible risks that may occur on a project. Some of these risks may be trivial in nature while others may be more important. The next step is to carry out a risk analysis and prioritize them so that suitable response can be designed. A qualitative analysis is first carried out and risks are prioritized. This is followed by a quantitative analysis of the high priority risks. A commonly used method for quantitative analysis is the scenario analysis in which the team assesses each risk in terms of:

1. The undesirable event
2. All the outcomes of the event's occurrence
3. The chance or probability that the event will occur
4. The magnitude of the impact of the event on the project
5. When the event might occur in the project
6. Its interrelationship with other parts of this project or other projects being undertaken by the organization
7. The ability to detect the event before its occurrence

The results of this analysis are normally tabulated in risk assessment forms. While there is no standard format, organizations design forms to suit their requirements. Let us consider the case of an information system project involving conversion of manual system to a computer-based automated system. Some of the risks may be user interface problems, database failure, hardware failure, user resistance to change and so on. A skeleton risk assessment form listing these risks is shown in Table 8.1.

The likelihood, impact and detection difficulty are arbitrarily rated on a scale of 1 to 5, with 1 being the least and 5 being the highest value on the scale.

Table 8.1 Risk assessment form

Risk event	*Likelihood*	*Impact*	*Detection difficulty*	*When*
Interface problems	3	4	4	Conversion
Database failure	3	4	5	System testing
Hardware failure	1	5	5	Installation
User resistance	4	3	3	Post-implementation

Risks are also prioritized using a probability and impact matrix. A typical probability impact matrix is shown in Figure 8.3. The matrix is divided into zones representing minor, moderate and major risks. The major zone is centred on the top right-hand corner, i.e. high impact and high likelihood of occurrence, while the minor zone is centred on the bottom left hand corner. The impact is considered more important than the likelihood. For instance, a 10% probability of losing ₹ 1,00,000 is rated higher than a 90% probability of losing ₹ 1000.

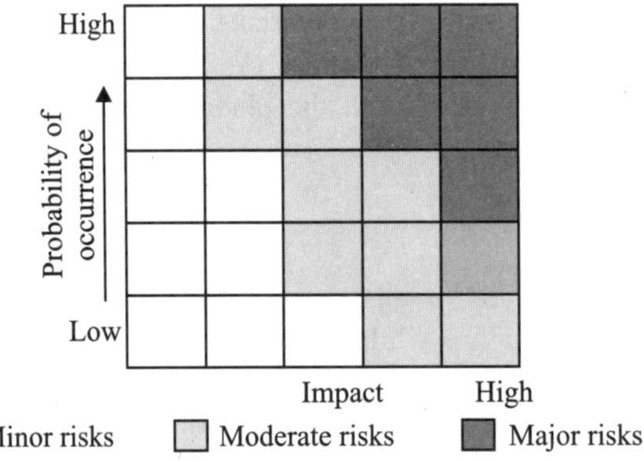

Figure 8.3 Probability impact matrix.

The risk impact matrix provides the basis for prioritization of risks. The major risks are priority one risks, followed by moderate risks and then minor risks.

8.4.1 Failure Mode and Effects Analysis

This is just an extension of the probability impact matrix. The ease of detection is included in the matrix.

$$\text{Risk value} = \text{Impact} \times \text{Probability} \times \text{Detection}$$

Each of the three dimensions is rated on a 5 point scale. The weightage of risks is then based on their risk value.

The high priority risks can be analyzed further by using quantitative techniques. Decision analysis using decision trees and decision matrix can be used to analyze risk. Probabilities are assigned to the occurrence of various events and the expected value criterion is used for evaluating risk. Another technique commonly used is simulation. Various scenarios can be simulated and risk assessment can be carried out. PERT also takes uncertainty into account by using three time estimates. Being a stochastic or probabilistic model, PERT simulation can also be carried out. The standard deviation and the mean time for each activity can be laid down and then the duration of each activity can be simulated using Monte Carlo simulation. Project durations and costs can be worked out. The impact of various risks can be assessed. Assessment of risk is the base for designing risk response.

Sensitivity analysis helps to determine which risks have the most impact on the project. It examines the extent to which each uncertain element affects the project when all other uncertain elements are held constant at their base level. Sensitivity analysis can be carried out to examine impact on different aspects of the project like time, cost, scope and quality.

Let us examine the quantitative methods for risk analysis with the help of an example.

EXAMPLE 8.1 During the construction of a bridge over a river, the soil conditions necessitate the use of a special boring machine, with which the company has little experience. If the machine is not operated properly, it is likely to be damaged. The damage to the machine will result in delay of the project and extra costs will be involved in repair of the machine. The damage to the machine may be to the tune of ₹ 2,00,000 with a probability of 0.20 and ₹ 5,00,000 with a probability of 0.10. There is also a remote probability of 0.01 that the machine may suffer irreparable damage and it may have to be written off. The machine costs ₹ 15,00,000. There shall be a setback of four to six weeks if the machine gets damaged. The task can be executed by outsourcing it to a company that specializes in such boring at a cost of ₹ 2,00,000. The company accepts the liability of carrying out repairs to the machine, if damaged, and the probability of damage is reduced to 0.03. Should the company accept the offer?

Solution The expected cost of damage to the machine is

$$2,00,000 \times 0.2 + 5,00,000 \times 0.1 + 15,00,000 \times 0.1 = 1,05,000$$

If the cost of delay per week is ₹ 2,00,000 and the probability of a four-week delay is 0.20 and the probability of a six-week delay is 0.10, then the expected cost of delay is

$$2,00,000 \times 4 \times 0.2 + 2,00,000 \times 6 \times 0.1 = 2,80,000$$

The total expected cost of damage and delay is ₹ 3,85,000.

If we accept the company's offer and outsource the task, our risk on damage and repairs becomes zero. However, our risk on delay (assuming that a five-week delay would occur) is

$$2,00,000 \times 5 \times 0.03 = 30,000$$

₹ 2,00,000 would be added to the cost of the project on outsourcing and a risk of ₹ 30,000 will be accepted as against a risk of ₹ 3,85,000 if the task is not outsourced. It is better to outsource the task.

The risk analysis can take the form as follows:

Definition

Condition The soil conditions in the area where the bridge crosses the river require the use of a special boring machine with which we have little experience.

Consequence Incorrectly operating the machine will damage it. Damage to the machine could cost from ₹ 2,00,000 to ₹ 15,00,000 in repairs and four to six weeks in lost time. A week's delay costs ₹ 2,00,000.

Probability

Probability of ₹ 2,00,000 damage—20%
Probability of ₹ 5,00,000 damage—10%
Probability of ₹ 15,00,000 damage—1%
Probability of no equipment damage—69%
Probable cost of equipment damage—₹ 1,05,000
Probable cost of delay—₹ 2,80,000

Strategy The task can be outsourced to another company for an estimated cost of ₹ 2,00,000. Using their operator reduces the chance of equipment damage to 3% and they will bear the cost of repair. The probability of delay is also reduced to 3%.

Note:

1. The probability was determined from the experience of this company and interviews with two other companies who have used the equipment.
2. The strategy adds ₹ 2,00,000 to the project cost but reduces the risk of cost damage to zero and the schedule risk to 3%.

8.5 RISK RESPONSE PLANNING

When a risk event has been identified and assessed, a decision has to be taken as to how to deal with it. Response to risks can be classified as mitigating, avoiding, transferring, sharing, or retaining.

8.5.1 Mitigating

The first alternative usually considered is to reduce the risk. This may be through reducing the likelihood that the risk event occurs and/or reducing the effect of the risk. For instance, we may reduce the risk of delays caused by rains in a construction project by scheduling most of the outdoor construction work during the dry season. Similarly, if there is a resource risk such as breakdown in the steady availability of raw material, the organization may mitigate the risk of stock-outs by maintaining inventory.

A mitigating strategy may aim at reducing the impact of the risk event. For instance, the risk of unexpected delays in receipt of cement or steel from the regular contracted supplier in an ongoing construction project may be mitigated by identifying alternate suppliers and having an understanding with them to supply certain quantities of cement and steel at short notice. This may involve buying the materials at a premium but it may well offset the increase in cost of the project due to delays.

8.5.2 Avoiding

Risk avoidance involves changing the project management plan to eliminate the threat of negative risks. For instance, we may have planned a project based on new but unproven technology. We could avoid the risk posed by the failure of unproven technology by using an older but proven technology for the project.

8.5.3 Transferring

This implies transferring the risk to another agency. For instance, we could outsource the project on a contract basis and transfer all risks to the contractor. Needless to say that transferring risk always involves a premium cost. The contractor, in the above example, would add a premium for the risk he will undertake to the costs quoted by him. Transferring of risk against natural calamities may be achieved through insurance. Performance bonds, guarantees and warranties are other means of risk transfer. Strategy referred to in Example 8.1 is a case of risk transfer.

8.5.4 Sharing

This involves allocating proportions of risk to different parties. For instance, the Airbus 340, research and development risks were allocated among European countries including Britain and France.

8.5.5 Retaining

Sometimes a conscious decision is taken to accept the risk. This may be because the chances of its occurring are very slim or it may not be feasible to transfer or share the risk. In such cases, contingency plans are prepared to deal with the risk event if it occurs.

Contingency planning

A contingency plan is an alternative plan which will be used if a foreseen risk event occurs. Like all plans, it answers what, when, where and how much action will take place. If contingency plans are not prepared, the management is surprised by the occurrence of a risk event. The management then either delays decision-making or takes decisions in panic, which may be counterproductive. The contingency plan must be known to all concerned and the person who will authorize a switch to the contingency must be nominated and given due authority so that the plan is smoothly executed. The conditions under which the contingency plan will be invoked should also be properly spelt out and documented. The cost of executing the contingency plan should be provided for, as invariably this will involve a disruption in the normal planned sequence of work.

Some of the common methods for handling risk are discussed in the following paragraphs.

8.5.6 Technical Risks

Technical risks are problematic and may even cause a project to be shut down. Contingency plans are made to cover such risks. For example, if we are planning to execute a project using new technology which may carry the risk of not working, we would have a contingency plan to execute the project with tested and proven technology, if and when failure of the new process occurs. Project managers must be able to quickly assess whether technical uncertainties can be resolved or not. The use of computer-aided design (CAD) has reduced such uncertainties to a great extent. It is further advocated that one should first identify high risk technical areas and then build models or design experiments to resolve the risk as quickly as possible.

8.5.7 Scheduling Risks

These generally involve trade-off decisions. Often managers increase these risks by their decisions. For instance, managers can become complacent when they see network slack in activities. They cease to worry about completing the activity on time. The use of slack may affect the availability of slack in later activities and may render some of them critical. Managing slack is an excellent method for reducing scheduling risks. The use of slack should be monitored and permitted only when it is a must. (Please also refer to the critical chain approach.)

Often someone in authority decides on the completion date of the project or on the completion of some milestone. These dates may be arbitrary or may be necessitated. For example, completion of a bridge by 26 January so that it can be inaugurated on the Republic Day by a suitable VIP, or the launch of a product to coincide with Diwali festival and so on. In such cases, schedules have to be compressed and methods have to be used which cost more than normal. Some activities on the critical path may have to be crashed and a time–cost trade-off may have to be undertaken.

Occasionally projects may have to be compressed midway through the project. This may be because the project is running behind schedule or some other avoidable reason. Such contingencies can be dealt with through cost crashing or through compromising and reducing the scope of the project or its quality.

8.5.8 Cost Risks

These risks are significant and carry heavy consequences. They generally occur because of errors in schedule and technical estimating. There is a dependency between time and costs and technical problems and costs. Any time overruns result in cost overruns. Technical problems also involve costs for their solution.

Cash flow risks are also present in a project. We have seen in Section 7.5 that we can use the early start and late start schedule to give us an idea of the required cash flows. It should be appreciated that making use of slacks in the schedule to manage cash flows will have a resultant effect on the time and resource schedule. Time, cost and resource schedules are interlinked and the linkages should be kept in mind while making plans or contingency plans to deal with these risks.

8.5.9 Contingency Funding

Contingency funds are established to cover project risks—identified and unknown. Often project 'owners' are reluctant to set aside contingency funds as they feel that this implies that the project is poorly planned. Some also feel that the contingency fund is just another slush fund and is likely to be misused. Such apprehensions can be overcome by laying down the conditions when such funds would be used and also delegating authority for sanctioning their use at the proper level. The size of these funds depends on the nature of the project and the uncertainty inherent in it. The uncertainty is reflected in the 'newness' of the project, inaccurate time and cost estimates, technical unknowns, changing scope and unforeseen problems. Contingency funding may vary from 1 to 10% based on experience of similar projects in the past. In projects involving new innovative technology the contingency funds may be as high as 20 to 60% of the estimated cost. It is not correct to arbitrarily lay down a percentage of the cost as contingency fund, nor is it prudent to base it on the sum total of all the contingencies included in estimate of each activity or work package. The contingency funding must be based on an assessment of risks.

The contingency reserve fund is divided into budget and management reserves for control purposes. A budget reserve covers identified risks and is allocated to specific segments or deliverables of the project. The management reserve is set up to cover unidentified risks and allocated to risks associated with the total project. The budget and management reserves are controlled at different levels and their use requires approval from different authority. The reserves are not included as part of the baseline. They are reserve funds available over and above the baseline to be used only if and when a risk event occurs. If the risk event for which a reserve fund was set up does not occur or its chance of occurring is past, the funds for that risk must be deducted from the available reserve. This will reduce the temptation to use budget reserves for other issues or problems. If the risk event occurs, the amount spent out of reserves is added to the cost baseline.

8.5.10 Time Buffers

Just as contingency funds are set up to absorb increases in cost because of occurrence of risk events, time buffers are set up to absorb the delays that may take place, throwing the project out of schedule. The amount of buffer time, just like the contingency funds, depends on the uncertainty associated with the project. The more the uncertainty, the more should be the time reserve for the schedule. Extra time is assigned at critical moments in the project, such as:

1. Activities with severe risk of time overruns.
2. Merge activities that are prone to delay as some preceding activity might get delayed.
3. Activities that use scarce resources, as the resource may not be available when required.
4. Non-critical activities which may become critical if slacks are used by earlier activities on the path.

A time buffer may also be added at the end of the project to cover the overall delay. This is somewhat akin to management reserve. Buffer management plays an important role in the critical chain approach.

8.6 RISK MONITORING AND CONTROL

Risk monitoring and control as per the *Project Management Book of Knowledge* is 'the process of identifying, analyzing, and planning for newly arising risks, keeping track of identified risks and those on the watch list, reanalyzing existing risks, monitoring trigger conditions for contingency plans, monitoring residual risks, and reviewing the execution of risk responses and evaluating their effectiveness'. It determines whether project assumptions are still valid and whether risk as assessed has changed from its previous state. We also monitor that the risk management policies and procedures are being correctly followed. Risk monitoring and control also includes setting up procedures to deal with events that require formal change in scope, budget or schedules.

Project managers should monitor risks and this should be part of project tracking and reporting system. They must be on the constant lookout for new risks. However, they must be aware that everyone is not keen to report problems or unforeseen risks. Admitting problems is perceived as poor performance by some individuals and this becomes more pronounced in organizations where mistakes are punished severely. If bad news is treated harshly then participants will be reluctant to speak freely and frankly. The trend to suppress bad news is further compounded if individual responsibility is not clearly defined and there is pressure on the project team to complete the project early. It is important that the top management fosters a culture where individuals can speak freely and frankly without fear of harsh punishments. The attitude of the management should be corrective and helpful rather than punitive, and 'witch hunting' should be avoided. It is more important to identify what went wrong and how to correct it and ensure that it does not happen again rather than finding out who is responsible and taking punitive action against the individual concerned.

An important factor in controlling costs because of risks is proper delegation of authority and responsibility. The line managers or person responsible for a particular task should have the authority to approve use of budget reserves and should be responsible for monitoring its rate of usage. If the risk event requires funds from the management reserve, the line person should play an active role in estimating additional costs and funds required to complete the project.

8.6.1 Managing Change

Projects will rarely go as per plan. In military parlance, it is often said that the first battle casualty is the plan. Coping with and controlling project changes poses a challenge to the project manager. Changes come from many sources, such as project owners and sponsors, project customers, project manager, project team and the occurrence of risk events. Most changes can be categorized as scope changes, improvement changes, and changes in baseline costs and schedules because of implementation of contingency plans on the occurrence of a risk event.

Since change is inevitable, a well-defined review and control system for change should be incorporated in the project plan. A change control system should be designed to achieve the following goals:

1. Identify proposed changes.
2. Identify effects of proposed change on budget and schedule.
3. Review, evaluate and approve or disapprove changes formally.
4. Negotiate and resolve conflicts arising from changes, especially in conditions and costs.
5. Disseminate information to all concerned about the change.
6. Assign responsibilities for implementing change.
7. Adjust master schedule and budget.
8. Track all changes that are to be implemented.

The process for approval of changes must be well defined. Authority to make changes must be delegated at the appropriate level. For instance, a change in the suppliers may require the approval of the project manager only, whereas a change in the scope of the project or the design may need the approval of an empowered committee comprising the project sponsor, the owner, the project manager and other stake holders. Approved changes must be incorporated into the baseline plan so that the changes can be tracked for their progress. Information about the changes must be intimated to all concerned so that they remain committed to them and implement them. Formalized procedures for approving changes will ensure that inconsequential changes are weeded out.

Risks need to be constantly monitored so that new risks that may be encountered as the project progresses can be identified and contingency plans can be made to cope with the risk event, if it occurs.

SUMMARY

Projects have inherent uncertainty in them and are, therefore, risk prone. A project risk is an uncertain event or condition that, if occurs, has a negative or positive effect on at least one of the project elements. Project management itself hinges on risk management. Correct choice of project ensures that the risk that the project will not conform to the objectives and goals of the organization is reduced. Defining the scope of the project reduces the risk of misunderstanding between the project owners and the project implementers. The WBS reduces the risk of omitting something important to the project. Good estimation reduces the risk of project overruns in terms of both time and cost.

Risk management essentially involves four steps—risk identification, risk analysis, risk response management and risk monitoring and control. All possible risks in various activities of the project are first identified and listed. The next step is to prioritize them according to the significance of the effect on the project if the risk event occurs. The significant risks are analyzed for their effect on the project in both qualitative and quantitative terms. The analysis also includes the probability of occurrence of the risk event and the ease with which the likelihood of occurrence of the risk event will be detected. The additional costs that may be incurred because of the occurrence of a risk event are also identified. Contingency plans are then drawn up to deal with the eventuality that a risk event will occur. The plans not only include the actions to be taken and by whom, but also make a provision for funds, time and resources. The plans also include the triggers that will set the plan in action and the authority that will approve the implementation of a contingency plan.

Contingency funds are provisioned to cater for contingency plans. The funds are broken down to budget reserves and management reserves. Budget reserves are assigned to identified risks and allocated for specific tasks. Management reserves are provisioned for unidentified risks that may affect the whole project. The usage of reserve funds must be closely monitored. In case the event for which they have been provided does not occur, the total availability of the fund should be decreased by the amount earmarked for the particular event. This will avoid the fund from being used on other activities. Time buffers are also provisioned in a manner similar to the contingency reserve funds.

Risk should be monitored and should form part of the project tracking system. The organization should encourage free and frank communication so that participants do not hide errors and risks. The attitude adopted should be corrective rather than punitive. When a risk event occurs and a contingency plan is invoked, it results in changes to schedule, budgets, and WBS. A formal process for approving and implementing changes should be in place.

Proper risk management will prevent the management from being surprised by events leading to either delay in decision-making or panic decision-making which is dysfunctional and leads to project delays and cost and time overruns.

QUESTIONS

1. The chances of risk events occurring and their respective costs increasing change over the project life cycle. What significance do these changes have for the project manager?
2. Explain the difference between risk avoidance, risk acceptance and transferring of risk with the help of suitable examples.
3. What do you understand by contingency planning?
4. Explain the difference between budget reserves and management reserves.
5. What aspects would you bear in mind while designing a change management control system?

PART III Project Execution, Monitoring and Control

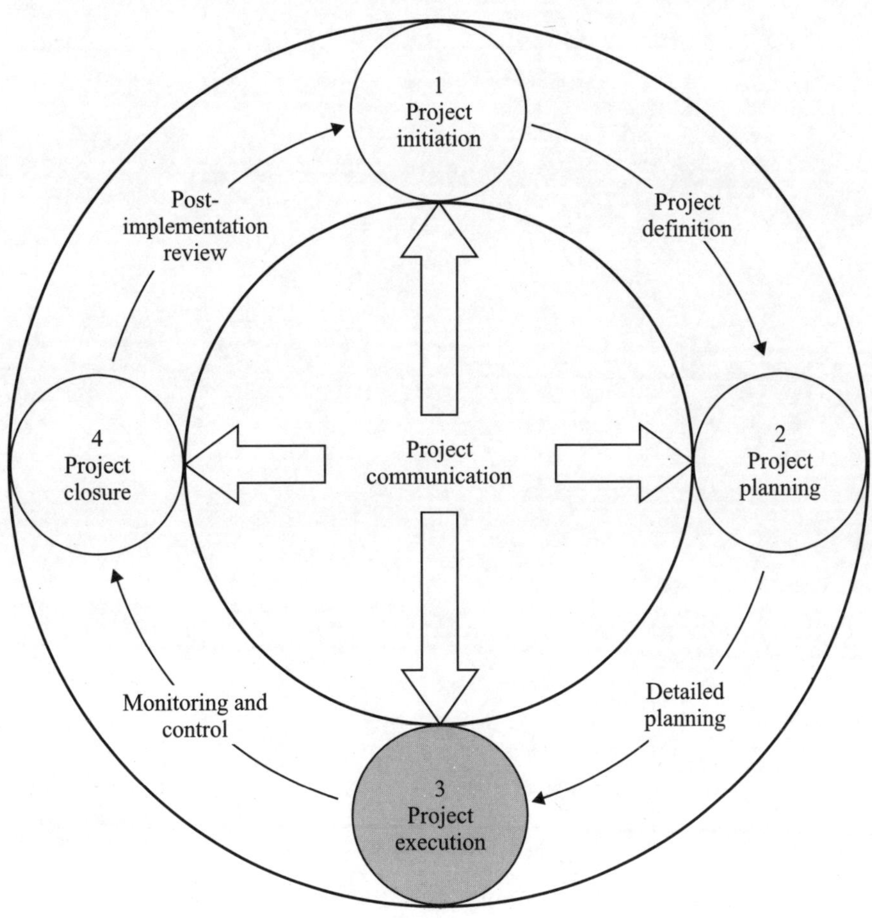

CHAPTER 9

Project Organization Structure and Culture

> *Innovative efforts should never report to line managers charged with responsibility for ongoing operations. ... The new project is an infant and will remain one for the foreseeable future, and infants belong in the nursery. The 'adults', that is, the executives in charge of existing businesses or products will have neither the time nor understanding for the infant.*
>
> —Peter Drucker

LEARNING OBJECTIVES

After reading this chapter, you will be able to:

- Understand the influence of organizational structure and culture on successful project management.
- Study different types of organizational structures—functional, project teams and matrix.
- Examine the determinants for choosing a particular organization structure.
- Study the effects of organizational culture on successful management of projects.

9.1 INTRODUCTION

You may wonder why we are talking of organization structure. Let us consider the case of a steel plant which is considering a project to double its existing capacity. You might say that an organization already exists, why then do we have to consider organizational structure for executing the project? Why can we not just task the production department to execute the project? The question is indeed valid.

Projects by definition are temporary endeavours undertaken to produce a unique product, service or result. Let us recall the implications of projects being temporary endeavours. The temporariness applies to the project as it has a definite beginning and a definite end and to the organization and infrastructure set-up to execute the project as there is no reason for the existence of the organization and the infrastructure once the project is terminated. Traditionally organizations are not designed to be temporary. They are designed to be permanent and to manage ongoing operations.

Most projects are multidisciplinary in nature because they require the coordinated efforts of various specialists. Traditional organizations are based on division of labour. They are organized into departments based on functional expertise. For instance, the production department has people who specialize in functions such as fabrication, assembly, testing and so on. Each department develops its own culture—customs, norms, values and working styles. Authority in organizations is distributed vertically in a hierarchical manner. Projects span across functional areas and identifying and legitimizing project manager's authority is often a problem. There are a number of possible ways to organize the execution of a project. Let us examine some of them and see their advantages and disadvantages.

9.2 TRADITIONAL OR FUNCTIONAL ORGANIZATION

Some organizations assign the responsibility of executing projects to the department where most of the work is to be carried out. For instance, the project for developing a new management information system may be assigned to the information services department, or a new product project may be assigned to the production department. Different parts of the project which require to be handled by different departments are given to them, whereas one department is given the task of coordinating the work. This has the advantage of the project being executed within the existing organization but it has its own drawbacks. The functional organization structure in shown in Figure 9.1.

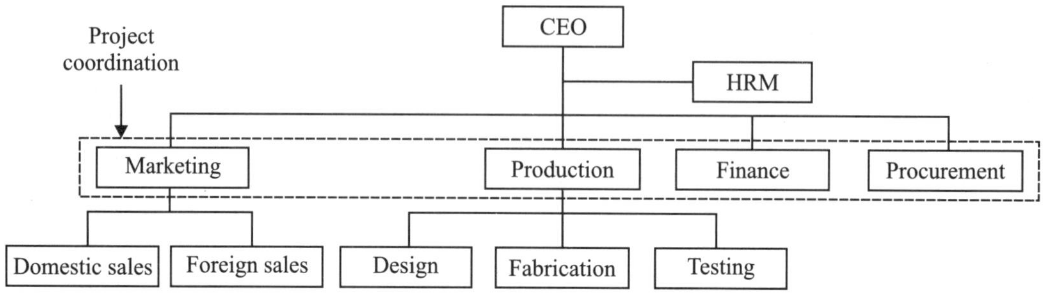

Figure 9.1 Functional organization.

The advantages of carrying out projects under the existing functional organization are as follows:

1. Projects are completed within the existing organizational framework. The existing channels of reporting, communication and control are used. Budgeting and control are easy.
2. Technical control is better. Individual experts can be utilized by many different projects.
3. Specialists in the division can be grouped to share knowledge and experience.

4. The functional division also serves as a base of technological continuity when individuals choose to leave the project.
5. The functional division contains the normal path of advancement for individuals whose expertise is in the functional area. Since individuals work on projects as part of their functional departments, advancement is not a cause for anxiety.
6. There is maximum flexibility in the use of staff. We can assign appropriate experts and specialists to the project from within the organization and they can revert to their original tasks on completion of the project.
7. Best suited for mass production.
8. Communication lines are well established.

Despite the aforementioned advantages, the system suffers from the following disadvantages:

1. A holistic approach is not possible. Complex projects cannot be undertaken. There may be poor integration across functional departments. Functional specialists may tend to be concerned only with their segment of the project and may not take a holistic view to do what is best for the project. Different departments may accord different priority to the project as it is not their main task. The project may get delayed on this account.
2. Project is not the main activity of department and focus is lost. It is often difficult to motivate people to work for project. They consider the project secondary to their normal tasks and may want to spend time on it only when they can spare it. Similarly, adequate resources may not be made available. The project is viewed as an imposition.
3. Sometimes there is a tendency to ignore activities not directly related to functional department.
4. Decision-making follows the normal hierarchical channels resulting in slow response. The project head approaches other functional heads only through the normal vertical channels of organizational communication.
5. No individual is responsible for the complete project and hence, there is no accountability. Coordination between different departments poses severe problems which are compounded by interpersonal rivalry and interpersonal conflicts.
6. It is difficult to motivate the project team as the project is not viewed as being linked to professional development and advancement. The team is not strongly committed to the project.

Some of the shortcomings of using the functional organization for executing projects can be overcome by laying down rules and procedures for resolving areas of conflict and instituting a hierarchical referral system. Commitment can be ensured by involving participating functional personnel in planning and establishing systems which permit direct contact between participating departments.

The shortcomings of using the traditional functional organization for managing projects gave rise to some modifications to the system and other organizational forms evolved. One of the earliest modifications was to add project leaders as staff at the departmental level (Figure 9.2). Their sole task was to coordinate project activities. However, being a part of the staff, they had little or no authority over the line functions and contributed marginally to obviate the shortcomings of the functional organization.

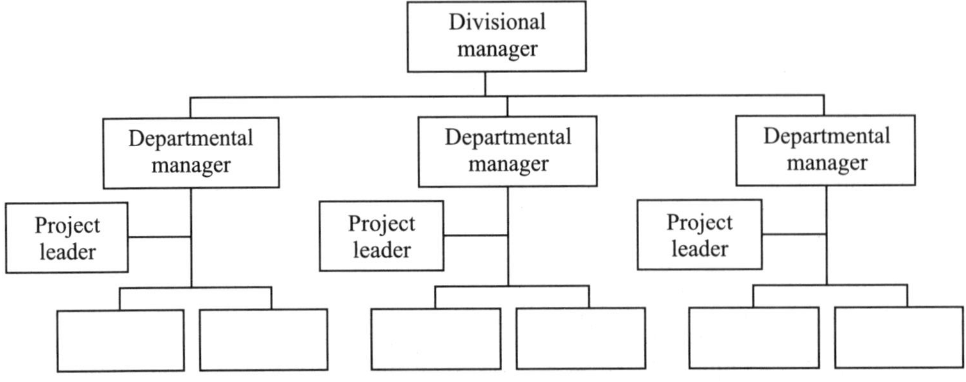

Figure 9.2 Project leaders at departmental level.

Another modification was to try and manage projects with the help of a task force comprising members from the involved departments (Figure 9.3). However, the task force's main task was to coordinate the effort on the project through frequent meetings and to review progress periodically. The task force had no authority and in case of conflicts referral was made to the top management. No team leader was appointed and the system suffered from disputes for leadership.

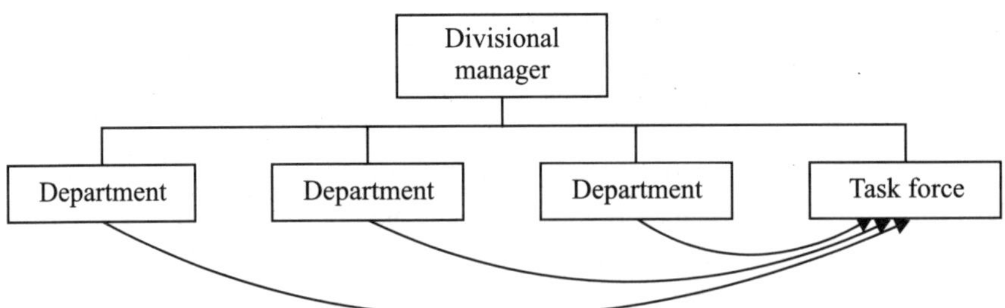

Figure 9.3 Managing projects through a task force.

9.3 PROJECT MANAGEMENT THROUGH DEDICATED TEAMS

The other extreme, as opposed to the functional organization, is to manage projects through the creation of independent teams (Figure 9.4). These teams operate as separate units from rest of the parent organization. Generally, a full-time project manager is appointed and is authorized to put together a team of specialists to work on the project. The personnel may be drawn from within the organization or hired from outside for the duration of the project. The interface between the team and the parent organization varies. The parent organization may lay down rules and procedures for administrative and financial control over the project. Generally, the project manager is given the maximum freedom to execute the project with resources allotted to him/her. The team is disbanded after the completion of the project. This may result in the loss of expertise gained on the project, especially if the team is composed mainly of experts and personnel hired from outside the organization. The experience gained from the project is lost to the organization.

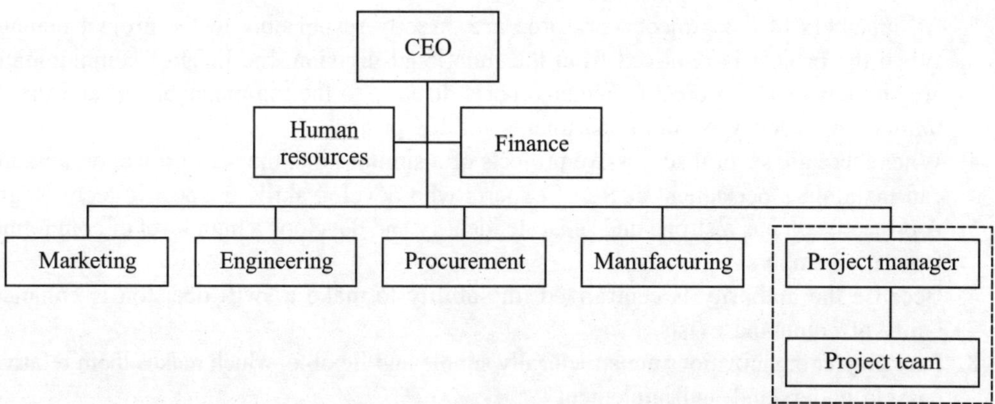

Figure 9.4 Managing projects through project teams.

Projects are the dominant form of business in some organizations like construction firms, consultancy firms, software development firms and so on. In such cases the entire organization is designed to support project teams. The organization consists of some centralized services provided by corporate departments and a set of quasi-independent project teams working on specific projects. The functional departments are set up to provide support to the project teams. For instance, the marketing department's task may be to generate new business that will lead to more projects; the human resource department is responsible for managing personnel issues as well as recruiting and training of new people for the organization. Such an organization is referred to as a projectized form of organization (Figure 9.5).

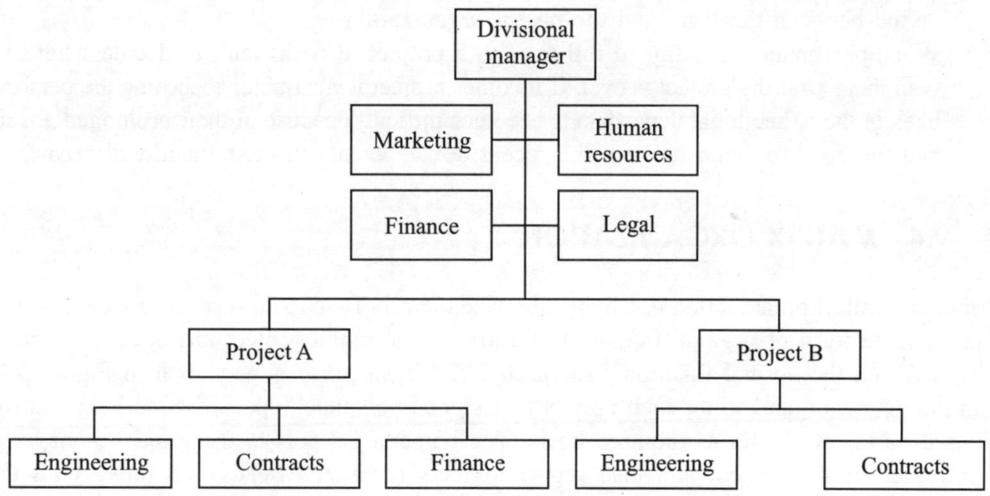

Figure 9.5 Projectized form of organization.

The advantages of such an organization are listed as follows:

1. The project manager has full line authority over the project and is responsible and accountable for its timely completion.

2. All members of the project workforce are directly responsible to the project manager.
3. When the project is removed from the functional division, the lines of communication are shortened. The project manager reports directly to the top management and there is limited dependency on the departments for the project.
4. When there are several successive projects of a similar kind, the pure project organization can maintain a permanent cadre of experts who develop skills in specific technologies.
5. A project team has a strong and separate identity and develops a high level of commitment from its members.
6. Because the authority is centralized, the ability to make a swift decision is enhanced.
7. Unity of command exists.
8. Pure project organizations are structurally simple and flexible, which makes them relatively easy to understand and implement.
9. The organizational structure tends to support a holistic approach to the project.

Some of the disadvantages of such an organization are as follows:

1. Each project tends to be fully staffed which can lead to a duplication of effort in every area from clerical staff to technological support. There is a tendency to have all the resources exclusively for the project so that time is not lost in coordinating their use. This leads to wasteful duplication.
2. There is a need to ensure access to technological knowledge and skills that result in an attempt by project managers to stockpile equipment and technical assistance.
3. The functional division is a repository of technical lore, but it is not readily accessible to team members of the pure project team.
4. Sometimes project teams develop a strong identity of their own resulting in a 'we–they' divide between the team and the parent organization.
5. When personnel are assigned full-time to a project, it is difficult to decide what to do with them after the project is over. If no other project is available, absorbing the personnel back in their functional departments becomes difficult because of their prolonged absence and the need to catch up with the recent developments in their functional areas.

9.4 MATRIX ORGANIZATION

The matrix form of organization is a hybrid between purely functional form of organization and the projectized form of organization. In this form, a horizontal project management structure is 'overlaid' on the normal functional hierarchy. The basic form is as shown in Figure 9.6.

In the matrix organization, each project is assigned personnel, specialists and experts from various departments on an as required basis. The personnel report to the project manager for the activities of the project and also report to their functional heads and liaise with their functional departments for the tasks pertaining to the project. The matrix organization optimally utilizes resources by having individuals work on multiple projects while retaining their capability of performing normal functional duties. Greater integration is achieved by creating and legitimizing the authority of the project manager. The project manager is responsible for integrating functional inputs and overseeing the completion of the project. The functional heads are responsible for overseeing the functional contribution to the project.

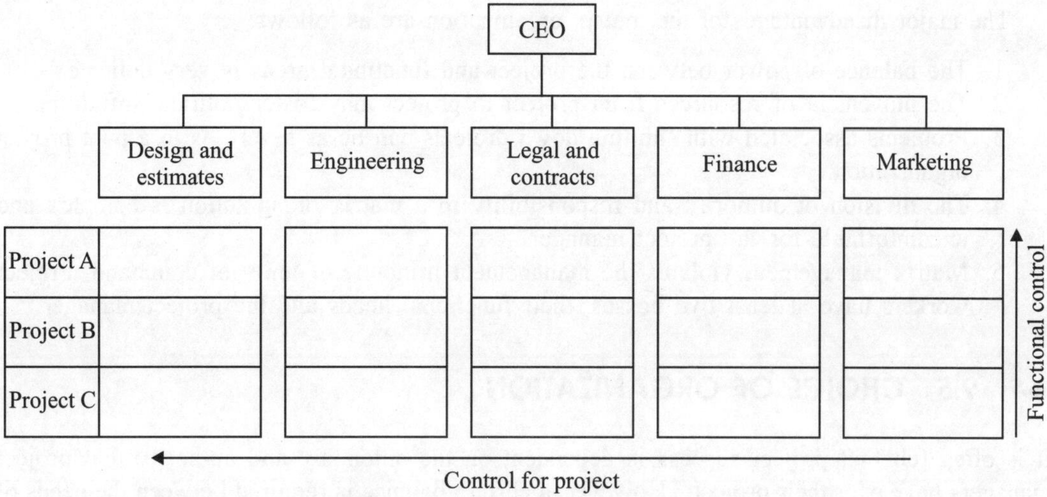

Figure 9.6 Matrix organization.

The matrix organization takes many forms. It may be a weak matrix where the balance of authority tilts in favour of the functional heads or it may be a strong matrix where the balance of authority is in favour of the project manager. A balanced matrix gives equal authority and importance to both the project manager and the functional heads.

In the weak matrix, the project manager coordinates the activities of the project but the functional heads are responsible for managing their segment of the project. The project manager draws indirect authority because of his proximity to the top management. He performs more of a staff function with little line authority. On the other hand, the strong matrix is similar to the project team. The project manager exercises control over the project and is the authority to decide what will be done and when it will be done. He takes most of the major decisions with regard to the project. While the matrix organization has numerous advantages, its biggest drawback is the violation of the principle of unity of command. Individuals report to both the project manager and their functional head and loyalty can be seriously jeopardized especially if there is interpersonal conflict between the project manager and the functional head.

The advantages of a matrix organization are listed as follows:

1. The project is the point of emphasis.
2. Because the project is overlaid on the functional divisions, the project has reasonable access to the reservoir of technology in all areas.
3. There is less anxiety amongst individuals about what happens to them when the project is completed, as they revert to their functional departments.
4. Response to client's needs is as rapid as in the pure project organization.
5. Matrix management gives the project access to representatives from the administrative units of the parent firm.
6. The matrix organization allows a better company-wide balance of resources to achieve goals. Resources can be shared across multiple projects.
7. There is a great deal of flexibility in precisely how the project is organized within the matrix.

The major disadvantages of the matrix organization are as follows:

1. The balance of power between the project and functional areas is very delicate.
2. The movement of resources from project to project may foster political infighting.
3. Problems associated with shutting down projects can be as severe as in a pure project organization.
4. The division of authority and responsibility in a matrix organization is complex and uncomfortable for the project manager.
5. Matrix management violates the management principle of unity of command. Project workers have at least two bosses, their functional heads and the project manager.

9.5 CHOICE OF ORGANIZATION

It is often felt that project success is dependent on the autonomy and authority that project managers have over their projects. However, a correct balance is required between the needs of the project and the needs of the parent organization. The choice of organization for managing a project depends on the organizational needs of the parent organization and the type of project.

At the organizational level, a key issue is the importance of project management to the firm. If most of the work of the firm involves managing projects then it is advisable to have a fully projectized organization. If the activities of the firm involve both standard products and projects, then a matrix organization may be more suitable. In the case of a firm which undertakes very few projects or deals with projects rarely, a less formal structure may be suitable. Temporary task forces or teams could be created on an as required basis. Alternatively, the project may even be outsourced as a turnkey activity.

Resource availability is another important consideration. A matrix organization is most suitable when resources have to be shared across multiple projects and across functional domains.

Organizations evolve over time out of the necessity to change. The functional organization cannot be converted to a matrix organization overnight. It will probably take the shape of a weak matrix to start with and will gradually evolve. Resistance to change is an important factor and functional heads will be reluctant to part with their authority or share it with the project manager.

Some organizations also set up Project Management Offices (PMO) to support project management efforts. The PMO's functions vary from organization to organization. As the PMO evolves and matures with time, it becomes a full service provider of project management expertise in the organzation. It may provide the following services:

1. Recruitment and selection of project managers from within and from outside the organization.
2. Creation and maintenance of internal project management system.
3. Establishment of standard project planning and reporting methods.
4. Training personnel in project management tools and techniques.
5. Development of comprehensive risk management systems.
6. Provision of in-house project management consultancy service.
7. Auditing of ongoing and completed projects.

8. Maintenance of all documents connected with projects, like project plans, funding reports, audit reports and so on.
9. Establishing and benchmarking best practices in project management.

The amount of autonomy required for the success of a project also determines the organizational structure best suited for it. Seven factors have been identified by Hobbs and Menard (1993) that have an impact on the organization structure. These are—size of the project; its strategic importance; the need for novelty and innovation in the project; need for integration of various functional domains; number of external interfaces required; budget and time constraints; and stability of resource requirements. The higher the level of these factors, the more autonomy and independence is required for the success of the project. This requires a project team structure or a matrix organization structure to be put into place.

Some organizations adopt a mixed structure especially if they have a variety of projects to undertake which may include high risk, medium risk and low risk projects. The organization may form dedicated project teams to execute high risk projects, a strong matrix organization may handle medium risk projects and the low risk projects may be handled through weak matrix organizations.

The choice of organization structure is determined by the nature of the project, and the characteristics and cultural preferences of the parent organization.

9.6 ORGANIZATIONAL CULTURE

Organizational culture is another major determinant of the type of organization structure to adopt for project management. What works fine for one organization may be totally unsuitable for another organization. What then is organizational culture? We all experience cultural differences when we travel to different parts of our big country or to different parts of the world. People behave differently and have different beliefs. They speak different languages and react differently to the same stimuli. Similarly, organizations also differ. Organization culture refers to "a system of shared norms, beliefs, values and assumptions which bind people together, thereby creating shared meanings". Each organization has its own customs, norms and habits that reflect the beliefs of the organization. Researchers have identified 10 dimensions of organizational culture. These are as follows:

(a) *Member identity.* It is the degree to which members identify themselves with the organization as a whole, rather than only with their job or professional functions. It is the difference between saying 'I am a good programmer' and 'I work for Wipro'.
(b) *Team emphasis.* The extent to which jobs are organized around groups as opposed to assigning jobs to individuals.
(c) *Management focus.* The degree to which the management is task oriented or people oriented.
(d) *Unit integration.* The extent to which units or departments within the organization are encouraged to function in a coordinated and interdependent manner.
(e) *Control.* The degree to which rules, policies and direct supervision are used to control the behaviour of employees.

(f) *Risk tolerance.* The extent to which employees are encouraged to be original and innovative even though such actions may invite risk.

(g) *Reward criteria.* The degree to which performance is rewarded with advancement and promotion rather than such awards being based on seniority, favouritism or other non-performance criteria.

(h) *Conflict tolerance.* The degree to which employees are encouraged to air conflicts and criticisms openly.

(i) *Means versus ends orientation.* The degree to which the management emphasizes results vis-à-vis the methods and procedures used to achieve them.

(j) *Open system focus.* The extent to which the organization responds to changes in the external environment.

ORGANIZATIONAL CULTURE—THE JAPANESE WAY

In a shoe factory, the employees had a dispute with the management. They decided to go on strike. However, it was not in their ethos to let production suffer. The workers produced only left shoes for three weeks in a novel form of protest. After the dispute was resolved, the workers only made right shoes and the overall production did not suffer. That's Japanese organizational culture for you.

Contrast this with our own country. Workers would have probably set a couple of buses on fire and caused damage to public property.

Each of these dimensions exists on a continuum. The characteristics of an organization which is successful at project management have values of the dimensions of organizational culture as shown in Figure 9.7.

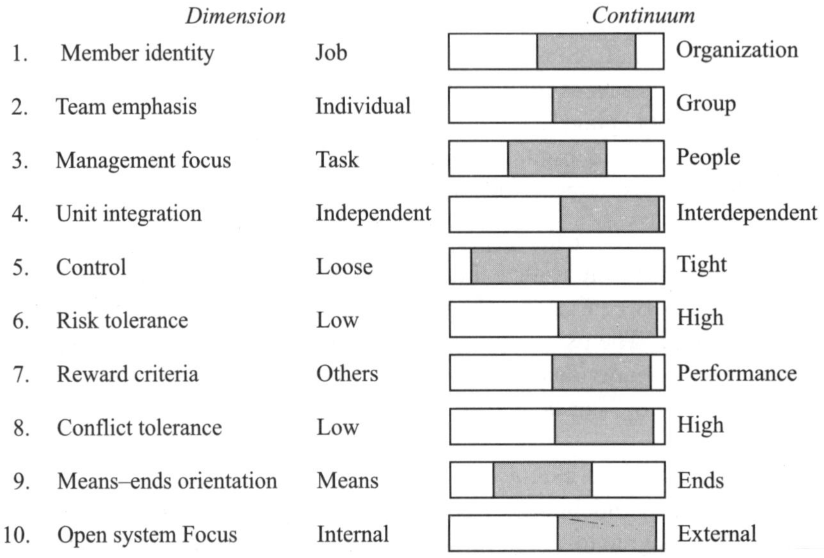

	Dimension		*Continuum*	
1.	Member identity	Job		Organization
2.	Team emphasis	Individual		Group
3.	Management focus	Task		People
4.	Unit integration	Independent		Interdependent
5.	Control	Loose		Tight
6.	Risk tolerance	Low		High
7.	Reward criteria	Others		Performance
8.	Conflict tolerance	Low		High
9.	Means–ends orientation	Means		Ends
10.	Open system Focus	Internal		External

Figure 9.7 Cultural dimensions of an organization which succeeds at projects.

As may be noted, the cultural dimensions do not necessarily have to lie at one extreme or the other. For instance, a balance is required between concern for task and concern for people. Similarly, an organization must draw a balance between means and ends. The ends do not always justify the means. Professional ethics must be maintained.

An organization that approaches close to these ideals is 3M. It is reputed for its innovativeness and its entrepreneurial culture in a large corporate framework. It encourages technical people to spend up to 55% of their time on their own projects. The firm has had to set up 40 separate product divisions. The culture of 3M is best portrayed in the phrases that they have often chanted—'Encourage experimental doodling'; 'hire good people and leave them alone'; 'if you put fences around people, you get sheep. Give people the room they need'.

Handling projects is easy if an organization has a culture conducive to project management. Much greater effort will be required to manage projects if the culture of the organization is not conducive. In an organization which has a supportive culture for project management needs, the project manager needs less authority and resources to complete the project.

A dedicated, self-sufficient project team or at least a strong matrix organization is advisable for organizations which have a culture which inhibits innovation and collaboration among departments and groups of people. This will encourage the creation of a sub-culture within the project team, in which a different set of norms, customs and values evolve, which are conducive to project completion.

SUMMARY

There are two critical factors of an organization that affect the successful implementation of projects. The first is the formal organizational structure vis-à-vis the structure created for project management. On one hand, there are organizations that carry out projects without making any structural changes and simply make a functional head responsible for the project. On the other extreme, there are organizations which set up dedicated independent teams for project implementation. A balance between the two is struck by having a matrix organization wherein a horizontal project management structure is superimposed on the hierarchical vertical structure of the organization. A project manager, having little or no influence over the organizational structure, would perform well if he understood the strengths and weaknesses of the organizational structure in which he had to work. He can then exploit the strengths and take adequate measures to mitigate the weaknesses of the system.

We have studied different organizational structures with this aim in view. A large number of organizations use the matrix structure so that resources can be shared in a multiple project environment. The matrix structure may be weak, balanced or strong—the strength being determined by the autonomy and independence enjoyed by the project manager vis-à-vis the functional heads.

Another important factor that affects an organization's ability to execute and undertake projects successfully is the organizational culture. The organizational culture is a set of norms, beliefs, values and assumptions which bind people together in an organization. The organizational culture has various dimensions which lie on a continuum. In some organizations, its culture encourages and facilitates the implementation of projects; while in others, the organization culture does not provide a conducive environment for project implementation. In an organization with a facilitating culture, the project management structure plays a less significant role in the successful implementation of projects. Conversely, in organizations where the organizational culture inhibits project implementation, the project management structure assumes significant importance. It is important for us to understand that while organizational culture cannot be changed overnight, we can and should structure the project management framework so that it can work efficiently and effectively in the prevailing organizational culture.

The project management structure and the culture of the organization are the major elements of the environment in which projects are implemented and the compatibility of project management structure with the culture of the organization helps successful implementation of projects.

QUESTIONS

1. What are the relative advantages and disadvantages of the functional, matrix and project team approaches to project management?
2. What is the difference between a weak matrix structure and a strong matrix structure?
3. How does culture affect the project management structure of an organization?
4. When would you prefer to use a project matrix as opposed to a dedicated project management team for project implementation?
5. Which do you think is more important—the project management structure or the organizational culture?

CHAPTER 10

Project Staffing

HR Issues

Get the right people. Then no matter what all else you might do wrong after that, the people will save you. That's what management is all about. —Tom DeMarco

LEARNING OBJECTIVES
After reading this chapter, you will be able to: • Understand the skill sets required by a project manager. • Study the traits of a project manager and the issues involved in selecting a project manager. • Study the problems of selecting and building project teams. • Understand the issues involved in managing project teams.

10.1 INTRODUCTION

The army maintains that it is the man behind the gun that matters and not the gun itself. The success of any system depends, to a large extent, on the men who operate it. Managing projects is no different. You may wonder why we are discussing project staffing. Is it really different from staffing any organization? The peculiar nature of projects—their temporariness in the main—creates a different environment for staffing. The project is not an ongoing activity and requires the coordination of activities across disciplines for its success. We shall deal with the selection of the project manager and the project team in this chapter.

The project staffing environment has some unique characteristics that make staffing problematic. Firstly, employees in a project organization face constant change, and unfortunately, change is an anathema for most of us. Most people prefer a stable working environment. The problem is further compounded as they have to report to more than one person. Some people treat the project as an opportunity to prove themselves. In their enthusiasm, they often experiment and want to do things differently which may not be in the best interest of the project. If they succeed, the project benefits, but failures do not constitute individual failures but result in the project going astray.

Reporting to two bosses creates its own stress. This is especially so when the functional head and the project manager give conflicting directions. The employee's loyalty tends to be seriously questioned. In such cases, he is most likely to toe the line of his functional head as he knows that he has to return to his functional department on completion of the project.

Some persons view the project as a quick stepping stone to personal advancement. Promotions and pay packages in the organization are governed by personnel policies. However, since the project is result oriented and is for a short duration, the project manager is generally permitted to decide on his own system of rewards for those who perform well. This is resented by others who do not work on the project leading to conflict within the organization.

The project manager's personality is another major factor affecting the project team. Is he viewed as a hard task master or a total professional? Is he a team builder or an autocrat? Can he lead from the front? How decisive is he? Is he supportive of the staff under him or does he pass the blame to his subordinates when things go wrong? The project manager's personal qualities will affect the pattern of staffing.

Let us first discuss the selection of the project manager.

10.2 THE PROJECT MANAGER

10.2.1 Leadership and Management Skills

In a perfect world, the project manager would just have to make a schedule, allocate resources, assemble a team and just tell them what to do. However, the world is anything but perfect. Things do not go according to plan. Delays occur; systems break down; the scope of the project changes; functional departments do not deliver as per schedule; risk events occur; interpersonal conflicts take place and the project manager has to cope with all these problems. But the project manager is not just a firefighter. He has to innovate and adapt to the ever-changing environment. He must be able to respond to changes in the plan, in the project scope, in the customer's requirements, in the team and so on.

The project manager must assign resources and see that the project is completed according to plan. At the same time, the project manager must be prepared to initiate change in plans because of the problems that beset it. According to Kotter (1990), managers cope with complexity and leaders cope with change. Managers direct, coordinate and control activities and people; the leader recognizes the need for change, redirects the efforts of the team and inspires them to move in a different direction. A project manager must not only be a good manager but also be a good leader. The degree of leadership required varies from project to project. A complex project with a high degree of uncertainty will require strong leadership at the top. A straightforward project, for example a construction project involving the construction of a series of apartment buildings, will require a lesser degree of leadership.

The qualities of exceptional leadership and management may not always be available in one person. Projects requiring high leadership should be led by people who are good leaders even if their management skills are not equally sharp. This can be compensated by having good managers as assistants. This is also conversely true.

10.2.2 Interpersonal Skills

A project manager has to manage a variety of people—some under his control and some over whom he has no control. He realizes that authority does not translate into influence and to be effective he has to manage a complex set of interfaces. In any project, the project manager has to deal with different groups of stakeholders. There may be a core group of specialists assigned on the project team. They may often be assisted by professionals and consultants who work on specific segments of the project. There are groups of people within the organization who are directly or indirectly involved with the project. Some of these are the top management; functional heads; administrative support groups, like the legal department, the finance department and the information systems department; the project sponsors; and other project managers. There are external agencies like the customers; various government agencies which give clearances for the project; contractors; suppliers; external consultants and so on. Figure 10.1 shows schematically the network of people that the project manager has to interact with. Some nuances of these interfaces are as follows:

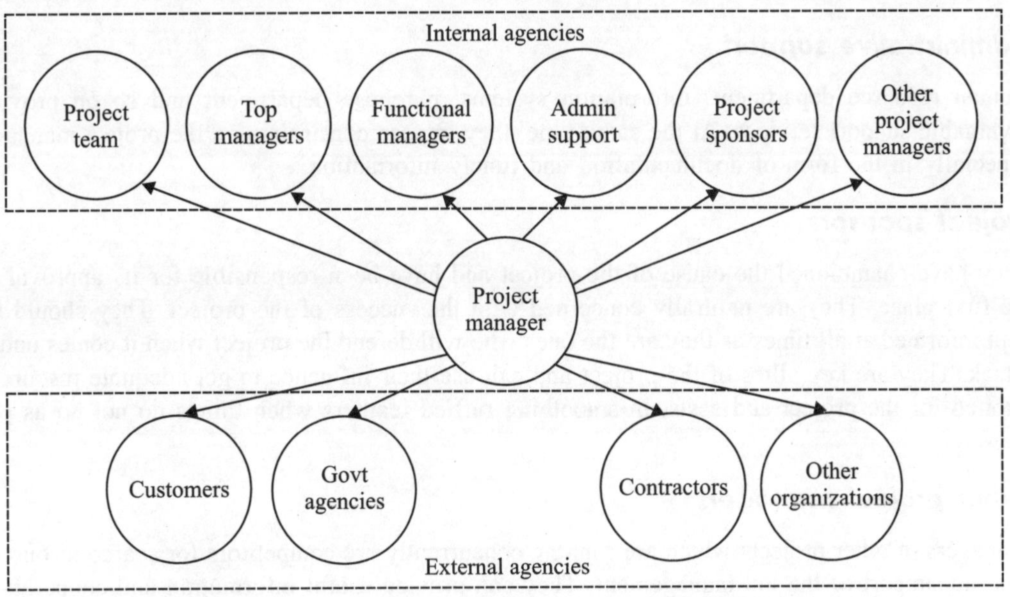

Figure 10.1 Networking requirements of a project manager.

Project team

These are the project participants who actually complete the project. While people do want to do the work well, they have some compulsions due to their commitments to their parent department. The project manager has to ensure that there is goal congruity and must address their concern and anxiety stemming from their commitment to the project and their functional department.

Top management

The top management has a natural vested interest in the project. They decide the priorities among projects for resources and funds. All major changes need their approval. They lay down success criteria and grant rewards for successful completion. It is important that the project manager constantly interacts with the top management and keeps them abreast of the progress of the project. He should develop a mutual trust with the top management so that he has their support even if things go wrong.

Functional managers

They make a contribution depending on the type of project organizational structure that exists. In a matrix set-up, they provide the personnel and resources to the project and may be responsible for certain segments of the project. Even in the case of a dedicated project team, the functional managers can give useful inputs to the project. They shall be willing to cooperate but only to a certain extent. As long as the project does not impinge on their own areas of interest, they shall cooperate with the project manager. But when there is a conflict of interest, they shall naturally accord greater priority to their own operations. They are also very status conscious and ego clashes can occur if the project manager is not skilled in handling interpersonal relations.

Administrative support

Human resource department, information systems, purchase department and so on provide invaluable support services. At the same time, they impose constraints on the project manager, especially in the form of documentation and timely information.

Project sponsors

They have championed the cause of the project and have been responsible for its approval in the first place. They are naturally concerned with the success of the project. They should be kept informed at all times as they are the ones who will defend the project when it comes under attack. They are key allies of the project and can use their influence to get adequate resources allotted for the project and assist in smoothing ruffled feathers when things do not go as per plan.

Other project managers

Managers of other projects which are running concurrently are competitors for scarce resources and the support of the top management. They can provide useful information and cooperation in sharing of resources.

Customers

They define the scope of the project and the success of the project lies in their satisfaction. Project managers must respond to customer needs and changing customer requirements to meet the customer's expectations.

Government agencies

The project has to obtain a number of approvals and clearances from government agencies. For instance, building construction has to conform to building codes. Environmental clearances are mandatory. Safety standards have to be met and so on. Bureaucracies work in their own rule-bound method and at their own pace. A project manager must deal with these agencies skilfully and patiently.

Contractors

A large part of the project may be done through contractors. The success of the project will depend on their ability to produce quality work on time. Project delays can occur if contracts are not properly handled.

Other organizations

A host of other organizations may impinge on the success or failure of a project. These include suppliers, auditors, public interest groups and so on. For instance, the inordinate delay in the execution of the Narmada Valley project and the Tehri Dam project can be attributed to public interest groups. Ms Medha Patkar and Shri Sunder Lal Bahaguna started movements against the projects. While the merits or otherwise of these moves are not being questioned here, it is important for the project manager to be aware of such threats and opportunities. (In more recent times, Tata's Nano Car project has had to shift from Nandigram, West Bengal to Gujarat despite suffering huge losses on account of sunk costs.)

Relationships are also interdependent. For instance, if the top management is perceived to be waning in its commitment to the project, the functional heads and others in the organization will also not accord it full cooperation. In the complexities of these relationships, the project manager has to create a cooperative network which will help to achieve the goals of the project. Such networks which are mutually beneficial are based on reciprocity or 'quid pro quo'. The project manager has to use his skills to influence others. Influence can be exerted through various means (similar to the '*daam, saam, dandh, bhed*' Indian philosophy). Cohen and Bradford (1990) have likened the domains of influence to 'currencies'. Just as one needs different currencies to do business in different countries, different types of influence can be used with different groups. Groups respond to different spheres of influence. Cohen and Bradford identify the following types of influence.

Task-related influence

This influence stems from the project manager's ability to help people to complete their tasks by making resources available to them as required. It can also extend to other project managers by sharing resources with them. It can also take the form of support to plans of others or cooperating with them by going out of one's way to help them to beat deadlines.

Position-related influence

This influence arises from the project manager's ability to enhance others' positions within the organization. This can be exercised by giving a person a chance to take up a challenging assignment and providing him the wherewithal to complete it. It can also take the form of letting others share glory and showcasing their achievements, especially in front of their superiors. The project manager can use this type of influence by promoting the abilities of other people and helping them to create their own network. It can take the form of making persons 'visible' to their higher ups. (See box.)

'VISIBILITY' TO THE BOSS

Our immediate superior, a Brigadier, in the Army HQ section where I was working, would call us periodically and ask us when we had last interacted with the Major General (our boss at the next hierarchical level) and the head of our functional department. He would then hand us a file and explain the case to us as well as the recommendations and his reasons for the same and then ask us to go and explain the matter to the Major General. He would ensure that we became visible to our functional head and won us over by this deliberate effort to build our images in the Major General's eyes. We all considered him a wonderful team builder and were ever willing to do anything for him, whether at the professional or at the personal level. Good leaders must learn to use all domains to influence people and get the best out of them.

Inspiration-related influence

Inspiration is a powerful form of influence. By creating a powerful vision of the project, it may draw extraordinary commitment from the team. Some projects by their nature are inspirational. For example, a team working on finding a cure for a dreaded disease, or working on a project that alleviates the misery of the poor and helpless makes people feel good about what they are doing and draws out the best in them. Inspiration pulls people towards doing something as opposed to pushing people into doing something.

Relationship-related influence

This influence is exerted by creating relationships rather than helping out in completing a task. Relationships extend beyond the professional interaction that we have. It is promoted through being friends, through listening to others, through sharing common interests, being there when people are feeling low and above all displaying a sense of humour to cheer others and giving them a feeling of belonging.

Personal-related influence

This type of influence stems from the project manager's ability to pander to a person's self-esteem. He can do this by assigning tasks to them that increase their skills and abilities. A person values his self-esteem and if he perceives that he is valued by others, he is likely to give his best. A person feels valued when his contribution is acknowledged and gratitude is expressed for what he has done.

A project manager must recognize the different means by which he can influence others, especially considering the different sets of people he has to deal with. He must be good at social networking. The first step is to identify those persons whose cooperation is needed; the people whose approvals are required and those whose opposition will result in the failure of the project. Having identified the persons concerned the project manager should try and view the project from their perspective, he should address their concerns and should then try and win them over. Project managers often spend a lot of their time meeting people and managing their support for the project. This is often referred to as managing by wandering around. The 'wandering around' refers to the manager's absence from his office. But the 'wandering around' is with a purpose. A project manager gets first-hand information about the situation on the ground by 'wandering around'. He spends a fair amount of time with those who are important to the project and gains their support through social and informal interaction.

10.2.3 Organizational Skills

Organizational skill is not restricted to drawing up an organizational chart linking all employees. It is the ability to design monitoring and control systems. The project manager should be able to design reporting relationships, lines of control and channels of information flow and make them work. He should be able to resolve conflicts when they become unproductive. In a project management situation, conflicts often arise due to a clash of goals and interests between the project requirements and the functional departmental requirements. Certain amount of conflict may lead to healthy competition which may give a boost to the morale and efficiency of the project team. The project manager should have the cognitive skill to recognize when conflict becomes dysfunctional and should step in to resolve it.

10.2.4 Duties of a Project Manager

The project manager has to perform a variety of duties. He is responsible for the overall completion of the project within the time frame allotted, within the budgeted costs and in conformity with the laid down quality standards. Some of his responsibilities are listed as follows:

1. Defining and maintaining the integrity of the project.
2. Developing executive plans for the project.
3. Organizing for execution of the project.
4. Setting of targets, development of reporting systems and ensuring accomplishment of targets.
5. Negotiating with those concerned for obtaining commitment to the project.
6. Directing, coordinating and controlling project activities.
7. Contract management.
8. Resource management.
9. Problem solving.
10. Relationship management.
11. Customer and stakeholder satisfaction.
12. Achievement of project objectives.

The responsibilities are not as simple as they appear. Effective project managers have to deal with the contradictory nature of their work. Some of the major contradictions are discussed below.

Project managers have to constantly draw a balance between innovation and stability. They have to deal with changing circumstances as mentioned earlier. At the same time, they must be innovative in their approach and constantly seek new and better methods of doing tasks. Innovations disturb the already established methods and routines and the project manager has to deal with these changes, ensuring that they do not cause unnecessary disruptions and delays.

Project managers have to encourage individuals to perform while maintaining teamwork and team spirit. They must endeavour to be perceived as fair and consistent in their treatment of team members while giving the impression to each individual member that he or she is special and important to the project. The project manager must be accomplished in interpersonal skills.

Project managers often have to interfere and resolve conflicts, solve technical problems, and insist on different approaches. They must act with equanimity and maintain their calm especially during moments of crisis. They should maintain a fine balance between intervention and allowing individuals to perform unhindered by unnecessary directions and 'spoon-feeding'.

Project managers have to build a project team dedicated and committed to the project. However, this sometimes becomes counterproductive and the team becomes overly cohesive refusing to accept outside ideas and suggestions. Team loyalty must be in consonance with organizational loyalty and project managers must ensure that there is no conflict between team and organizational loyalty.

As a leader the project manager has to use a flexible style of leadership. He may adopt a participative style of management but may have to switch to an autocratic mode when circumstances so warrant. The style must suit the situation in hand. While project managers generally adopt a consultative approach and involve the team, they must be firm in their decision-making and maintain finesse and poise.

10.2.5 Traits of a Project Manager

Volumes can be written on the traits of leadership without involving a consensus. Good project managers have some common traits and the most important of these are discussed in the following paragraphs.

Holistic foresight

A project manager should be able to take a systems view of the project. He should not attempt to break the project into its various phases and then try, understand and manage each phase. Instead, the project manager should have the vision to foresee the project as a whole and to realize how the various factors collectively interact to produce project outcomes. The interaction between the parts should take precedence over the parts themselves.

Personal integrity

A project manager must have unimpeachable personal integrity. To be a good leader, one must establish a firm sense of one's self and one's principles. A project manager must lead by example and there must be congruence between 'being' and 'seeming' behaviour. He must practise what he preaches. It is essential to have a credible image in order to enjoy the trust of the team and to obtain their loyalty and commitment. Respect can only be commanded and not demanded. Others genuinely respect you for the image they perceive of you and not because of your authority and organizational position. The respect accorded to you on the basis of your authority or position is merely superficial and does not come from the heart.

Proactive

A good project manager must be proactive in his approach. He should take timely action so that small concerns do not escalate into major problems.

High tolerance for ambiguity and stress

A project manager's task is stressful. He has to cope with deadline pressures, a high degree of technical uncertainty and difficult interpersonal situations. Even stubborn professionals can generate a great deal of stress. The project manager should have the resilience to tackle stress and physical exercise, a healthy diet and life style and a supportive domestic environment can help in coping with stress.

Good communication skills

A project manager must be a good communicator. He has to communicate widely with different people and he must be able to convey his ideas correctly to them. He must also be a good and empathetic listener and should be able to draw out the true meaning of what others are saying to him.

Effective time manager

Time is at a premium for a project manager. He must be able to manage his time effectively. He should be able to prioritize his activities and yet give the impression that he has time for every one.

Skilful politician

We have already seen the different sets of people with whom a project manager has to interact. Each set of people have their own agendas and the project manager must be able to influence them and balance their particular agendas to obtain their support for the project.

Optimist

A project manager must be a diehard optimist. Even when faced with adverse circumstances he should believe in the success of the project and should be able to instil confidence in his team that things will work in the manner they want them to. A good sense of humour and a positive playful attitude are often the project manager's greatest strengths.

10.2.6 Issues Involved in Selection of a Project Manager

The various issues involved in the selection of a project manager are discussed in the following paragraphs.

External or internal source

A question that organizations often need to answer is whether the project manager should be appointed from within the organization or a person be inducted from outside. If the organization is seriously considering appointing an 'outsider' as a project manager, it should consider the adverse effect this will have on the morale of managers within the organization. In any case, an outsider will take time to familiarize himself with the structure and functioning of the organization. He will have to understand the organizational climate and the internal relationships between various persons who will be important to the success of the project. He will also have to establish his credentials and find acceptance within the organization. In spite of this, an outsider may have to be appointed as the required technical competence may not be available within the organization. On occasions, internal strife and competition between the internal managers may be so predominant that an outsider may be selected to avoid conflict within the organization. An outsider also brings fresh thinking and new ideas to an organization. If the project is in a new field of business, it may be prudent to appoint a project manager from outside the organization. It must, however, be borne in mind that if project managers are always appointed from outside, the organization will not develop expertise in the field of project management and managers within the organization will not get an opportunity to develop the skills necessary for project management.

Experience

Organizations generally give a lot of weightage to experience in project management when selecting project managers. A veteran who has successfully managed some projects is preferred over a younger person who lacks experience even though he may be more knowledgeable and technically more qualified. This is because project management is a difficult task requiring more of general management skills than specialist skills. Because of the unique nature of projects, the scope for making mistakes is limited. A veteran would have learnt a lot from his past mistakes. On the other hand, the youngster will start making mistakes now, which is best avoided.

Technical competence or interpersonal skills

Ideally a project manager should have both technical competence and good interpersonal skills. However, this ideal is rarely achieved. A technocrat tends to consider himself as a top specialist and gets too involved with the technical details of the project overlooking the more important skills of handling human beings. Instead of getting things done through others, he tends to become a doer himself. This is best avoided. The interpersonal skills should take priority over technical skills. The lack of technical expertise with the project manager can be made up by having technically skilled staff to assist him, but interpersonal skills cannot be easily taught. They are acquired over time.

Tough task master

Appointing a tough task master as a project manager may not work out well. Line employees, who enjoy considerable freedom with their line managers, may feel stifled if the project manager applies too much pressure. Line managers have considerable authority over their line employees and can 'influence' them to suit their convenience. A project manager lacks such authority and must motivate people to give their best not out of fear of punishments but by obtaining their commitment to the project. A project manager has to be both people and task oriented.

Maturity

Some companies employ older people as project managers on the assumption that they are mature. Grey hair or a balding pate is no measure of a person's maturity. A project manager acquires maturity through working on different types of projects and handling a variety of situations. Unless a person is exposed to different types of projects and situations and learns to handle them, spending years or even decades in project management may not be of much use. For instance, aerospace projects may take a decade to complete. A project manager who has worked on such a project may have 10 years experience but has actually seen only one type of project and may not be able to handle a different situation. Experience should not be viewed only in terms of the length of time spent in project management but in terms of the variety of situations to which one has been exposed.

10.3 THE PROJECT TEAM

10.3.1 Problems of Managing a Project Team

The success of a project is attributable not only to the project manager but also in a large measure to the successful handling of the project team. The project manager should be able to enthuse and motivate the team and draw positive synergy from them. He can do this if he can form and build the team properly. The team poses its own problems. The team may be formed from within the organization or from outside or a combination of the two. Often the team may not have full-time members, and experts may join the team for various components of the project as and when required.

A team drawn from within the organization may bring in members who are known to each other. While this may be a plus point, it can also cause conflict of interest as the members bring with them their load of inter-department rivalries, their personal likes and dislikes for each other and their perceptions of others. In a matrix organizational structure, the functional managers generally decide who is to be assigned to the project. The project manager will have to work with functional heads to get the persons he needs for the project. If he uses his clout with the top management to obtain persons from functional departments, he will be perceived as unnecessarily robbing departments of their essential personnel. As far as possible, the team should comprise persons who volunteer to work on the project. This will ensure their commitment to the project.

Teams which are a mix of persons from within the organization and outsiders pose their own problems. It may take some time before the outsiders are accepted by the team and fully amalgamated in it. Similarly, the part-time members may not be readily accepted. Unless properly inducted to the team they may be viewed with awe because of their expertise in a particular field and with some misgivings by the other members of the team.

Project managers should consider the following factors while recruiting team members:

Problem-solving ability

Complex projects require members who are skilled at problem solving. However, one must be cautious that such members may become bored and disinterested in the project if it does not pose any challenge to them.

Technological expertise

While technological expertise in certain fields may be required for the project, managers should be wary of technology buffs. Often they tend to make too much of technology and may be involved more in studying or implementing technology for the sake of technology rather than for its contribution towards the goals of the project. For instance, in implementation of information systems projects, often very high technology is advocated by the experts when simple solutions would serve the purpose equally well.

Availability

Often the members available for the project may not be the ones that the project manager requires on his team. A balance will have to be struck between availability and requirement.

Reputation

Team members who have a reputation for being 'winners' lend credibility to the project and make it easier for the manager to promote it with the stakeholders.

Relationship with stake holders

Often it may be helpful to include members who enjoy a good relationship with the project stakeholders and the top management as they will be able to resolve issues that may be irksome to the stakeholders. This is especially true in a matrix structure. Any conflicts of interest between the project requirements and the functional departments can be resolved better through a team member who enjoys a good working relationship with the functional head.

10.3.2 Team Building

The project manager must endeavour to build a high performance team. Teams that exhibit high positive energy and high performance generally have the following characteristics:

1. They share a common goal and every member is willing to work towards the achievement of that common goal.
2. Members recognize individual strengths and expertise and utilize these towards achieving the goals of the project. They accept the influence of those whose skills are relevant at the particular stage of the project.
3. The team exerts its efforts towards problem solving ignoring interpersonal issues and competitive struggles.

4. Differences of opinion are encouraged and freely expressed. But once a course of action is arrived at, all members give total commitment and their unquestioned support to it.
5. Mistakes are treated as opportunities for learning rather than for punishment. Witch-hunting is avoided. Members are encouraged to be creative and to take reasonable risks.
6. Members identify with the team and have a high sense of personal commitment to the project. They consider it as an opportunity for professional and personal growth.

The project manager must realize that teams cannot be formed overnight. An understanding of the team development process can go a long way to building high performance teams. Groups generally go through five stages of development in a project. The first stage is termed as *forming*. In this stage, the group gets acquainted with each other and with the objectives and goals of the project. The members identify and understand their individual roles and the interpersonal relationships with regard to their working. Responsibility and reporting relationships are established. Members establish ground rules for their conduct with respect to the project (roles and performance expected from them) and with respect to the behaviour expected from them towards each other. Once the members start thinking of themselves as a part of a cohesive group, the next stage begins.

The next stage is termed as *storming*. This stage is marked by a high degree of conflict. The conflict arises due to the resistance of members to the constraints and restrictions imposed by the project on their individuality. While the members accept they are a part of a group, it takes the members some time to accept the project manager's leadership as to how decisions will be made and control will be exercised. As these conflicts are resolved and the project manager's leadership is accepted, the members move on to the next stage.

The third stage is referred to as *norming*. During this stage, the group develops close relationships and cohesiveness. The group develops a strong sense of camaraderie and starts identifying itself with the project. The group is now set to give its best. The next stage is *performing*. As the name suggests, the team is now fully functional. The energies of the group are no longer directed towards getting to know each other but are directed towards achieving the goals of the project.

Once the project is completed the team has to be disbanded. This stage of disbandment is peculiar to projects and is often emotionally disturbing for some members. While some members bask themselves in the team's project accomplishments, others may be depressed over the loss of friendship and camaraderie gained during the currency of the project. This stage may be termed as *adjourning*.

The project manager needs to make a concerted effort at team building. He has to take an active role in setting the group norms which will lead to positive synergy and the success of the project. The project manager must lay down the ground rules as early as possible. These not only involve organizational and procedural issues but also include the norms on how the team will interact with each other. The decision-making process must be clearly defined and authority–responsibility relationships must be clearly spelt out. Each member of the team must be clear as to his role and that of others. A proper management control system should be put in place. It should lay down the form of reporting, the frequency of reports and what actions to take with regard to exception reporting.

Some of the norms associated with high performance teams are as follows:

1. Confidentiality is maintained and information is not shared outside the team without its concurrence.
2. It is acceptable to go wrong, but unacceptable to surprise others. If deadlines or milestones are likely to be delayed, others must be informed. The tendency to hide 'bad news' must be curbed. This can be ensured only if the project manager removes the fear of punishment and stresses on the need to be corrective instead of punitive.
3. Disagreements between individuals are only natural, but once a decision is taken, it must enjoy everyone's support irrespective of personal feelings.
4. Outside experts must be respected for their knowledge and the team should cooperate with them.
5. Hard work does not imply lack of fun. The team should be able to indulge in fun and the working environment should be pleasant and congenial.

Project managers should set and follow these norms.

The project manager has an important role to play in establishing an identity for the team to which they become emotionally attached. This can be achieved through team meetings, co-location of team members, team names and team rituals. Periodic team meetings provide not only a forum for exchanging information about the project but also an opportunity for team members to meet and experience that they are not alone on the project. They have the support and assistance of colleagues when required. Meetings promote a sense of belonging and help in establishing a team identity. Teams which work in a common workplace quickly identify themselves to the workplace. However, this is not always possible, especially in matrix organizational structures where members may work on the project only part-time. The project manager should insist on a suitable project office with a place for holding meetings. The walls can be covered with Gantt charts, cost charts and other output associated with planning and control of the project. These serve as tangible signs of project effort. Project identity can also be established by giving the team a tangible name such as 'Geeta's Group' or 'Chopra's Crusaders' and so on. The team may also develop a logo for itself which can be affixed to stationery, T-shirts, coffee mugs and so on. This helps in giving a unique identity to the project team of which they are proud. The social aspects of team building must also be paid attention to and the occasional dinner or get-together can go a long way to developing teams.

10.3.3 Managing Conflict

Disagreements and conflicts often arise between team members during the life of the project. There may be disagreement on the priorities, allocation of resources, suggested solutions to problems and so on. Some conflicts support the goals of the project. For instance, two members may argue passionately on how a particular task should be implemented. The argument may lead to a review of the method and an evolution of a better method of handling the task in hand. Such conflicts help in improving performance. On the other hand, members may get into a heated debate and storm out of the room refusing to work together. The project manager has to use his skills to decide when conflict is healthy, leading to synergy and when it is dysfunctional, requiring resolution at the earliest.

Conflict occurs at all stages of the project. During the planning stage, conflict mainly arises on priorities and schedules. At the execution stage, friction may occur over schedule slippages, technical problems and staff issues. Pressures to achieve milestones without compromising on quality or increase in cost often lead to conflict within the team. The team members are stressed by the need to meet deadlines and the tension leads to conflict between members.

The project manager must encourage functional conflict. There is no clear-cut demarcation between functional and dysfunctional conflict. While in one team, members may have a heated argument with exchange of expletives and yet resolve their differences, members in another team may have an outwardly polite argument but may simmer inwardly to the point of having irreconcilable differences leading to a division of the team. The project manager should see the effect that the conflict has on the project performance and not how it affects the feelings of individuals. Situations where teams work in total harmony often result in complacency. Members may agree with suggestions of others just to maintain harmony even when they know that the suggestions are impractical and unworkable. The project manager should be wary of this absence of conflict. Conflict is like nuclear energy. If properly harnessed it can yield positive results but if uncontrolled can be vastly destructive. Disagreement on issues often leads to a review of the situation resulting in better solutions. A discussion on possible alternatives or the questioning of a particular course of action may throw up better options. The project manager may enforce disagreement by appointing someone as the devil's advocate. He may also resort to asking the group to come up with reasons as to why a particular course of action generally agreed upon should not be followed. Constructive criticism should be accepted and functional conflict should be encouraged.

On the other hand, dysfunctional conflict must be dealt with as quickly as possible. As mentioned earlier, it is difficult to discern when conflict is functional or dysfunctional. For instance, two team members may hate each other's guts but may produce excellent results due to intense competition and the desire to surpass each other. Is this congenial to the working environment? Certainly not. Is it functional? Yes, as long as it contributes to the project. Alternatively, a disagreement over some technical matter may degenerate into an irrational personality clash or failure to resolve an issue may lead to unnecessary delays in the execution of the project. There is no easy method of dealing with dysfunctional conflict and the manager must use various strategies to deal with it.

The manager may mediate between the conflicting parties. He may negotiate a resolution by using reasoning, persuasion, suggesting alternatives and so on. He may use his negotiating skills, find common ground and point out that the win/lose situation has devolved into a lose/lose situation for every one. Compromises and adjustments are necessary.

Managers may have to act as arbitrators in a conflict. The manager has to act fairly and ensure that he is not perceived as taking sides. Sometimes he can use his guile by suggesting a solution which he knows would be unacceptable to both sides and then ask them to revert to him with their suggestions or a better solution (King Solomon's strategy—'cut the child into two pieces and take a piece each').

Often the situation can be diffused with the help of humour or adjourning the discussion to a later time so that tempers can cool down and the protagonists view the situation more rationally. Reassignment of tasks so that parties in conflict do not work together is another way of dealing with conflict.

If situations go totally beyond control, the project manager may have to remove the members involved in the conflict from the team. It is normal to remove both parties since both are usually at fault. The removal of members also sends a clear message to others that conflict beyond a point will not be tolerated.

The project manager must develop and use his interpersonal skills to deal with conflict. He should develop the cognitive ability to distinguish between functional and dysfunctional conflict and must promptly intervene when the conflict becomes dysfunctional.

10.3.4 Other Issues

High performance teams produce dramatic results. However, they have a flip side and often succumb to their own illusions of invincibility and self-grandeur leading to pitfalls in their behaviour and performance. Members in highly cohesive groups often tend to lose their critical evaluation capabilities and get entrapped in 'group think'. Pressures for conformity and the illusion of invincibility of the group lead them to suspend critical evaluation of situations and decisions. The group tends to make decisions hastily without due consideration of all the alternatives, sometimes resulting in fiascos which in hindsight appear totally improbable. Groups with very high espirit de corps, high degree of confidence in their own capabilities and inordinately high degree of optimism sometimes suffer from illusions of infallibility and tend to overlook all alternatives while making decisions. Such groups may stifle any voices of dissent by emphasizing the need to conform rather than disagree as a group. The lack of critical evaluation leads to faulty decisions.

Project teams are sometimes permitted to bypass procedures that are normally followed in the organization for greater expediency. However, this must not become a habit with the project team. The bypassing of bureaucratic hurdles is attractive and tempting but bureaucratic procedures form the backbone of any organization's working. Excessive attempts at bypassing bureaucratic channels will only lead to alienation from the rest of the organization as those within the organization have to work under the bureaucratic constraints. The bureaucrats themselves will resent this attitude of the project team and may create unnecessary hurdles in their functioning just to 'get even'.

Members of high performance teams enjoy great personal satisfaction from the challenges thrown up by the project. They become infatuated with the challenge of the project and the talent around them to such an extent that when the project finishes, they suffer from burnout and disorientation. They find it difficult to fit into their original slots to which they have to revert on completion of the project.

Project teams act closely with clients and sometimes their identity with client becomes so strong that the client's interests start taking priority over the organization's interests. This results in excessive project creep and in extreme cases an open defiance of corporate policy and interests.

These maladies are difficult to deal with as they are a distortion of something good, rather than simply evil. Managers must ensure that a balance is maintained between the project team and the parent organization. In a matrix organizational structure, balance is maintained as members have to keep in touch with their functional departments. In the case of dedicated project teams, balance can be maintained by having members of the parent organization actively involved at project status meetings and so on. When managers detect the onset of group think, they should introduce dissent by playing the role of a devil's advocate. Formal team-building sessions may help to refocus attention of the team on project objectives.

SUMMARY

Project staffing is different from staffing of other organizations because of the peculiar nature of projects. Essentially, the project organization is temporary in nature and ceases to exist after the completion of the project. This characteristic of the organization poses its own peculiar problems with regard to staffing. In typical matrix organizations, project team members are sometimes torn between loyalties to the project vis-à-vis loyalty to their functional department. There is also some anxiety as to the future once the project is over.

The project manager has to be a leader and a manager as he must be able to cope with the changing environment. He should be adept at handling people and should have high interpersonal skills. During the course of his duties, he has to interact with a large set of people varying from top management, stakeholders, suppliers, contractors, government agencies, project team members, other project managers, technical experts and so on. He should be able to influence and motivate the project team towards achieving the project goals.

Selection of a project manager involves some issues such as whether he should be from within the organization or brought in from outside, whether he should be a technocrat or a generalist, whether we should prefer experience or knowledge in the related field and so on. The project manager has a very important role to play and he should be carefully selected.

The team members should be selected on the basis of their problem-solving abilities, their technical skills, their reputation as 'winners', their relationship with other stakeholders and above all their availability. Project teams go through the normal team-building process which involves norming, storming, forming, performing and adjourning.

Conflict is an inherent part of working in teams and groups. Project managers should be skilled at conflict resolution. Conflict may be dysfunctional or functional. Dysfunctional conflict must be resolved as soon as possible. The project manager may act as a mediator or as an arbitrator amongst members involved in a conflict. He should, however, be very wary of excessive cohesiveness and conformity as this gives rise to 'group think', as a result of which groups take decisions without rationally considering all alternatives or the implications of their decisions. They tend to avoid all conflicts and dissensions within the team so that harmony is maintained. The project manager may have to consider the use of conflict stimulation techniques, such as appointing a devil's advocate, asking the group to come up with reasons why the decision or plan made by them will not work, introducing 'outsiders' to air different views and so on.

The success of a project depends not only on a well-conceived project plan but also on the team which is to execute it. Having the right people, with the right skills and the right attitudes can be a major success factor in the execution of a project. A project is a one-time activity and there is no room for mistakes—nor can one learn from mistakes as these may prove disastrous for the project in hand. Project staffing, therefore, assumes great importance.

QUESTIONS

1. What are the problems peculiar to project staffing?
2. What are the traits common to successful project managers?
3. What are the duties of a project manager?
4. What are the issues involved in the selection of a project manager?
5. A project manager must be a good leader. Comment.
6. Why is it important for a project manager to have good interpersonal skills?
7. What are the problems of selecting and managing project teams?
8. As a project manager, how would you influence members of your project team?
9. What strategies can you adopt for conflict management?

CHAPTER 11

Project Monitoring and Control

If you can interpret project status data in several different ways, only the most painful interpretation will be correct.
—Stephen Seay

LEARNING OBJECTIVES

After reading this chapter, you will be able to:

- Appreciate the problems of project monitoring and control.
- Develop a management information system for project monitoring and control.
- Study the methods of monitoring and controlling time performance on projects.
- Study the monitoring and control of time performance on projects through network analysis.
- Study the method of monitoring and controlling projects through the earned value method.
- Understand and interpret status reports.

11.1 INTRODUCTION

Plans are made with the best of intentions, but seldom do things go exactly as per plan. It is important to monitor projects during their execution and exercise control over them so that time and cost overruns are avoided. Projects rarely, if ever, lend themselves to the conventional budgetary control. Traditionally, the budgeted costs are broken down into costs to be incurred over a period of time. Comparison is then done between the budgeted cost and the actual cost incurred during a review period. The variation forms the basis of control. This poses its own problems when dealing with projects. Let us take an example.

A firm is executing a high-tech project of construction of an oil refinery. The planned budgeted costs for the first three months are ₹ 5,00,000, while the actual costs are ₹ 6,00,000. The accounting department may conclude that the project has a cost overrun of ₹ 1,00,000, whereas the project may be ahead of schedule and the extra cost represents the cost of doing the extra work. Alternatively, the project may be behind schedule and may have also had a cost overrun. The data does not tell the full story. Similarly, if the actual cost incurred is less than the planned budgeted cost, is the project saving money, or is it behind schedule, or both? It may be appreciated that traditional cost budgeting control methods prove inadequate in dealing with projects.

What exactly is control and how does it work? Control is the process of measuring the current state of a system, comparing it with a desired state and then taking adequate measures to reduce the variance between the current state and the desired state. It presupposes that there is a 'desired state' or a baseline with which comparisons are to be made. There must be a means to measure the current state. This may involve different parameters depending on the system under study. There must be a corrective mechanism to deal with variance. A thermostat in a refrigerator is a typical example of control. The temperature inside the refrigerator is measured and compared with the temperature set by the user. If the interior's temperature is found to be higher than the set temperature, relays are activated which turn the compressor on, and if the temperature is lower, the relay switches the compressor off. In the case of a project, the important variables requiring control are time, cost and quality.

The planning process sets the baseline in regard to these parameters. A project control information system must be incorporated so that the state of these variables—time, cost and quality—can be measured. Corrective measures must then be initiated to reduce the variances, if any.

11.2 SETTING A BASELINE

The baseline is set based on the schedules prepared during the planning stage. It is the planned cost and the expected scheduled performance against which actual cost and performance are measured. The project network schedule derived from the WBS serves as a baseline to compare against actual performance. The Gantt chart is a typical tool used to track performance. Its easy-to-understand visual format makes it a favourite tool to convey project status to top management who do not have time for details. Gantt charts were also referred to in Chapter 6. An example of a Gantt chart is shown in Figure 11.1.

The data on the Gantt chart can be set as a baseline, and actual progress and revised time estimates can be added to give an overview of the project at a glance.

11.3 PROJECT MANAGEMENT INFORMATION SYSTEM

Monitoring the progress of the project requires reliable, relevant, accurate and timely information. We must identify what data needs to be collected, who will collect it, how will he collect it and when will it be collected. The system must also lay down how the data will be analyzed, processed and disseminated. In order to identify the data to be collected we should first analyze the information needs of the different stakeholders. The information should answer the following:

1. What is the current status of the project in terms of schedule and costs?

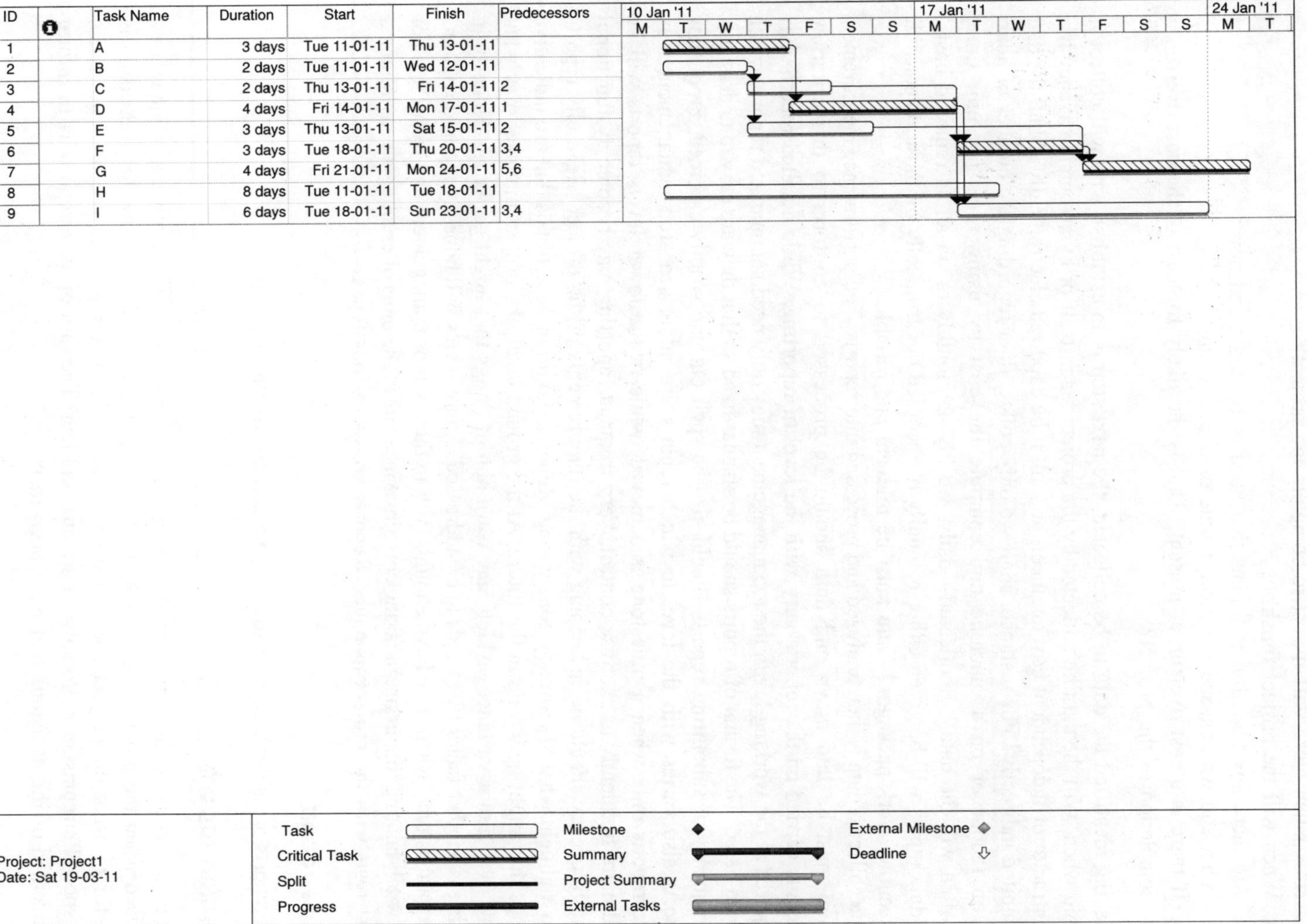

ID		Task Name	Duration	Start	Finish	Predecessors
1		A	3 days	Tue 11-01-11	Thu 13-01-11	
2		B	2 days	Tue 11-01-11	Wed 12-01-11	
3		C	2 days	Thu 13-01-11	Fri 14-01-11	2
4		D	4 days	Fri 14-01-11	Mon 17-01-11	1
5		E	3 days	Thu 13-01-11	Sat 15-01-11	2
6		F	3 days	Tue 18-01-11	Thu 20-01-11	3,4
7		G	4 days	Fri 21-01-11	Mon 24-01-11	5,6
8		H	8 days	Tue 11-01-11	Tue 18-01-11	
9		I	6 days	Tue 18-01-11	Sun 23-01-11	3,4

Figure 11.1 Gantt chart showing the project network.

2. How much more will it cost to complete the project?
3. When will the project finish?
4. Are there any potential problems that need to be addressed now?
5. What and who caused the project time or cost overrun?
6. If there is a cost overrun at present, what is the likely forecast of the cost overrun at completion of the project?

Having identified the data to be collected, the next step is to establish who will collect it, how and when. Will the data be collected by the project team itself or by an outside agency like the contractor or independent cost engineer, or shall it be captured electronically? Shall the data be compiled indirectly? For instance, shall we only collect data regarding the number of hours spent on labour or on a machine and compute the cost by using rates per unit time? How often will the data be collected—daily, weekly or monthly or on an as required basis? What data inputs will be given either manually or recorded electronically by those responsible for executing work packages? Data must be relevant and reliable.

The collected data is then analyzed and processed into reports. The performance measurement criterion must be laid down and data should be processed to conform to this criterion. The details carried on the reports vary with the level of reporting. While detailed reports may be required at the working level, the top management may only need summarized reports which are broad based. The format of reports should be standardized so that they are easy to understand. The frequency of submitting reports should also be spelt out and strictly enforced. Frequency of reports also varies with the level to which reports are addressed. Top management may require reports only when a milestone is achieved, while at the lower levels reports will be needed more frequently to exercise control. Very frequent reporting may become dysfunctional and the frequency should be in keeping with the requirements of the project. Generally reports tend to highlight what has already gone wrong. Reports should include trends that are indicative of things that might go wrong in the future. At the ground level, the project manager may want to know even minor variances which may warn him of things that might go wrong. Honesty in reporting is another factor that needs to be addressed. Junior levels will honestly report deviations and variations only when they have enough faith in their senior management and trust them not to go 'witch-hunting' but assist in taking corrective measures. The onus of creating an environment of trust rests with the project manager. Reports are of various types.

Routine reports

These reports are submitted periodically and contain routine information.

Exception reports

As the name indicates, these are raised in exceptional circumstances. Generally exception reports are raised when the project is off track and the management needs to know that a decision is called for to bring the project back on track. They are also raised when decisions are taken under special circumstances to solve a serious problem. The aim of such reports is to inform all concerned of the decisions that have been taken.

Special reports

These are based on analysis or studies carried out either as part of the project or to overcome some special problem connected with the project. They aim to share the experience gained on the project or the special situation with others in the organization, who may be interested or may face similar situations in the future.

Reporting systems often become unwieldy and ineffective because of information overload, poor coordination and irrelevant data. Sometimes the reports contain too many details which make them difficult to comprehend. At times the decision-makers ask for too many details, irrespective of whether they need the information or not. This results in making the task of compiling such reports boring and tedious. Information tends to follow Finagale's law:

> *Information that we have is not what we want. The information we want is not what we need and the information that we need is generally not available.*

Very often reports become meaningless as there is poor coordination between the project information system and that of the firm. Methods of accumulating costs and overheads may be different for the firm and different for the project, making the data incompatible and incomparable. Project information systems should follow the same methodologies as the information systems of the firm to overcome this problem.

Reports must contain information that is relevant to the issue and to the recipient's information needs. Sometimes the project reports are integrated with the other routine reports pertaining to functional departments. These do not facilitate proper control over the project.

11.4 MONITORING AND CONTROLLING TIME PERFORMANCE

The baseline for measuring time performance is generally set using a Gantt chart. The progress at the end of a review period can be incorporated in the Gantt chart and the network can be updated. A tracking Gantt chart can be used to show the revised schedule and the progress. MS Office Project and similar project management software cater for all these functions. The project used in Section 11.2 is being used to illustrate the use of MS Office Project software. The original Gantt chart shown in Figure 11.1 has been saved as the baseline. The Gantt chart in Figure 11.2 shows the progress of the project as on 18 January 2009. Activity A, instead of starting on 11 January 2009 and finishing on 13 January 2009, actually commenced on 13 January and finished on 16 January. The activity B also commenced on 13 January instead of 11 January and finished on 15 January instead of 12 January. The effect of this delay on the rest of the project is shown on the updated Gantt chart. The project will now finish on 1 February, whereas it was to finish on 28 January as per plan. Activity H started on 12 January instead of 11 January and by 18 January only 25% of the work was completed.

Figure 11.3 shows the tracking Gantt chart for the same data. The chart has been generated using MS Office Project software.

Let us study how we can control the schedule aspect through networks with the help of Example 11.1.

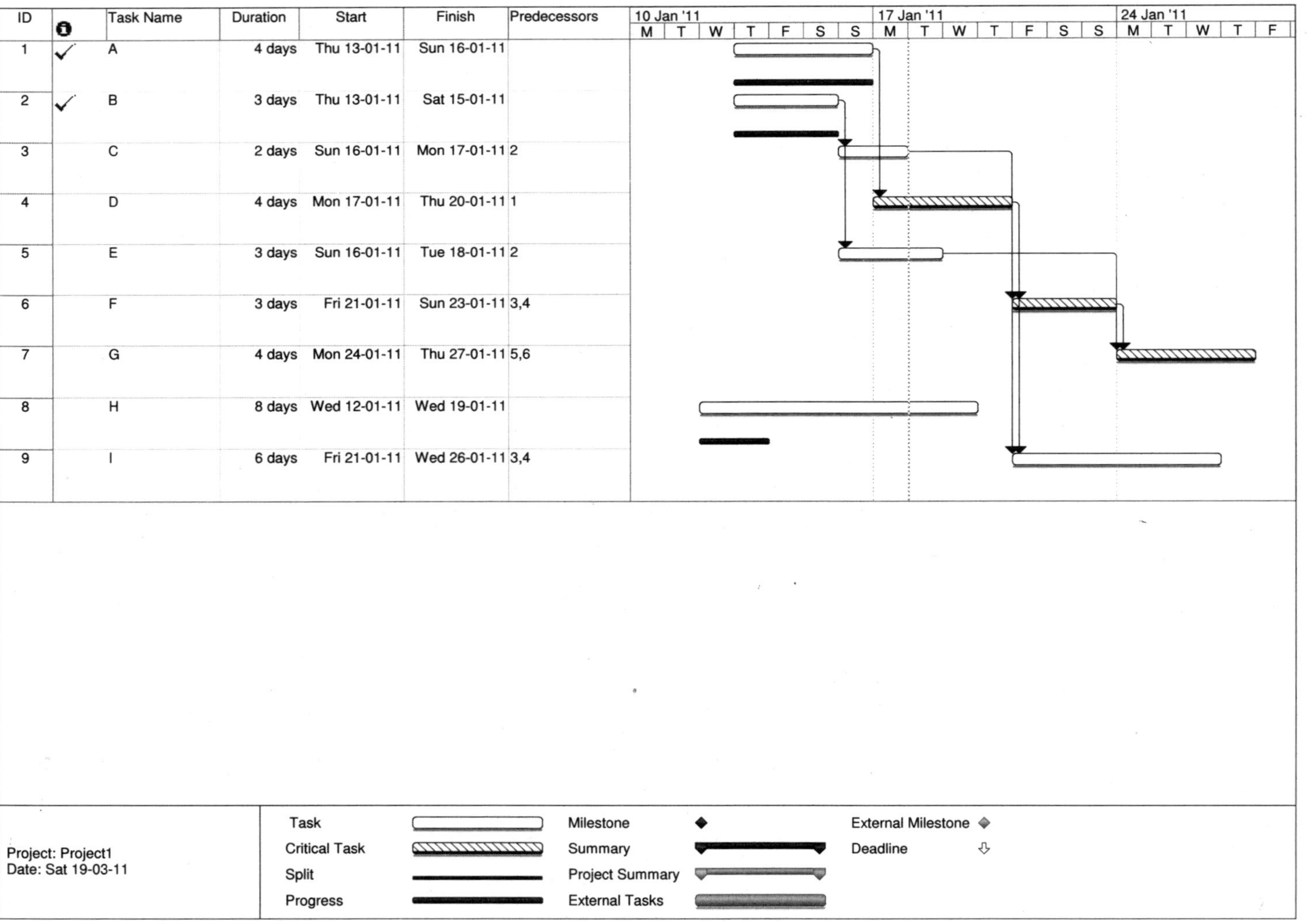

ID		Task Name	Duration	Start	Finish	Predecessors
1	✓	A	4 days	Thu 13-01-11	Sun 16-01-11	
2	✓	B	3 days	Thu 13-01-11	Sat 15-01-11	
3		C	2 days	Sun 16-01-11	Mon 17-01-11	2
4		D	4 days	Mon 17-01-11	Thu 20-01-11	1
5		E	3 days	Sun 16-01-11	Tue 18-01-11	2
6		F	3 days	Fri 21-01-11	Sun 23-01-11	3,4
7		G	4 days	Mon 24-01-11	Thu 27-01-11	5,6
8		H	8 days	Wed 12-01-11	Wed 19-01-11	
9		I	6 days	Fri 21-01-11	Wed 26-01-11	3,4

Figure 11.2 Gantt chart showing project status as on 18 January.

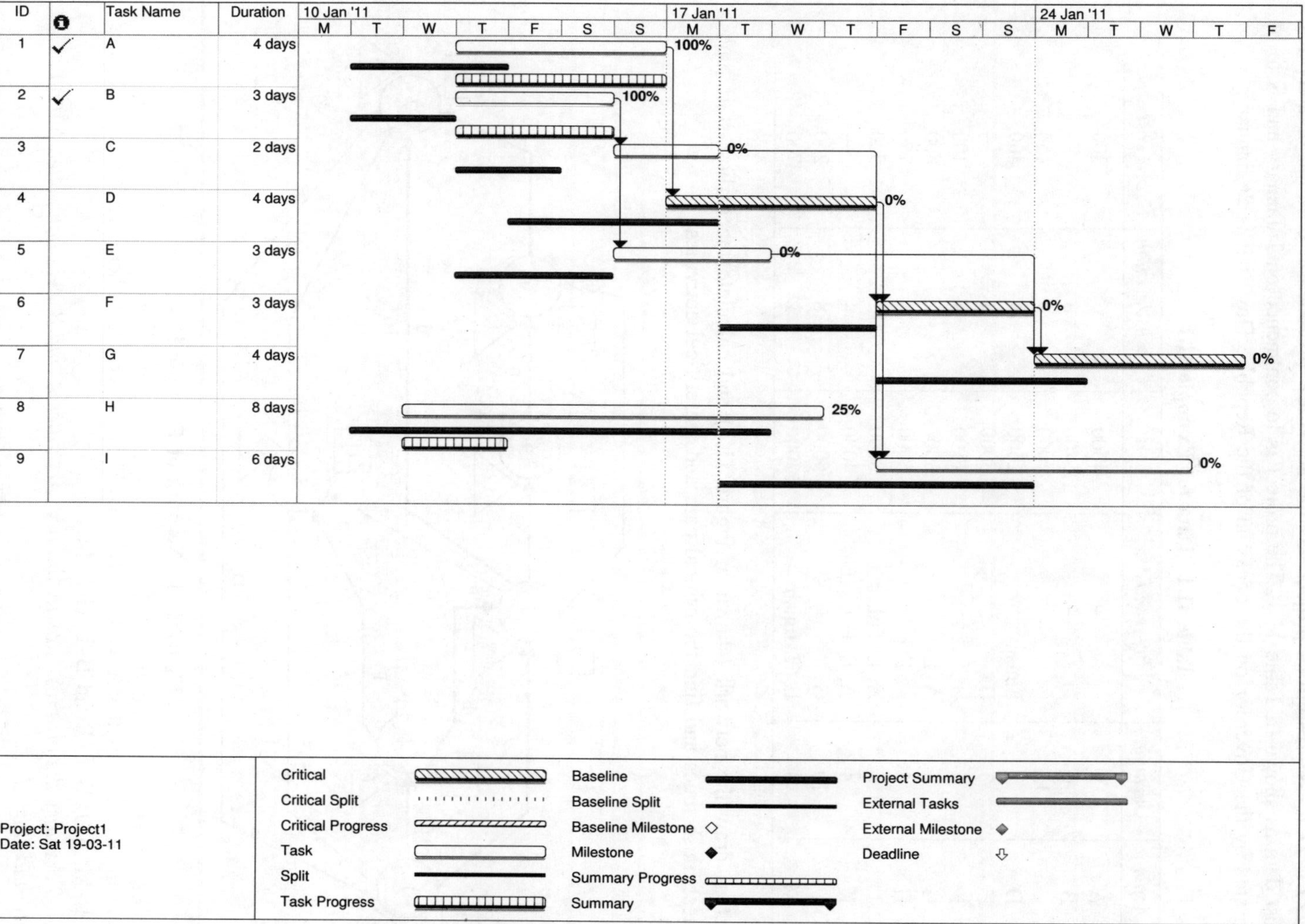

Figure 11.3 Tracking Gantt chart showing project status as on 18 January.

EXAMPLE 11.1 A prestigious project has the activities, precedence, duration of activities, and cost data as shown in Table 11.1. The project is to commence on 1 January and is to be inaugurated by the Governor on the occasion of the Republic Day, that is 26 January.

Table 11.1 Data for Example 11.1

Activity	*Duration*	*Preceded by*	*Cost*	*Crash duration*	*Crash cost/day*
A	9	—	4500	6	300
B	6	—	5400	6	—
C	11	—	4000	9	150
D	5	Finish	2500	4	400
E	3	B	3000	3	—
F	5	B	1500	4	100
G	3	A, E	3000	2	600
H	6	A, E	5000	4	750
J	16	A, E, finish	8000	12	500
K	4	A, E, F, C, finish	4000	4	—
L	10	G	5000	8	250
M	3	L, H, finish	3000	2	700

Let us draw the network (shown in Figure 11.4) and calculate the earliest start times, the latest finish times and find the critical path and the critical activities.

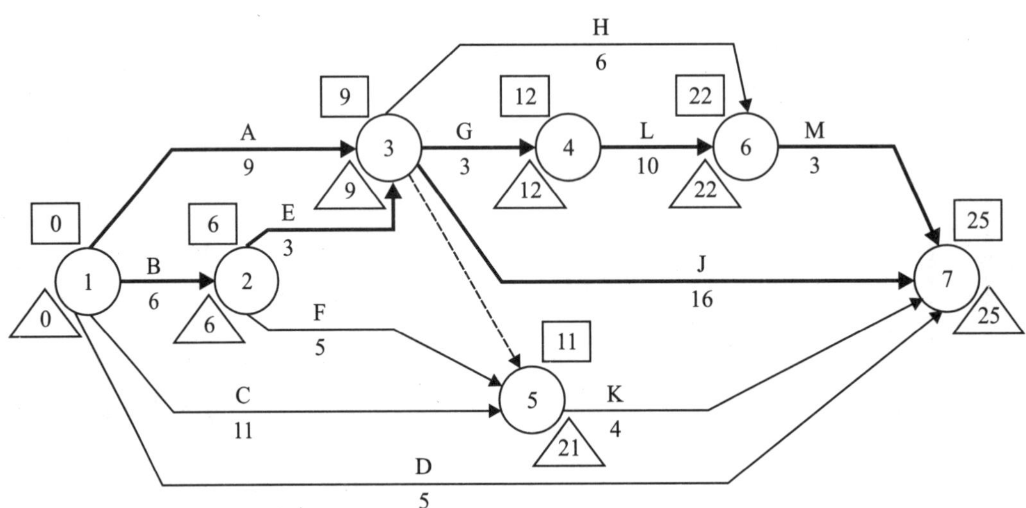

Figure 11.4 Network of Example 11.1.

As can be seen activities A, B, E, G, L, J and M are all critical. There are four critical paths: A–G–L–M; A–J; B–E–J and B–E–G–L–M.

On 9 January the progress was as follows: Activities A and B were completed but no other activity had started.

Let us now revise the network (shown in Figure 11.5).

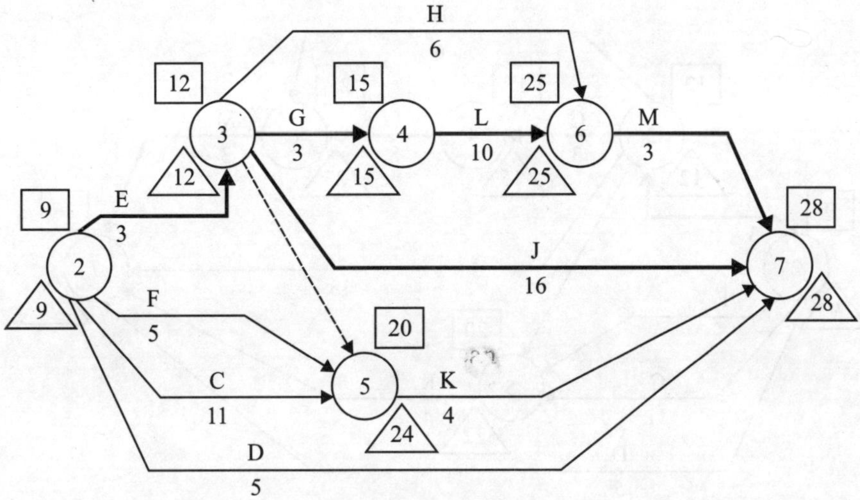

Figure 11.5 Revised network for Example 11.1.

We have removed the activities A and B since they are completed, and we are assuming that we would now start all activities on 10 January that are required to be started. We now find that the project cannot be completed before 29 January. Since it is an important project and must be inaugurated by the Governor on 26 January, we must now crash it by three days. The critical activities are E, G, L, M and J. The critical paths are E–G–L–M and E–J. Activity E cannot be crashed. The cheapest activity to crash is L which can be crashed by two days at a cost of ₹ 250 per day. Let us crash L by two days and revise the network (shown in Figure 11.6).

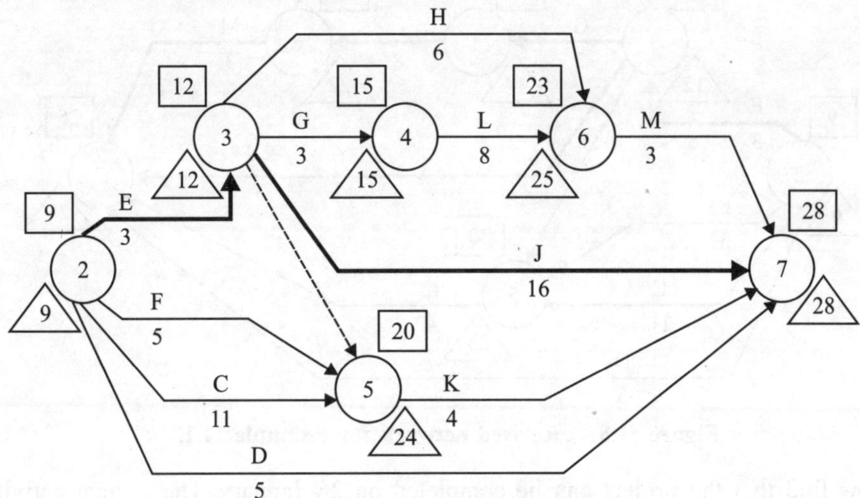

Figure 11.6 Revised network for Example 11.1.

It can now be seen that the duration of the project has not changed and the critical activities are E and J. Since E cannot be crashed, let us crash J by three days and revise the network (shown in Figure 11.7).

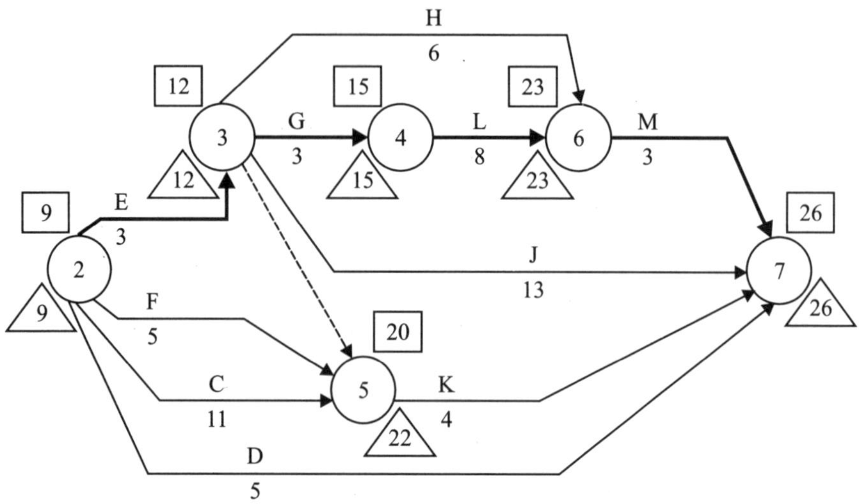

Figure 11.7 Revised network for Example 11.1.

We now find that the project duration has decreased by two days and we still need to crash it by one more day. The critical activities are E, G, L and M. Of these, E cannot be crashed and L has been crashed to its maximum limit. We can consider crashing G or M. The cheaper option is to crash G by one day. Let us revise the network (shown in Figure 11.8).

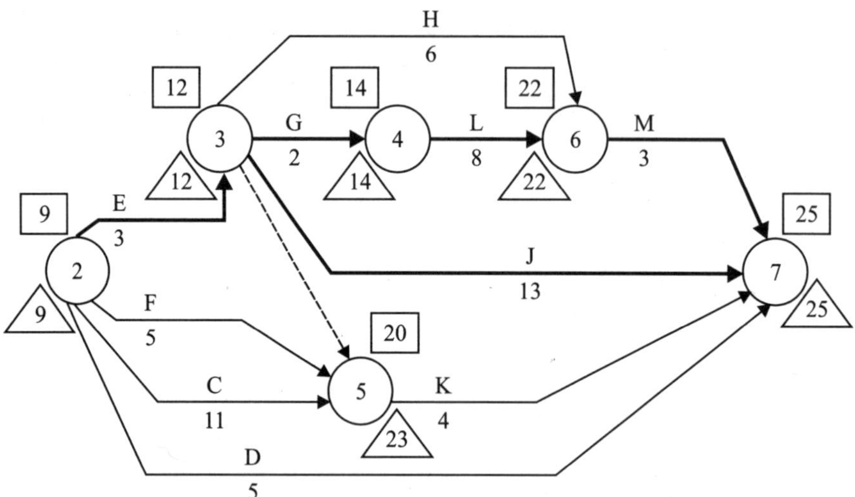

Figure 11.8 Revised network for Example 11.1.

We now find that the project can be completed on 26 January. The critical activities are E, G, L, M and J and the critical paths are E–G–L–M and E–J.

As can be seen, the network must be revised periodically so that it can serve as a tool for control.

Gantt charts produced for this project with the help of MS Office Project software are shown in Figures 11.9–11.11.

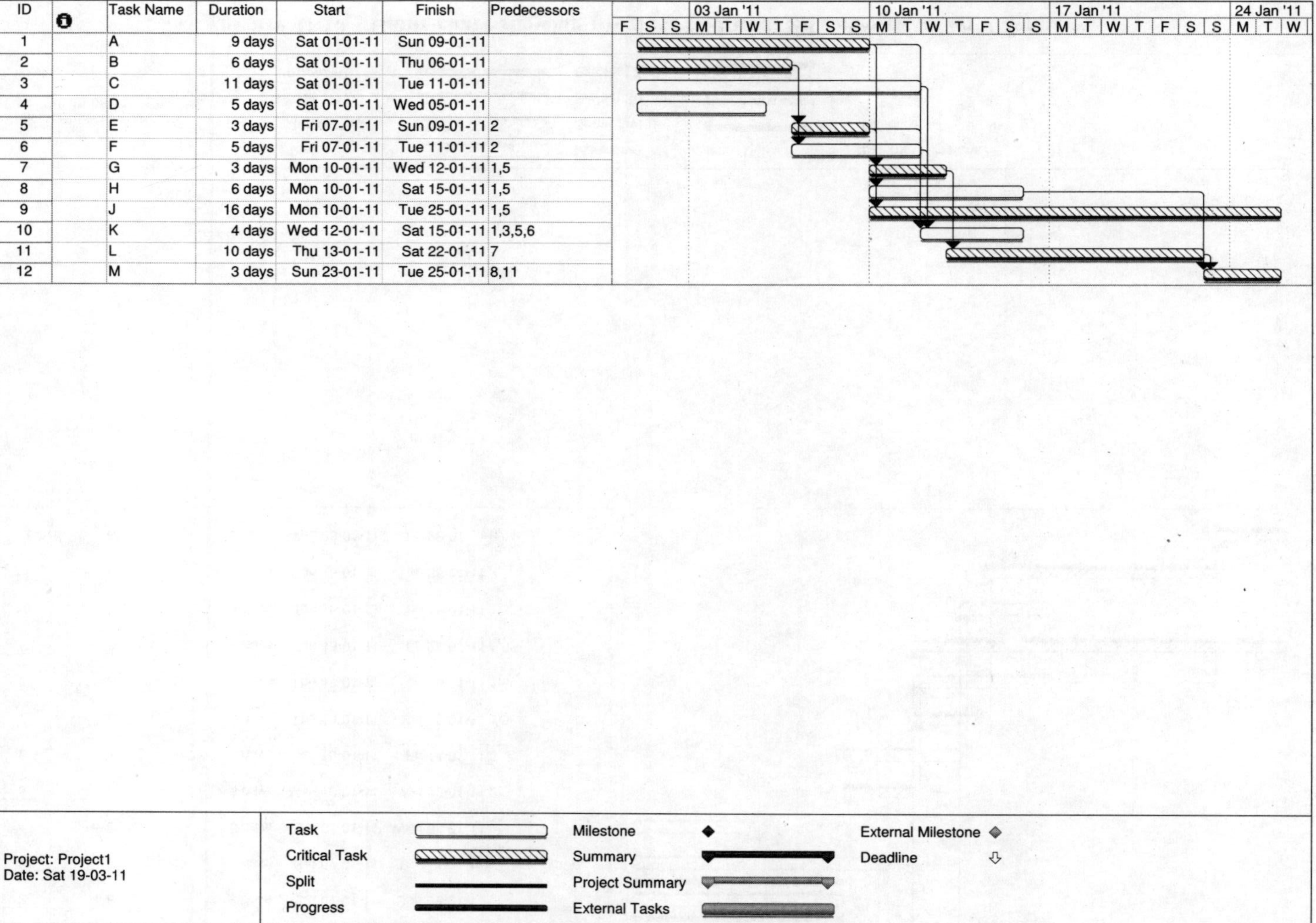

ID	Task Name	Duration	Start	Finish	Predecessors
1	A	9 days	Sat 01-01-11	Sun 09-01-11	
2	B	6 days	Sat 01-01-11	Thu 06-01-11	
3	C	11 days	Sat 01-01-11	Tue 11-01-11	
4	D	5 days	Sat 01-01-11	Wed 05-01-11	
5	E	3 days	Fri 07-01-11	Sun 09-01-11	2
6	F	5 days	Fri 07-01-11	Tue 11-01-11	2
7	G	3 days	Mon 10-01-11	Wed 12-01-11	1,5
8	H	6 days	Mon 10-01-11	Sat 15-01-11	1,5
9	J	16 days	Mon 10-01-11	Tue 25-01-11	1,5
10	K	4 days	Wed 12-01-11	Sat 15-01-11	1,3,5,6
11	L	10 days	Thu 13-01-11	Sat 22-01-11	7
12	M	3 days	Sun 23-01-11	Tue 25-01-11	8,11

Figure 11.9 Gantt chart showing the project planned schedule.

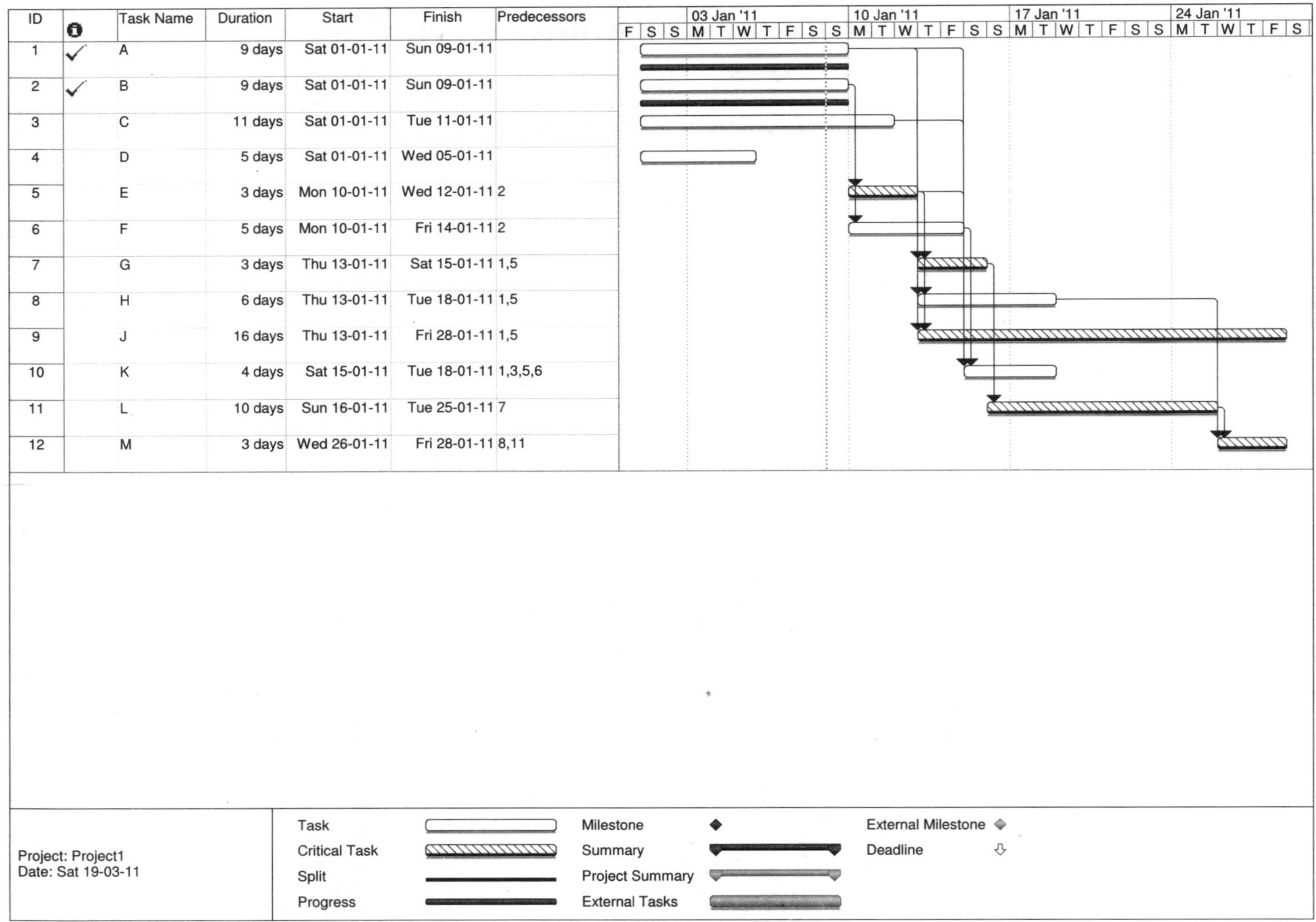

ID		Task Name	Duration	Start	Finish	Predecessors
1	✓	A	9 days	Sat 01-01-11	Sun 09-01-11	
2	✓	B	9 days	Sat 01-01-11	Sun 09-01-11	
3		C	11 days	Sat 01-01-11	Tue 11-01-11	
4		D	5 days	Sat 01-01-11	Wed 05-01-11	
5		E	3 days	Mon 10-01-11	Wed 12-01-11	2
6		F	5 days	Mon 10-01-11	Fri 14-01-11	2
7		G	3 days	Thu 13-01-11	Sat 15-01-11	1,5
8		H	6 days	Thu 13-01-11	Tue 18-01-11	1,5
9		J	16 days	Thu 13-01-11	Fri 28-01-11	1,5
10		K	4 days	Sat 15-01-11	Tue 18-01-11	1,3,5,6
11		L	10 days	Sun 16-01-11	Tue 25-01-11	7
12		M	3 days	Wed 26-01-11	Fri 28-01-11	8,11

Figure 11.10 Gantt chart showing progress and updated network as on 9 January.

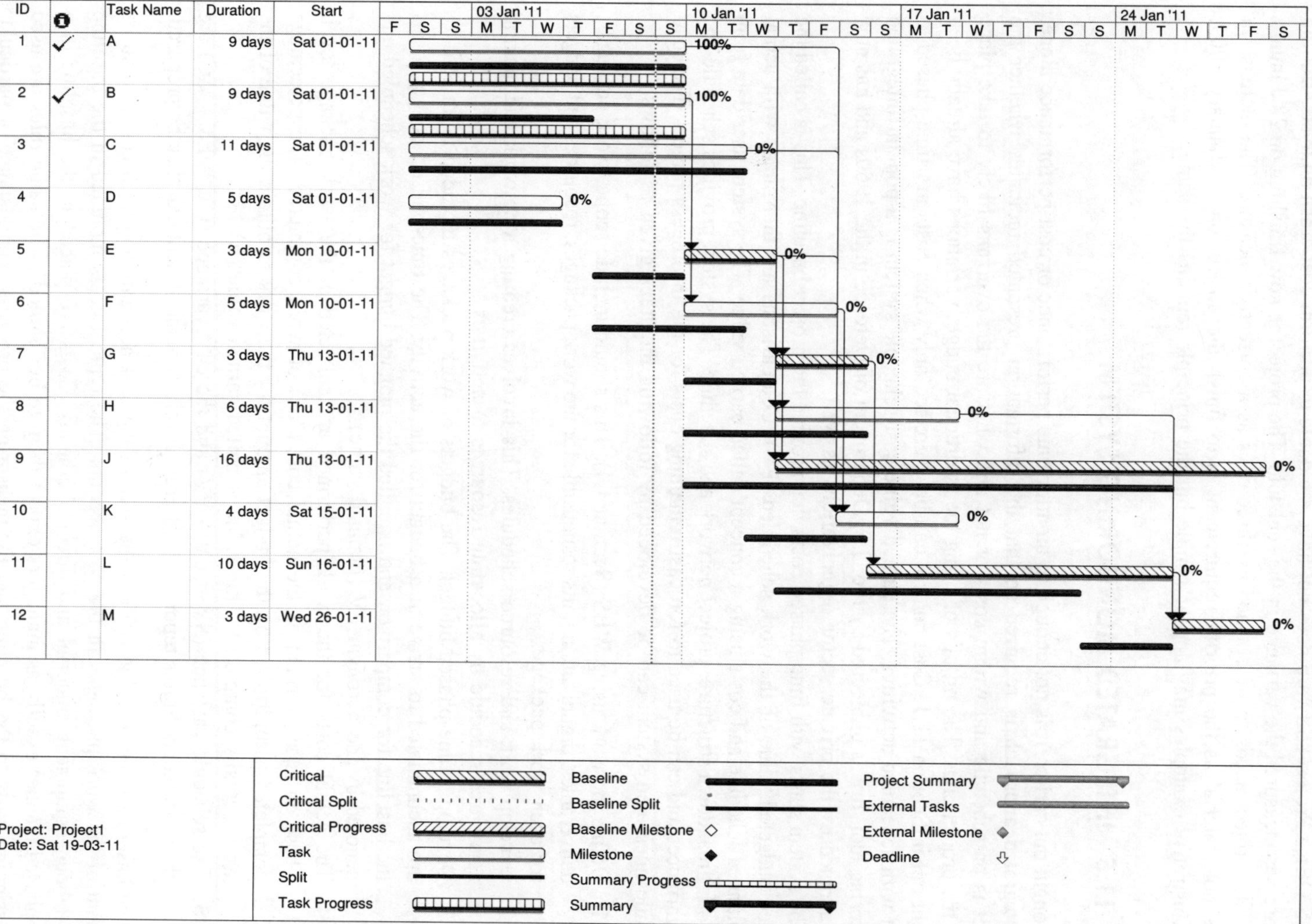

Figure 11.11 Tracking Gantt chart showing project status on 9 January after updating.

MS Office Project software does not have a module to perform cost crash analysis. But the software has measured the variance in the schedule. The project is now finishing on 28 January 2009. The project needs to be crashed by three days as a corrective measure. The increase in cost is not material as the priority requirement is to finish the project on 25 January 2009. The illustrative examples may appear simple but the principle remains the same.

11.5 INTEGRATED MONITORING SYSTEM

As brought out earlier, it is not enough to monitor time performance or cost performance alone. An integrated approach is required so that the information presented indicates whether the project is on schedule and within costs or not and what are the overruns likely to take place when the project ends. The pitfalls of using the traditional budget variations have already been brought out in Section 11.1. Cost control can be exercised only when costs are time-phased to match with scheduled activities. The earned value cost schedule system is a popular integrated monitoring tool. It was pioneered by the U.S. Department of Defence in the 1960s and has now been adopted by the private sector organizations as well.

The system starts with time-phased costs that provide the project baseline. This is called the planned budgeted value of the work scheduled (PV). Comparisons are then made with actual and planned schedule and costs using a concept called earned value. The system uses data from the work breakdown structure, project network and schedule. The system provides schedule and cost variances and can be used to forecast remaining costs for the in-process project. The cost/schedule integrated system can be developed by following the steps given as follows:

Step 1 Define the work using WBS (Section 4.4). This should include scope, work packages, deliverables, organization units responsible for the work packages, resources and budgets for each work package.

Step 2 Develop work and resource schedules. This involves creating a network and making a resource schedule by allocating resources to activities.

Step 3 Develop a time-phased budget. The budgets of work packages included in an activity are accumulated to arrive at a budget for the activity. The time-phased budget forms the baseline for comparison and is called the planned budget for work scheduled and denoted by the acronym PV (planned value).

Step 4 The actual costs for the work performed are collected at the work package level. These costs are termed as the actual cost (AC) of work completed. The percentage completed is multiplied by the budget amount for the work to obtain the value of the work actually completed. This value is called earned value (EV).

Step 5 The schedule variance (SV = EV – PV) and the cost variance (CV = EV – AC) are then computed. Status reports for different levels of management can then be prepared.

The baseline planned value (PV) is the sum of the cost accounts and each cost account is the sum of the work packages in the cost account. The typical costs included in the baseline are—labour, equipment, material and direct overheads. Costs are placed in the baseline in a time-phased manner exactly as managers expect them to be ‘earned’. The same rules are used for assigning costs to the baseline and for measuring the progress. For instance, a particular activity extending over a period of 10 days may involve different types and units of work over each day and hence different costs. If these costs and the progress of work can be related, then they would be reflected accordingly in the baseline and would be measured accordingly too. As this poses some problems, the most commonly used rule for assigning and measuring costs is the *per cent complete* rule. Under this rule, frequent check points are established over the duration of the work package and completion percentages are assigned in monetary terms (₹). For instance, if a work package involves excavation of 7000 cubic metres of earth and its planned cost is ₹ 1,40,000, then each cubic metre of excavation completed would be assigned a cost of ₹ 20. If at a review period 700 metres of excavation have been completed, we can say that 10% of the work package has been done. The earned value (EV) of this work would be obtained by multiplying the budgeted value with this percentage, that is,

$$1{,}40{,}000 \times 0.10 = 14{,}000 \text{ (₹ 14,000)}$$

The variance analysis compares the earned value (EV) with the expected schedule value (PV) to obtain schedule variance and the earned value (EV) with the actual cost (AC) to obtain the cost variance. A positive variance indicates a desirable condition while a negative variance indicates that things have gone wrong.

Cost variance indicates whether the work accomplished has cost more or less than was planned at any point over the life of the project. A positive variance indicates that the accomplished work has cost less than planned and a negative cost variance indicates a cost overrun. If separate cost accounts are maintained for labour, materials and equipment, the cause of the variance can be isolated and corrective action can be taken.

Schedule variance presents only an overall assessment of all the work packages in the project scheduled to date. It does not contain any critical path information. It measures the progress in rupee terms rather than in time units. Therefore, it does not give accurate information on whether any milestone or critical activity is late or early. The only accurate method of obtaining the true time progress of the project is to compare the baseline network with the actual network through a tracking Gantt chart as explained in the preceding section. However, the scheduled variance is an indicator of the direction the project is taking—after about 20% of the project is complete.

Sometimes alternate rules are used for computing earned value. These help to reduce the cost of data collection and remove subjective judgements of people involved as to how much work has been completed. The commonly followed alternate rules are as follows:

0/100 per cent rule

The rule assumes that credit is earned for the work only when it is completed. Hence, 100% of the budget is earned when the package is completed. This rule is used for work packages having very short durations.

50/50 per cent rule

This rule permits 50% of the value of the work package budget to be earned when the work is started and 50% to be earned when the work is completed. This rule is generally applied to work packages of short duration and small total costs.

Let us understand the procedure with the help of an example. For the sake of simplicity and ease of understanding it is assumed that there is only one cost account (labour) and each activity on the network is only using labour and no other costs are assigned. It has also been assumed that the project earliest start times will be used as a baseline. The percentage complete rule will be used for assigning and measuring costs.

The basic data for the project is given in Table 11.2.

Table 11.2 Basic data for a project

Activity	*Preceded by*	*Duration*	*Manpower required*	*Cost per day*
A	Start	3	3	3000
B	Start	2	2	2000
C	B	2	3	3000
D	A	4	2	2000
E	B	3	3	3000
F	D, C	3	3	3000
G	F, E, finish	4	3	3000
H	Start, finish	8	1	1000
I	D, C	6	2	2000

The Gantt chart for the project is shown in Figure 11.12.

Table 11.3 shows the baseline costs on a daily basis using the earliest start times as the baseline. Double lines indicate critical activities. Normal activities are shown by dotted lines.

Table 11.3 Base line costs on a daily basis

S. No.	*Activity*	*EST*	*LFT*	*Cost/day*	1	2	3	4	5	6	7	8	9	10	11	12	13	14
1	A	0	3	3000														
2	B	0	5	2000														
3	C	2	7	3000														
4	D	3	7	2000														
5	E	2	10	3000														
6	F	7	10	3000														
7	G	10	14	3000														
8	H	0	14	1000														
9	I	7	14	2000														
Daily costs (000s)					6	6	10	9	6	3	3	6	5	5	5	5	5	3
Cumulative costs (000s)					6	12	22	31	37	40	43	49	54	59	64	69	74	77

A status report presents a snapshot of the project. It uses earned value to measure schedule and cost performance. Work packages may be in one of the following three conditions:

1. Finished
2. Not yet started
3. Partially completed and in progress

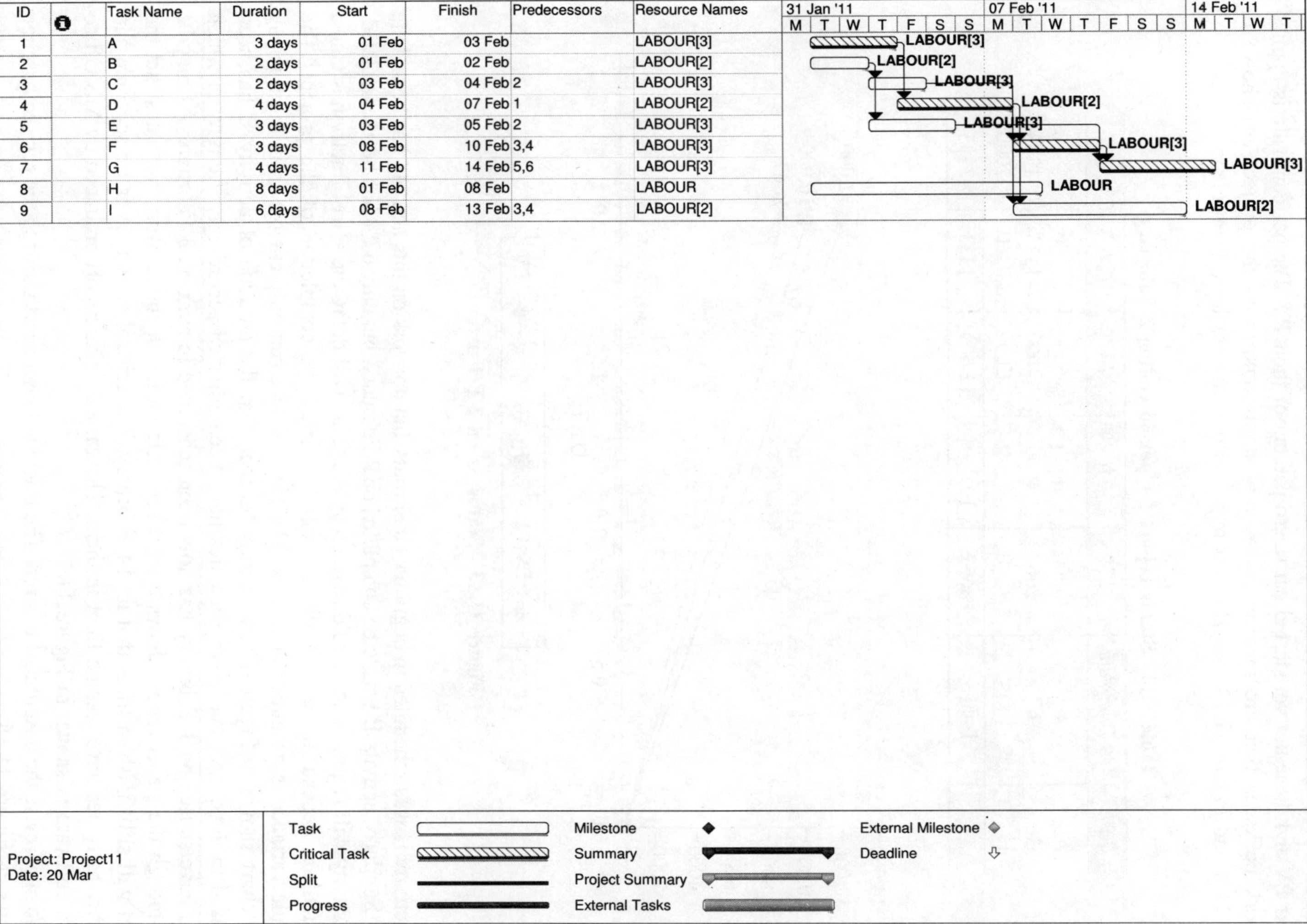

ID	Task Name	Duration	Start	Finish	Predecessors	Resource Names
1	A	3 days	01 Feb	03 Feb		LABOUR[3]
2	B	2 days	01 Feb	02 Feb		LABOUR[2]
3	C	2 days	03 Feb	04 Feb	2	LABOUR[3]
4	D	4 days	04 Feb	07 Feb	1	LABOUR[2]
5	E	3 days	03 Feb	05 Feb	2	LABOUR[3]
6	F	3 days	08 Feb	10 Feb	3,4	LABOUR[3]
7	G	4 days	11 Feb	14 Feb	5,6	LABOUR[3]
8	H	8 days	01 Feb	08 Feb		LABOUR
9	I	6 days	08 Feb	13 Feb	3,4	LABOUR[2]

Figure 11.12 Gantt chart showing the earliest time schedule for the project.

The first two conditions pose no problems. The work packages that are finished earn 100% of their PV and those not yet started earn zero percent of their PV. The per cent rule is applied for work packages that are in progress. A few status reports on the project are shown in Table 11.4 and Figure 11.13. Suitable assumptions on progress have been made.

Table 11.4 Status report for period ending 2 February

Task	*% Complete*	*EV*	*AC*	*PV*	*CV*	*SV*
A	67	6000	6000	6000	0	0
B	67	2667	4000	4000	–1333	–1333
H	0	0	0	2000	0	–2000
	Total	8667	10,000	12,000	–1333	–3333

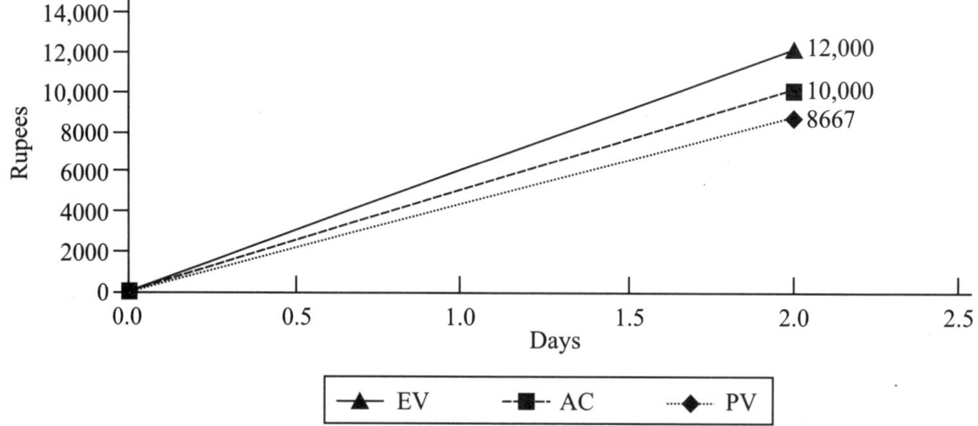

Figure 11.13 Status as on 2 February.

Activity H was scheduled to begin on 1 February but no work on this activity has been done so far. Similarly, activity B was to be completed on 2 February, but only 67% has been completed. The activity will require one more day to complete. This will delay the start of activities C and E which are dependent on B. Will this actually delay the completion of the project? The schedule variance is no indicator of this. The clear picture can only emerge from the tracking Gantt chart shown in Figure 11.14. It may be seen that the duration of activity B has been increased to three days and other activities have been adjusted accordingly. Activity H which should have started on 1 February has now been scheduled to start on 3 February. As may be seen, though the status report shows a total schedule variance, the network indicates that the project will still finish in time, that is, 14 February. The critical activity A is on schedule and the other activities have enough float in them. The earned value report produced by MS Office Project software is shown in Figure 11.15.

We may revise the baseline, if desired. The tracking Gantt chart showing the revised baseline is shown in Figure 11.16.

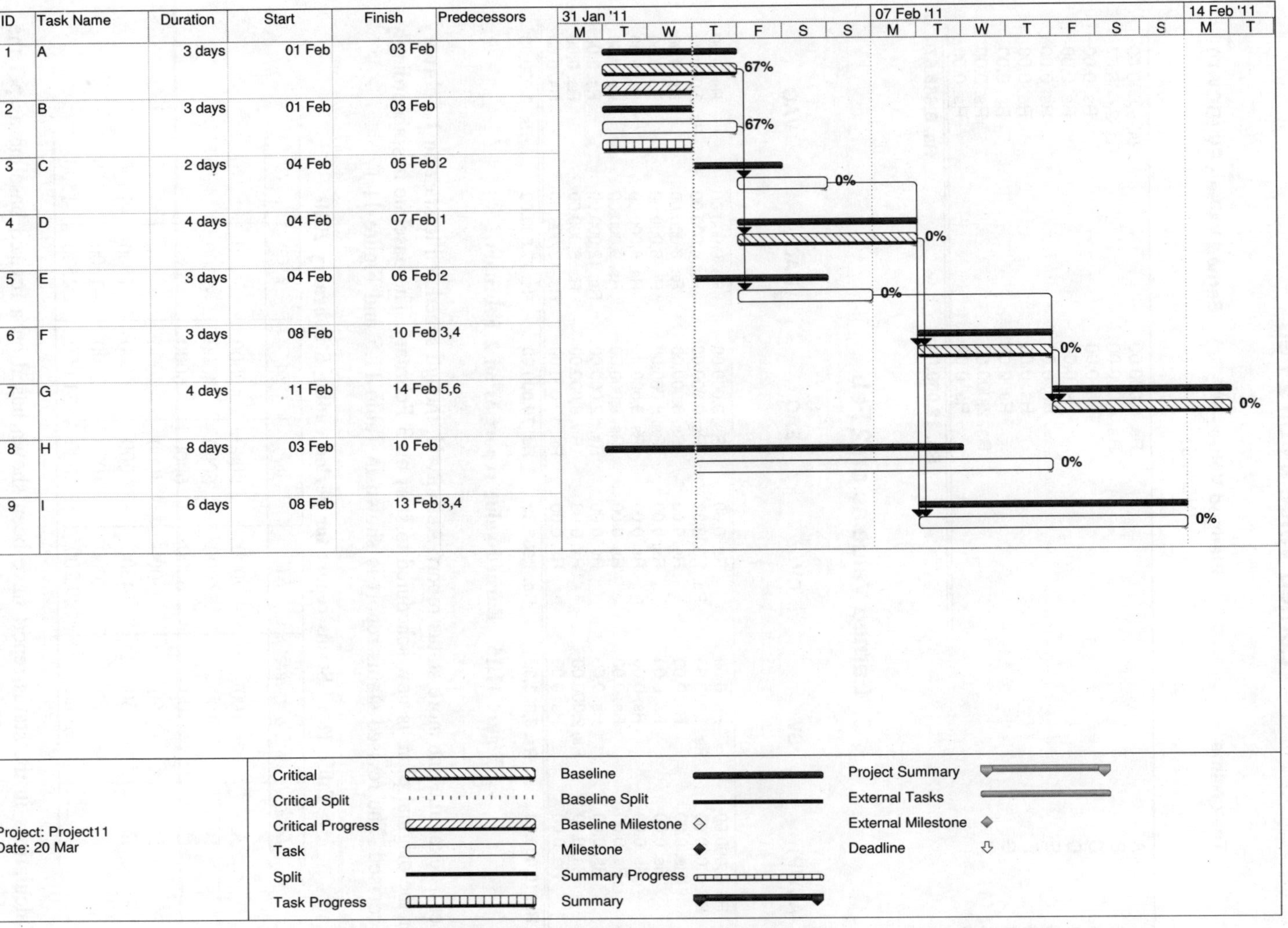

Figure 11.14 Tracking Gantt chart showing progress as on 2 February.

Earned Value as on 2 Feb

ID	Task Name	Planned Value - PV (BCWS)	Earned Value - EV (BCWP)
1	A	Rs. 6,000.00	Rs. 6,000.00
2	B	Rs. 4,000.00	Rs. 2,666.67
3	C	Rs. 0.00	Rs. 0.00
4	D	Rs. 0.00	Rs. 0.00
5	E	Rs. 0.00	Rs. 0.00
6	F	Rs. 0.00	Rs. 0.00
7	G	Rs. 0.00	Rs. 0.00
8	H	Rs. 2,000.00	Rs. 0.00
9	I	Rs. 0.00	Rs. 0.00
		Rs. 12,000.00	**Rs. 8,666.67**

Earned Value as on 2 Feb

AC (ACWP)	SV	CV	EAC	BAC	VAC
Rs. 6,000.00	Rs. 0.00	Rs. 0.00	Rs. 9,000.00	Rs. 9,000.00	Rs. 0.00
Rs. 4,000.00	-Rs. 1,333.33	-Rs. 1,333.33	Rs. 6,000.00	Rs. 4,000.00	-Rs. 2,000.00
Rs. 0.00	Rs. 0.00	Rs. 0.00	Rs. 6,000.00	Rs. 6,000.00	Rs. 0.00
Rs. 0.00	Rs. 0.00	Rs. 0.00	Rs. 8,000.00	Rs. 8,000.00	Rs. 0.00
Rs. 0.00	Rs. 0.00	Rs. 0.00	Rs. 9,000.00	Rs. 9,000.00	Rs. 0.00
Rs. 0.00	Rs. 0.00	Rs. 0.00	Rs. 9,000.00	Rs. 9,000.00	Rs. 0.00
Rs. 0.00	Rs. 0.00	Rs. 0.00	Rs. 12,000.00	Rs. 12,000.00	Rs. 0.00
Rs. 0.00	-Rs. 2,000.00	Rs. 0.00	Rs. 8,000.00	Rs. 8,000.00	Rs. 0.00
Rs. 0.00	Rs. 0.00	Rs. 0.00	Rs. 12,000.00	Rs. 12,000.00	Rs. 0.00
Rs. 10,000.00	**-Rs. 3,333.33**	**-Rs. 1,333.33**	**Rs. 79,000.00**	**Rs. 77,000.00**	**-Rs. 2,000.00**

Figure 11.15 Earned value report as on 2 February.

Let us examine one more status report. Activity H, though scheduled to start on 1 February as per the original plan, is now scheduled to start on 3 February. The baseline has accordingly been revised. The revised status report is shown in Table 11.5 and Figure 11.17.

Table 11.5 Status report for period ending 5 February 2010

Task	*% Complete*	*EV*	*AC*	*PV*	*CV*	*SV*
A	100	9000	9000	9000	0	0
B	100	4000	6000	4000	–2000	0
C	100	6000	6000	6000	0	0
D	50	4000	4000	4000	0	0
E	50	4500	6000	6000	–1500	–1500
H	25	2000	3000	2000	–1000	0
	Total	29,200	34,000	31,000	–4500	–1500

Calculations in the status report have been shown based on a revised baseline as per the progress on 2 February. The updated tracking Gantt chart is shown in Figure 11.18.

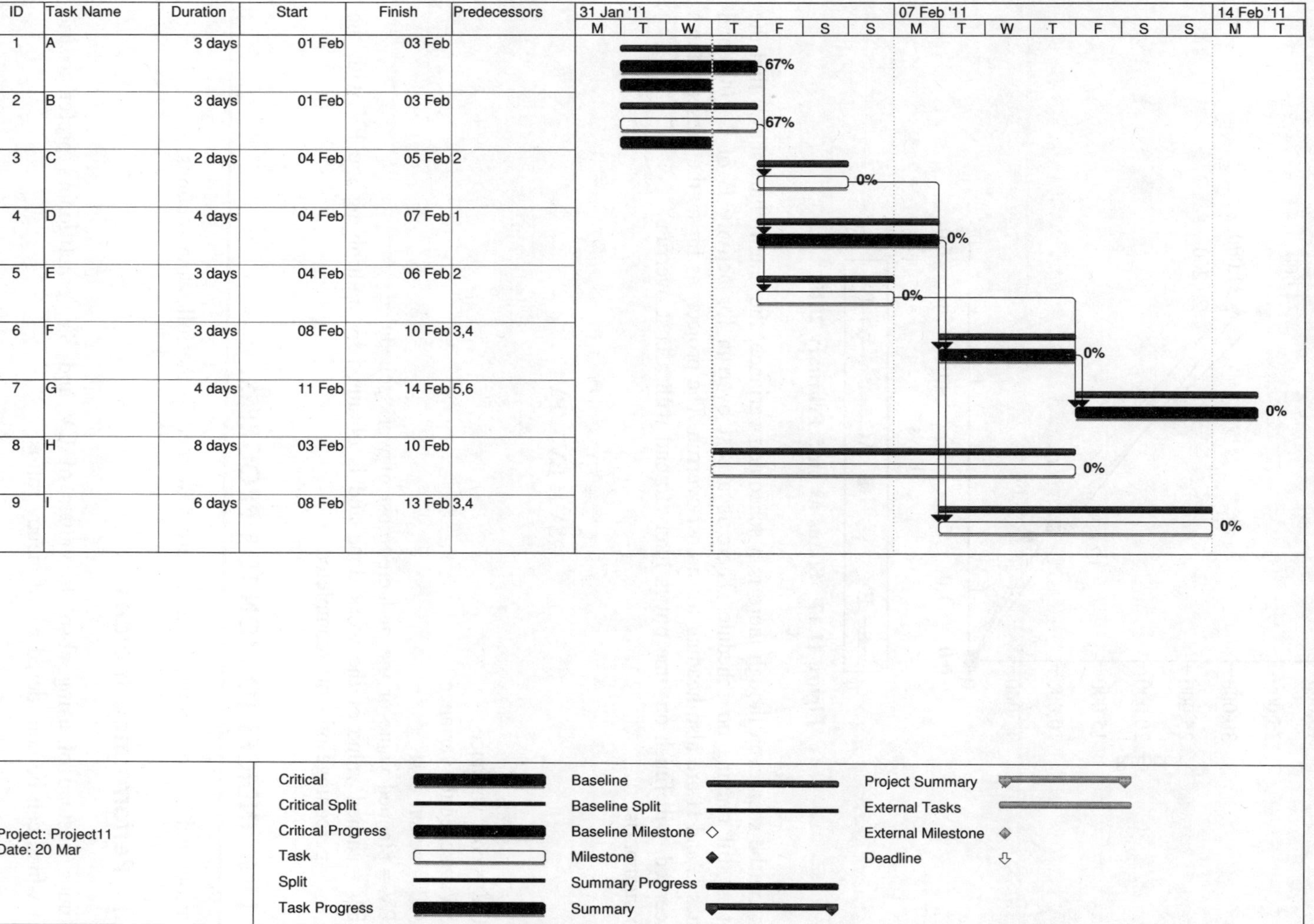

Figure 11.16 Tracking Gantt chart showing revised baseline as on 2 February.

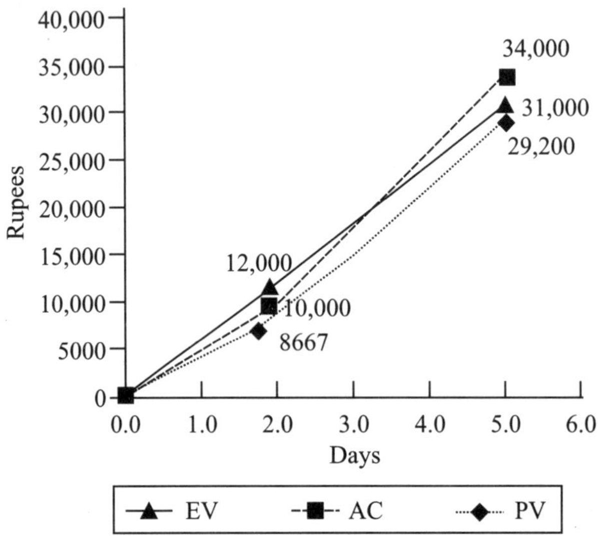

Figure 11.17 Status as on 5 February 2010.

As can be seen even though there is a scheduled variance, the Gantt chart shows that the project is still running on schedule. There is a cost overrun for activity B of ₹ 2000 and activities E and H are also heading for a cost overrun. The project, as far as the present status is concerned, will finish on time but is likely to end with a cost overrun.

To summarise,

$$CV = EV - AC$$
$$SV = EV - PV$$

where

CV = cost variance
SV = schedule variance
AC = actual cost
PV = planned value or the budgeted cost of work scheduled
EV = earned value of the work done and is obtained by multiplying the PV with the percentage of work completed

11.6 INDICES TO MONITOR PROGRESS

The various indices to monitor progress are described in the following sections.

11.6.1 Performance Indices

Sometimes, instead of using absolute values of CV and SV, practitioners prefer to use indices which can be considered as efficiency ratios.

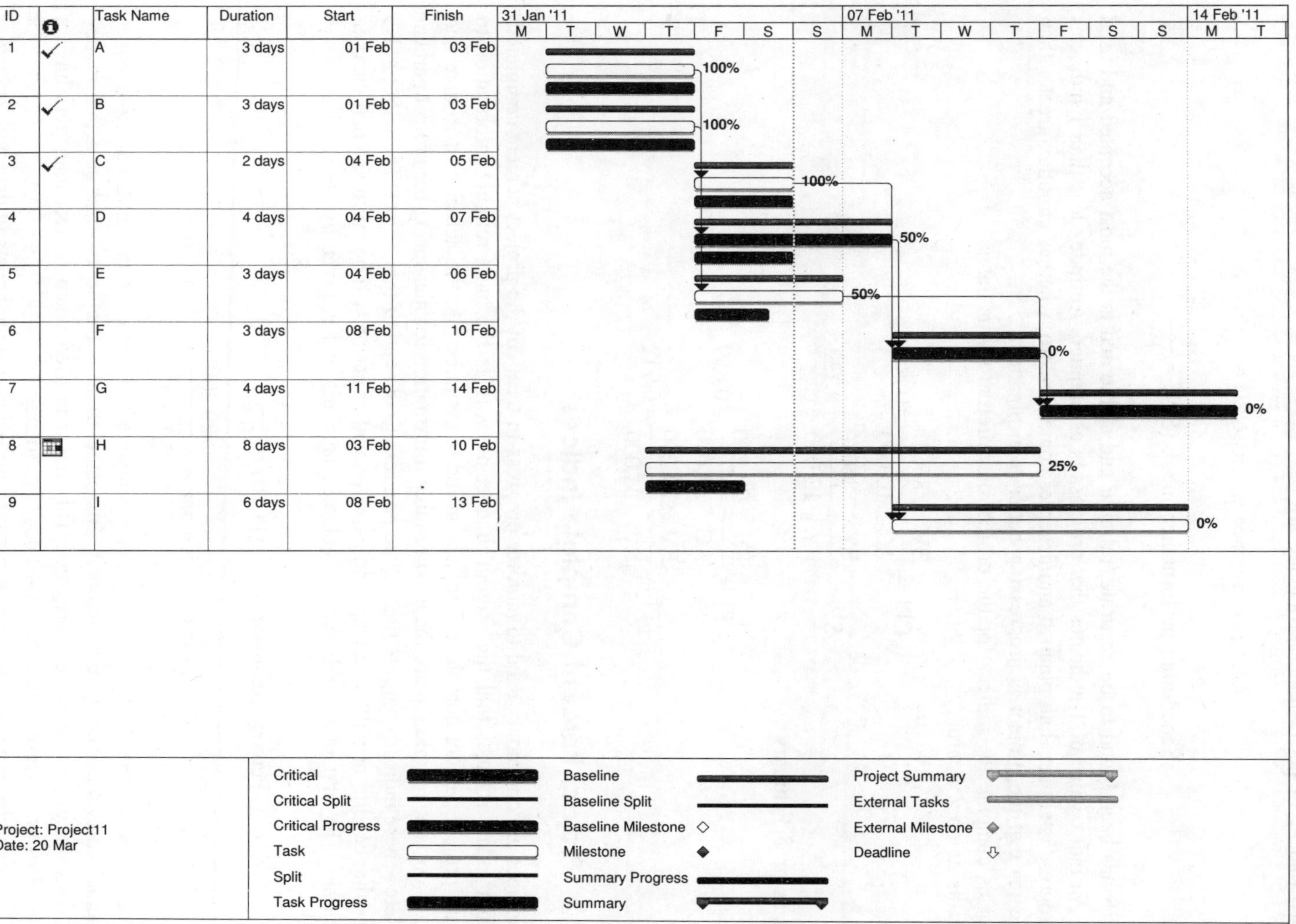

Figure 11.18 Tracking Gantt chart showing status as on 5 February.

The two indices of performance efficiency are:

$$\text{Cost performance index (CPI)} = \frac{\text{EV}}{\text{AC}}$$

$$\text{Scheduling performance index (SPI)} = \frac{\text{EV}}{\text{PV}}$$

The CPI has been found to be accurate, reliable and stable and is the most accepted and used index. An index value of 1 indicates that progress is as planned. An index less than 1 indicates that progress is slower than planned and deserves some concern, whereas an index greater than 1 indicates that the project is progressing better than planned.

Let us compute the indices for the project on different status dates.

Status as on 2 February

$$\text{CPI} = \frac{\text{EV}}{\text{AC}} = \frac{8667}{10{,}000} = 0.867$$

$$\text{SPI} = \frac{\text{EV}}{\text{PV}} = \frac{8667}{12{,}000} = 0.722$$

Status as on 5 February

$$\text{CPI} = \frac{\text{EV}}{\text{AC}} = \frac{29{,}200}{34{,}000} = 0.859$$

$$\text{SPI} = \frac{\text{EV}}{\text{PV}} = \frac{29{,}200}{31{,}000} = 0.942$$

11.6.2 Project Percent Complete Indices

Two indices are commonly used to monitor progress in terms of the project percent completed. The first index assumes that the original budget of work is the most reliable information to measure project percent complete. The second index assumes that the actual cost to date and expected costs at completion are the most reliable information for measuring the project percent complete. These indices compare the to date progress to the end of the project. The indices also assume that conditions will not change, no improvement or action will be taken and that the data is accurate. The first index is based on budgeted amounts and is given by:

$$\text{Percent complete index (PCIB)} = \frac{\text{EV}}{\text{BAC}}$$

$$\text{PCIB (as on 5 February)} = \frac{29{,}200}{77{,}000} = 0.38\% \ (38\%)$$

The index reveals that 38% work has been completed in terms of the total budgeted costs. The actual costs incurred do not figure in this calculation as the actual cost or actual money spent does not guarantee project progress. This index is used when project managers have a high level of confidence in the original budget estimates.

The second index views the percent complete in terms of actual costs to date and the actual costs expected for the completion of the project (EAC—expected actual cost). For instance, if on 5 February the staff estimates that the actual cost of completion of the project will be ₹ 95,000, then the index is calculated as follows:

$$\text{Percent complete index (PCIC)} = \frac{\text{AC}}{\text{EAC}}$$

$$= \frac{34{,}000}{95{,}000} = 0.36\,(36\%)$$

This index is preferred by some managers as it is based on actual and revised estimates which incorporate newer and more complete information.

The two indices present different views of the project. The estimates for the actual costs needed till completion of the project will need to be revised at every review period.

11.6.3 Technical Performance Measurement

It has been stressed time and again that the project should satisfy the parameters of time, cost and quality. While the indices and methods discussed so far address the measurement of time and cost performance, the measurement of quality is equally important. The specifications of the project must be checked and it should be ensured that the quality requirements are met. For instance, the cost of the project may be reduced by compromising on its qualitative performance. No standard indices can be laid down for measuring quality. However, management must lay down measurable performance parameters to ensure that the qualitative performance requirements of the project are met.

11.7 FORECASTING FINAL PROJECT COST

The final cost of the project may be forecast by experts based on the actual costs incurred to date and the additional information available to them. Such revision is used on smaller projects and when the new information indicates that the original estimates are not accurate.

Another method of forecasting final project cost is to use the actual costs to date plus an efficiency index. This method is invariably used in large projects where the original budget is less reliable. The first step is to calculate the estimated cost to complete remaining work. This is computed as follows:

$$\text{ETC} = \frac{\text{Work remaining}}{\text{CPI}} = \frac{\text{BAC} - \text{EV}}{\text{EV/AC}}$$

$$\text{EAC} = \text{ETC} + \text{AC}$$

where

ETC = estimated costs to complete remaining work
CPI = cumulative cost index to date
EV = cumulative budgeted cost of work completed to date
AC = cumulative actual cost of work completed to date

BAC = total budget of the baseline
EAC = estimated total cost at completion

Let us forecast the cost of project completion based on the status report of 5 February for the project considered in the example.

Total baseline budget (BAC) = ₹ 77,000
Cumulative earned value (EV) to date = ₹ 29,200
Cumulative actual cost (AC) to date = ₹ 34,000

$$\text{ETC} = \frac{77,000 - 29,200}{29,200/34,000} = 55,711$$

$$\text{EAC} = 55,711 + 34,000 = 89,711$$

The forecast for the final cost of the project is ₹ 89,711 as against the original budgeted cost of ₹ 77,000.

Another popular index is the 'To Complete Performance Index'. It measures the amount of value that each remaining rupee in the budget must earn to stay within the budget. It is expressed as:

$$\text{TCPI} = \frac{\text{BAC} - \text{EV}}{\text{BAC} - \text{AC}}$$

For the example under study,

$$\text{TCPI} = \frac{\text{BAC} - \text{EV}}{\text{BAC} - \text{AC}} = \frac{77,000 - 29,200}{77,000 - 34,000} = 1.11$$

TCPI of 1.11 implies that each remaining rupee in the budget must earn ₹ 1.11 in value. There is more work to be done than budget left and the project is likely to end up with a cost overrun.

The model assumes that conditions will not change, the cost database is reliable and past progress is representative of future progress.

11.8 CHANGING A BASELINE

Changes during the life cycle of a project are inevitable. While some changes may have beneficial effects on the project, others have a negative effect on the project and every effort must be made to avoid them. If the project is not properly defined, changes will occur resulting in cost or time overrun, or have an effect on the quality parameters of the project. Most changes occur due to change in scope of the project. Unless the change is sought for by the client or the change is considered vital to the efficiency of the end result of the project, these should be avoided. Changes should be approved by the client and he should be willing to pay for incorporating them. As brought out in an earlier chapter, making changes once the project is underway is always a much costlier proposition than incorporating them at the early stages of project formulation and project definition. Scope creep can cause major cost overruns. Minor changes in the scope seem innocuous at first sight, but the cumulative effect of all these changes can be quite substantial. Changes in scope will affect the baseline and will necessitate changes to the baseline. However, care should be taken not to incorporate changes in the baseline to hide poor performance on past or current work.

Let us study the effect of the change in baseline with the help of the previous example where we had shown a changed baseline after 2 February. Refer to the tracking Gantt chart shown in Figure 11.18.

As can be seen, the activity H can start only on 3 February, as no work was carried out on the activity till 2 February. By shifting the baseline for activity H, the planned budget has also been disturbed. The planned cumulative costs till 5 February as per Table 11.3 were ₹ 37,000. If we had taken the planned budgeted costs as the planned value (PV), the schedule variance (SV) would be much greater, as follows:

$$SV = EV - PV = 29{,}200 - 37{,}000 = -7800$$

We can see from the revised network that the project is unlikely to be delayed as the activity H has a slack of six days available to it and no critical activity has been delayed. Performance on time schedule can be judged realistically only from an updated network. The schedule variance is not a true indicator of time performance.

Retrospective changes in the baseline for work that has already been completed should not be permitted. Transfer of money between cost accounts should not be allowed after the work is completed. Unforeseen changes can be handled through the contingency reserve.

Contingency reserve is provided to cope with the risk and the uncertainty associated with the project. The amount of contingency reserve is related to the risk and uncertainty. If the project presents little that is new to the project team, the contingency reserve may be 1 or 2% of the total cost of the project. However, if the project is something that is new to the project team, 5 to 20% of the total project cost may be provisioned as reserve for contingencies.

SUMMARY

Projects need to be controlled so that time and cost overruns are avoided, while maintaining the quality performance of the project. Conventional methods of budget control do not prove adequate for monitoring projects. For instance, if expenditure in excess of budgeted expenditure results in more work being completed than planned, there may be no cost overrun despite the budget variance. Control implies comparing current status with desired status and taking action to reduce variances. An information system by itself does not exercise control. Control is exercised through actions by project managers to reduce variance between status of the project at review period and the plan. It involves setting a baseline in terms of time-phased costs. The baseline forms the time-phased 'desired state' of the project. Time performance of the project is tracked by means of Gantt charts. Monetary indices are not necessarily an indicator of time performance.

Time performance of the project can be monitored through networks and Gantt charts. The networks must be updated as per the current state of the project on the review date and analyzed for delays, especially in critical activities.

Cost control is generally maintained through the earned value method. The 'earned value' is the percentage work completed multiplied by the planned cost for that work. The earned value is compared with actual costs incurred and the planned value of the work that was scheduled for the period. Schedule and cost variances are then computed as follows:

Cost variance (CV) = Earned value (EV) – Actual cost (AC)
Schedule variance (SV) = Earned value (EV) – Planned value (PV)

Other indices that help to monitor the project can also be computed.

The earned value or the integrated cost/schedule model provides the project manager and other stake holders with a snapshot of the current and future status of the project. The method helps to track problems early and identify the same so that corrective action can be taken. The best of plans fail unless there is proper monitoring and control and the success of a project depends, to a large extent, on adequate monitoring and control systems.

QUESTIONS

1. Why are conventional methods of budgetary control inadequate for monitoring and control of projects?
2. How does the earned value provide a better picture of the current status of a project?
3. Although the earned value method calculates schedule variance, why is this insufficient for controlling time performance?
4. How can we forecast the final cost of a project?
5. In Month 4, the actual cost incurred on a project is ₹ 20,000, the earned value is ₹ 22,000 and the planned cost is ₹ 24,000. Prepare a status report for the project.
6. The following table gives the details of activities of a project, their duration, dependency, cost and cost distribution. All figures are in thousands of rupees.

				Cost distribution by weeks					
Task	*Duration*	*Predecessor*	*Cost*	1	2	3	4	5	6
A	2	—	4	2	2				
B	5	A	15	2	3	5	3	2	
C	6	A	24	3	5	3	5	3	5
D	3	B	9	3	4	2			
E	4	C	16	4	4	4	4		
F	3	D, E	6	1	2	3			

Draw a network. Set up a baseline as shown in Table 11.3. By the end of Week 4, the progress is as follows:
Task A complete at an actual cost of ₹ 3000.
Task B 50% complete at an actual cost of ₹ 10,000.
Task C 33% complete at an actual cost of ₹ 8000.
Make a status report for the project for the period ending Week 4. Calculate EV, PV, CV and SV.

7. In the above project, progress at the end of Week 8 is as follows:
Task A complete at an actual cost of ₹ 3000.

Task B complete at an actual cost of ₹ 18,000.
Task C complete at an actual cost of ₹ 24,000.
Task D 33% complete at an actual cost of ₹ 300.
Task E 25% complete at an actual cost of ₹ 3000.
Make a status report for the period ending Week 8. Calculate EV, PV, CV and SV.

8. For the above project, calculate SPI, CPI and PCIB for periods ending Week 4 and Week 8.
9. The following table gives the details of activities of a project, their duration, dependency, cost and cost distribution. All figures are in thousands of rupees.

				Cost distribution by weeks					
Task	*Duration*	*Predecessor*	*Cost*	1	2	3	4	5	6
A	2	—	20	10	10				
B	5	A	25	8	8	4	4	1	
C	6	A	30	5	5	10	5	3	2
D	2	A	24	16	8				
E	4	B	20	5	5	6	4		
F	4	D	16	4	4	4	4		
G	2	E, F	10	5	5				

Draw a network. Set up a baseline as shown in Table 11.3. By the end of Week 3, the progress is as follows:
Task A complete. Actual cost ₹ 15000.
Task B 20% complete. Actual cost ₹ 5000.
Task C 10% complete. Actual cost ₹ 2000.
Task D 0%. Work not yet started.
Prepare a status report. Calculate EV, PV, CV and SV. Also compute SPI, CPI and PCIB.

10. Progress at the end of Week 6 for the above project is as follows:
Task A complete. Actual cost ₹ 15,000.
Task B 80% complete. Actual cost ₹ 18,000.
Task C 80% complete. Actual cost ₹ 21,000.
Task D complete. Actual cost ₹ 22,000.
Task E 0%. Work not yet started.
Task F 50% complete. Actual cost ₹ 6000.
Prepare a status report. Calculate EV, PV, CV and SV. Also compute SPI, CPI and PCIB.

CHAPTER 12

Contract Management and Partnering

It must be considered that there is nothing more difficult to carry out nor more doubtful for success nor more dangerous to handle than to initiate a new order of things.

—Machiavelli

LEARNING OBJECTIVES

After reading this chapter, you will be able to:

- Understand the types of contracts.
- Understand the types of tenders.
- Study the tendering process.
- Appreciate the basis for registration of contractors.
- Understand the difference between conciliation and arbitration.
- Study the activities involved in contract closure.
- Appreciate the advantages of partnering and study the partnering process.
- Understand the concept of public private partnership.

12.1 INTRODUCTION

Most large projects are executed through contractors. This is because often the sponsoring or project organization may not have the requisite expertise to undertake all the activities associated with the project. The success of a project depends on the proper execution of contracts. Contractors must be carefully selected and the terms of the contract must be given adequate attention when contracts are drafted. Ambiguous or inconsistent contracts are difficult to understand and enforce.

A contract is a formal agreement between two parties wherein one party (the contractor) agrees to perform a service and the other party (the client) agrees to do something in return, usually in the form of payment to the contractor. A contract is legally binding. It defines the responsibilities of both the parties and the conditions under which the contract is operative. The contract defines the rights of the parties in relationship to each other and the remedies available to thc partics in case the other party breaches the contract and fails to discharge its obligations.

12.2 TYPES OF CONTRACTS

There are basically two types of contracts—fixed price contracts and cost plus contracts. In a 'fixed price' contract, a price is agreed upon in advance and remains fixed as long as there are no changes to the scope or provisions of the agreement. In a 'cost plus' contract, the contractor is reimbursed for all or some of the expenses incurred during the performance of the contract. Unlike the fixed price contract, the final price of the project is not known until the project is completed. There are several variations within these basic types.

12.3 FIXED PRICE CONTRACT

Under a fixed price contract or a lump sum contract, the contractor agrees to carry out all the work specified in the contract at a fixed price. The client can obtain a minimum price through competitive bidding. Normally, sealed bids are invited and the contract is awarded to the lowest bidder. Fixed price contracts are preferred by both the clients and the contractors when the scope of the project is well defined, the costs can be estimated fairly accurately and the project has low implementation risks. As the costs are fixed, the clients do not have to be concerned with the costs and can focus on monitoring the progress of the work and ensuring that the project specifications are met. Contractors prefer fixed price contracts because clients are unlikely to request changes in the project scope or specifications. This reduces the uncertainty in a project and consequently the risk involved. Contractors can plan efficient use of resources as changes and uncertainty are minimal.

However, the contractor has to be careful in estimating costs. If the estimates are too high, the contractor may lose out to competitors with lower bids, and if the estimates are on the lower side, the contractor may make little or no profit even after bagging the contract.

The disadvantage of a fixed price contract for the client is that it is more difficult and more costly to prepare. The specifications have to be spelt out in sufficient detail so that the contractor is absolutely clear as to what is to be done. Since changes to the contract once it is assigned will generally not be made, it is imperative that a detailed description of the task to be performed is included in the contract. As the contractor's profits are restricted to the difference between the actual costs and the bid price, the contractor may be tempted to use cheaper quality materials and lower quality workmanship, or may extend the completion date to reduce costs. The client should guard against this through specifying all details of the end item in the contract and through proper supervision of the work. Sometimes clients hire expert consultants to supervise and oversee the contractor's work so that their interests are safeguarded.

The biggest disadvantage of such contracts for the contractor is the risk of underestimation. If the work does not proceed as per schedule, the project may end up with time and cost overruns leading to losses for the contractor. This can be obviated by devoting time to ensure that estimates are accurate.

Some variations to the fixed price contract are discussed in the succeeding sections.

12.3.1 Economic Price Adjustment Contracts

Escalation clauses are sometimes included in fixed price contracts, especially in case of projects with a long lead time such as construction projects. Such provisions protect the contractor against increases in cost of materials, labour and overhead expenses. For instance, the price may be linked to an inflation index or to the wholesale price index or to some other relevant index which measures the increase in costs of the inputs used by the project.

Sometimes the contract may have provision for revising the price as the costs become known. The redetermination of price may be once at the end of the project or may be over a number of times at periodic intervals. Some contracts permit only a downward revision of price, while others may have provision for both upward and downward adjustments. Such contracts are appropriate when it is difficult to estimate price because of lack of accurate cost data. While the purpose of such economic price adjustment contracts is to make appropriate adjustments in case of cost uncertainties, they are sometimes misused. An unscrupulous contractor may win a contract on a low bid, start work and then 'discover' that the costs are much higher than expected. The contractor can take advantage of the redetermination of price clauses and justify increasing the cost of the contract.

12.3.2 Fixed Price Incentive Contracts

Often fixed price contracts are accompanied by incentive clauses to motivate the contractor to reduce costs and improve efficiency. Fixed price incentive contracts are often used when there is some uncertainty in the cost of the work, particularly when a product is being built to unique specifications, and does not use off-the-shelf components. This is common in contracts involving test programs or new technology or processes. A fixed price incentive contract specifies a target cost, a target profit, a price ceiling (but not a profit ceiling or floor), and a profit adjustment formula. These elements are all negotiated at the outset. The price ceiling is the maximum that may be paid to the contractor, except for any adjustment under other contract clauses. When the contractor completes performance, the parties negotiate the final cost, and the final price is established by applying the formula.

For example, the contract may include a formula based on cost sharing ratio (CSR). Let us assume that the CSR is 75/25. This implies that if the target cost is exceeded, the contractor will bear 25% of the excess cost and the client will bear 75% of the excess cost subject to the maximum cost ceiling. In other words, for every rupee in excess of the target cost but within the maximum cost, the contractor loses 25 paise thus resulting in a reduction of his profits.

When the final cost is less than the target cost, application of the formula results in a final profit greater than the target profit. Using the data of the above example, every rupee below the target cost will be shared between the contractor and the client in a ratio of 25/75. The contractor thus stands to gain 25 paise profit for every rupee of cost below the target cost, resulting in an increase in his profits. If the final negotiated cost exceeds the price ceiling, the contractor absorbs the difference as a loss. Because the profit varies inversely with the cost, this contract type provides a positive, calculable profit incentive for the contractor to control costs.

The drawback of such contracts is that they involve more administrative work. Detailed cost accounting and performance monitoring are required to determine accurate cost figures.

Other incentive contracts may be tied to schedule rather than cost. The contract specifies a completion date which must be met in order for the contractor to receive his full fee, or profit. Positive incentives can be built-in which increase the fee for early completion. Conversely, negative incentives can also be included which reduce the fee if the schedule date is not met. This can be tied to one final completion date, or can be structured incrementally to a series of timeline milestones.

If a contract has certain performance specifications, then the supplier is expected to meet those for the given price. In some cases, however, the buyer is interested in obtaining a product with better performance than what the minimum specifications dictate. To accomplish this, performance incentive contracts may be designed which reward the contractor financially if the product exceeds the specifications in performance areas such as speed, noise reduction, reduced weight or increased strength. These contracts can give a contractor a financial incentive to invest more capital in additional research and development.

In the case of new technology or research, it is not always possible to come up with target and maximum costs in advance. For these situations, incentive contracts may use a successive target rather than a firm cost. Estimated costs are established at the beginning of contract performance, with an agreement that firm costs will be determined at some future point, such as after a design review or upon test program completion. Regardless of the nature of the work to be done, incentive contracts can be designed to make certain both buyer and seller are adequately protected.

12.4 COST PLUS CONTRACT

Under this contract, the contractor is reimbursed for all direct allowable costs, like materials, labour, travel and so on and an additional fee to cover overheads and profit. The fee is negotiated in advance and is usually in the form of a percentage of the total costs. On small projects, this type of contract is a 'time and materials' contract in which the client agrees to reimburse the contractor for labour and material costs. Labour costs are based on an hourly or daily wage rate, which includes direct and indirect costs as well as profits.

Such contracts put the burden of risk on the client. The final cost of the project is not indicated in the contract and becomes known only when the project ends. The contractor is supposed to do his best to meet the specifications of the project in terms of cost, timely completion and quality, but cannot be held responsible if the specifications are not met. The biggest disadvantage of such a contract is that it provides no incentive to the contractor to complete the project within costs and within the stipulated time, as he will be paid regardless of the final cost. The only motivation for the contractor to keep the project within cost and time is the loss of reputation that he will suffer if the project ends up with cost and time overruns. This may also affect his ability to secure contracts in the future.

Sometimes the additional fee may be specified as a fixed amount rather than as a percentage of costs. This may provide some incentive to the contractor to complete a project within time as he does not earn any extra fee even if the project is delayed.

12.5 INDEFINITE DELIVERY CONTRACT

It is a contract awarded to one or more vendors to deliver supplies and services. There are three types of indefinite delivery contracts—definite quantity contracts, requirements contract and indefinite quantity contracts.

(a) *Definite quantity contract.* A definite quantity contract provides for delivery of a definite quantity of specific supplies or services for a fixed period, with deliveries or performance to be scheduled at designated locations upon order. Such a contract is used when it can be determined in advance that a definite quantity of supplies or services will be required during the contract period and that these are regularly available after a short lead time.

(b) *Requirements contract.* It is a contract under which the contractor commits to fulfil the client's entire requirements for certain goods or services at specified prices during the contract period. The deliveries or performance are scheduled by placing orders with the contractor. It is appropriate for acquiring any supplies or services when the client anticipates recurring requirements but cannot predetermine the precise quantities of supplies or services that he will need during a definite period.

(c) *Indefinite quantity contracts.* Under this contract, the contractor commits to provide an indefinite quantity, within stated limits, of supplies and services during a fixed period of contract. The minimum quantity below which orders will not be placed and the maximum quantity beyond which supplies or services will not be accepted are clearly stated in the contract. Orders are placed for individual requirements. The contract may also spell out the total minimum quantity and maximum quantity to be supplied during the period of contract.

12.6 TENDERS

Tendering is the process in which a detailed specification of goods or services to be provided is circulated to a number of potential contractors. The contractors bid for the work by providing a tender document that includes the price for the work, a timetable and an explanation of how it will be carried out. The tendering authority is free to select from the tenders supplied, though public bodies are generally forced to accept the lowest bid or the cheapest tender on grounds of principle. Sometimes selection may be based on quality, reliability, projected speed of operations, and the track record of the contractor rather than the price. The main focus through tender is on competition of price and quality.

12.7 TYPES OF TENDERS

The following are the main types of tenders.

12.7.1 Global Tender

A global tender is floated with a view to elicit offer or response from any contractor situated anywhere in the world. The need for a global tender arises either when the client does not know about the contractors for a particular task in question or when one thinks that a wider choice of contractors is possible through a global tender. Such a tender may be floated when there is lack of information on vendors or when only a few vendors are known. If there are chances that the known vendors may form a cartel, global tenders may be floated.

Global tenders may be floated by listing them in international trade journals, international newspapers and business magazines. The Internet has made it possible to resort to e-tendering and listing tenders on Internet portals specially designed for this purpose.

12.7.2 Open Tender

An open tender is similar to global tender except that it restricts the choice of contractors to those within the country. Open tenders may be listed in national dailies, internal trade and business bulletins and magazines. It may also be listed on the Internet. Since any information on the Internet is globally available, the difference between a global and an open tender is gradually fading away.

12.7.3 Limited or Restricted Tender

In this type of tender, only a limited number of contractors are invited to make a bid for the contract. This method is resorted to when the capabilities of the contractor to undertake the contract are well established. The client may make advertisements seeking an expression of intent for tendering from contractors. In response, contractors have to submit a filled-in pre-qualification questionnaire to show that they have sufficient knowledge, experience and the resources to fulfil the obligations of the contract. Contractors, who are shortlisted on the basis of their pre-qualification responses, are invited to bid for the contract. Organizations also maintain a list of registered approved contractors whose capabilities are checked periodically. The contractors may be further classified according to their capabilities and financial standing.

12.7.4 Single Tender

When the goods or services involved in a contract are proprietary in nature, that is, only one contractor is capable of meeting the requirement, a single tender may be issued. Single tendering may also be resorted to when sufficient time is not available to evaluate the offers of other contractors and a contractor with a proven delivery record is available.

12.7.5 Negotiated Tender

As suggested by the name, in this type of tender, the client invites a few shortlisted contractors and negotiates the terms of the contract with them. There may also be competitive dialogue, wherein contractors, shortlisted on the basis of their pre-qualification responses, are invited to participate in competitive dialogue with the client. The dialogue is flexible and may include written or verbal submissions and interviews. A number of rounds of dialogue may be carried out to reduce the number of potential contractors. The client then invites the contractors to make their final bid for the contract.

12.8 TENDERING PROCESS

The steps followed in the tendering process are listed below. Some of these steps may be eliminated depending on the type of tender that is being called for.

1. Issue advertisements to the press/magazines inviting expression of interest for the project.
2. Receive response to pre-qualification questionnaires from interested contractors.
3. Analyze pre-qualification responses and shortlist potential contractors based on selection criteria as stated in the advertisements.
4. Carry out negotiations or competitive dialogue with potential contractors identified in step 2. This may be required only in the case of negotiated contracts. In some cases, even pre-qualification requirements may not be necessary.
5. Invite all contractors identified (after negotiations or competitive dialogue, if undertaken) to bid for the contract.
6. Arrange a site visit for identified contractors in case of projects involving construction or other work at site.
7. Receive filled-in tenders from selected contractors along with earnest money as specified in the tender documents. Earnest money is a sum of money deposited at the time of submitting tenders to ensure the seriousness of the contractor towards the bidding process. The earnest money is refunded to unsuccessful bidders, while it is converted to guarantee money in the case of the successful bidder. Tender boxes for receiving tenders are sealed by the authority appointed for the purpose at the time intimated in the tender documents. Late tenders are not allowed to be put in the tender box.
8. Open the tenders together at the place and on the date and time fixed for the same. Tenders are opened in the presence of bidders and the person opening them reads out the amounts quoted by each bidder. The opening authority makes a comparative statement and hands over the same to the contract section for their further action.
9. Evaluate the tenders against the award criteria.
10. Select the successful tender.
11. Issue contract to the successful contracting firm.
12. Inform the unsuccessful contracting firms about their non-selection.

12.9 REGISTRATION OF CONTRACTORS

Registration is the process of obtaining the credentials of the contractor and maintaining the lists of such contractors. Registration could be category-wise such as buildings, roads, water supply, electrification, air-conditioning and so on based on certain criteria. The registration is also done monetary limit-wise. Public sector undertakings and government organizations have laid down the following criteria for registration of contracting firms:

1. Constitution of the firm, its legal status and partners.
2. Immovable and movable properties and bank deposits held by the firm. This gives an idea about the financial standing of the firm and whether it shall be able to undertake the project with the payment schedules envisaged.

3. Turnover during last five years, balance sheets.
4. Valid ITCC.
5. Performance from previous employers.
6. Major equipment held.
7. Qualifications and experience of key personnel.
8. Information regarding litigations.
9. List of works carried out in time.
10. Engineers proposed to be employed and technical capability of the firm.
11. Whether proprietorship or partnership firm.

12.10 CONTRACT LAW

All contracts in India are subject to the Indian Contract Act, 1872. The Act comprehensively covers the various aspects of contracts and the obligations of parties to the contract. The Act applies throughout India except in the State of Jammu and Kashmir.

Disputes arising between the parties may be settled through conciliation or arbitration. These are governed by the Conciliation and Arbitration Act, 1996.

12.10.1 Conciliation

Conciliation is the process by which the parties are facilitated to reach an amicable settlement of their disputes (part III of the Conciliation and Arbitration Act, 1996). It is adopted prior to arbitration. Conciliation takes place only if the parties agree to it. A conciliator is appointed as per contract provision. He shall be guided by the principles of objectivity, fairness and justice. He facilitates the parties to come together for an agreed settlement. When the parties sign settlement agreement, it shall be final and binding on the parties. The conciliator authenticates settlement agreement and the settlement agreement shall have the status of arbitral award.

Conciliation can take place only when both parties agree to solve the dispute through this method. The party initiating conciliation invites the other party through written invitation to conciliate and proceedings commence only when the other party accepts the invitation in writing. Normally one conciliator is appointed with both parties agreeing to his name. If two conciliators are appointed, each party may appoint a conciliator. In the case of three conciliators, the two conciliators, one nominated by each party, select the third conciliator.

The conciliator asks each party to submit their statements and their pleas before him. He may seek further details as required and may propose a settlement at any stage of the proceedings. Once the parties reach settlement of the dispute, the conciliator may assist them to draw up a settlement agreement. The agreement once accepted and signed by both parties is binding on them and has the same effect as an award by an arbitration tribunal.

12.10.2 Arbitration

The Conciliation and Arbitration Act, 1996 applies to any arbitration conducted in India and its awards and to enforcement of foreign awards. Arbitration may be institutional or ad hoc. Despite the advantages of institutional arbitration, ad hoc arbitration is more in vogue in India.

In ad hoc arbitration, the procedures have to be agreed upon by the parties and the arbitrator. This requires cooperation between the parties and involves a lot of time. When a dispute is in existence, it is difficult to expect cooperation between the parties. In institutional arbitration, on the other hand, the procedural rules are already established by the institution. Formulating rules is, therefore, no cause for concern. The fees are also fixed and regulated under rules of the institution.

In ad hoc arbitration, infrastructure facilities for conducting arbitration pose a problem and parties are often compelled to resort to hiring facilities of expensive hotels, which increase the cost of arbitration. Other problems include getting trained staff and library facilities for ready reference. In contrast, in institutional arbitration, the institution will have ready facilities to conduct arbitration, trained secretarial/administrative staff, as well as library facilities. There will be professionalism in conducting arbitration.

In institutional arbitration, the arbitral institutions maintain a panel of arbitrators along with their profiles. The parties can choose the arbitrators from the panel. Such arbitral institutions also provide for specialized arbitrators. These advantages are not available to the parties in ad hoc arbitration.

In institutional arbitration, many arbitral institutions such as the International Chamber of Commerce (ICC) have an experienced committee to scrutinize the arbitral awards. Before the award is finalized and given to the parties, the experienced panel scrutinizes it. As a result, the possibilities of the court setting aside the award is minimal, because the scrutiny removes possible legal/technical flaws and defects in the award. This facility is not available in ad hoc arbitration, where the likelihood of court interference is higher.

In institutional arbitration, the arbitrators are governed by the rules of the institution, and they may be removed from the panel for not conducting the arbitration properly. In ad hoc arbitration, the arbitrators are not subject to such institutional removal sanctions.

In the event the arbitrator becomes incapable of continuing as arbitrator in an institutional arbitration, substitutes can be easily located and the procedure for arbitration remains the same. This advantage is not available in an ad hoc arbitration, where one party (whose nominee arbitrator is incapacitated) has to reappoint the new arbitrator. This requires cooperation of the parties and can be time consuming.

In institutional arbitration, as the secretarial and administrative staff are subject to the discipline of the institution, it is easy to maintain confidentiality of the proceedings. In ad hoc arbitration, it is difficult to expect professionalism from the secretarial staff.

Theoretically, arbitration is designed to provide speedy justice at lesser costs than litigation, but in practice, there are frequent delays because of adjournments. The awards can be challenged in courts and judicial intervention results in delays and additional costs.

12.11 CONTRACT CLOSEOUT

Whenever a contract is completed, it should be properly closed out. The contractor should give a notice of completion to the client. A joint inspection of the work is carried out after which the client also issues a completion certificate. A list of defects to be rectified is prepared. The defects are intimated to the contractor, who then rectifies the defects. The client should be informed of completion of rectification of defects by the contractor. And a request is made for performance certificate on satisfactory completion of defect liability period. Once the client is satisfied that all defects have been rectified, the security performance guarantee sum is released to the contractor.

12.12 PARTNERING

Partnering is a process for transforming contractual agreements into a cohesive, collaborative team that deals with issues and problems encountered in implementing projects. It improves performance through enhanced teamwork. Through partnering, the customer, community, consultants, prime contractor, major subcontractors and suppliers form as one project team and cooperate, share goals, communicate openly and resolve issues speedily. It offers an alternative style of management by promoting trust and respect to complete the project successfully in keeping with the stakeholder's expectations.

The origins of partnering can be traced to the construction industry where partnering was developed to promote cooperation and beneficial relations between the various agencies that contribute to planning, designing and the actual construction and execution of projects. It has gradually spread to other industries because of the benefits that it provides.

Project partnering has been defined as "a method of transforming contractual relationships into a cohesive, cooperative project team with a single set of goals and established procedures for resolving disputes in a timely manner" (Cowan, Gray and Larson, 1992).

Partnering aims at transforming the traditionally adversarial relationship between the contractor and the client to one of cooperation. The adversarial relationship originates from the inherent conflict between the cost to the owner and the profit to the contractor. This is essentially a zero sum game where the gains of one are the losses of the other. This makes owners and contractors suspicious of each other. The owner reacts by monitoring the contractor's performance aggressively and questioning every request made for adjustments in plan or budget. The contractor on his part exploits any loopholes in the contract. Mistakes are often hidden and a blame game starts with each one claiming that the other is responsible for the mistakes and also responsible for rectifying them. This results in delays, additional costs and often long and costly litigation or arbitration. Partnering aims at overcoming these drawbacks. Some of the benefits of partnering are reduced administrative costs, more efficient utilization of resources, improved communication, improved innovation and improved performance.

12.13 STEPS TO PARTNERING

Partnering entails considerable time and effort spent on forging a common team identity among participants from different organizations. It involves the creation of systems designed to sustain and expand collaboration over the activities of the project. Since it involves an attitudinal change from adversarial to cooperative and collaborative, it requires members from all partnering agencies to get together and develop plans and processes to deal with the issues involved in the project. The partnering process may take many forms.

The steps involved in partnering are as follows:

(a) *Introduction.* The decision to apply formal partnering should be based on two criteria: a commitment by the organizations' leaders to support partnering methods, and a business decision that the project benefits will exceed their costs. In the introduction stage, the senior managers are introduced to the concept of partnering and commitment of the CEOs concerned is obtained. The principal stakeholders are invited for partnering. The invitation can be made by any of the principals to the other stakeholders on a project. It may be a formal invitation or as simple as a telephone call. An initial partnering workshop is planned. A professional partnering facilitator may be appointed.

(b) *Preparation.* In this stage, preparations for conducting the initial workshop are completed. A neutral partnering facilitator and a neutral venue are selected for the initial workshop. The participants are identified. The facilitator helps in bringing about attitudinal change in all the members of the team and helps them move from 'individual interest first' to a 'project interest first basis'. An agenda is established based on the potential project issues, opportunities and risks, and potential breakthroughs.

(c) *Workshop.* The next stage involves the conduct of the workshop. The focus should be on building relationships, individual and team goals, project issues and risks and development of accepted and agreed upon management processes.

(d) *Application.* The project team applies the partnering processes that have been designed in the workshop. Open communications are established and rapid issue resolution processes are put in place. Efforts are made to induce others to join in partnering the project. Measures of performance are established and results are reviewed for their effectiveness. Course corrections are made as necessary and steps are taken to reinforce the new partnering culture that is established.

Partnering provides a venue where project teams, with contributions and guidance by participating executives, establish direction. They consider the goals of each of the organizations and craft a partnering charter to establish a mission and the goals that when met will be a successful project for all. They also establish guidelines for conduct between the organizations and people supporting the project. It raises the art of team-building a notch—from aligning people to aligning organizations to "buy in" for the success of the project. It motivates and inspires individuals to become active members of the winning team. The team feels motivated and inspired as they determine their own goals and resort to structured processes to evaluate and renew joint commitment to success of the project.

12.14 PUBLIC–PRIVATE PARTNERSHIP

"The public–private partnership (PPP) project means a project based on contract or concession agreement between a government or statutory entity on the one side and a private sector company on the other side, for delivering an infrastructure service on payment of user charges."

PPPs are being promoted for implementation of infrastructure projects. PPP is often described as a private business investment where two parties comprising government as well as a private sector undertaking form a partnership. The private party assumes substantial financial, technical and operational risk in the project. There are various types of PPPs. In some cases, the cost of using the service is borne exclusively by the users of the service, as is the case with using roads or bridges where a toll charge is recovered from those using the road or the bridge. In other types of PPPs, the capital investment is made by the private sector and it agrees to provide services, the cost of which is borne wholly or partly by the government. The government may also provide capital subsidy in the form of a one-time grant or provide revenue subsidies in the form of tax breaks and guaranteed annual revenues for a fixed period.

Generally, a private sector consortium forms a special company called a *special purpose vehicle* (SPV) to develop, build, operate and maintain the asset for the contracted period. The consortium consists of the contractor, a maintenance company and the financial institutions which have loaned funds for the project. The contract is signed between the government and the SPV. Typical examples of PPP projects are the new highway projects being undertaken in India. The road is developed and built by a private consortium and then maintained and operated by them for a certain period. A toll charge is recovered from the users for the service. The new airports in the country have also been undertaken as PPP projects.

12.14.1 Build-Operate-Transfer (BOT) or Build-Own-Operate-Transfer (BOOT)

BOT or BOOT is a form of project financing wherein the private entity receives a concession, that is the right to operate the business (for example, a parking lot), from the government to finance, design, construct and operate a facility stated in the contract. For instance, the new airports being constructed in India are being undertaken as BOT projects. This enables the project builder to recover investment, operating and maintenance expenses incurred on the project. Traditionally such projects are transferred to the government at the end of the contracted concession period.

BOT or BOOT is a type of project financing. It differs from traditional financing as follows:

1. The lenders to the project look primarily at the earnings of the project as the source from which loan repayments will be made. Their credit assessment is based on the project, and not on the creditworthiness of the borrowing entity.
2. The security taken by the lenders is largely confined to the project assets. As such, project financing is often referred to as 'limited recourse' financing because lenders are given only a limited recourse against the borrower.

More recently, organizations around the globe have been involved in adopting the BOT model in a unique manner. For example, a company called 'The Venture Street' in India has adopted and modified BOT model and made it build-operate-associate-transfer (BOAT). Additionally the company has expanded the scope of the model in public health, hospitals, pharmaceutical and information technology (IT) sector. The company is a venture capital company.

SUMMARY

Most large projects are executed through contractors and subcontractors. A contract is a formal agreement between two parties wherein one party (the contractor) agrees to perform a service and the other party (the client) agrees to do something in return, usually in the form of payment to the contractor. A contract is legally binding. There are mainly two types of contracts—the fixed price contract and the cost plus contract. Another variation is the indefinite delivery contract.

Tendering is the process in which a detailed specification of goods or services to be provided is circulated to a number of potential contractors with the aim of selecting a contractor for the envisioned task. Tenders may be global, open, limited or restricted, single, or negotiated. It is important for project managers to be aware of the tendering process. The process generally involves advertizing the tender in the press, analyzing responses to pre-qualification questionnaires, inviting shortlisted contractors to bid, evaluating bids against a selection criterion and finally awarding the contract to the selected contractor.

Contractors can be registered by the organization according to their performance capabilities and their financial standing so that the process of tendering can be simplified.

Contracts in India fall under the purview of the Indian Contract Act, 1872. Disputes are governed by the Conciliation and Arbitration Act, 1996.

Partnering is a process for transforming contractual agreements into a cohesive, collaborative team that deals with issues and problems encountered in implementing projects. It improves performance through enhanced teamwork. It aims at changing the traditional confrontationist and adversarial relationship between clients and contractors to one of cooperation and collaboration. It attempts to make the contractor and other parties as part of the project team and moves them from an 'individual's interest first' to a 'project interest first' basis.

Public–private partnership (PPP) project means a project based on contract or concession agreement between a government or statutory entity on the one side and a private sector company on the other side, for delivering an infrastructure service on payment of user charges. PPP projects are being increasingly undertaken for infrastructure in India. The projects may be on a build-own-operate-transfer (BOOT) or on a build-operate-transfer (BOT) basis. Major highways and airport projects have been undertaken on BOT basis. The private party is given a concession to design, build, operate and maintain the facility over the period of the contracted concession.

QUESTIONS

1. What is a contract? Explain the different types of contracts.
2. What is the difference between a negotiated tender and a restricted tender?
3. What points would you bear in mind while registering contractors?
4. What is the difference between conciliation and arbitration?
5. How is partnering different from contracting?
6. What do you understand by public–private partnership?

PART IV Project Closure

Chapter 13 Project Audit and Closure

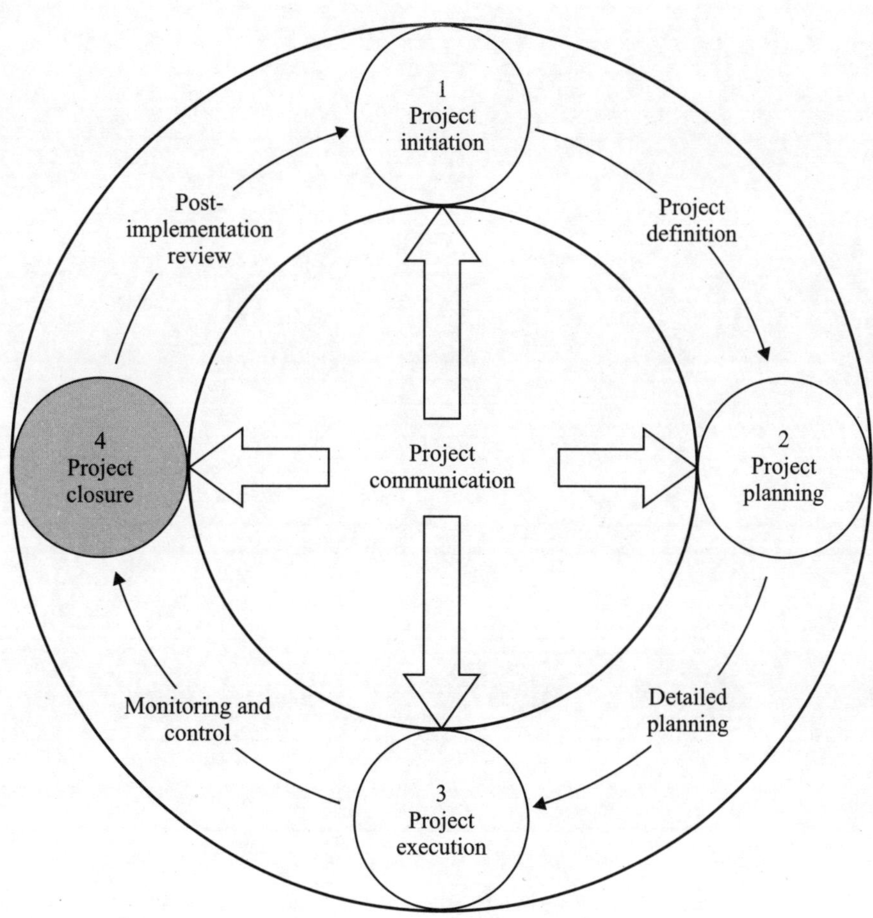

CHAPTER 13

Project Audit and Closure

Know when to cut your losses if necessary. Don't let your desire to succeed be the enemy of good judgement. If Napoleon had left Moscow immediately, he may have returned with a salvageable army.

—Jerry Manas

LEARNING OBJECTIVES

After reading this chapter, you will be able to:

- Appreciate the need to carry out project audit.
- Understand the difference between in-process project audit and post-project audit.
- Study the methodology for carrying out a project audit.
- Appreciate the content required in a project audit report.
- Understand the different circumstances under which projects are closed and the activities involved in project closure.
- Appreciate the need for carrying out a performance review of the project team, the team members and the project manager.

13.1 INTRODUCTION

The best of plans will go awry. Things will go wrong. A successful organization is a learning organization, which not only learns from its mistakes but also imbibes the best practices that have given successful results in the past. It is prudent for organizations that have a number of projects going on simultaneously, to carry out a periodic reality check to see where they stand. Project audit is carried out with the following objectives:

1. It evaluates the efficiency and effectiveness with which the project was managed, the level of customer satisfaction and the extent to which the project delivered the expected benefits to all the stakeholders.

2. It assesses what was done wrong and what contributed to success.
3. It identifies lessons which will improve the delivery of future projects.

However, a large number of organizations do not carry out a project audit on the plea that they are too busy to spare time for this activity. Quite often, project audits are carried out only for projects that are major failures or disasters. While this may highlight the major mistakes that were made, the best practices which led to success are lost. It is, therefore, important to carry out a project audit of all projects, irrespective of the fact that they were major failures or successes.

Project audits are more than regular status reports. Even though they use performance measures and forecast data, they are more inclusive. Project audits review why the project was selected in the first place and what its role in the organization's priorities was. They also check on whether the organizational culture is suitable for undertaking such projects, and whether the project team was suitably staffed and provided the wherewithal to successfully undertake the project.

13.2 WHEN TO AUDIT?

Project audit can be performed while a project is in process or after it is completed.

13.2.1 In-Process Project Audit

An in-process project audit is concerned with the progress and performance of the project so that corrective changes can be made. The audit reviews and checks if conditions have changed. For instance, is the project still relevant? Have the priorities changed, and so on? In rare cases, the audit may even suggest a premature closure of the project. This may be the case if the project is found to have become irrelevant or the need which the project was to satisfy no longer exists. The tendency to overlook recommendations for premature closure because of the huge sunk costs involved must be avoided. It is better to accept the loss on account of sunk costs than to foolishly persevere to complete the project when its very raison d'être has ceased to exist.

13.2.2 Post-Project Audit

The emphasis of a post-project audit is towards managing projects in a better manner in the future. Though it examines the performance on the project, it is aimed at long-term perspective of managing future projects. It takes a much broader view and would evaluate the strategic implications of the project. Did the project actually deliver the strategic benefits that were visualized at the selection stage? What best practices were followed which could enhance management of projects in future? What errors were committed which need to be guarded against in future project undertakings?

13.3 HOW TO AUDIT?

Every effort should be made to make the project audit a normal process. A project team should not perceive that it has been singled out for audit. The manner in which audit is carried out depends on the size of the project and the size of the organization. Some other factors that may affect the audit are project importance, project type, risk associated with the project and the problems facing the project. A large-sized organization handling a number of projects may lay down that project audits will be carried out at certain stages of the project life cycle. For instance, it may as a matter of policy carry out audits when the task is 25% complete, 50% complete and on final completion. In a small organization, where face-to-face contact is prevalent at all levels, the project audit may take the form of a special staff meeting. In other organizations, the project audit may be assigned to an outside agency.

The top management must ensure that the project audit is not perceived as a witch-hunt. It should address project issues and refrain from commenting on individual performances. It is important to know what went wrong and why it went wrong, and how such mistakes can be avoided in the future. The project audit is not for the purpose of apportioning blame or finding out who was responsible for the mistakes. The audit must be constructive and corrective and not punitive in its observations. Audit activities should be sensitive to human emotions and reactions, and the inherent threat to those being evaluated should be reduced to the minimum.

The senior management must show open support for the audit to ensure that the audit team receives cooperation from those concerned and all information, data and facts required by them are made available to them. The data and facts should be verifiable. The project audit team should have access to the project participants and the project customers. The project audit team should be friendly, empathetic and objective while carrying out the audit. This will reduce anxiety and ensure cooperation from those being audited.

The project audit should be completed as quickly as possible. An in-process project audit can be disruptive and should therefore be finished in a couple of days or so, depending on the size and nature of the project.

13.4 WHO SHOULD AUDIT?

Project audits may be carried out by teams designated from within the organization or by special teams of experts hired from outside. The outcome of a project audit must represent an independent, outside view of the project. Audits are invariably viewed negatively by the project stakeholders. There is a certain inherent apprehension about an audit and it is important that the independence and an objective view are maintained. Careers and reputations can be irreparably damaged even in organizations that accept mistakes. If the project audit is favourable, careers and reputations can be enhanced. Since audit is a human activity, it is susceptible to internal politics and some firms prefer assigning the responsibility of audit to an outside consulting agency.

Irrespective of the origin of the project audit team, the leader must have no direct involvement or direct interest in the project. He should command the respect of the senior management and other project stakeholders. He should be perceived to be impartial and fair. He should be willing to listen empathetically to all concerned. The person selected should be perceived to have the best interests of the organization in mind. He should have a broad-based experience in the organization and the industry and should have independence and authority to submit the audit report without fear of recriminations from parties with vested interests.

Other members should also possess similar characteristics and may be selected for their special expertise. Some project team members also need to be co-opted into the audit team. A post-project audit will have more members from the audit team than an in-process project audit, as it may not be possible to take away members from their primary task of managing the project. The organization may also like to nominate some persons who are likely to be given the opportunity of handling projects in the future. The conduct of a project audit is a good opportunity for training future project managers as they can be exposed to both the mistakes and the best practices followed on the project being audited. It is sometimes felt that inclusion of project team members on a project audit may bring in undue biases. However, such misgivings are generally ill-founded as project team members do have a genuine interest in improving the future project management process.

13.5 THE AUDIT REPORT

Project audit reports generally cover two perspectives—one evaluates the project from the organization's point of view and the other carries out an evaluation from the project team's point of view. The organization's perspective focuses on the following issues:

Organization culture

Was it supportive towards the project and is it suitable for this type of project? Are any corrective steps required?

Senior management support

Did the senior management provide adequate support to the project, in terms of resources as well as moral support?

Project goals

Were the objectives of the project fulfilled? Has the environment changed to nullify the need for the project (in case of ongoing projects)? Did the project fit in with the overall strategic plan of the organization? Did it deliver the benefits as visualized at the selection and planning stages?

Risk management

Were the risks involved properly identified and assessed? Were contingency plans formulated? Were contingency plans used? If so, what was the actual impact of the risk events which occurred? Were they assessed realistically?

Project team

Did the personnel assigned to the project have the required talents and skills, or were compromises made while drawing up the project team? If the project has been completed, have the members of the project team been fairly assigned to new projects or tasks?

External evaluation

What are the suggestions, if any, from the outside agencies like contractors and so on?

Customer satisfaction

Are the clients satisfied with the manner in which the project was executed and finally handed over to them?

The evaluation from the project team's perspective focuses on the following issues:

Planning and control systems

Were the planning and control systems used for the project adequate? Should such systems be used for similar projects in the future? If so, why? If not, why not?

Conformity

Did the project conform to the planned schedule, cost and quality? If not, why did deviations occur? What steps can be taken to avoid such deviations in future?

Management information system

Was the management information system adequate? Did it provide effective interfaces and communication with the project stakeholders?

Resources

Was the team assigned adequate resources in terms of money, personnel, equipment, machinery and other support? Were there resource conflicts with other ongoing projects? Were such conflicts adequately resolved? Was the team managed well?

Many checklists for project audit have been compiled by different sources and are easily available on the Internet for use on a project. Essentially they cover the issues that have been discussed in the preceding paragraphs.

The audit, based on authentic and verifiable data, should lead to recommendations that represent major corrective actions that should be initiated. The recommendations should also highlight the practices that led to positive successes and that should be continued with and used in the future projects. The lessons learned from the project should form a separate section. These may not be in the form of recommendations. These include mistakes and pitfalls that are easily avoided and actions are taken to ensure success. These can be of immense value to project teams managing future projects. The recommendations and lessons learnt may also be compiled in the form of a summary booklet for ease of reference in the future.

13.6 PROJECT CLOSURE

All projects eventually come to an end. Theoretically, the scope statement defines a clear ending for the project; however, the actual ending may not correspond to the planned ending. Some projects may have to be closed prematurely while others may extend into seeming perpetuity.

Regular project audits and reviews will identify projects which should have endings different from those that were planned.

13.6.1 Normal Project Closure

The most common circumstance for project closure is simply a completed project. In the case of a new production facility, or a building, the finish is marked by the handing over the ownership to the customer. The completion of a development project may be marked by the handing over of complete designs and so on. For example, a project for new product development may be finished when the design is handed over to production. The finish of system upgrades, development of new management processes, development of new information systems and so on occurs when the system goes on stream and outputs are incorporated into ongoing operations.

13.6.2 Premature Closure

Sometimes projects may have to be closed prematurely with some parts of the project eliminated. For instance, a marketing manager may insist that the product design be given to production without going through the market testing phase as he will otherwise lose the first mover advantage in the market. Such requests should be carefully weighed before a decision to close the project prematurely is taken. While it may lead to short-term profits because of the early mover's advantage, the product may have to undergo costly redesigning at a later stage to keep up with the competition. Before closing a project prematurely, we must ask ourselves why the original project scope and objectives have changed. Premature closure should have the approval of all project stakeholders, and such decisions should be taken by the senior management.

13.6.3 Perpetual Projects

Some projects never seem to end. Even though they are unduly delayed, they appear to carry on forever. Typically, they suffer from project creep. Seemingly small add-ons keep increasing the scope of the project. For instance, adding features to product design, or software, which on the face of it are to improve the project outcome—product or service. We must question why these 'extras' were not thought of at the project formulation stage. Scope creep of this nature results in time and cost overruns. The project manager or the project audit team must at some stage declare a 'freeze' on the project design or scope and steer the project towards closure. The project scope can be redefined so that closure is forced. Other methods that could be adopted may include reduced budgets, time deadlines and a limit on resources.

13.6.4 Failed Projects

At times, projects may have to be declared as failures and closed. There may be various reasons for failure. For instance, there may be technological changes. A company working on a computer game based on 32-bit technology may suddenly find that a competitor has come up with a 64-bit game. It is better to write off the amount already spent on the project as 'sunk cost' rather than send 'good money to chase bad money'. A pharmaceutical company may have to abandon its new drug project as the side effects of the drug may be deemed unacceptable. In the rapidly changing world around us, we must have the ability to identify our competition. The introduction of the digital watch ruined the Swiss watch industry, which failed to adapt to the changing technology because of its blinkered perception of superiority. Sony has managed to do the same to Kodak. The digital camera revolutionized photography. Currently, cell phones with their emphasis on mobility are revolutionizing the photography and music industry. Income generated through sale of ring tones has outstripped the revenues generated through sale of music CDs.

Closure of perpetual projects and failed projects needs careful handling as project participants must not be left with the stigma of working on a project that failed. As far as possible, project failure should not be attributed to individuals. Other modes should be used to 'justify' early project closure or to identify a project problem—such as a change in customer needs or preferences, changes in technology, or competitors coming up with better or more advanced products and services. These are external causes and are perceived as beyond anyone's control. Early closure of projects can hurt reputations, egos and may even affect jobs. The human aspect of early closure must not be lost sight of.

13.7 PROJECT CLOSURE PROCESS

As the project nears completion, equipment and people are reallocated to other activities or projects. Managing the closure phase is as important as managing the other phases of the project. There is a sense of euphoria that the major challenges of the project are over. But wrapping up the project is as important as executing it. However, accounting for equipment, preparing final reports and so on are considered boring tasks by the project team which consists of action-oriented people. If due care is not taken, the closure tasks can take an inordinately long time. It is necessary to develop a plan for project closure and ensure its implementation. The closure plan should address the following issues:

1. What tasks are required to close the project?
2. Who will be responsible for these tasks?
3. When will closure begin and end?
4. How will the project be delivered?

Unless a project is closed prematurely, the task of closure is entrusted to the project manager. The project manager's next assignment should be communicated to him, as this will provide him with an incentive to close the project as quickly as possible and move on to new challenges.

The closure plan and schedule is communicated to the project team as early as possible. This helps them to psychologically accept that the project will end and helps them to prepare to move to their next assignments. The team members' next assignment should be ready when the termination of the project is announced. Conversely, it may be argued that the members may not take adequate interest in the closure activities as they are looking forward to their new assignments. The project manager is faced with the task of keeping the team focused on closure activities and ensuring that deadlines are met. These are prone to slip during the closure phases.

The major activities included in the closure phase are as follows:

1. Getting delivery acceptance from the customer.
2. Shutting down resources and shifting them to new uses.
3. Closing accounts and seeing that all outstanding bills are cleared.
4. Reassigning project team members.
5. Evaluating the project team, team members and the project manager.

Many organizations have come up with elaborate checklists for closing projects. The experience of such organizations can be used to ensure that nothing is missed out during the closure phase.

The closure phase has emotional connotations for the project team. While they bask in the glory of the successful completion of the project, there is a sense of loss and sadness as friendships and relations forged during the project are about to be terminated and members will go their separate ways. We have earlier emphasized that the project team builds an identity of its own. The loss of this identity can be emotionally disturbing to the members. It is customary to arrange a celebration of the completion of the project. This may range from an office high tea to an elaborate banquet with speeches, award of certificates and mementoes for the participants. This provides an emotional release to the members as they bid farewell to each other. Even when projects have to be prematurely closed, this aspect should be kept in mind.

13.8 PERFORMANCE EVALUATIONS

Auditing includes performance evaluations of the project team, individual team members and the project manager. A performance evaluation is necessary to identify the developmental needs of the individual as well as for continuous improvement in the organization through organizational learning. Performance evaluation implies measurement against predefined specific criteria, or laid down standards. In the case of a project, it should also be ensured that all supportive measures needed by the team to meet the expected criteria are in place before the commencement of the project.

In practice, it is generally observed that performance evaluation is not carried out in a satisfactory manner. The major drawbacks are that the performance evaluation of individuals is still left to superiors in the team member's home department and the team's performance is measured mostly against the criteria of time, cost and specifications. The aspects of team building, performing as an effective team, effectiveness of group decisions, group cohesiveness, trust amongst members, and commitment to the team task and so on are often ignored. These are important issues from an organization's point of view and should be included in the evaluation criteria. The performance of the team collectively, team members individually, and the project manager must be evaluated.

13.8.1 Team Evaluation

Before the project begins, certain minimum conditions should be met. These help in setting standards and criteria against which performance of the project team can be measured.

Some of these are as follows:

(a) *Goals.* Clear, measurable, challenging but attainable goals should be set for the team and the individual members. These can form the basis for standards against which performance can be measured.
(b) *Responsibilities and performance standards.* Ensure that the team and individual members are fully aware of their responsibilities and the performance standards required of them.
(c) *Reward system.* An adequate system of team rewards should be instituted so that a clear signal is sent that the management values the synergy of the team.
(d) *Career planning.* A clear career path should be in place for successful project managers.
(e) *Authority.* The project team should have enough discretionary authority to enable it to deal with short-term difficulties.
(f) *Trust.* The organization culture should promote a high level of trust.
(g) *Evaluation criteria.* Team performance should be measured beyond the conventional time, cost and specifications criteria. Some of the team characteristics mentioned in Section 10.3.2 can be used to set performance criteria.

The actual team performance can take many forms. A commonly used method is to conduct a survey generally restricted to the team members. Sometimes other project stakeholders may also be included in the survey. The team members are asked to respond to a questionnaire based on the performance criteria. Responses may be on a numerical point scale. The responses are tabulated and consolidated and the results are reviewed at a meeting of the team members and the senior management. Some examples of questions that may be included are as follows:

	Disagree				*Agree*
1. The team shared a sense of common purpose and members were willing to work towards achieving project goals.	1	2	3	4	5
2. Differences of opinion amongst the members were encouraged and freely expressed without showing any disrespect to others' point of view.	1	2	3	4	5

The performance evaluation of the team helps in the development of the team, assessing its strengths and weaknesses, and drawing lessons for the future. It can bring about behavioural changes amongst the team members and ensure continuous improvement for the organization.

13.8.2 Evaluation of Individual Team Members

Organizations carry out performance appraisals of individuals as these form the basis for making decisions regarding promotions, future job assignments and pay increments and other rewards. Persons working on project teams also need to be evaluated for their performance, but the extent to which project managers are involved in performance appraisal varies from organization to organization. When projects are managed within functional organization—that is, where the project is under the control of a functional department with inputs from other departments as required—appraisals are carried out by the functional head of department to which the individual belongs and not by the project manager. The functional head may request for inputs from the project manager and incorporate these in the individual's appraisal. In a matrix organization, appraisal may be carried out by both the project manager and the functional head of the individual's department. In project organizations, where most of the work is performed under the project manager, the responsibility of carrying out individual performance appraisals may be given to the project manager. The '360-degree feedback' or multirater appraisal system is also gaining acceptance in some organizations. The process involves obtaining feedback on the individual's performance from all people who are affected by the individual's performance at work.

Performance appraisal should ideally fulfil two needs. It should identify the strengths and weaknesses of the individual and assist in developing action plans for improving the individual's performance. It should also help in assessing the potential of the individual for promotion and identify special training needs, if any, so that the individual can be developed to fulfil roles identified for him in the future. It may also form the basis of adjusting salaries and other monetary rewards. The requirements are not compatible. People get over-obsessed with the salary and merit adjustments angle of a performance appraisal and lose sight of it as a tool for effective constructive feedback which may help the individual to improve his performance.

Performance appraisals by project managers may take the form of an essay on each individual describing his or her performance, or questionnaires may be designed on the lines of the one suggested for evaluating the project team. Some organizations may use elaborately designed forms using rating scale or even behaviourally anchored rating scale (BARS). A self-assessment by the individual concerned may also be incorporated in the system. Irrespective of the system used, it is imperative that the individual's performance be reviewed with him by the project manager.

Performance reviews are looked upon as unpleasant tasks. The project manager should call each individual and discuss his performance with him. While carrying out a review, care should be taken not to compare individuals. The individual should be assessed against the established standards. When being critical, the focus should be on specific instances of the individual's behaviour than on the individual personally. The effect of the behaviour on the project should be described in specific terms. Criticism should be constructive in nature. Performance reviews should be conducted fairly and more importantly should be perceived as such by those being evaluated. The review should be treated as part of an ongoing process and should be used to reach an agreement with the individual as to how he or she can improve his or her performance.

The project manager's performance is evaluated in a similar manner. As the project manager performs a very important role and has to interact with various stakeholders with varying interests in the project, a 360-degree appraisal is becoming increasingly popular. Information on the performance of a project manager can be collected from customers, vendors, team members, peers and other managers.

SUMMARY

Project audit is an important step in knowledge management of the organization. It is aimed at highlighting both the mistakes which occurred in the undertaking of the project and the good practices that led to success. The lessons learnt from the project, both positive and negative, can help an organization in the future.

Project audits may be carried out when the project is still in process or post-completion of the project. Organizations which carry out a large number of projects may even lay down certain milestones when audits will be carried out, for example, when the project is 25% complete, 50% complete and 100% complete.

The audit team may be drawn either from internal sources or from external sources. It should be perceived as being fair and impartial. The audit team should co-opt some members from the project team. It should be emphasized that the project audit is not a 'witch-hunt' and stress should be on what went wrong and why, and how it can be avoided in the future. It is not important as to who was responsible for the error. Similarly, the good practices followed by the project team must also be noted so that the same practices can be followed in the future. The project audit report should present perspectives from the organizational point of view and the project team's point of view.

Once a project is finished it must be properly closed. Closure involves a transfer of ownership of the project from the project team to its client. It also involves reallocation of resources, equipment and personnel to other tasks, a finalization and closure of all accounts and performance evaluation of the project team, its members as individuals, and the project manager. A closure plan with start and finish dates for each activity should be drawn up as otherwise closure may take unduly long. Projects may be closed normally, that is, when the project goals are achieved or closed prematurely in case changes in environment dictate their premature closure. Some projects tend to go on forever due to project scope creep. Such projects should be forced to close by redefining their scope and putting an end to scope creep.

The project team's performance should be evaluated. The evaluation should go beyond measuring its performance against time, cost and quality. Aspects such as team building, performing as an effective team, effectiveness of group decisions, group cohesiveness, trust amongst members, and commitment to the team task should also be included in the evaluation.

Individual performance evaluations may be carried out by the project manager or by the individual's functional head. In the latter case, it would be prudent to obtain inputs from the project manager and incorporate them in the individual's performance appraisal.

A 360-degree appraisal may be carried out for the project manager.

The project closeout phase includes project closure, project audit and performance evaluation.

QUESTIONS

1. What do you understand by project audit? Why is a project audit undertaken?
2. What points will you bear in mind while carrying out a project audit?
3. When would a project have to be closed prematurely?
4. What are the activities associated with the closure of a project?
5. "We cannot afford to terminate the project now. We have already spent 50% of the planned budget." Comment on the statement.
6. What would you include in a project audit report?

CHAPTER 14

Public Projects
Indian Context

Large-scale public projects require the agreement of large numbers of people.

—Thom Mayne

LEARNING OBJECTIVES

After reading this chapter, you will be able to:

- Acquire knowledge of the various agencies involved in formulating, appraising and approving government-funded plan schemes and projects.
- Understand the appraisal and approval limits of the agencies involved.
- Study the process followed for appraisal and approval of government-funded schemes and projects.
- Familiarize yourself with the generic structure of a detailed project report.
- Examine the salient features of the guidelines laid down for the preparation of feasibility reports.

14.1 INTRODUCTION

Public sector projects are undertaken by the Government of India. The Planning Commission is responsible for formulating the five-year plan. The plan spells out the broad strategy and the role of each sector. It also lays down the physical targets and the financial outlays for each sector. Based on the plan, the administrative ministries develop their own plans and programmes. Public sector investments came into their own with the introduction of the Five-Year Plans in the 1950s. A large number of projects were planned and undertaken in many basic industries. Despite the large investments and outlays, the process of appraisal and selection of projects was ad hoc and perfunctory till the middle 60s. For a long time, the important proposals were appraised by the Expenditure Finance Committee of the Ministry of Finance. The methods and procedures used left a lot to be desired. A slew of reforms were introduced in the 60s. However, systems were still tardy leading to massive project cost and time overruns. Periodic reviews are carried out to improve systems and 'Guidelines for the Formulation, Appraisal and Approval of Government-Funded Plan Schemes/Projects' were issued by the Ministry of Finance, Department of Expenditure in May 2003. These were revised in November 2007 and the present guidelines arc applicable to the 11th plan. This chapter aims to familiarize the reader with the laid down government procedures for project appraisal and approval, and the guidelines for preparation of feasibility reports and project reports.

14.2 AGENCIES INVOLVED

The following agencies are involved in formulating, appraising and approving government-funded plan schemes and projects.

14.2.1 The Planning Commission of India

The Planning Commission was set up by a Resolution of the Government of India in March 1950. It is responsible for making assessment of all resources of the country, augmenting deficient resources, formulating plans for the most effective and balanced utilization of resources and determining priorities. The Prime Minister is the Chairman of the Planning Commission.

The first five-year plan was launched in 1951 and two subsequent five-year plans were formulated till 1965, when there was a break because of the Indo-Pakistan conflict. Two successive years of drought, devaluation of the currency, a general rise in prices and erosion of resources disrupted the planning process and after three Annual Plans between 1966 and 1969, the fourth five-year plan was started in 1969. The eighth plan was again delayed due to the fast changing political situation at the Centre and the years 1990–91 and 1991–92 were treated as Annual Plans. The eighth plan was finally launched in 1992 after the initiation of structural adjustment policies. For the first eight plans, the emphasis was on a growing public sector with massive investments in basic and heavy industries, but since the launch of the ninth plan in 1997, the emphasis on the public sector has become less pronounced and the current thinking on planning in the country, in general, is that it should increasingly be of an indicative nature. The 11th five-year plan is currently being implemented.

The functions of the Planning Commission as laid down in the Parliamentary Resolution are as follows:

1. Make an assessment of the material, capital and human resources of the country, including technical personnel, and investigate the possibilities of augmenting such of these resources as are found to be deficient in relation to the nation's requirement.
2. Formulate a plan for the most effective and balanced utilization of the country's resources.
3. On a determination of priorities, define the stages in which the plan should be carried out and propose the allocation of resources for the due completion of each stage.
4. Indicate the factors which are tending to retard economic development, and determine the conditions which, in view of the current social and political situation, should be established for the successful execution of the plan.
5. Determine the nature of the machinery which will be necessary for securing the successful implementation of each stage of the plan in all its aspects.

6. Appraise from time to time the progress achieved in the execution of each stage of the plan and recommend the adjustments of policy and measures that such appraisal may show to be necessary.
7. Make such interim or ancillary recommendations as appear to it to be appropriate either for facilitating the discharge of the duties assigned to it, or on a consideration of prevailing economic conditions, current policies, measures and development programmes or on an examination of such specific problems as may be referred to it for advice by Central or State Governments.

The role of the Planning Commission is gradually shifting from providing a highly centralized planning system towards indicative planning which includes formulation of a long-term strategic vision and deciding on the priorities of the nation. It works out sectoral targets so that the economy can grow in the desired direction.

14.2.2 Project Appraisal and Management Division (PAMD)

It was set up in 1972 as a special division of the Planning Commission under the name Project Appraisal Division. The name was later changed to Project Appraisal and Management Division. The PAMD is responsible for techno-economic appraisal of all plan projects or schemes of Ministries and Departments of Government of India. The appraisal facilitates investment decisions by the Expenditure Finance Committee (EFC)/Public Investment Board (PIB). The investment proposals of the Ministry of Defence and the Department of Atomic Energy and Space do not fall within the purview of the PAMD.

The PAMD is also responsible for evolving research methodology and other steps required for systematic project planning in India. It develops formats and guidelines for the submission of proposals for projects/programmes. It is also associated with other divisions of the Planning Commission in examining proposals received from Ministries and Departments for grant of 'in-principle' approval for new schemes and projects. The PAMD appraises all projects costing ₹ 50 crores or more and prepares appraisal notes before the projects are considered by the PIB, EFC, or other bodies like the Committee of Public Investment Board and Expanded Board of Railways.

The PAMD has also published 'Guidelines for the Preparation of Feasibility Reports' for industry (including mines), coal and power sectors in 1992. These are modified and updated from time to time.

14.2.3 Other Institutions

The Ministry of Finance, Department of Expenditure, Plan II Division has an institutional set-up for project appraisal. The various committees and boards along with their composition and their financial limits are listed below:

(a) *Standing Finance Committee (SFC).* The Standing Finance Committee is responsible for carrying out appraisals of projects costing over ₹ 15 crores and less than ₹ 50 crores. Its composition is as follows:

 (i) Secretary of the Administrative Ministry/Department—Chairperson

(ii) Financial Advisor of the Administrative Ministry/Department—Member
(iii) Joint Secretary in Charge of the Subject Division—Member
(iv) Representative of the Planning Commission, Department of Expenditure and any other Ministry/Department that the Secretary/Financial Advisor may suggest can also be invited, as per requirement

(b) *Expenditure Finance Committee (EFC)*. It is responsible for appraisal of projects costing more than ₹ 50 crores. Its composition is as follows:

(*For proposals costing less than* ₹ 150 *crores*)

(i) Secretary of the Administrative Ministry/Department—Chairman
(ii) Secretary (Planning Commission) or his representative—Member
(iii) Secretary (Department of Expenditure) or his representative—Member
(iv) Financial Advisor of the Administrative Ministry/Department—Member Secretary

(*For proposals costing above* ₹ 150 *crores*)

(i) Secretary (Department of Expenditure)—Chairman
(ii) Secretary (Planning Commission) or his representative—Member
(iii) Secretary of the Administrative Ministry—Member
(iv) Financial Advisor of the Administrative Ministry/Department—Member Secretary

(c) *Public Investment Board (PIB)*. The Board is responsible for appraising all projects above ₹ 150 crores where financial results are quantifiable. The composition of the Board is as follows:

(i) Secretary (Department of Expenditure)—Chairman
(ii) Secretary (Department of Economic Affairs)—Member
(iii) Secretary (Planning Commission)—Member
(iv) Secretary (Ministry of Statistics and Programme Implementation)—Member
(v) Secretary (Ministry of Environment and Forests)—Member
(vi) Secretary of the Administrative Ministry concerned with the public investment proposal—Member
(vii) Joint Secretary (PF.II), Department of Expenditure—Member Secretary

Meetings of PIB shall be attended, in normal course, by the nominated Member personally. The next senior most officer representing the Ministry/Department may be nominated only in most extraordinary circumstances when the nominated principal Member is unable to participate personally.

(d) *Power Projects Investment Committee (PPIC)*. All power-related projects are appraised by the PPIC. The composition of the PPIC is as under:

(i) Secretary (Ministry of Power)—Chairman
(ii) Secretary (Department of Expenditure)—Member
(iii) Secretary (Department of Economic Affairs)—Member
(iv) Secretary (Planning Commission)—Member
(v) Secretary (Ministry of Statistics and Programme Implementation)—Member
(vi) Secretary (Ministry of Environment and Forests)—Member

(vii) Financial Advisor, Ministry of Power Member—Secretary
(viii) Chairman, Central Electricity Authority—Special Invitee
(ix) Chairman, Central Water Commission—Special Invitee

(e) *Committee of Public Investment Board.* It is composed as under:

(i) Secretary (Department of Expenditure)—Chairman
(ii) Secretary (Planning Commission)—Member
(iii) Secretary of the Administrative Ministry/Department concerned with the public investment proposal—Member
(iv) Joint Secretary (PF.II), Department of Expenditure—Member Secretary

The broad functions of the various committees are as follows:

1. To examine, in detail, an investment proposal at the project formulation stage, and to decide whether investment of public funds therein is justified on socio-economic considerations.
2. To examine whether the objectives sought to be met by the project/scheme and/or activities proposed can be combined in existing projects/schemes in a more rational manner and unwanted proliferation/multiplicity of implementation structures and mechanisms can be avoided.
3. To examine whether issues relating to displacement, resettlement and rehabilitation of affected families/persons have been suitably taken care of.
4. To examine, in detail, whether risk factors in project execution and management are expressly specified and taken note of; and mitigation strategies are spelt out in detail in respect of the same.
5. To recommend the proposal, to the appropriate forum of approval, if the factors stated above and other factors found to be relevant in the peculiar circumstances in which the project/scheme has been formulated, have been addressed to the satisfaction of the appraisal forum.

14.3 APPRAISAL AND APPROVAL LIMITS

The appraisal and approval limits as laid down by the government are as follows:

Appraisal limits

Limit (₹, crore)	*Appraisal forum*
<15.0	Ministry in normal Course
≥15.0 and <50.0	Standing Finance Committee (SFC)
≥50.0 and <150.0	Expenditure Finance Committee (EFC) chaired by Secretary of Administrative Ministry/Department
≥150.0	Public Investment Board (PIB)/Expenditure Finance Committee (EFC) chaired by Secretary (Expenditure); projects/schemes where financial returns are quantifiable will be considered by PIB and others by EFC

Approval limits

Limit (₹, crore)	*Appraisal forum*
<15.0	Secretary Administrative Ministry/Department
≥15.0 and <75.0	Minister-in-Charge of Ministry/Department
≥75.0 and <150.0	Minister-in-Charge of Ministry/Department and Minister of Finance
≥150.0	Cabinet Committee on Economic Affairs (CCEA)

The limits refer to the total size of the project or scheme, which may include budgetary support, internal resources, external aid, loans and so on.

14.4 GUIDELINES FOR FORMULATION, APPRAISAL AND APPROVAL OF GOVERNMENT-FUNDED PLAN PROJECTS AND SCHEMES

Step 1. Project identification—feasibility report

The project preparation commences with the preparation of a feasibility report (FR) by the Administrative Ministry. The project is considered for 'in-principle' approval by the Planning Commission for inclusion in the plan based on the FR. The FR should focus on analysis of the existing situation, nature and magnitude of the problems to be addressed, need and justification for the project in the context of national priorities, alternative strategies, initial environmental and social impact analysis, preliminary site investigations, stakeholder commitment and risk factors. The FR should establish whether the project is conceptually sound and feasible and enable a decision to be taken regarding inclusion in the plan and preparation of a detailed project report (DPR). The FR should present a rough estimate of the project cost. Consultation with stakeholders should be held to ensure involvement of stakeholders in the project concept and design. The Financial Advisor should be involved in this exercise.

Step 2. In-principle approval of Planning Commission

The Administrative Ministry sends the FR to the Planning Commission for 'in-principle' approval, to enable the project/scheme to be included in the plan of the Ministry/Department.

Step 3. Preparation of DPR

The Administrative Ministry prepares the DPR for the project/scheme after obtaining 'in-principle' approval of the Planning Commission. The various stakeholders in the project continue to be associated while preparing the DPR. The services of experts/professional bodies may be hired for preparation of the DPR, if considered necessary. The Financial Advisor is also associated. The DPR must address all issues related to the justification, financing and implementation of the project/scheme. A generic structure of the DPR as given in the guidelines is discussed in Section 14.6. The Terms of Reference (TOR) for preparation of the DPR should cover all aspects of the generic DPR structure. In addition, sector/project-specific aspects should be incorporated in the TOR as required. The requirements of the EFC/PIB format should also be kept in view.

Step 4. Inter-ministerial consultations

The final DPR is circulated along with draft EFC/PIB memo to the Department of Expenditure, Planning Commission and any other concerned Ministries for seeking comments before official level appraisal. Techno-economic clearance is obtained from agencies like CEA and CWC wherever required. Thereafter, the EFC/PIB memo along with appraisal note/comments of the relevant Ministries and Planning Commission is placed before the EFC/PIB for consideration.

After approval by the EFC/PIB, the proposal is put up for approval of the Minister of the Administrative Ministry and the Finance Minister. If required, the proposal is put up for approval by the CCEA.

These guidelines apply to all plan schemes/projects, including social sector schemes/projects, costing ₹ 50 crores and above over a five-year plan period. In sectors where a number of sub-projects are taken up under a scheme, this limit will apply to the umbrella project under which the sub-projects are included. 'In-principle' approval is not required for power and coal sector projects.

14.5 APPROVAL PROCEDURE

The approval procedures are as follows:

1. 'In-principle' approval based on feasibility report (FR)
2. Preparation of DPR by Administrative Ministry/Department and circulating it along with draft EFC/PIB memo
3. Comments to be offered on DPR and draft EFC/PIB memo by Planning Commission and concerned Ministries/Departments/Agencies
4. Preparation of final EFC/PIB memo based on DPR and comments received, and circulating the same to Planning Commission, Department of Expenditure and other concerned Ministries/Departments/Agencies
5. Convening of EFC/PIB meeting after receiving final EFC/PIB memo
6. Issue of minutes after EFC/PIB meeting
7. Submission of proposal for approval of Administrative Minister and Finance Minister
8. Circulation of draft CCEA note
9. Issue of comments by different Ministries/Departments on draft CCEA note with approval of Minister-in-Charge
10. Forwarding the proposal finalized by Administrative Ministry to Cabinet Secretariat for consideration by CCEA
11. Meeting of CCEA and final approval

14.6 GENERIC STRUCTURE FOR DETAILED PROJECT REPORT (DPR)

The detailed project report should include the following as per the guidelines:

(a) *Context/background.* This section should provide a brief description of the sector/ sub-sector, the national priority, strategy and policy framework as well as a brief description of the existing situation.

(b) *Problems to be addressed.* This section should elaborate the problems to be addressed through the project/scheme at the local/regional/national level, as the case may be. Evidence regarding the nature and magnitude of the problems should be presented, supported by baseline data/surveys/reports. Clear evidence should be available regarding the nature and magnitude of the problems to be addressed.

(c) *Project objectives.* This section should indicate the *development objectives* proposed to be achieved, ranked in order of importance. The deliverables/outputs for each development objective should be spelt out clearly. This section should also provide a general description of the project.

(d) *Target beneficiaries.* There should be clear identification of target beneficiaries. Stakeholder analysis should be undertaken, including consultation with stakeholders at the time of project formulation. Options regarding cost sharing and beneficiary participation should be explored and incorporated in the project. Impact of the project on weaker sections of society, positive or negative, should be assessed and remedial steps should be suggested in case of adverse impact.

(e) *Project strategy.* This section should present an analysis of alternative strategies available to achieve the development objectives. Reasons for selecting the proposed strategy should be brought out. Involvement of NGOs should be considered. Basis for prioritization of locations should be indicated (where relevant). Options and opportunity for leveraging government funds through public–private partnership must be given priority and explored in depth.

(f) *Legal framework.* This section should present the legal framework within which the project will be implemented and strengths and weakness of the legal framework insofar as it impacts on achievement of project objectives.

(g) *Environmental impact assessment.* Environmental impact assessment should be undertaken, wherever required and measures should be identified to mitigate adverse impact, if any. Issues relating to land acquisition, diversion of forest land, rehabilitation and resettlement should be addressed in this section.

(h) *Ongoing initiatives.* This section should provide a description of ongoing initiatives and the manner in which duplication will be avoided and synergy will be created through the proposed project.

(i) *Technology issues.* This section should elaborate on technology choices, if any, evaluation of options, as well as the basis for choice of technology for the proposed project.

(j) *Management arrangements.* Responsibilities of different agencies for project management and implementation should be elaborated. The organization structure at various levels as well as monitoring and coordination arrangements should be spelt out.

(k) *Means of finance and project budget.* This section should focus on means of finance, evaluation of options, project budget, cost estimates and phasing of expenditure. Options for cost sharing and cost recovery (user charges) should be considered and built into the total project cost. Infrastructure projects may be assessed on the basis of the cost of debt finance and the tenor of debt. Options for raising funds through private sector participation should also be considered and built into the project cost.

(l) *Time frame.* This section should indicate the proposed 'zero' date for commencement and also provide a PERT/CPM chart, wherever relevant.

(m) *Risk analysis.* This section should focus on identification and assessment of project risks and how these are proposed to be mitigated. Risk analysis could include legal/contractual risks, environmental risks, revenue risks, project management risks, regulatory risks, and so on.

(n) *Evaluation.* This section should focus on lessons learnt from evaluation of similar projects implemented in the past. Evaluation arrangements for the project, whether concurrent, mid-term or post-project, should be spelt out. It may be noted that continuation of projects/schemes from one plan period to another will not be permissible without an independent, in-depth evaluation being undertaken.

(o) *Success criteria.* Success criteria to assess whether the development objectives have been achieved should be spelt out in measurable terms. Baseline data should be available against which success of the project will be assessed at the end of the project (impact assessment). In this regard, it is essential that baseline surveys be undertaken in case of large, beneficiary-oriented projects. Success criteria for each deliverable/output of the project should also be specified in measurable terms to assess achievement against proximate goals.

(p) *Financial and economic analysis.* Financial and economic analysis of the project may be undertaken where the financial returns are quantifiable. This analysis would generally be required for investment and infrastructure projects, but may not always be feasible for social sector projects where the benefits cannot be easily quantified.

(q) *Sustainability.* Issues relating to sustainability, including stakeholder commitment, operation and maintenance of assets after project completion, and other related issues should be addressed in this section.

14.7 GUIDELINES FOR PREPARATION OF FEASIBILITY REPORT

Guidelines for preparation of feasibility report were issued by the PAMD in 1966. These were revised in 1987 and fresh guidelines have been now issued in 1992. The guidelines spell out the details required for the preliminary feasibility report (PFR) which is needed to accord 'in-principle' approval, and the details to be included in the detailed feasibility report (DFR). The guidelines also give details for specific sectors—cement, paper, engineering industry, metal and other mining/non-ferrous metallurgy, iron and steel ferrous metallurgy and processing industry.

The information to be included in the PFR is as follows:

1. Brief outline/salient features of the proposal.
2. Need and justification of the project based on technical necessity and/or demand–supply analysis of the product. The need for the project must be justified from a broad assessment of demand and supply. The basis and assumptions underlying the demand and supply projections should be spelt out in detail. Technical necessity must be supported by adequate details in quantitative terms about the benefits likely to accrue from the project.

3. Identification and analysis of broader alternatives available for meeting the objectives or need. Broad or macro level alternatives that can replace the proposal in toto should be considered. The comparative analysis of alternatives should be based on a realistic set of assumptions and the qualitative and quantitative criteria for determining the inter se priorities should be clearly brought out.
4. Location, technology, feedstock, capacity of the plant and the product mix proposed for each techno-economically feasible alternative should be included.
5. Broad item-wise estimate of capital cost together with the basis and year-wise phasing of capital expenditure for all the alternatives considered should be included.
6. Broad item-wise estimate of operating and maintenance costs and financial and economic benefits from the project for each alternative.
7. Linkages of raw materials and details of infrastructural facilities, such as land, water, power, transport and environmental quality of the region.
8. Economic and financial viability analysis of the project including determination of IRR/NPV, cost of production and generation, domestic resource cost, breakeven point, payback period and so on. The data is required for each alternative considered.
9. Complete list of studies and investigations proposed to be carried for preparation of DFR.
10. For location-specific projects, the clearance for site and acquisition of land required, if any, should be considered at this stage. The environmental and forest clearance for studies and investigations and for the site should be obtained before putting up a PFR. While the requirements of an environmental appraisal are to be met separately, the PFR should include the following information:
    (i) Quantification of characteristics of effluent emissions and waste from different technology options.
    (ii) Land use of proposed site, soil conditions with respect to microbes and leachability, distance from sanctuaries, baseline information on meteorology, noise level, existing flora and fauna and so on.
11. Estimate of costs and time frame involved for studies and investigations proposed and preparation of DFR.

It may be observed that the feasibility report includes the various studies and analysis included in Chapter 3, namely, market analysis, technical analysis, financial analysis, economic analysis and environmental analysis.

After the 'in-principle' approval is received, the studies and investigations as approved are carried out and a feasible option is developed into a project. A DFR is prepared and submitted for further processing and approval. This report gives a detailed description of the project parameters, based on the investigations and studies, to enable the appraising agencies to evaluate the technical feasibility and the economic and financial viability of the project. The information to be included in the DFR is listed as follows:

1. Demand–supply position and other information about the sector or industry including market studies
2. Policies

3. Project in the framework of corporate and national plan
4. Alternatives
5. Technical aspects
   (i) Location and site
   (ii) Production build-up
   (iii) Plant size
   (iv) Technology
   (v) Feedstocks/raw materials
   (vi) Energy consumption
   (vii) Equipment and construction requirements
   (viii) Manpower requirements
   (ix) Transport and communications requirements
   (x) Utilities
   (xi) Linked projects
6. Organizational and managerial aspects
7. Environmental aspects
8. Project costs
   (i) Capital cost requirements
   (ii) Operating requirements and costs
   (iii) Total system cost
9. Financial analysis
10. Economic analysis
11. Sensitivity analysis

The details required to be given under each head and subhead are elaborated upon in the guidelines. For instance, under 'organizational and managerial aspects', the DFR should elaborate on implementation plan, state of preparedness, marketing plan and other clearances required for the project. The guidelines also include suggested formats for the preparation of the FR and the DFR. The guidelines run into 173 pages, divided into five chapters. A chapter dealing with revision of cost estimates is also included.

SUMMARY

The success of any project depends on its proper formulation and appraisal and this is equally true for projects entailing public spending. The Planning Commission is responsible for formulating the five-year plan. The plan spells out the broad strategy and the role of each sector. It also lays down the physical targets and the financial outlays for each sector. Based on the plan, the Administrative Ministries develop their own plans and programmes.

The agencies involved in project formulation and project appraisal are the Administrative Ministries, Project Appraisal and Management Division of the Planning Commission of India, Standing Finance Committee (SFC), Expenditure Finance Committee (EFC), Public Investment Board (PIB), Power Projects Investment Committee (PPIC), and Committee of Public Investment

Board. The authorities are empowered to appraise projects and appraisal limits are specified based on the total cost of the project. The authority to approve projects rests with the Secretary of the Administrative Ministry for projects below ₹ 15 crore and with the Minister-in-Charge Administrative Ministry for projects between ₹ 15 crore and ₹ 75 crore. Projects costing more than ₹ 75 crore but less than ₹ 150 crore need the approval of the Minister-in-Charge Administrative Ministry and the Finance Minister. All projects costing ₹ 150 crore or more are approved by the Cabinet Committee on Economic Affairs and then approved by the Cabinet.

The Ministry of Finance, Department of Expenditure, Plan Finance II Division laid down elaborate guidelines for formulation, appraisal and approval of government-funded plan schemes/projects in May 2003. These were subsequently revised in November 2007. The revised guidelines are applicable during the 11th five-year plan. The guidelines also include a generic format for detailed project reports.

The Project Appraisal and Management Division of the Planning Commission lays down guidelines for preparation of preliminary feasibility reports and detailed feasibility reports from time to time. The currently applicable guidelines were issued in April 1992. The guidelines are very elaborate and include formats to which various sections of the feasibility report must conform.

It may be observed that the guidelines require a market study, a technical analysis, an environmental analysis, a financial analysis and an economic analysis to be carried out. Salient features of all these studies are included in Chapter 3.

QUESTIONS

1. What are the functions of the Planning Commission of India?
2. Explain the procedure for approval of government-funded projects and schemes.
3. What are the main contents of a feasibility report?
4. What is the role of Administrative Ministry and the Finance Ministry in the planning and approval of government-funded projects and schemes?

Case Studies

CASE 1 TEZ TAAR ELECTRONICS

Tez Taar Electronics, an electronics product firm, was established in 2002. During the past few years, it has established itself in the market as a manufacturer of innovative electronic products. The company specializes in electronic household products like television sets, microwave ovens, electronic games, and desktop and laptop computers. It has now decided to launch a new product which would combine an electronic game and a musical keyboard aimed at children in their teens. The project involved a hand-held device with a touch screen and a touch keypad. The project was scheduled over a period of six months.

The design phase of the project was nearly completed, when the marketing department came up with the idea of incorporating a digital camera in the device as well. After some delay and discussions, the recommendation was accepted. The product had to undergo major design changes and a new design was prepared which incorporated a 1.2 mega pixel camera in the design. The design phase which was originally scheduled for two months had a time overrun of one month because of the changes in the scope of the project.

Before the design was handed over to the production department, the marketing department requested for a change in the specification of the digital camera. 1.2 mega pixel cameras were being incorporated in most hand-held devices including mobile phones. The marketing department was of the view that a 3 mega pixel camera would differentiate the product from other similar products launched by the competitors. On the face of it, the change appeared minor but the product had to be sent back to the design team as the running of the game on the high resolution screen had not been built in and the display was not up to the mark. This recommendation was also accepted. The designers spent another two weeks tweaking the software to run on a high resolution screen. By now the project was running well behind schedule.

A prototype of the product was produced, but before it could be test marketed, a competitor came up with a hand-held device that had a musical keyboard capable of producing the sound of three different instruments. The sponsors again suggested changes and wanted the incorporation of multiple instrument sounds in the musical keyboard. The design was again modified to incorporate these changes.

By then the company had acquired mobile telephony technology. A suggestion was made that the device should also incorporate a mobile telephone. The project originally scheduled for six months was already in its tenth month and prototypes, testing and test marketing phases were yet to take off.

The Vice President of the Gaming Division called for a high-level meeting and you, as the project manager of this new product, have to brief the Vice President and his team and address their concerns on the time and cost overruns occurring on this project.

What do you think are the major causes for the delay in this project and what action would you recommend?

CASE 2 ACME SECURITIES LIMITED

Acme Securities Limited is a company that specializes in security systems. Two years ago, the strategic management team of the company set a goal of developing a close circuit camera based security system for homes at an affordable price of ₹ 2000 per unit. A few months later, the senior management met to discuss the new product. The meeting resulted in the drawing up of a set of general specifications for the new product along with major deliverables, a product launch date and a cost estimate based on previous experience of the company.

Some time later, a meeting was held to brief middle management on the goals and objectives of the new product, allocate major responsibilities, set a project start and finish date and to emphasize the need to launch the project as planned and to keep it within the estimated costs. The meeting was attended by members of all departments. Although everyone realized the risks attached with the project were high, there was a great deal of enthusiasm for it. Some doubts were raised about the suggested time frame and the estimated costs, but these were swept away in the wave of euphoria over doing something new. The provision of a close circuit camera based home security system at such an affordable cost held a lot of promise in terms of its demand. Everyone agreed that the project was worth doing and appeared doable. It was to be accorded the highest priority in the company.

Mr. Ajay Kapoor was selected as the project manager. Mr. Kapoor had successfully launched two new systems earlier and had some experience of project management. Since he had some reservations about the time frame and the cost of the project, he called a meeting of his team and in consultation with them created a work breakdown structure (WBS). The work packages were identified and assigned to the organizational units responsible for their execution. He then asked the organizational units responsible to prepare time and cost estimates. The team was also encouraged to obtain estimates from other sources also.

The estimates were compiled and aggregated upwards. The estimates were not compatible with the estimates of the senior management. The cost estimate was ₹ 5 lakh in excess of the estimate provided by the senior management—an overrun of 20%. The time estimate was also four months over the estimate provided by the senior management. A review of the estimates was carried out and Mr. Kapoor concluded that the estimates prepared by his team were reasonable. He held another meeting of his staff to brainstorm for alternative solutions. Some of the suggestions received by him included cancellation of the project; changing the scope of the project; going into a partnership with a research agency so that costs of developing new technology and production processes could be shared; and outsourcing of technology design. However, nothing significant in terms of cost reduction emerged. Everyone was of the opinion that the project launch date should be met so that first mover advantage is not lost. This would mean compressing the time schedule at extra cost.

Mr. Kapoor met with the marketing, production and design managers and shared his problem with them. Though some ideas were generated, reduction in cost was not considered feasible with the current specifications and time frame. Mr. Kapoor was faced with the daunting task of apprising the top management that their estimate was out by ₹ 5 lakh.

At this stage, what would you do if you were the project manager?

CASE 3 PARKLAND

The Jaipur Development Authority (JDA) is planning a Community Centre building. The building is located in a large area on the outskirts of the town. In keeping with its policy of beautification of the town and making it an attractive tourist centre, JDA plans to landscape the area surrounding the building. The plan visualizes contouring of the landscape, manicured lawns, shrubs, trees, a sprinkler-based watering system, fountains and lily ponds. Accordingly, a sum of ₹ 20,00,000 was allocated for the landscaping project and a tender document was developed so that the landscaping work would be completed in the next 24 months. Quotations were then called for and response to the tender was invited.

Parkland, a Delhi-based landscape architectural firm, won the contract on the basis of a sketch that they had submitted along with their proposal. They were also the lowest bidders and were awarded the contract for ₹ 17,50,000. Parkland then prepared a detailed landscaping plan based on the drawings of the site included in the tender documents. This was followed by a meeting with the JDA officials to decide on the start of the project and access and security of plant and equipment. A fixed cost contract was duly signed.

Parkland scoped and planned the project with specific milestones for site preparation, irrigation, turf laying and tree and shrub planting. Parkland had carried out a number of similar projects at other sites. From their past experience, they felt that it was not necessary to have a formal project plan. They merely wanted an agreement on the scope of the project and the key deliverable dates. They also requested JDA to nominate a single person with whom they would have to deal. JDA nominated Mr. Sharma, their senior administrative and estate officer and assigned him the responsibility of overseeing the project.

Parkland commenced work in November and by January had completed the site preparation. At this time, the roof of the building was being constructed. Heavy concrete mixers carrying premixed concrete for the roof lost their way and traversed over the prepared site causing damage to the newly prepared and levelled ground for the lawns.

The Parkland site manager met Mr. Sharma and apprised him of the damage caused. The site would have to be repaired and a week would be needed to bring things back to shape. While Mr. Sharma agreed that it was not Parkland's fault, he emphasized the need to complete the project within the budgeted amount. He suggested that some savings be effected by reducing the scope of some other work. No records of these discussions were maintained, nor were any written reports submitted by Parkland to JDA.

Accordingly, Parkland proceeded to repair the site. Shrubs and small trees were planted as per the original schedule. After some days, it was noticed that though the plants had initially taken root, they had begun to wilt despite watering. A horticulturist was called in and he attributed the damage to the plants to the presence of termites in the area. It was suggested that the area be treated with anti-termite compounds. The task involved drilling 10-foot deep holes at every 10-foot interval and pouring an anti-termite chemical in them. The treatment added to the costs and had not been initially foreseen or catered for. The matter was brought to the notice of Mr. Sharma. He gave a patient hearing but insisted that Parkland should have foreseen such a problem. He again suggested that savings be made in some other work associated with the project.

Parkland carried out the anti-termite treatment and replanted the shrubs and small trees. Despite the setback, by March, things appeared to be progressing well. Work on the pipeline and sprinkler system commenced. The project manager decided to cut back on the scope of this work so that the additional costs incurred on the anti-termite treatment could be made up. The bore of the pipeline was reduced and the number of sprinkler nozzles was also reduced. Work also commenced on the fountains. Heavy rains during July and August caused the construction work to stop but helped the shrubs and trees. By November, the trees and shrubs were well established. The contoured landscape had also stabilized. Some damage caused due to the rains was repaired. Work on the pipeline and sprinkler system recommenced and work on the fountains also commenced. By May, the following year, Parkland commenced work on planting the turf. The rains, in the previous year, had been good and Parkland expected that rains in June and July would help in establishing the lawns.

Unfortunately, the weather turned for the worse. A very hot spell ruled over Northern India. The freshly put turf began to wither. The sprinklers were found to be inadequate. The dry weather continued and the monsoons failed.

By September, the project was three months behind schedule. The lawns were patchy and had big bare patches in them. A large number of shrubs had also died during the dry period because of inadequate watering. The site looked a shadow of the drawing that had won Parkland the contract in the first place. Costs were rising and Parkland had already spent ₹ 19,00,000 on the project. Parkland requested a meeting with the top management of JDA. The Vice President of Parkland was to head the team at the meeting. Parkland raised the issue of extra costs, but JDA turned down their request for additional funds saying that Parkland should have visualized these contingencies and included them in their estimates. JDA further claimed that at no stage had Parkland made any written referrals to its problems. JDA and Parkland referred the dispute to their legal experts but no agreement was in sight.

As an experienced project manager, you have been approached by both the parties to conduct a project audit. You have been selected for your impartiality and lack of any vested interest in the dispute.

1. How would you go about carrying out a project audit?
2. What would you include in your audit report?
3. Would you co-opt any experts in your audit team, and if so, from what areas?
4. What advice would you give to JDA and Parkland?
5. How would you resolve the issue and bring the project to closure?

In your opinion, could the project be handled better? What was the main cause of the project failing to deliver?

CASE 4 RASOI APPLIANCES

Rasoi Appliances is a white goods manufacturer. It manufactures kitchen appliances like food processors, food warmers, ovens, toasters, grills, refrigerators and other household goods. It has recently received a suggestion for developing a microwave oven especially for Indian conditions. The microwave oven should not only include the functions of microwave cooking, grilling and conventional oven, but should also have a facility to turn over the food or stir it with the help of a timer. The design should also preserve the flavour of Indian spices.

The suggestion was passed on to the product design team. The product development team consists of the following persons:

1. Marketing Executives (3)
2. Design Engineers (3)
3. Production Engineers (3)
4. Industrial Engineers (3)
5. Purchase Officer (1)

The team studied the problem and came up with the following list of activities:

Task	*Description*	*Duration*	*Predecessor*	*Resources*
1	Market research and analysis	3 weeks		Marketing Executives (3) Design Engineer (1)
2	Product design	6 weeks	1	Design Engineers (3) Production Engineer (1) Industrial Engineer (1) Marketing Executive (1)
3	Process study	3 weeks	1	Production Engineers (2) Industrial Engineers (3)
4	Product design selection	1 week	2, 3	Marketing Executives (2) Design Engineers (3) Production Engineers (2) Industrial Engineers (2)
5	Detailed marketing plan	2 weeks	4	Marketing Executives (3)
6	Setting up manufacturing process	4 weeks	4	Design Engineer (1) Production Engineers (2) Industrial Engineers (3)
7	Detailed product design	6 weeks	4	Marketing Executive (1) Design Engineers (3) Production Engineers (2) Industrial Engineer (1)
8	Test prototype	1 week	7	Design Engineers (3) Production Engineers (2)
9	Finalize product design	3 weeks	6, 8	Design Engineers (3) Production Engineers (2) Industrial Engineers (2) Marketing Executive (1)

(Contd...)

(Contd...)

Task	*Description*	*Duration*	*Predecessor*	*Resources*
10	Procure components	3 weeks	9	Purchase Officer (1)
11	Procure additional production equipment	4 weeks	9	Purchase Officer (1)
12	Install production equipment	3 weeks	10, 11	Production Engineers (3) Industrial Engineers (2)

1. When is the project likely to be finished?
2. What is the critical path and what are the critical activities?
3. What are the slacks in the activities?
4. Which activities involve overloading of resources?
5. If the project is time constrained, attempt to level the resources within the available slacks. What would be the impact of such levelling?
6. If the project is resource constrained and no additional personnel are available, when will the project be completed?

CASE 5 ARUN FINANCIAL CONSULTANTS

Part 1

Arun Financial Consultants is a firm of chartered accountants and financial consultants. Amongst its many activities, it specializes in arranging finance for new entrepreneurs. It helps them in evaluation, preparing viable reports, documentation, legal documentation and finally obtaining a loan from banking or financial institutions. The task involves preparing a proposal, checking the background of the client firm for its creditworthiness, preparing pro forma balance sheets and profit and loss accounts for the term of the loan, carrying out a need analysis, preparing loan agreement documents and finally obtaining the loan for the client. To facilitate better management, the firm uses PERT. It is currently processing the proposed loan for Alfa Enterprises. The team assigned for this project has identified the following activities:

Activity	*Description*	*Immediate predecessor*
A	Start preparing proposal as per template	—
B	Check credit worthiness of firm	—
C	Create a rough draft proposal	A, B
D	Carry out need analysis with client	C
E	Estimate future cash outflows and inflows	C
F	Prepare pro forma financial statements	E
G	Prepare and obtain approval of legal documents	C
H	Integrate all documents and produce proposal	D, F, G
I	Identify potential sources of capital and select	G, F
J	Check, approve and print final legal proposal	H
K	Sign agreement and transfer funds	I, J

Three time estimates for activities are given as follows:

Activity	*Time optimistic*	*Time most likely*	*Time pessimistic*
A	4	7	10
B	2	5	8
C	2	5	8
D	16	19	28
E	6	9	24
F	1	7	13
G	4	10	28
H	2	5	14
I	5	8	17
J	2	5	8
K	19	28	37

1. What is the mean time for completion of the project?
2. If the company has a policy of setting up a project with 95% probability of achieving the plan, what time frame should the company set for this project?

Part 2

The project team has estimated the following cost data for the project. The team also discussed how it could compress the timing of the project and came up with crash costs and crash durations possible for the activities as shown in the following table. The normal time for the activities is to be taken as the mean time required for each activity as derived from the three time estimates.

Activity	*Normal cost*	*Maximum crash possible*	*Crash cost per day*
A	4000	3	500
B	5000	2	1000
C	7000	—	—
D	20,000	3	2500
E	11,000	2	1000
F	7000	1	1100
G	24,000	2	3000
H	8000	1	2000
I	6000	1	2000
J	7000	1	1000
K	14,000	6	1000

Total normal cost is ₹ 1,13,000.
Overhead costs for the project are ₹ 1000 per day.

1. What is the optimal duration of the project?
2. An error was made in the estimates for the overhead costs. The revised figure for overhead costs was ₹ 1200 per day. Will the optimal duration of the project change?
3. What is the earliest time by which the project can be finished?

CASE 6 WHITE WATER RAFTING EXPEDITION

The Department of Management Studies, IIT Roorkee is planning to take its MBA students for a team-building camp. The camp will be held at a site known as Marine Drive about 15 km from Rishikesh. The camp will be of three-day duration and will include white water rafting over the Ganges, a trekking trip to Shakumbhari Devi Temple and some team-building exercises. The Dean contacted the Manager of Ganga Adventures, a firm which organizes rafting tours and camps and asked him to submit a proposal for the trip.

As manager of Ganga Adventures, you have organized similar trips before. Based on an earlier proposal, details of which are given below, carry out a risk analysis and identify the risks associated with this project. How would you deal with each of these risks?

Project objective

To organize a three-day adventure camp at Marine Drive Camp Site, Rishikesh for 100 students of MBA, IIT Roorkee from 21 May to 23 May at a cost of ₹ 1500 per head.

Deliverables

1. Provide four luxury buses for transporting students by road from Roorkee to camp site and for use during the duration of the camp.
2. Provide packed breakfast for all students on 21 May.
3. Provide tented accommodation for students (four persons to a tent) for 21 and 22 May night. Cots, lighting arrangements, adequate water arrangements and toilet tents should be provided.
4. Provide all meals till 23 May, when students will return to Roorkee.
5. Arrange campfire on 21 May night.
6. Provide 12 rafts for white water rafting along with a guide each on 22 May for a rafting trip down the Ganges.
7. Provide medical cover and rescue boat during the rafting expedition.
8. Arrange for cross country trekking trip to Shakumbhari Devi Temple on 23 May.
9. Arrange for refreshments at Shakumbhari Devi Temple.
10. Transport students back to Roorkee to arrive no later than 23:00 hours on 23 May.

CASE 7 R & D PROJECT

Bharat Telecom, a firm dealing in electronic products, approved an R & D project for developing a new mobile handset in August 2001, which required technical breakthroughs. The product was to be developed by July 2002 so that it could be introduced into the market quickly as the life cycle of the product was relatively short due to very rapid changing technologies. The Marketing Department was of the view that the product would not survive longer than a year in the market. A budget of ₹ 6,00,000 was allotted for the project.

Bharat Telecom had a well-established project management methodology with periodic reviews. At the first review, the project showed good signs of progress though the technological breakthrough had yet to be achieved. The project team was enthusiastic and optimistic about the project.

By the time the second review was carried out, the project had still not been able to develop the technology as visualized in the original plan. The other components of the project seemed in place, but the breakthrough to achieve a battery that would have lasted a long period without charging was still not in sight. The long life of the battery had been touted as the selling point for the project. The project was already one month behind schedule. A suggestion was made by one of the senior executives that the project be cancelled. However, the project sponsor managed to convince the executive committee that the project would be successfully completed.

At the next review meeting, the technical breakthrough was still a distant dream. The project was already running four months behind schedule. The cost had also exceeded the budgeted amount. The project team requested for another ₹ 1,00,000 for the project.

The executive committee was sharply divided in its views. Most of the members were of the view that the product would not hit the market in time and reduce the marketing window available to it. They felt that the firm may not break even with the short period for sales available to them. The Senior Marketing Manager conveyed to the committee that marketing may not be able to meet the planned sales target. The Chairman of the executive committee was reluctant to cancel the project. Already ₹ 6,00,000 had been spent on it. R & D further added that the technological breakthrough would also be exploited in future products and the effort spent thus far should not be allowed to go waste.

1. What would you do if you were the Chairman of the executive committee, and why?
2. What aspects would you consider while taking your decision?
3. How would you ensure that the R & D team does not get demotivated, if the project is cancelled?

CASE 8 SUPREME CERAMICS LIMITED

Supreme Ceramics is a company that manufactures and supplies sanitary hardware and fittings. Its products range from wall and floor tiles, wash basins, toilet seats, water taps and fittings to toilet accessories and fixtures. Each product is made in various designs and colours. The design of water taps and other fittings not only has to be functional but also has to be artistic to attract attention. The competition in the market is fierce. Supreme Ceramics targets big clients like construction companies and builders through aggressive marketing as these provide them with a good source of revenue. For instance, a builder could pick up 5000 or more components for a single hotel or a single block of residential apartments.

Unfortunately, Supreme suffers from a non-cooperative culture. Each department functions as though it is an independent entity and is the sole contributor to the profits of the company. The Marketing Department and the Production Department are always at loggerheads. While Production concentrates on producing new designs and products, Marketing insists that they should have the final say since they are in direct contact with the customers and understand their needs.

The CEO of Supreme realized that if the organization was to compete successfully in the market, it would have to adopt a project management approach towards developing new products. However, the attempt to implement project management met with great resistance. No one was willing to take on the mantle of the project manager. Functional heads refused to cooperate and kept working on their own 'pet' projects. Functional team members stayed away from project meetings on one pretext or the other. Line managers did not support project management.

The CEO was perturbed at this and emphasized the urgent need for implementing project management practices. The Vice Presidents, Marketing and Production reluctantly agreed to make another attempt but were not sure whether the effort would succeed. An external expert was called in to help implement project management in the organization. He decided to first tackle the issue of conflict between different departments. Strangely, while everyone was aware of the existing conflict, no one knew its exact origin or source. The expert interviewed key personnel and the gist of what he gathered is given below.

Production department

The production department was of the view that Marketing interfered too much with their work. Production was keen to emphasize that they had a lot of load besides new product development. They faced a major problem as Marketing would insist on last minute changes to design, necessitating rework and loss of production hours. The loss of production time occurred because these changes were often intimated after Production had scheduled the facilities for the particular product. Rescheduling involved changing set-ups of machines and delays. Production engineers felt that the Marketing personnel did not perform their own task properly and were never clear as to what they wanted. Last minute changes were not conducive to the efficient working of the Production Department.

Marketing department

The marketing department contended that in order to meet the fierce competition, they passed on ideas for new products to the Production Department as soon as they got them from the customers. This was necessary as the products took four to six months to develop and the products had a short life cycle. Often, these ideas were not complete and a good definition of what was required was not available. The customers were then approached for further clarifications and specifications. Last minute changes were thus unavoidable. Marketing personnel felt that Production should accept and make these changes as the product must meet the customer's needs.

1. What do you think is the critical issue?
2. How would you resolve the differences between the Marketing and Production Departments?
3. How would you implement project management in the organization?

APPENDIX A

Finance for Project Managers

1. Cost of Capital

- Introduction
- Cost of Term Loans
- Cost of Debentures
- Cost of Preference Equity
- Cost of Equity
- Cost of Retained Earnings and Cost of External Equity
- Weighted Average Cost of Capital
- Application to Project Management

2. Cash Flows

- Introduction
- Principles
- Determining Cash Flows—Equity Funds
- Cash Flows—Long-term Funds
- Cash Flows—Total Funds
- Cash Flows for a Replacement Project
- Cash Flows and Taxation
- Cash Flows and Inflation
- Application to Project Management

A.1 COST OF CAPITAL

A.1.1 Introduction

Projects are financed through various sources of funds like equity, preference equity, debentures, long or short-term borrowings and so on. The cost of capital is defined as the minimum rate of return that the organization must earn on its investments so that it can satisfy and meet the expectations of its investors. When people invest money in an organization, they expect certain returns on their investment. If the returns fall short of their expectations, they are likely to withdraw their invested funds and shift them to more promising avenues. For instance, when an investor buys equity shares of an organization, he expects a certain return which may be by way of dividends declared by the organization or by way of an increase in the market price of the share. It is, therefore, imperative that the organization earns a rate of return in keeping with the expectations of the investor. The organization also incurs certain costs when it raises capital. These costs must also be recovered through the returns on investment in addition to the returns expected by the investors.

Since the organization may raise funds through different sources, the cost of capital is the weighted arithmetic average of the cost of various sources of finance that have been used by it. Let us understand this with the help of an example. Suppose an organization has a total capital base of ₹ 700 lakh consisting of ₹ 400 lakh of equity and ₹ 300 lakh of debt funds, and the cost of equity and debt funds is 15% and 8%, respectively. Then the cost of capital is:

$$\frac{400}{700} \times 15\% + \frac{300}{700} \times 8\% = 12\%$$

In order to compute the cost of capital, the first step is to compute the cost of funds obtained from various sources by the organization. Let us now examine the method of computing cost of capital for various sources of funds.

A.1.2 Cost of Term Loans

All term loans, whether short-term or long-term, are made available by the source at a certain rate of interest. This has to be paid to the source from whom funds have been borrowed. However, the borrower does not pay any tax on interest paid by him, and this results in a saving to him. The actual amount paid is the interest as calculated by the interest rate less the amount of saving of tax. Let us understand this with the help of an example. Suppose a firm has obtained a term loan of ₹ 100 lakh from a bank at 15% interest and the tax rate is 40%. Then the firm will actually pay:

$$\begin{aligned} \text{Interest at } 15\% &= ₹\ 15 \text{ lakh} \\ \text{Savings due to non-taxation} &= ₹\ 15 \times 0.40 \\ &= ₹\ 6 \text{ lakh} \\ \text{Net cost} &= ₹\ 9 \text{ lakh} \end{aligned}$$

Generalizing, we can say that:

$$\text{Cost of term loan} = \text{Interest rate } (1 - \text{tax rate})$$
$$k_i = I(1 - t)$$

where

k_i = Cost of term loans
I = Interest rate of term loan
t = Corporate tax rate

A.1.3 Cost of Debentures

Debentures carry an annual rate of interest and are redeemed either completely after a period of time or through part payments spread over a number of years. The cost of floatation of the debentures may be amortized over the life of the debentures or may not be amortized. Let us understand the concept of computing cost of debentures with the help of an example.

EXAMPLE A.1 A company raises debentures of face value ₹ 100 each. The debentures carry an interest rate of 12% per annum and are to be redeemed at face value after five years. Tax rate is 40%. Let us assume that the cost of floatation is ₹ 5 per debenture and is not being amortized.

The interest to be paid annually on one debenture = ₹ 15

The interest on debentures is also non-taxable.

Hence, actual cash outflow due to interest = 15(1 – 0.4) = ₹ 9

Since the cost of floating the debenture is ₹ 5, the net amount realized per debenture is ₹ 100 – ₹ 5 = ₹ 95. The cost of floatation should be distributed over the life of the debenture, that is, five years in this case.

$$\text{Annual cost of floatation} = ₹\ 5/5 = ₹\ 1$$

A total cost of ₹ 10 has been incurred on average investment, i.e. (95 + 100)/2.

$$\text{Cost of debenture} = \frac{9+1}{195/2} = \frac{20}{195} = 10.25\%$$

Generalizing,

$$k_d = \frac{I(1-t) + \dfrac{F-P}{n}}{\dfrac{F+P}{2}}$$

where

k_d = Post-tax cost of debenture capital
I = Annual interest rate per debenture
t = Corporate tax rate
F = Redemption value of debenture
P = Net amount realized per debenture
n = Maturity period

If the cost of floatation of the debenture is amortized, then the cost is annually written off just like depreciation, and is not taxed. Hence, amortization leads to tax savings on the floatation costs and the above relationship is modified as shown below:

$$k_d = \frac{I(1-t) + \dfrac{F-P}{n}(1-t)}{\dfrac{F+P}{2}}$$

A.1.4 Cost of Preference Equity

Preference shares carry a fixed rate of dividend and are generally redeemed after a certain number of years. Since the dividend is paid out of appropriations made after tax, there is no tax saving in the case of preferential share dividend. The cost of capital can be worked out in the similar manner as for debentures:

$$k_p = \frac{D + \dfrac{F-P}{n}}{\dfrac{F+P}{2}}$$

where

k_p = Cost of preference capital
D = Preference dividend payable annually per share
t = Corporate tax rate
F = Redemption value of preference share
P = Net amount realized per preference share
n = Maturity period

A.1.5 Cost of Equity

Calculating the cost of equity shares is more complex as they do not carry a fixed rate of dividend. The dividend may vary from year to year. The earning per share is also neither constant nor is it completely distributed. The organization may retain some earnings to meet future investments. Various approaches can be adopted. We shall examine the dividend forecast approach, realized yield approach and the earning price ratio approach.

Dividend forecast approach

It is difficult to forecast the complete dividend stream. If we assume that the dividend per year has a constant annual growth rate g, then the cost of equity is given by the relationship:

$$k_e = \frac{D_1}{P_e} + g$$

where

k_e = Cost of equity
D_1 = Dividend expected at the end of the year
P_e = Current price of equity (price per share)
g = Growth rate.

EXAMPLE A.2 The market price per share of Alpha Chemicals is ₹ 125. The company is expected to pay a dividend of ₹ 25 at the end of the year, and the dividend per share (DPS) is expected to grow at a rate of 8%. What is the cost of equity?

Solution

$$k_e = \frac{D_1}{P_e} + g = \frac{25}{125} + .08 = 0.28$$

Cost of equity is 28%.

Realized yield approach

As per this approach, the past returns from the equity are taken as a proxy for future returns. The approach assumes that the past returns were in keeping with expectations of the investors and that the investors will continue to have the same expectations from the equity. These assumptions do not generally hold good in real life. The cost of equity calculated by this approach forms a start point for the estimation of the required return.

The realized return over a period of n years is given by

$$k_e = (W_1 \times W_2 \times W_3 \times \cdots \times W_n)^{1/n} - 1$$

where

k_e = Cost of equity
W_t = Wealth ratio and is computed as

$$W_t = \frac{D_t + P_t}{P_{t-1}}$$

D_t = Dividend at the end of year t
P_t = Price per share at the end of year t
P_{t-1} = Price per share at the beginning of year t (or end of year $t - 1$)

EXAMPLE A.3 The following table gives the dividend per share and the price per share for the past four years:

	Year			
	1	2	3	4
Price per share at beginning of year	10.00	12.00	11.00	12.25
Dividend per share	1.50	2.00	1.75	2.00

What is the cost of equity?

Solution

Year	1	2	3	4
Wealth ratio	$\frac{1.50+12.00}{10.00}=1.35$	$\frac{2.00+11.00}{12.00}=1.08$	$\frac{1.75+12.25}{11.00}=1.27$	

$$k_e = (1.35 \times 1.08 \times 1.27)^{1/3} - 1 = 0.227 \text{ or } 22.7\%$$

Earning price ratio approach

As per this approach, the cost of equity is:

$$k_e = \frac{E_1}{P}$$

where

k_e = Cost of equity
E_1 = Expected earning per share (EPS) for the next year
P = Current market price per share
$E_1 = E(1 + g)$, where E is the current EPS and g is the growth rate.

The model gives accurate results when either all the earnings are paid out as dividends or the retained earnings also earn a rate of return equal to the cost of equity.

EXAMPLE A.4 The current market price per share of Beta Enterprises is ₹ 80 and the current EPS is ₹ 15. The growth rate is 5%. Calculate the cost of equity.

Solution

$$k_e = \frac{E(1+g)}{P} = \frac{15(1+.05)}{80} = 0.196 \text{ or } 19.6\%$$

A.1.6 Cost of Retained Earnings and Cost of External Equity

When a company incurs floatation cost to raise equity from the external market, the cost of external equity is involved. The floatation costs imply that the actual amount realized is not the market price of the share but the price less the cost of floatation. The cost of external equity in the case of the dividend forecast method is given by:

$$k_e' = \frac{D_1}{P_e(1-f)} + g$$

where

k_e' = Cost of external equity
D_1 = Dividend expected at the end of the year
P_e = Current price of equity (price per share)
g = Growth rate
f = Cost of floatation expressed as a percentage of the current market price

There is no particular method for accounting of floatation costs in other approaches used to compute the cost of equity. An approximation for the cost of external equity can be obtained from the following relation:

$$k_e' = \frac{k_e}{1-f}$$

where

k_e' = Cost of external equity
k_e = Cost of equity or rate of return required by investors
f = Floatation cost expressed as a percentages of the current market price

EXAMPLE A.5 Beta Enterprises has ₹ 200 lakhs of retained capital and raises ₹ 100 lakhs as fresh equity from the market. The investors expect a return of 18% and the cost of floatation is 5%. What is the cost of retained earnings and the cost of external equity?

Solution Cost of retained earnings

$$k_r = k_e = 18\%$$

Cost of external equity

$$k_e' = \frac{k_e}{1-f} = \frac{0.18}{1-0.05} = 18.95\%$$

A.1.7 Weighted Average Cost of Capital

The cost of capital is the weighted arithmetic average of the cost of various sources of finance that have been used by the company. Let us understand this with the help of an example.

EXAMPLE A.6 The capital structure of Delta Durables is given in the following table:

	(₹, lakh)
Equity capital (20 lakh shares of face value ₹ 10 each)	200
15% preference shares (2 lakh shares of face value ₹ 10 each)	20
Retained earnings	130
12% non-convertible debentures (50,000 debentures of face value ₹ 100 each)	50
14% loan from HDFC	100

The current market price per share is ₹ 30. The next expected dividend per share is ₹ 3 and the dividend is expected to grow at a constant rate of 8%. The preference shares are redeemable at par after five years and are currently quoted at ₹ 7.50 per share at the stock exchange. The debentures are redeemable at par after seven years and the current price is ₹ 90 per debenture. The tax rate applicable to the firm is 40%. Calculate the cost of capital to the firm.

Solution

Step 1 Determine the cost of various sources of finance.

Cost of equity using dividend forecast method is:

$$k_e = \frac{D_1}{P_0} + g = \frac{3}{30} + 0.08 = 0.18$$

Cost of preference capital

$$k_p = \frac{D + \frac{F - P}{n}}{\frac{F + P}{2}} = \frac{1.5 + \frac{10 - 7.5}{5}}{\frac{10 + 7.5}{2}} = 0.229$$

Cost of retained earnings is the same as the cost of equity, that is,

$$k_r = k_e = 0.18$$

Cost of debentures

$$k_d = \frac{I(1-t) + \frac{F - P}{n}}{\frac{F + P}{2}} = \frac{12(1 - 0.4) + \frac{100 - 90}{7}}{\frac{100 + 90}{2}} = 0.09$$

Cost of term loan

$$k_i = I(1 - t) = 0.14(1 \times 0.4) = 0.084$$

Step 2 Determine the weights associated with the various sources of finance. The weights may be based on book values of the sources of finance included in the present capital structure of the company, or on the present values of the sources of finance included in the present capital structure, or on the basis of proportions of financing planned. Let us follow the book value approach.

$$\text{Weight of equity } (W_e) = \frac{200}{500} = 0.40$$

$$\text{Weight of preference capital } (W_p) = \frac{20}{500} = 0.04$$

$$\text{Weight of retained earnings } (W_r) = \frac{130}{500} = 0.26$$

$$\text{Weight of debentures } (W_d) = \frac{50}{500} = 0.10$$

$$\text{Weight of term loans } (W_i) = \frac{100}{500} = 0.20$$

Step 3 Determine the weighted average cost of capital

$$= W_e \times k_e + W_p \times k_p + W_r \times k_r + W_d \times k_d + W_i \times k_i$$

$$\text{Cost of capital} = 0.40 \times 0.18 + 0.04 \times 0.20 + 0.26 \times 0.18 + 0.10 \times 0.09 + 0.20 \times 0.084$$

$$= 0.1526$$

Weighted average cost of capital is 15.26%.

A.1.8 Application to Project Management

The cost of capital is used as the discount rate when computing the NPV of a project or for comparison with the computed internal rate of return when appraising projects for selection.

A.2 CASH FLOWS

A.2.1 Introduction

Financial appraisal of projects involves the estimation of costs and investments to be made; an estimation of income as a result of the project in terms of either profits or cash flows and a comparison of the investments made and the income derived.

Projects are appraised and compared on the basis of their net present value, or internal rate of return, or payback period. Each of these methods requires a knowledge of the stream of cash flows which are likely to occur in future as a result of the project. The net present value also involves a discounting rate. The internal rate of return is compared to a base rate of return which is in keeping with the expectations of the investors. The cost of capital can be used as a discount rate while calculating net present value. It also serves as the base rate of return with which the internal rate of return is compared. We have seen how to compute the cost of capital in the previous section. We shall now examine how to compute cash flows.

A.2.2 Principles

Estimation of cash flows is based on the following principles:

1. All costs and benefits are measured in terms of cash flows. Non-cash charges like depreciation which are considered for the purpose of determining the profit after tax are added back to the profit after tax to obtain the net cash flow.
2. Net cash flows are those that accrue after paying tax. Cash flows are defined in post-tax terms.
3. Cash flows are measured in incremental terms. Only the increments that occur in the present level of costs and benefits on account of the project are considered relevant.

Cash flows have three basic components:

(a) *Initial investment.* This includes the cost of the project plus the working capital required for operations. In case of a replacement project, the after tax salvage value realized from the disposal of the old asset and the net working capital required for operation of the old asset is deducted in keeping with the principle of measuring cash flows in incremental terms.

(b) *Operating cash flows.* These constitute the after tax cash flows obtained from operating the assets created by the project. In case of a replacement project, the operating cash flows from the old asset, had it not been replaced, are deducted.

(c) *Terminal cash flow.* This consists of the after tax salvage value of the assets and the recovery of net working capital associated with it. In case of a replacement project, the after tax salvage value, had the asset not been replaced, and the recovery of net working capital associated with the old asset is deducted.

A.2.3 Determining Cash Flows—Equity Funds

Cash flows can be viewed from different perspectives. The most commonly used perspective is from the point of view of the owners or equity holders of the project. We shall understand the method of calculating cash flows with the help of some illustrations.

EXAMPLE A.7 Alfa Technologies is considering a new product project with the following information:

1. The total outlay of the project is expected to be ₹ 100 million, which consists of ₹ 70 million in fixed assets and ₹ 30 million in current assets.
2. The total outlay of ₹ 100 million is proposed to be financed as follows:

	(₹, million)
Equity	40
12% preference equity redeemable after five years	5
15% term loan	30
18% short-term bank borrowings	15
Trade credit	10
Total	100

3. The term loan is payable in five equal instalments of ₹ 6 million each, starting at the end of the first year. The levels of bank finance for working capital and trade credit will remain constant at ₹ 15 million and ₹ 10 million, respectively, till they are paid back or retired at the end of the product life of five years.
4. The expected revenue from the new product will be ₹ 120 million per year and the operating costs including depreciation will be ₹ 80 million annually. Depreciation on fixed assets will be 30% as per the written down value method. The net salvage value of the fixed assets and current assets at the end of five years will be ₹ 12 million and ₹ 30 million, respectively.
5. The tax rate applicable to the firm is 40%.

The equity-related cash flow stream represents the costs and benefits of the equity shareholders (owners) of the firm. The cash flows can be divided into three components as follows:

Initial investment = Equity capital
Operating cash flows = Profit after tax
+ Depreciation
– Preference dividend
– Loan repayments
– Redemption of preference equity/debentures
+ Other non-cash charges

Terminal cash flow = Net salvage value of fixed assets
+ Net salvage value of current assets
– Repayment of term loans
– Repayment of working capital advances
– Repayment of trade credits and other dues
– Redemption of preference equity/debentures

Depreciation

Depreciation can be either on a straight line basis or on a written down value basis. For calculation of tax, the written down value method is used. It implies that the asset is depreciated at a fixed rate of the written down value every year. For instance, if the value of the asset is ₹ 100 and the depreciation rate is 25%, then in the first year, the depreciation will be 25% of ₹ 100, that is, ₹ 25. In the second year, the depreciation will be 25% of ₹ 75 (which is the written down value of the asset after the first year's depreciation is deducted), that is ₹ 18.75.

The cash flow stream is tabulated as follows:

		(₹, million)					
		Year					
		0	1	2	3	4	5
1	Equity	–40.00	—	—	—	—	—
2	Revenues		120.00	120.00	120.00	120.00	120.00
3	Operating cost		80.00	80.00	80.00	80.00	80.00
4	Depreciation		21.00	14.70	10.29	7.20	5.04
5	Interest on working capital (STBB)		2.70	2.70	2.70	2.70	2.70
6	Interest on term loan		4.50	3.60	2.70	1.80	0.90
7	Profit before tax (2 – 3 – 4 – 5 – 6)		11.80	19.00	24.31	28.30	31.36
8	Tax		4.72	7.60	9.72	11.32	12.54
9	Profit after tax (7 – 8)		7.08	11.40	14.59	16.98	18.82
10	Preference dividend		0.60	0.60	0.60	0.60	0.60
11	Repayment of term loan		6.00	6.00	6.00	6.00	6.00
12	Operating cash flow (9 – 10 – 11 + 4)		21.48	19.50	18.28	17.58	17.26
13	Net salvage value of fixed assets						12.00
14	Net salvage value of current assets						30.00
15	Repayment of short-term borrowings						15.00
16	Redemption of preference equity						5.00
17	Net cash flow (12 + 13 + 14 – 15 – 16)	–40.00	21.48	19.50	18.28	17.58	39.26

Note: Item 6, interest on term loan, is decreasing as the loan is being paid back in instalments every year and interest is calculated only on the remaining balance.

One may wonder why dividends, if any, paid to the shareholders have not been deducted from the cash flows. The cash flows accrue to the equity holders and any dividend paid to them would accrue to them. The retained earnings and the dividends belong to the equity holders and, therefore, there is no requirement to account for them separately.

A.2.4 Cash Flows—Long-term Funds

Cash flows may be determined from a long-term funds perspective. It is akin to assuming that all providers of long-term finance, that is, equity holders and providers of long-term finance, are considered as owners. This affects the initial, operating and terminal cash flows. The initial cash flows consist of all long-term finance. While computing operational cash flows, the interest paid on long-term finance is added back to the profit after tax as it is paid to the assumed owners. However, since no tax has been deducted on it, its post-tax value is taken. The terminal cash flow does not include the repayment of long-term finance. The changes are summarized as follows:

Initial investment = Equity + Long-term funds
Operating cash flows = Profit after tax
+ Depreciation
+ Interest on term loan (1 – Tax rate)
– Preference dividend
– Redemption of preference equity/debentures
+ Other non-cash charges
Terminal cash flow = Net salvage value of fixed assets
+ Net salvage value of current assets
– Repayment of working capital advances
– Repayment of trade credits and other dues
– Redemption of preference equity/debentures

Cash flows from a long-term finance perspective with the data given in Example 1 are as follows:

		(₹, million)					
		Year					
		0	1	2	3	4	5
1	Equity	–40.00	—	—	—	—	—
2	Long-term borrowings	–30.00	—	—	—	—	—
3	Revenues		120.00	120.00	120.00	120.00	120.00
4	Operating cost		80.00	80.00	80.00	80.00	80.00
5	Depreciation		21.00	14.70	10.29	7.20	5.04
6	Interest on working capital (STBB)		2.70	2.70	2.70	2.70	2.70
7	Interest on term loan		4.50	3.60	2.70	1.80	0.90
8	Profit before tax (3 – 4 – 5 – 6 – 7)		11.80	19.00	24.31	28.30	31.36
9	Tax		4.72	7.60	9.72	11.32	12.54
10	Profit after tax (8 – 9)		7.08	11.40	14.59	16.98	18.82
11	Preference dividend		0.60	0.60	0.60	0.60	0.60
12	Operating cash flow [10 – 11 + 5 + 7(1 – 0.4)]		30.18	27.66	25.90	24.66	23.80
13	Net salvage value of fixed assets						12.00
14	Net salvage value of current assets						30.00
15	Repayment of short-term borrowings						15.00
16	Redemption of preference equity						5.00
17	Net cash flow (12 + 13 + 14 – 15 – 16)	–70.00	30.18	27.66	25.90	24.66	45.80

A.2.5 Cash Flows—Total Funds

Cash flows may be viewed from the perspective of total funds. It is assumed that all providers of funds are the owners of the enterprise. The effect on initial, operating and terminal cash flows is as follows:

$$\begin{aligned}
\text{Initial investment} &= \text{Total funds}\\
\text{Operating cash flows} &= \text{Profit after tax} + \text{Depreciation}\\
&\quad + \text{Interest on term loan}(1 - \text{Tax rate})\\
&\quad + \text{Interest on short-term borrowings}(1 - \text{Tax rate})\\
&\quad + \text{Other non-cash charges}\\
\text{Terminal cash flow} &= \text{Net salvage value of fixed assets}\\
&\quad + \text{Net salvage value of current assets}
\end{aligned}$$

Cash flows from a total funds perspective for the data given in Example C.7 are as follows:

		(₹, million)					
		Year					
		0	1	2	3	4	5
1	Total funds	–200.00	—	—	—	—	—
2	Revenues		120.00	120.00	120.00	120.00	120.00
3	Operating cost		80.00	80.00	80.00	80.00	80.00
4	Depreciation		21.00	14.70	10.29	7.20	5.04
5	Interest on working capital (STBB)		2.70	2.70	2.70	2.70	2.70
6	Interest on term loan		4.50	3.60	2.70	1.80	0.90
7	Profit before tax (2 – 3 – 4 – 5 – 6)		11.80	19.00	24.31	28.30	31.36
8	Tax		4.72	7.60	9.72	11.32	12.54
9	Profit after tax (7 – 8)		7.08	11.40	14.59	16.98	18.82
10	Operating cash flow [9 + 4 + (5 + 6) (1 – 0.4)]		32.40	29.88	28.12	26.88	26.02
11	Net salvage value of fixed assets						12.00
12	Net salvage value of current assets						30.00
13	Net cash flow (10 + 11 + 12)	–200.00	32.40	29.88	28.12	26.88	68.02

A.2.6 Cash Flows for a Replacement Project

As mentioned earlier, cash flows for a replacement project are calculated on an incremental basis. Let us examine this with the help of an example.

EXAMPLE A.8 A company is determining the cash flows for a project involving the replacement of an old machine with a new machine. The book value of the old machine is ₹ 5,00,000 and it can be sold for ₹ 4,00,000. The machine has a residual life of five years after which its salvage value will be ₹ 1,00,000. It is being depreciated at 25% annually under the written down value method. The working capital requirement is ₹ 4,00,000.

The new machine costs ₹ 20,00,000. It needs a working capital of ₹ 6,00,000. The machine is depreciated at a rate of 25% by the written down value method for five years after which the machine will no longer be required. It will fetch a net salvage value of ₹ 5,00,000. The machine will result in a saving of ₹ 4,00,000 annually in operating costs (other than depreciation). The corporate tax rate is 40%.

The cash flows are determined as follows:

		(₹, million)					
		Year					
		0	1	2	3	4	5
1	Cost of new asset	–2000.00					
2	Salvage value of old machine	400.00					
3	Increase in net working capital	–200.00					
4	Incremental increase in revenue		400.00	400.00	400.00	400.00	400.00
5	Depreciation on new machine		500.00	375.00	281.25	210.94	158.20
6	Depreciation on old machine		125.00	93.75	70.31	52.73	39.55
7	Incremental depreciation		375.00	281.25	210.94	158.20	118.65
8	Incremental profit before tax (4 – 7)		25.00	118.75	189.06	241.80	281.35
9	Tax		10.00	47.50	75.63	96.72	112.54
10	Profit after tax		15.00	71.25	113.44	145.08	168.81
11	Cash flow (10 + 7)		390.00	352.50	324.38	303.28	287.46
12	Net terminal value of new machine						500.00
13	Net terminal value of old machine						100.00
14	Recovery of incremental net working capital						200.00
15	Net cash flow (11 + 12 – 13 – 14)	–1800.00	390.00	352.50	324.38	303.28	487.46

A.2.7 Cash Flows and Taxation

It should be noted that tax is only deducted on profits. There is no taxation on losses. The losses can be carried forward to the next year and tax is deducted when the firm earns positive profits after all losses incurred to date have been carried forward. A simplified method of calculating cash flows is to compute negative tax on losses and deduct it from the tax whenever tax becomes due. Let us examine this aspect with the help of an example.

EXAMPLE A.9 XYZ Company is thinking of investing ₹ 100 lakh on a project. The life of the project is eight years and the estimated salvage value of the assets is ₹ 4 lakh at the end of eight years. The company follows a straight line method of depreciation, and the corporate tax rate is 40%. The estimated cash flows before tax and depreciation are as follows:

Year	*Estimated cash flow before tax*
1	8.0
2	10.0
3	18.0
4	22.0
5	30.0
6	36.0
7	38.0
8	40.0

Calculate the cash flows.

The cash flows are as follows:

		(₹, million)								
		Year								
		0	1	2	3	4	5	6	7	8
1	Initial investment	–100								
2	Estimated cash flow		8.00	10.00	18.00	22.00	30.00	36.00	38.00	40.00
3	Depreciation		12.00	12.00	12.00	12.00	12.00	12.00	12.00	12.00
4	Profit before tax		–4.00	–2.00	6.00	10.00	18.00	24.00	26.00	28.00
5	Tax		–1.60	–0.80	0.00	4.00	7.20	9.60	10.40	11.20
6	Net profit after tax					6.00	10.80	14.40	15.60	16.80
7	Net cash flow		8.00	10.00	18.00	18.00	22.80	26.40	27.60	28.80
8	Salvage									4.00
9	Net cash flow		8.00	10.00	18.00	18.00	22.80	26.40	27.60	32.80

As can be seen, the firm suffers a loss in the first two years. In the third year, the firm has a profit before tax of ₹ 6 lakh. The tax on this works out to ₹ 2.4 lakh (40%). The negative tax carried forward for the first two years is ₹ 2.40 lakh (1.60 + 0.80) and hence zero tax is paid in the third year.

If we carry the losses forward, the loss of ₹ 4 lakh of first year is carried to the second year, and the accumulated loss carried forward to the third year would be ₹ 6 lakh. This would result in a zero profit before tax and hence a zero tax liability in the third year.

A.2.8 Cash Flows and Inflation

There is often a misconception that inflation can be ignored since both revenues and costs will be affected. While this is true, the depreciation is charged on the book value and this will affect the resultant cash flows. Let us examine the effect of inflation on cash flows with the help of an example.

EXAMPLE A.10 A project involves a cash outlay of ₹ 3,00,000 and has a life of five years. The salvage value at the end of five years is ₹ 50,000. The estimated maintenance and operating costs and revenues at the beginning of the project are given in the following table:

	(₹, 000s)
Annual revenue	225
Maintenance and operating costs	100
Depreciation (written down value method)	25% annually
Tax rate	40%

Inflation rate is 5% annually.

Let us first determine the cash flows without the effect of inflation. The cash flows are as follows:

		(₹, 000s)					
		Year					
		0	1	2	3	4	5
1	Initial investment	–300.00					
2	Revenue		225.00	225.00	225.00	225.00	225.00
3	Operating costs		100.00	100.00	100.00	100.00	100.00
4	Depreciation		75.00	56.25	42.19	31.64	23.73
5	Profit before tax (2 – 3 – 4)		50.00	68.75	82.81	93.36	101.27
6	Tax		20.00	27.50	33.13	37.34	40.51
7	Profit after tax (5 – 6)		30.00	41.25	49.69	56.02	60.76
8	Operating cash flow (7 + 4)		105.00	97.50	91.88	87.66	84.49
9	Salvage						50.00
10	Net cash flow (8 + 9)	–300.00	105.00	97.50	91.88	87.66	134.49

Let us now consider the inflation. The inflation rate is 5% annually. The effect is being compounded, and the inflation rate is $(1 + r)^t$, where r is the inflation rate and t is the time period. The cash flows are as shown in the following table:

		(₹, 000s)					
		Year					
		0	1	2	3	4	5
	Inflation factor $(1 + r)^t$	0.00	1.05	1.10	1.16	1.22	1.28
1	Initial investment	–300.00					
2	Revenue		236.25	248.06	260.47	273.49	287.16
3	Operating costs		105.00	110.25	115.76	121.55	127.63
4	Depreciation		75.00	56.25	42.19	31.64	23.73
5	Profit before tax (2 – 3 – 4)		56.25	81.56	102.52	120.30	135.80
6	Tax		22.50	32.63	41.01	48.12	54.32
7	Profit after tax (5 – 6)		33.75	48.94	61.51	72.18	81.48
8	Operating cash flow (7 + 4)		108.75	105.19	103.70	103.82	105.21
9	Salvage						63.81
10	Net cash flow	–300.00	108.75	105.19	103.70	103.82	169.03
11	Cash flows adjusted for inflation (10/inflation factor)	–300.00	103.57	95.41	89.58	85.41	132.44

As may be observed, the net cash flows after being adjusted for inflation are lower than the cash flows without inflation. This will affect the net present value (NPV) and the internal rate of return of the project. Assuming a discount rate of 20%, the NPV of the project without considering inflation is ₹ 4.70 lakh, and the NPV after considering inflation is ₹ –1.18 lakh. If inflation exists, the project should not be undertaken as it has a negative NPV.

A.2.9 Application to Project Management

Cash flows are required to consider the profitability of the project. They are also needed to compare and appraise projects. Project appraisal is carried out using methods such as the (NPV), internal rate of return (IRR), return on investment, benefit–cost ratio and payback period. These have been adequately described in Chapter 3 (Section 3.4).

APPENDIX B

The Standard Normal Probability Distribution

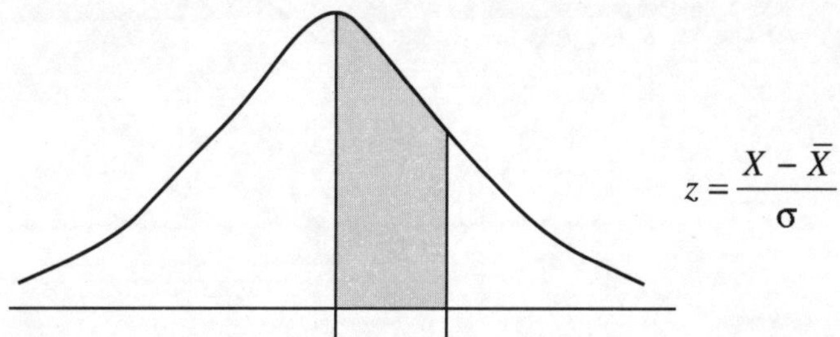

$$z = \frac{X - \bar{X}}{\sigma}$$

Z	.00	.01	.02	.03	.04	.05	.06	.07	.08	.09
0.0	0.0000	0.0040	0.0080	0.0120	0.0160	0.0199	0.0239	0.0279	0.0319	0.0359
0.1	0.0398	0.0438	0.0478	0.0517	0.0557	0.0596	0.0636	0.0675	0.0714	0.0753
0.2	0.0793	0.0832	0.0871	0.0910	0.0948	0.0987	0.1026	0.1064	0.1103	0.1141
0.3	0.1179	0.1217	0.1255	0.1293	0.1331	0.1368	0.1406	0.1443	0.1480	0.1517
0.4	0.1554	0.1591	0.1628	0.1664	0.1700	0.1736	0.1772	0.1808	0.1844	0.1879
0.5	0.1915	0.1950	0.1985	0.2019	0.2054	0.2088	0.2123	0.2157	0.2190	0.2224
0.6	0.2257	0.2291	0.2324	0.2357	0.2389	0.2422	0.2454	0.2486	0.2517	0.2549
0.7	0.2580	0.2611	0.2642	0.2673	0.2704	0.2734	0.2764	0.2794	0.2823	0.2852
0.8	0.2881	0.2910	0.2939	0.2967	0.2995	0.3023	0.3051	0.3078	0.3106	0.3133
0.9	0.3159	0.3186	0.3212	0.3238	0.3264	0.3289	0.3315	0.3340	0.3365	0.3389
1.0	0.3413	0.3438	0.3461	0.3485	0.3508	0.3531	0.3554	0.3577	0.3599	0.3621
1.1	0.3643	0.3665	0.3686	0.3708	0.3729	0.3749	0.3770	0.3790	0.3810	0.3830
1.2	0.3849	0.3869	0.3888	0.3907	0.3925	0.3944	0.3962	0.3980	0.3997	0.4015
1.3	0.4032	0.4049	0.4066	0.4082	0.4099	0.4115	0.4131	0.4147	0.4162	0.4177
1.4	0.4192	0.4207	0.4222	0.4236	0.4251	0.4265	0.4279	0.4292	0.4306	0.4319
1.5	0.4332	0.4345	0.4357	0.4370	0.4382	0.4394	0.4406	0.4418	0.4429	0.4441
1.6	0.4452	0.4463	0.4474	0.4484	0.4495	0.4505	0.4515	0.4525	0.4535	0.4545

(Contd...)

(Contd...)

Z	.00	.01	.02	.03	.04	.05	.06	.07	.08	.09
1.7	0.4554	0.4564	0.4573	0.4582	0.4591	0.4599	0.4608	0.4616	0.4625	0.4633
1.8	0.4641	0.4649	0.4656	0.4664	0.4671	0.4678	0.4686	0.4693	0.4699	0.4706
1.9	0.4713	0.4719	0.4726	0.4732	0.4738	0.4744	0.4750	0.4756	0.4761	0.4767
2.0	0.4772	0.4778	0.4783	0.4788	0.4793	0.4798	0.4803	0.4808	0.4812	0.4817
2.1	0.4821	0.4826	0.4830	0.4834	0.4838	0.4842	0.4846	0.4850	0.4854	0.4857
2.2	0.4861	0.4864	0.4868	0.4871	0.4875	0.4878	0.4881	0.4884	0.4887	0.4890
2.3	0.4893	0.4896	0.4898	0.4901	0.4904	0.4906	0.4909	0.4911	0.4913	0.4916
2.4	0.4918	0.4920	0.4922	0.4925	0.4927	0.4929	0.4931	0.4932	0.4934	0.4936
2.5	0.4938	0.4940	0.4941	0.4943	0.4945	0.4946	0.4948	0.4949	0.4951	0.4952
2.6	0.4953	0.4955	0.4956	0.4957	0.4959	0.4960	0.4961	0.4962	0.4963	0.4964
2.7	0.4965	0.4966	0.4967	0.4968	0.4969	0.4970	0.4971	0.4972	0.4973	0.4974
2.8	0.4974	0.4975	0.4976	0.4977	0.4977	0.4978	0.4979	0.4979	0.4980	0.4981
2.9	0.4981	0.4982	0.4982	0.4983	0.4984	0.4984	0.4985	0.4985	0.4986	0.4986
3.0	0.4987	0.4987	0.4987	0.4988	0.4988	0.4989	0.4989	0.4989	0.4990	0.4990

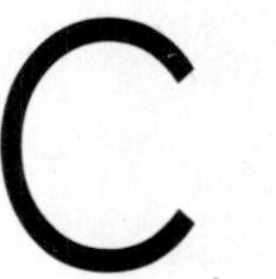

APPENDIX C

Financial Tables

Future value of ₹ 1 invested for period t at a rate $k = (1 + k)^t$

Period	Rate																			
	1%	2%	3%	4%	5%	6%	7%	8%	9%	10%	11%	12%	13%	14%	15%	16%	17%	18%	19%	20%
1	1.010	1.020	1.030	1.040	1.050	1.060	1.070	1.080	1.090	1.100	1.110	1.120	1.130	1.140	1.150	1.160	1.170	1.180	1.190	1.200
2	1.020	1.040	1.061	1.082	1.103	1.124	1.145	1.166	1.188	1.210	1.232	1.254	1.277	1.300	1.323	1.346	1.369	1.392	1.416	1.440
3	1.030	1.061	1.093	1.125	1.158	1.191	1.225	1.260	1.295	1.331	1.368	1.405	1.443	1.482	1.521	1.561	1.602	1.643	1.685	1.728
4	1.041	1.082	1.126	1.170	1.216	1.262	1.311	1.360	1.412	1.464	1.518	1.574	1.630	1.689	1.749	1.811	1.874	1.939	2.005	2.074
5	1.051	1.104	1.159	1.217	1.276	1.338	1.403	1.469	1.539	1.611	1.685	1.762	1.842	1.925	2.011	2.100	2.192	2.288	2.386	2.488
6	1.062	1.126	1.194	1.265	1.340	1.419	1.501	1.587	1.677	1.772	1.870	1.974	2.082	2.195	2.313	2.436	2.565	2.700	2.840	2.986
7	1.072	1.149	1.230	1.316	1.407	1.504	1.606	1.714	1.828	1.949	2.076	2.211	2.353	2.502	2.660	2.826	3.001	3.185	3.379	3.583
8	1.083	1.172	1.267	1.369	1.477	1.594	1.718	1.851	1.993	2.144	2.305	2.476	2.658	2.853	3.059	3.278	3.511	3.759	4.021	4.300
9	1.094	1.195	1.305	1.423	1.551	1.689	1.838	1.999	2.172	2.358	2.558	2.773	3.004	3.252	3.518	3.803	4.108	4.435	4.785	5.160
10	1.105	1.219	1.344	1.480	1.629	1.791	1.967	2.159	2.367	2.594	2.839	3.106	3.395	3.707	4.046	4.411	4.807	5.234	5.695	6.192
11	1.116	1.243	1.384	1.539	1.710	1.898	2.105	2.332	2.580	2.853	3.152	3.479	3.836	4.226	4.652	5.117	5.624	6.176	6.777	7.430
12	1.127	1.268	1.426	1.601	1.796	2.012	2.252	2.518	2.813	3.138	3.498	3.896	4.335	4.818	5.350	5.936	6.580	7.288	8.064	8.916
13	1.138	1.294	1.469	1.665	1.886	2.133	2.410	2.720	3.066	3.452	3.883	4.363	4.898	5.492	6.153	6.886	7.699	8.599	9.596	10.699
14	1.149	1.319	1.513	1.732	1.980	2.261	2.579	2.937	3.342	3.797	4.310	4.887	5.535	6.261	7.076	7.988	9.007	10.147	11.420	12.839
15	1.161	1.346	1.558	1.801	2.079	2.397	2.759	3.172	3.642	4.177	4.785	5.474	6.254	7.138	8.137	9.266	10.539	11.974	13.590	15.407
16	1.173	1.373	1.605	1.873	2.183	2.540	2.952	3.426	3.970	4.595	5.311	6.130	7.067	8.137	9.358	10.748	12.330	14.129	16.172	18.488
17	1.184	1.400	1.653	1.948	2.292	2.693	3.159	3.700	4.328	5.054	5.895	6.866	7.986	9.276	10.761	12.468	14.426	16.672	19.244	22.186
18	1.196	1.428	1.702	2.026	2.407	2.854	3.380	3.996	4.717	5.560	6.544	7.690	9.024	10.575	12.375	14.463	16.879	19.673	22.901	26.623
19	1.208	1.457	1.754	2.107	2.527	3.026	3.617	4.316	5.142	6.116	7.263	8.613	10.197	12.056	14.232	16.777	19.748	23.214	27.252	31.948
20	1.220	1.486	1.806	2.191	2.653	3.207	3.870	4.661	5.604	6.727	8.062	9.646	11.523	13.743	16.367	19.461	23.106	27.393	32.429	38.338

Future value of an annuity of ₹ 1 received for period t at a rate $k = [(1 + k)^t - 1]/k$																				
	Rate																			
Period	1%	2%	3%	4%	5%	6%	7%	8%	9%	10%	11%	12%	13%	14%	15%	16%	17%	18%	19%	20%
1	1.000	1.000	1.000	1.000	1.000	1.000	1.000	1.000	1.000	1.000	1.000	1.000	1.000	1.000	1.000	1.000	1.000	1.000	1.000	1.000
2	2.010	2.020	2.030	2.040	2.050	2.060	2.070	2.080	2.090	2.100	2.110	2.120	2.130	2.140	2.150	2.160	2.170	2.180	2.190	2.200
3	3.030	3.060	3.091	3.122	3.153	3.184	3.215	3.246	3.278	3.310	3.342	3.374	3.407	3.440	3.473	3.506	3.539	3.572	3.606	3.640
4	4.060	4.122	4.184	4.246	4.310	4.375	4.440	4.506	4.573	4.641	4.710	4.779	4.850	4.921	4.993	5.066	5.141	5.215	5.291	5.368
5	5.101	5.204	5.309	5.416	5.526	5.637	5.751	5.867	5.985	6.105	6.228	6.353	6.480	6.610	6.742	6.877	7.014	7.154	7.297	7.442
6	6.152	6.308	6.468	6.633	6.802	6.975	7.153	7.336	7.523	7.716	7.913	8.115	8.323	8.536	8.754	8.977	9.207	9.442	9.683	9.930
7	7.214	7.434	7.662	7.898	8.142	8.394	8.654	8.923	9.200	9.487	9.783	10.089	10.405	10.730	11.067	11.414	11.772	12.142	12.523	12.916
8	8.286	8.583	8.892	9.214	9.549	9.897	10.260	10.637	11.028	11.436	11.859	12.300	12.757	13.233	13.727	14.240	14.773	15.327	15.902	16.499
9	9.369	9.755	10.159	10.583	11.027	11.491	11.978	12.488	13.021	13.579	14.164	14.776	15.416	16.085	16.786	17.519	18.285	19.086	19.923	20.799
10	10.462	10.950	11.464	12.006	12.578	13.181	13.816	14.487	15.193	15.937	16.722	17.549	18.420	19.337	20.304	21.321	22.393	23.521	24.709	25.959
11	11.567	12.169	12.808	13.486	14.207	14.972	15.784	16.645	17.560	18.531	19.561	20.655	21.814	23.045	24.349	25.733	27.200	28.755	30.404	32.150
12	12.683	13.412	14.192	15.026	15.917	16.870	17.888	18.977	20.141	21.384	22.713	24.133	25.650	27.271	29.002	30.850	32.824	34.931	37.180	39.581
13	13.809	14.680	15.618	16.627	17.713	18.882	20.141	21.495	22.953	24.523	26.212	28.029	29.985	32.089	34.352	36.786	39.404	42.219	45.244	48.497
14	14.947	15.974	17.086	18.292	19.599	21.015	22.550	24.215	26.019	27.975	30.095	32.393	34.883	37.581	40.505	43.672	47.103	50.818	54.841	59.196
15	16.097	17.293	18.599	20.024	21.579	23.276	25.129	27.152	29.361	31.772	34.405	37.280	40.417	43.842	47.580	51.660	56.110	60.965	66.261	72.035
16	17.258	18.639	20.157	21.825	23.657	25.673	27.888	30.324	33.003	35.950	39.190	42.753	46.672	50.980	55.717	60.925	66.649	72.939	79.850	87.442
17	18.430	20.012	21.762	23.698	25.840	28.213	30.840	33.750	36.974	40.545	44.501	48.884	53.739	59.118	65.075	71.673	78.979	87.068	96.022	105.931
18	19.615	21.412	23.414	25.645	28.132	30.906	33.999	37.450	41.301	45.599	50.396	55.750	61.725	68.394	75.836	84.141	93.406	103.740	115.266	128.117
19	20.811	22.841	25.117	27.671	30.539	33.760	37.379	41.446	46.018	51.159	56.939	63.440	70.749	78.969	88.212	98.603	110.285	123.414	138.166	154.740
20	22.019	24.297	26.870	29.778	33.066	36.786	40.995	45.762	51.160	57.275	64.203	72.052	80.947	91.025	102.444	115.380	130.033	146.628	165.418	186.688

Present value of ₹ 1 received at period t discounted at a rate $k = 1/(1+k)^t$																				
	Rate																			
Period	1%	2%	3%	4%	5%	6%	7%	8%	9%	10%	11%	12%	13%	14%	15%	16%	17%	18%	19%	20%
1	0.990	0.980	0.971	0.962	0.952	0.943	0.935	0.926	0.917	0.909	0.901	0.893	0.885	0.877	0.870	0.862	0.855	0.847	0.840	0.833
2	0.980	0.961	0.943	0.925	0.907	0.890	0.873	0.857	0.842	0.826	0.812	0.797	0.783	0.769	0.756	0.743	0.731	0.718	0.706	0.694
3	0.971	0.942	0.915	0.889	0.864	0.840	0.816	0.794	0.772	0.751	0.731	0.712	0.693	0.675	0.658	0.641	0.624	0.609	0.593	0.579
4	0.961	0.924	0.888	0.855	0.823	0.792	0.763	0.735	0.708	0.683	0.659	0.636	0.613	0.592	0.572	0.552	0.534	0.516	0.499	0.482
5	0.951	0.906	0.863	0.822	0.784	0.747	0.713	0.681	0.650	0.621	0.593	0.567	0.543	0.519	0.497	0.476	0.456	0.437	0.419	0.402
6	0.942	0.888	0.837	0.790	0.746	0.705	0.666	0.630	0.596	0.564	0.535	0.507	0.480	0.456	0.432	0.410	0.390	0.370	0.352	0.335
7	0.933	0.871	0.813	0.760	0.711	0.665	0.623	0.583	0.547	0.513	0.482	0.452	0.425	0.400	0.376	0.354	0.333	0.314	0.296	0.279
8	0.923	0.853	0.789	0.731	0.677	0.627	0.582	0.540	0.502	0.467	0.434	0.404	0.376	0.351	0.327	0.305	0.285	0.266	0.249	0.233
9	0.914	0.837	0.766	0.703	0.645	0.592	0.544	0.500	0.460	0.424	0.391	0.361	0.333	0.308	0.284	0.263	0.243	0.225	0.209	0.194
10	0.905	0.820	0.744	0.676	0.614	0.558	0.508	0.463	0.422	0.386	0.352	0.322	0.295	0.270	0.247	0.227	0.208	0.191	0.176	0.162
11	0.896	0.804	0.722	0.650	0.585	0.527	0.475	0.429	0.388	0.350	0.317	0.287	0.261	0.237	0.215	0.195	0.178	0.162	0.148	0.135
12	0.887	0.788	0.701	0.625	0.557	0.497	0.444	0.397	0.356	0.319	0.286	0.257	0.231	0.208	0.187	0.168	0.152	0.137	0.124	0.112
13	0.879	0.773	0.681	0.601	0.530	0.469	0.415	0.368	0.326	0.290	0.258	0.229	0.204	0.182	0.163	0.145	0.130	0.116	0.104	0.093
14	0.870	0.758	0.661	0.577	0.505	0.442	0.388	0.340	0.299	0.263	0.232	0.205	0.181	0.160	0.141	0.125	0.111	0.099	0.088	0.078
15	0.861	0.743	0.642	0.555	0.481	0.417	0.362	0.315	0.275	0.239	0.209	0.183	0.160	0.140	0.123	0.108	0.095	0.084	0.074	0.065
16	0.853	0.728	0.623	0.534	0.458	0.394	0.339	0.292	0.252	0.218	0.188	0.163	0.141	0.123	0.107	0.093	0.081	0.071	0.062	0.054
17	0.844	0.714	0.605	0.513	0.436	0.371	0.317	0.270	0.231	0.198	0.170	0.146	0.125	0.108	0.093	0.080	0.069	0.060	0.052	0.045
18	0.836	0.700	0.587	0.494	0.416	0.350	0.296	0.250	0.212	0.180	0.153	0.130	0.111	0.095	0.081	0.069	0.059	0.051	0.044	0.038
19	0.828	0.686	0.570	0.475	0.396	0.331	0.277	0.232	0.194	0.164	0.138	0.116	0.098	0.083	0.070	0.060	0.051	0.043	0.037	0.031
20	0.820	0.673	0.554	0.456	0.377	0.312	0.258	0.215	0.178	0.149	0.124	0.104	0.087	0.073	0.061	0.051	0.043	0.037	0.031	0.026

Present value of an annuity of ₹ 1 paid for period t at a rate $k = [1 - 1/(1 + k)^t]/k$

Period	Rate																			
	1%	2%	3%	4%	5%	6%	7%	8%	9%	10%	11%	12%	13%	14%	15%	16%	17%	18%	19%	20%
1	0.990	0.980	0.971	0.962	0.952	0.943	0.935	0.926	0.917	0.909	0.901	0.893	0.885	0.877	0.870	0.862	0.855	0.847	0.840	0.833
2	1.970	1.942	1.913	1.886	1.859	1.833	1.808	1.783	1.759	1.736	1.713	1.690	1.568	1.647	1.626	1.605	1.585	1.566	1.547	1.528
3	2.941	2.884	2.829	2.775	2.723	2.673	2.624	2.577	2.531	2.487	2.444	2.402	2.361	2.322	2.283	2.246	2.210	2.174	2.140	2.106
4	3.902	3.808	3.717	3.630	3.546	3.465	3.387	3.312	3.240	3.170	3.102	3.037	2.974	2.914	2.855	2.798	2.743	2.690	2.639	2.589
5	4.853	4.713	4.580	4.452	4.329	4.212	4.100	3.993	3.890	3.791	3.696	3.605	3.517	3.433	3.352	3.274	3.199	3.127	3.058	2.991
6	5.795	5.601	5.417	5.242	5.076	4.917	4.767	4.623	4.486	4.355	4.231	4.111	3.998	3.889	3.784	3.685	3.589	3.498	3.410	3.326
7	6.728	6.472	6.230	6.002	5.786	5.582	5.389	5.206	5.033	4.868	4.712	4.564	4.423	4.288	4.160	4.039	3.922	3.812	3.706	3.605
8	7.652	7.325	7.020	6.733	6.463	6.210	5.971	5.747	5.535	5.335	5.146	4.968	4.799	4.639	4.487	4.344	4.207	4.078	3.954	3.837
9	8.566	8.162	7.786	7.435	7.108	6.802	6.515	6.247	5.995	5.759	5.537	5.328	5.132	4.946	4.772	4.607	4.451	4.303	4.163	4.031
10	9.471	8.983	8.530	8.111	7.722	7.360	7.024	6.710	6.418	6.145	5.889	5.650	5.426	5.216	5.019	4.833	4.659	4.494	4.339	4.192
11	10.368	9.787	9.253	8.760	8.306	7.887	7.499	7.139	6.805	6.495	6.207	5.938	5.687	5.453	5.234	5.029	4.836	4.656	4.486	4.327
12	11.255	10.575	9.954	9.385	8.863	8.384	7.943	7.536	7.161	6.814	6.492	6.194	5.918	5.660	5.421	5.197	4.988	4.793	4.611	4.439
13	12.134	11.348	10.635	9.986	9.394	8.853	8.358	7.904	7.487	7.103	6.750	6.424	6.122	5.842	5.583	5.342	5.118	4.910	4.715	4.533
14	13.004	12.106	11.296	10.563	9.899	9.295	8.745	8.244	7.786	7.367	6.982	6.628	6.302	6.002	5.724	5.468	5.229	5.008	4.802	4.611
15	13.865	12.849	11.938	11.118	10.380	9.712	9.108	8.559	8.061	7.606	7.191	6.811	6.462	6.142	5.847	5.575	5.324	5.092	4.876	4.675
16	14.718	13.578	12.561	11.652	10.838	10.106	9.447	8.851	8.313	7.824	7.379	6.974	6.604	6.265	5.954	5.668	5.405	5.162	4.938	4.730
17	15.562	14.292	13.166	12.166	11.274	10.477	9.763	9.122	8.544	8.022	7.549	7.120	6.729	6.373	6.047	5.749	5.475	5.222	4.990	4.775
18	16.398	14.992	13.754	12.659	11.690	10.828	10.059	9.372	8.756	8.201	7.702	7.250	6.840	6.467	6.128	5.818	5.534	5.273	5.033	4.812
19	17.226	15.678	14.324	13.134	12.085	11.158	10.336	9.604	8.950	8.365	7.839	7.366	6.938	6.550	6.198	5.877	5.584	5.316	5.070	4.843
20	18.046	16.351	14.877	13.590	12.462	11.470	10.594	9.818	9.129	8.514	7.963	7.469	7.025	6.623	6.259	5.929	5.628	5.353	5.101	4.870

Bibliography

Adams, J.R. and Campbell, B., *Roles and Responsibilities of the Project Manager*, Upper Darby, PA: Project Management Institute, 1982 [4th printing, 1990].

Baker, S. and Baker, K., *The Complete Idiot's Guide to Project Management*, New York: Alpha Books, 1998.

Berkun, S., *The Art of Project Management*, Cambridge MA: O'Reilly Media, 2005.

Block, T.R. and Frame, J.D., *The Project Office*, Menlo Park, CA: Crisp Publications, 1998.

Boardman, A. et al., *Cost Benefit Analysis: Concepts and Practice*, 3rd ed., Upper Saddle River, New Jersey: Prentice Hall, 2005.

Brooks, F., *The Mythical Man-Month: Essays on Software Engineering*, Reading, MA: Addison-Wesley, 1982.

Cable, D. and Adams, J.R., *Organizing for Project Management*, Upper Darby, PA: Project Management Institute, 1982 [3rd printing, 1989].

Callahan, K.R., Gary, S.S. and Lynne, M.B., *Project Management Accounting: Budgeting, Tracking, and Reporting Costs and Profitability*, Hoboken, NJ: John Wiley & Sons, 2007.

Campbell, C.A., *The One-Page Project Manager: Communicate and Manage Any Project with a Single Sheet of Paper*, Hoboken, NJ: O.C. Tanner, 2007.

Cavendish, P. and Martin, MD., *Negotiating and Contracting for Project Management*, Upper Darby, PA: Project Management Institute, 1982 [2nd printing, 1987].

Chandra P., *Projects: Planning, Analysis, Financing, Implementation, and Review*, 5th ed., New Delhi: Tata McGraw-Hill, 2002.

Charvat, J., *Project Management Methodologies: Selecting, Implementing, and Supporting Methodologies and Processes for Projects*, Hoboken, NJ: John Wiley & Sons, 2003.

Choudhary, S., *Project Management*, New Delhi: Tata McGraw-Hill, 1988.

Clough, R., Sears, G., and Sears K., *Construction Project Management*, 4th ed., New York: John Wiley & Sons, 2000.

Cohen, A.R and Bradford, D.L., *Influence without Authority*, New York: John Wiley & Sons, 1990.

Cohn, M., *Agile Estimating and Planning*, Upper Saddle River, New Jersey: Prentice Hall, 2005.

Cowan C., Gray, C., and Larson, E., "Project partnering," *Project Management Journal*, 1992.

DeWeaver, M.F. and Gillespie, L.C., *Real-World Project Management: New Approaches for Adapting to Change and Uncertainty*, New York: Quality Resources, 1997.

Dinsmore, P.C., *Human Factors in Project Management*, New York: AMACOM, 1990.

Dreger, J.B., *Project Management: Effective Scheduling*, New York: Van Nostrand Reinhold, 1992.

Eriksen, D., *A Project Manager's Team Building Tool—Project Partnering*, ATI Systems, 2007.

Esque, T.J., *No Surprises Project Management: A Proven Early Warning System for Staying on Track*, Mill Valley, CA: ACT Publishing, 1999.

Ferry, D.D. and Noelle, F., *77 Sure-Fire Ways to Kill a Software Project*, San Jose: Author's Choice Press, 2000.

Fleming, Q.W. and Koppleman, J.M., *Earned Value Project Management*, 2nd ed., Upper Darby, PA: Project Management Institute, 2000.

Frame, J.D., *Managing Projects in Organizations: How to Make the Best Use of Time, Techniques, and People*, San Francisco: Jossey-Bass, 1995.

Gates, B., *Business @ the Speed of Thought*, New York: Warner Books, 1999.

Gilbert, S., *90 Days to Launch: Internet Projects on Time and on Budget*, New York: John Wiley & Sons, 2001.

Graham, R.J. and Englund, R.L., *Creating an Environment for Successful Projects: The Quest to Manage Project Management*, San Francisco: Jossey-Bass, 1997.

Gray, C.F. and Larson, E.W., *Project Management: The Managerial Process*, 3rd ed., New Delhi: Tata McGraw-Hill, 4th reprint 2008.

Greer, M., *The Project Manager's Partner: A Step-by-Step Guide to Project Management*, Amherst, MA: HRD Press, 1996.

Greer, M., *Project Management for Workgroups: Facilitator's Guide for the Project Manager's Partner*, Amherst, MA: HRD Press, 1997.

Greer, M., *The Manager's Pocket Guide to Project Management*, Amherst, MA: HRD Press, 1999.

Hallows, J., *Information Systems Project Management: How to Deliver, Function & Value in Information Technology Projects*, New York: AMACOM, 1998.

Harvard Business School Press. *Managing Projects: Expert Solutions to Everyday Challenges*, Boston, MA: Harvard Business School Press, 2006.

Haugan, G.T., *Effective Work Breakdown Structures*, Vienna, VA: Management Concepts, 2002.

Hendrickson, C., *Project Management for Construction: Fundamental Concepts for Owners, Engineers, Architects and Builders,* Pittsburgh, PA: Department of Civil and Environmental Engineering, Carnegie Mellon University, 1999.

Highsmith, J., *Agile Project Management: Creating Innovative Products*, New York: Pearson Education, 2004.

Hill, G.M., *The Complete Project Management Office Handbook*, Arlington, VA: Auerbach Publications, 2003.

Hobbs, B. and Menrad, P., "Organizational choices for project management," In: Paul Dinsmore (Ed.), *The AMA Handbook of Project Management*, New York: AMACOM, 1993.

House, R.S., *The Human Side of Project Management*, New York: Addison-Wesley, 1988.

Ireland, L., *Quality Management for Projects and Programs*, Upper Darby, PA: Project Management Institute, 1991.

Kendrick, T., *The Project Management Took Kit: 100 Tips and Techniques for Getting the Job Done Right*, New York: AMACOM, 2004.

Kerzner, H., *Project Management: A Systems Approach to Planning, Scheduling, and Controlling*, 9th ed., Hoboken, NJ: John Wiley & Sons, 2005.

Kirchof, N. and Adams, J., *Conflict Management for Project Managers*, Upper Darby, PA: Project Management Institute, 1982 [3rd printing, 1989].

Kotter, J.P., What Leaders Really Do, *Harvard Business Review*, May–June 1990.

Laufer, A. and Hoffman, E., *Project Management Success Stories: Lessons of Project Leaders*, New York: John Wiley & Sons, 2000.

Lewis, J.P., *Fundamentals of Project Management*, New York: AMACOM, 1997.

Lock, D., *Project Management*, 6th ed., New York: John Wiley & Sons, 1996.

Magness, F., *Fundamentals of Project Management*, Washington: Qualitech Systems, 1990.

Martin, M., Teagarden, C.C., and Lambreth, C., *Contract Administration for the Project Manager*, Upper Darby, PA: Project Management Institute, 1983 [3rd printing, 1990].

Manus, J., *Napoleon on Project Management*, Nashville, TN: Thomas Nelson Inc., 2006.

McConnell, S., *Software Project Survival Guide*, Redmond, WA: Microsoft Press, 1998.

McCormack, M., *What They Don't Teach You at Harvard Business School: Notes from a Street-Smart Executive*, New York: Bantam, 1986.

Nelson, B. and Economy, P., *Managing for Dummies*, Foster City, CA: IDG Books, 1996.

Newell, M.W. and Marina, N.G., *The Project Management Question and Answer Book*, New York: AMACOM, 2004.

Panneerselvam, R. and Senthilkumar, P., *Project Management*, New Delhi: PHI Learning, 2010.

Pell, A., *Complete Idiot's Guide to Team Building*, New York: Alpha Books, 1999.

Peters, T. and Waterman, R., *In Search of Excellence: Lessons from America's Best-Run Companies*, New York: Harper & Row, 1982.

Peters, T., *Reinventing Work: The Project 50 [Or, Fifty Ways to Transform Every "Task" Into a Project That Matters]*, New York: Alfred A. Knopf, 1999.

Pinto, J.K. and Kharbanda, O.P., *Successful Project Managers: Leading Your Team to Success*, New York: Van Nostrand Reinhold, 1995.

Portney, S.E., *Project Management for Dummies*, 2nd ed., Hoboken, NJ: Wiley Publishing, 2006.

Prahlad, C.K. and Hamel, G., The Core Competence of the Corporation, *Harvard Business Review*, May–June 1990.

Project Management Institute, *People in Projects*, Upper Darby, PA: Project Management Institute, 2001.

Project Management Institute, *Project Management Institute Practice Standard for Work Breakdown Structures*, Upper Darby, PA: Project Management Institute, 2001.

Project Management Institute Standards Committee, *A Guide to the Project Management Body of Knowledge (PMBOK)*, Upper Darby, PA: Project Management Institute, 2004.

Richman, L., *Project Management: Step by Step*, New Delhi: PHI Learning, 2008.

Roman, D.D., *Managing Projects: A Systems Approach*, New York: Elsevier Science Publishing, 1986.

Sontakki, V.C., *Project Management*, Mumbai: Himalaya Publishing House, 2006.

Stuckenbruck, L.C. and Marshall, D., *Team Building for Project Managers*, Upper Darby, PA: Project Management Institute, 1985 [3rd printing, 1990].

Stuckenbruck, L.C. (Ed.), *The Implementation of Project Management: The Professional's Handbook*, Upper Darby, PA: Project Management Institute, & Reading, MA: Addison-Wesley Publishing Co., 1981 [12th printing, 1995].

Verzuh, E., *The Fast Forward MBA in Project Manaagement*, New York: John Wiley & Sons, 1999.

Verma, V.K. and Thamhain, H.J., *Human Resource Skills for the Project Manager: The Human Aspects of Project Management, Volume 2*, Upper Darby, PA: Project Management Institute, 1996.

Wideman, R.M. (Ed.), *Project and Program Risk Management: A Guide to Managing Project Risks and Opportunities*, Upper Darby, PA: Project Management Institute, 1992.

Wysocki, R.K. et al., *Building Effective Project Teams*, New York: John Wiley & Sons, 2001.

Wysocki, R.K. et al., *Effective Project Management*, 3rd ed. New York: John Wiley & Sons, 2003.

Answers to Selected Questions

Chapter 2

4. Project A

Chapter 3

5. Project A. Payback period 3.75 years
6. NPV ₹ 11,834.49, IRR 29.82%
7. NPV ₹ 17,138.47
8. Project A

Chapter 5

5. Estimated cost ₹ 28,00,000; savings ₹ 1,68,000

Chapter 6

6. Critical path is 1–3–6–9. Duration is 15 months. We do not need another crane. It can be scheduled as follows: Activity 3–7 from month 2 to month 7, activity 2–5 from month 7 to month 11, and activity 8–9 from month 11 onwards.
7. Critical path is A–C–D–E–F–I–J. Duration is 98 days.
8. Critical path is B–C–F–G–H–I–J–M. Duration is 22 days
9. Critical path are B–E–F–H–I–J. A–E–F–H–I–J. Duration is 25 months.
10. Critical path is A–D–E–F–I–J. Duration is 32 weeks.
11. Critical path is A–E–H–I–K. Duration is 40 days.
12. Critical path is A–B–D–F–G–H–I. Duration is 41 Weeks.
13. Critical path is A–E–F–C–D–H. Duration is 57 days.
14. Critical path is B–F–K–L. Duration is 24.67 weeks. Variance on critical path is 4.0555. Probability to finish in 26 weeks or less is 0.746. Probability of finishing in 23 weeks

or less is 0.2039. Probability of finishing in 25 weeks or more is 0.4343. At 95% confidence level, completion time is 27.97 weeks.

15. Critical path is A–D–F. Duration is 18 weeks. Probability of completing in 20 weeks or less is 84.14%.
16. Expected duration of the project is 17 weeks. There is a 0.16 probability of the project being completed at least three weeks earlier than expected.
17. Optimal duration of the project is 11 days. Crash 1–2 by two days, 2–5 by five days and activity 4–5 by one day. Optimal cost of project is ₹ 17,600.
18. Normal duration is 45 days. Critical path is A–C–E–F. Shortest duration is 33 days. Optimal duration is 38 days at a cost of ₹ 64,400. Crash E by three days and F by four days.
19. Normal time is 21 days. Shortest time is 16 days. Most economical time is 19 days. Cost is ₹ 73,550.
20. Optimal duration is 24 days at a cost of ₹ 1,75,000.
21. Expected completion time is 160.17 days. Probability of completion in 165 days is 0.9478.
22. Expected completion time is 53 days. Critical paths are B–D–E–G–H and B–F–G–H. Probability of completing within 60 days is 0.9659.
23. Expected time of completion is 53.67 days. Critical paths are A–B–E–F–H–I and A–B–E–H–I. Probability of completing within 56 days is 0.5849.
24. Critical paths are A–C–E–G–J and A–C–E–H–J. Project completed in 124 weeks.
25. 73 days.
26. Expected time of completion is 64.83 weeks. Probability of completing in 52 weeks is 0.0001. Probability of completing in 65 weeks is 0.5198, and probability of completing in 70 weeks is 0.9378.

Chapter 7

5. Original duration is 12 days. Critical activities are A, D and F. Revised duration after resource levelling is 15 days. Critical activities are B, F, C and G.
6. Original duration is 15 days. Critical activities are B, D and F. After resource levelling duration is 18 days. Critical activities are B, E and F.
7. Original duration is 9 months. Critical activities are C, E and F. After resource levelling duration is 11 months. Critical activities are A, D and F. Project can be completed with two bulldozers in 11 months.

Chapter 11

5. SV = ₹ –2000; CV = ₹ 2000.
6. Status report for period ending Week 4

Task	*% Complete*	*EV*	*AC*	*PV*	*CV*	*SV*
A	100	4000	3000	4000	1000	0
B	50	7500	10,000	5000	–2500	2500
C	33	8000	8000	8000	0	0
Total		19,500	10,000	17,000	–1500	2500

7. Status report for period ending Week 8

Task	*% Complete*	*EV*	*AC*	*PV*	*CV*	*SV*
A	100	4000	3000	4000	1000	0
B	100	15,000	18,000	15,000	–3000	0
C	100	24,000	24,000	24,000	0	0
D	33	3000	3000	3000	0	0
Total		46,000	48,000	46,000	–2000	0

8.

	Week 4	*Week* 8
SPI = EV/PV	1.15	1
CPI = EV/AC	1.95	0.958
PCIB = EV/BAC	0.26	0.62

9. Status report for period ending Week 3

Task	*% Complete*	*EV*	*AC*	*PV*	*CV*	*SV*	*SPI*	*CPI*	*PCIB*
A	100	20,000	15,000	20,000	5000	0			
B	20	5000	5000	8000	0	–3000			
C	10	3000	2000	5000	1000	–2000			
D	0	0	0	16,000	0	–16,000			
Total		28,000	22,000	49,000	6000	–21,000	0.57	1.27	0.19

10. Status report for period ending Week 6

Task	*% Complete*	*EV*	*AC*	*PV*	*CV*	*SV*	*SPI*	*CPI*	*PCIB*
A	100	20,000	15,000	20,000	5000	0			
B	80	20,000	18,000	24,000	2000	–4000			
C	80	24,000	21,000	25,000	3000	–1000			
D	100	24,000	22,000	24,000	2000	0			
E	0	0	0	0	0	0			
F	50	8000	6000	8000	2000	0			
Total		96,000	82,000	1,01,000	14,000	–5000	0.95	1.17	0.66

Index